BLACK BARTY

BLACK
BARTY

BARTHOLOMEW ROBERTS
AND HIS PIRATE CREW
1718–1723

AUBREY BURL

SUTTON PUBLISHING

This book was first published in 1997 by Alun Books

This new edition first published in 2006 by
Sutton Publishing Limited · Phoenix Mill
Thrupp · Stroud · Gloucestershire · GL5 2BU

British Library Cataloguing in Publication Data
A catalogue record for this book is available from the British
Library.

ISBN 0 7509 4312 2

Typeset in 11/13pt Goudy.
Typesetting and origination by
Sutton Publishing Limited.
Printed and bound in Great Britain by
J.H. Haynes & Co. Ltd, Sparkford.

Contents

Barti Ddu o Gas Newy'Bach
Y morwr tal a'r Chwerthiniad iach
Efo fydd y llyw
Ar y llong a'r criw –
Bartu Ddu o Gas Newy'Bach.

Black Barty of Little Newcastle
The tall seaman of the hearty laugh,
He guides the rudder
Over the ship and the crew –
Black Barty of Little Newcastle.

from 'Barti Ddu',
I.D. Hooson (1880–1948)

At the pleasant village of Little Newcastle, Dyfed, five miles south of
Fishguard, a gaunt and slender stone stands on the green in front of the
church. On it is a metal sign:

CAS NEWYDD BACH
yn y pentref yma y ganed
BARTI DDU
y mör-leidr enwog
(1682–1722)

LITTLE NEW CASTLE
in this village was born
BLACK BARTY
the famous pirate
(1682–1722)

'In an honest service there is thin commons, low wages, and hard
labour. In this, plenty and satiety, pleasure and ease, liberty and power.
And who would not balance creditor on this side, when all the hazard
that is run for it, at worst, is only a sour look or two at choking? No, a
merry life and a short one shall be my motto.

Damnation to him who ever lived to wear a halter'.

Bartholomew Roberts.

List of Plates

Introduction

This is the true story, recovered from original sources, of a band of pirates who from 1718 until 1723 terrorised the seas off the African coast, in the West Indies, and in the American colonies. It begins with the suppression of a pirate base on New Providence and ends near the cold shores of Newfoundland.

During those years the pirates had four captains: Howel Davis, the imaginative Welshman; Thomas Anstis, the deserter; John Phillips, the murderer. But it is with the fourth that this book is chiefly concerned because he was the greatest pirate of the age, a tea-drinking marauder of astonishing audacity. His name was Bartholomew Roberts.

He lived at a vintage time for rogues, an age of criminals whose names are household: Captain Kidd, privateer turned pirate, hanged at Execution Dock in 1701; the infamous Blackbeard, Edward Teach the pirate, who was killed in 1718, the year in which this story begins; the pirate women, Anne Bonny and Mary Read at whose trial in 1720 they 'pleaded their bellies', confounding the court who did not expect pregnancy in pirates; Jack Sheppard, pickpocket and locksmith, admired for his ingenious escapes from prisons, arduously breaking through padlocked door after door and thick wall after wall at Newgate. He was hanged at Tyburn in 1724.

There was Dick Turpin in 1739, arrested for the unprovoked shooting of his landlord's gamecock, and who courageously leapt neck-snappingly off the gallows steps to avoid a more lingering death by slow strangulation. Others were almost as well known: Jonathan Wild the thief-taker, Claude Duval, courteous highwayman. But of all of them Bartholomew Roberts was outstanding for his daring, effrontery, and success.

Pirates must be seen against their historical background. The laws of Britain, the state of the American colonies, the self-seeking captains of the Royal Navy, unemployment amongst sailors, all of them contributed to piracy. Although the majority of Britons deplored Roberts they also helped to make him.

Pirates are not to be confused with buccaneers, privateers or corsairs, all of whom were more or less honest. Buccaneers, the Brethren of the Coast, were in the beginning only involved with profitable recriminations against the restrictive trading practices of Spain. Privateers and corsairs were a kind of civil navy with governmental permission to attack their country's enemies. Loot was an added incentive for patriotism.

Pirates were the enemies of all who sailed the sea. Plunder was their only object, intimidation their chief weapon, corrupt shore officials and trade embargoes their secret allies. Their calling is no more to be defended than that of housebreakers, footpads and highwaymen. Yet no apology is required for this book. Biographies of pirates are rare. Books have been written about piracy in general, usually relishing the atrocities, but until recently most were plagiarisms of earlier works and in them the pirates were puppets. The element that set these criminals apart, the sea, was rarely mentioned. Their ships and the conditions in them were ignored. Content with reporting corpse after corpse such books could as well have been written about Bluebeard the child-murderer as Blackbeard the pirate.

Commendable exceptions to this criticism are the books by David Cordingly, formerly of the National Maritime Museum, Greenwich. His *Life Among the Pirates* is a masterly historical review of the facts and fictions that colour the images of the ruffians and blackguards called pirates.

The present book describes how pirates lived and I have chosen to write about one man because his history includes the squalor, the temptations, the fear, the triumphs and the debaucheries that pirates knew. He was also brave, ambitious and successful.

Most pirate books are embellishments of Captain Charles Johnson's classic, *A General History . . . of the Most Notorious Pyrates . . .* first published in 1724. Its details and current knowledge make it the foundation stone for any new work. That it is also very readable is unsurprising because 'Captain Johnson' was possibly Daniel Defoe who had already written two novels about pirates, *The King of the Pirates*, 1719, and *Captain Singleton*, 1720. Johnson's *History . . .* is generally accurate but it does contain errors and omissions that contemporary documents and records of trials expand and rectify.[1]

'Johnson' is more reliable about Bartholomew Roberts than of other pirates and better about the end of Roberts' career than its beginning because he had spoken with naval officers who were at the final trial, one of his informants being the surgeon of the warship, *Swallow*, John Atkins, who recorded the proceedings at Cape Coast Castle.

The attacks, plunderings, violence described here did happen. There are, perhaps, a dozen minor incidents which are uncorroborated although these are probable. They are identified as such in the Notes. Where a speech is quoted it comes from Johnson and is therefore fictitious but it gives the vocabulary and syntax of the day. What it must lack are the local dialects, regional Welsh, lowland Scottish, Cockney, the rich diversity of pronunciations of those pronouncedly parochial days.

Many events are attested in manuscript in the Public Records Office: the letters of colonial governors; the Calendar of State Papers (Colonial Series); or were admitted by pirates at their various trials. Lurid accounts of brutalities were reported in broad-sheets such as *The Original Weekly Journal* and others whose copies survive in the Burney Collection of the British Museum's Reading Room. These bulletins are often the only source for such distant and ephemeral occurrences, the writers obtaining their copy from the returning captains and seamen who had suffered from piracy. References to them are provided in the Notes.

There is a coincidence. Fate brought together two men who by chance were associated with the events in this book, one with their beginning, the other with the end. In 1719 Daniel Defoe wrote *Robinson Crusoe*, a novel based on the desert island castaway, Alexander Selkirk, who had been rescued by Captain Woodes Rogers in 1709. Selkirk was in the naval warship, *Weymouth*, as it prepared to attack Bartholomew Roberts.

There are thanks to be offered: to Patrick Pringle for his stirring and exciting book, *Jolly Roger*, that stimulated my own interest in piracy and for his encouragement; to the Revd W. Lewis, rector of Little Newcastle; to Professor P.N. Furbank for his advice about the authorship of Daniel Defoe; to the staff of the Science Museum, London, who advised me on the technicalities of 18th century ship design; the Public Records Office; the Scottish Records Office; the British Museum Reading Room; the Bodleian Library, Oxford; the pirate library of the National Maritime Museum, Greenwich; the Guildhall Library, London; the National Library of Scotland; the National Library of Wales; the libraries of Hull College of Higher Education, the University of Birmingham, and the Society of Antiquaries of London.

I am most grateful to Sally Jones of Alun Books, Port Talbot, for having the initiative to publish the story of just one pirate, albeit Welsh, however successful he was. Equally I am delighted at the enthusiasm of Sarah Flight of Sutton Publishing, Stroud, who has reincarnated that tea-drinking, Sabbath-observing, richly-apparelled scoundrel.

Finally, to the many friends and colleagues whose help and interest has saved this book from fading into a bloodthirsty dream.

PART ONE

Captain Howel Davis

July 1718–June 1719

1

Captain Howel Davis

1718–1719

'The pyrates off the coast of Guinea in Africa have taken goods to the value of £204,000'.
The Weekly Journal or British Gazetteer, 9 April 1720

Early in January, 1709 the winter in England was so bitter that the Thames turned to ice and Dean Swift, author of *Gulliver's Travels*, ate gingerbread at one of the fairground stalls set up on the frozen river. A few weeks later but eight thousand miles away Robinson Crusoe was rescued.

'Crusoe' was not his real name. It was invented by Daniel Defoe ten years later when he wrote his first novel after forty impoverished years as a pamphleteer. 'Robinson Crusoe' was Alexander Selkirk and his rescuer was Captain Woodes Rogers, a privateer famous for his raids on the American possessions of England's enemy, Spain. It is a minor irony of history that it was Rogers who saw the start of the greatest reign of piracy the seas had known and it was Selkirk who almost saw its end which came only two months after his death on board a man-of-war pursuing Bartholomew Roberts.

Defoe had read Rogers' account of his privateering expedition, *A Cruising Voyage Round the World*, 1712, as the similarity of extracts from the two books show. Rogers, an

experienced seaman and navigator had been commissioned by
Bristol merchants to attack and plunder Spanish territories in
the Pacific in retaliation for Spain's unremitting harrassment of
British shipping. Despite mutiny, near-starvation and battles at
sea in which he was twice wounded Rogers returned in 1711
with a rich cargo of some £170,000, a huge sum when a soldier
maimed in the wars might receive a pension of £18 a year.
Rogers also brought back Selkirk who had been marooned in
1704 for more than four years on Màs-a-Tierra, now renamed
Isla Robinson Crusoe, the largest of the Juan Fernandez islands
off the coast of Chile, after refusing to sail in an unseaworthy
vessel. He was discovered only by accident when Woodes
Rogers sent a boat ashore for fresh water.[1]

Rogers had been so successful that on his return to England he
was rich enough to rent the West Indian islands of the Bahamas,
with the appointment as governor, for twenty-one years. But
there was a problem. Piracy flourished there. It was a perfect time
for pirates. Cargoes were plentiful, merchant ships were poorly
armed, naval protection was slight and there was little chance of
capture. Wherever there was trade whether on the American
coast, in the West Indies or off Africa pirates lurked.

Although the war with Spain was officially over in 1713
skirmishes continued and the British Navy was occupied in the
Mediterranean with few ships available for duties elsewhere. Yet
trade was expanding. Chartered companies, The East India
Company, the Hudson's Bay Company, the Royal African
Company and scores of others prospered from the riches of virgin
territories. New lands were acquired, new settlements established.
Trading sloops and sailing galleys with auxiliary oars for calm
weather travelled the long triangular route from Britain with cloth,
hardware and weapons to Africa; from Africa across the Atlantic
with slaves for the Americas; from America back to Britain with
spices, rum, tea and, above all, money. Unprotected by the navy but
bringing wealth to their employers the merchant captains, relied on
the vastness of the oceans to save them from pirates. In vessels with

inadequate armament and with unenthusiastic crews they were defenceless. Pirates thrived on such easy pickings. As the colonies and commerce increased so did piracy. To the aphorism, 'Trade follows the flag' can be added, 'and piracy follows trade'.

In the colonies defence was often left to the private owner who had little incentive to resist pirates. To the contrary it was easier, safer and more profitable to trade with them. Life was hard, income was low and piratical goods were cheap. It was a time for the rich man and the business man but not for the poor.

In Britain there was wealth and luxury. The first English banknotes were issued in 1718. The streets of London offered the best shopping in Europe and everywhere tradesmen's signs hung, elaborate and brightly coloured. After the Great Fire of 1666 the heart of the city was being rebuilt. The elegant squares, Cavendish, Grosvenor, Hanover, were rising. The church of St Mary-le-Strand was finished in 1717. The nobility gamed for fortunes, duelled in their fashionable grey-powdered wigs, lace cravats, satin waistcoats and breeches. Merchants met in aromatic coffee-houses. The South Sea Company would soon tempt investors with its promise of swift gains.

But the times were uneasy. The king, George I from Germany, speaking no English, had been on the throne only since 1714, there had been a Jacobite rising the next year and there was a persistent dread of a second invasion.

For those without money there were greater fears. In London the poor existed within a few yards of prosperity but were a lifetime of deprivation from it. Unemployment brought starvation but with the naval war over there were hundreds of seamen without ships. Laws were harsh, prisons were pits of corruption and fever, there was a gallows near every town. No job meant the misery of the workhouse or, worse, transportation. The colonies needed labour and many penniless men, women and children were condemned to near-slavery on the plantations.

Poverty meant degradation, even death. Despite the risks many sailors were lured by the pleasures of piracy. It offered easy money. Instead of hard labour there were the sirens of drink, idleness, wealth and women. Woodes Rogers was warned that in the Bahamas he might find hundreds of pirates.

In April, 1718, he sailed from England in the *Delicia*, a thirty-gun, 460-ton merchantman that he had used on an earlier trip to Madagascar. With him was the *Willing Mind* of twenty guns, and two 20-metre long trading sloops, the *Buck* and the *Samuel*, two-masted vessels of 100 tons, fore-and-aft rigged, each with six guns on their upper decks. There was also a strong though temporary naval escort, the *Milford*, a 5th-rate man-of-war of 32 guns, and a pair of naval sloops, bigger and more heavily-armed than their civilian counterparts, the *Rose* and the *Shark*.[2] With him Rogers carried a General Pardon for those pirates who cared to accept it.

> . . . and we do hereby promise and declare that in case of any of the said Pirates shall, on or before 5 September, in the year of our Lord, 1718, surrender him or themselves, to one of our principal Secretaries of State in Great Britain or Ireland, or to any Governor or Deputy Governor of any of our Plantations beyond the seas; every such Pirate or Pirates so surrendering him or themselves, as aforesaid, shall have our gracious Pardon of and for such, his or their piracy or piracies, by him or them committed before the 5 of January next ensuing.

Rewards for taking:
      pirate captain, £100
      Lt, master, boatswain, carpenter, gunner, £40
      inferior officer, £30
      private man, £20

A pirate turning renegade and capturing or causing to be captured a pirate to receive £200.

Lord Treasurer or Commissioner of Treasury to pay accordingly.

Hampton Court, 5.9.17

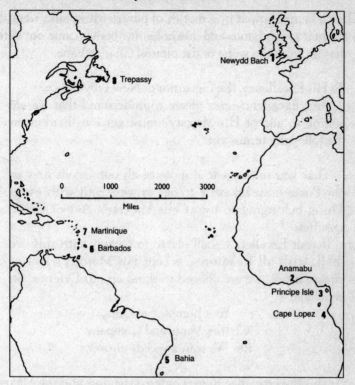

The World of Bartholomew Roberts. Triumphs and Disasters

Early in July Rogers reached New Providence. Over six hundred pirates loitered there, indifferent to his arrival. So content were they with their life, so profligate with their riches, that once when they had captured a merchantman laden with fine brocades they casually tore the fine cloths into strips to tie to the horns of goats to distinguish between the herds of different settlements.[3] Rogers seemed no threat. They had already ignored one appeal and the new governor could not anticipate any better response to this. Events proved him right.

For a day his little fleet lay in the harbour at whose mouth an island created two entrances making any blockade difficult.

Then a launch rowed by a motley of pirates whose silks went ill with their rough hands and unwholesome bodies came out with a message from the worst of the pirates, Charles Vane.

To His Excellency, the Governor of New Providence.

Your Excellency may please to understand that we are willing to accept His Majesty's most gracious Pardon on the following terms, viz:

That you suffer us to dispose of all our Goods now in our Possession. Likewise to act as we see fit with every Thing belonging to us, as His Majesty's Act of Grace specifies.

If your Excellency shall please to comply with this, we shall, with all Readiness, accept His Majesty's Act of Grace. If not, we are obliged to stand on our Defence. So conclude,

Your humble Servants,
Charles Vane, and Company.
P.S. We wait a speedy answer.[4]

At this impertinence Rogers ordered the *Rose* and the *Milford* to block the harbour. The *Rose*'s captain, Whitney, sent a lieutenant under a flag of true to talk with Vane. The officer reported that the pirates were drunk and were threatening to kill Rogers and all his force rather than give in. There was little to do except to attempt a blockade.

It was cannonfire from the burning ship that roused the fleet next night. She came flaming out of the darkness with guns firing erratically like a sputtering grenade, slicing into the rigging of the *Rose*. The naval vessels cut their cables and ran to sea pursued by mocking, undirected shots. Rogers watched helplessly. Flames lit the harbour and by their light he could see Vane's vessel, black flag at the mizzen, sailing out through the dangerous narrows of the eastern channel. Then, as the fire reached her magazine, the fireship exploded in a blast that flared across the New Providence and left the *Delicia* rocking and tossing at her anchorage.

Vane had escaped accompanied by rebellious pirates including 'Calico Jack' Rackam, who was later to depose him. Only a drift of smoke remained of his fireship. Rogers sent the *Buck* and *Samuel* after him but the pirate eluded them only to be shipwrecked later, saved, recognised and sentenced to death on Jamaica in 1719. Johnson recorded that he 'betray'd the Coward when at the Gallows, and died in Agonies equal to his Villainies'.[5]

With Vane gone Rogers acted decisively. He sent a second copy of the Pardon ashore hoping that the pirate had taken all the irredeemable criminals with him. It was a hope that seemed justified when he landed next day. He was met by men who said they would accept the Pardon. Most of them had pistols or curving cutlasses, they were filthy and the town of Nassau behind them was no more prepossessing with its rough shacks, tents and taverns. Raw hides rotted and stank at the waterside. Sailors said that when the wind blew offshore ships could smell New Providence before it came into view. Rogers had the Pardon read out and chose a dwelling larger and less dirty than the rest for his headquarters.

The *Milford* left for duties on the North American coast. Whitney of the *Rose* also was impatient to depart. So was the *Shark* but Rogers could not spare them until his worst problems were solved. Law had to be established on the island and the fortifications had to be strengthened in case the pirates returned. Vane was still free but Whitney refused to pursue him. The perversity of naval captains in foreign places where they could make money was widespread and of them Whitney was to become notorious. Only a few months later in January 1719 Rogers was to write to his friend Sir Richard Steele, dramatist and editor of the *Spectator*, complaining about the captain.

'Captain Whitney, Commander of H.M. Ship, the *Rose* man of war, being one of the three that saw me into this place, and left me in an utmost danger so long ago - he also pretends to have a knowledge of you, and several of my friends in London; but he has behaved so ill that I design to forget him as much as I can; and if he is acquainted with you, and sees you in London before me, I desire he might know his character from the several accounts I have sent hence, with what gives from other parts, may serve to convince all his friends that he is not the man he may appear to be at home'.

Whitney continued to follow his own interests.[6]

Rogers' third problem was his greatest. There was Spanish territory all around him and Spain allowed no country to trade with her colonies. To prevent smuggling there were coastguard vessels, *costagardas*, whose suspicions were intense and whose methods unpleasant. Paradoxically, it was a system that encouraged piracy. Spanish merchants with their monopoly charged high prices. To the colonists pirates who sold stolen goods cheaply were welcome guests. Pirates and *costagardas* fought each other ferociously but both were menaces to honest British, French or Dutch trading ships.

By September Woodes Rogers was worried. Provisions were scarce and money scarcer. Only a trading expedition could obtain supplies but the nearest island, Hispaniola, was Spanish. There was no choice. Two ships had to be sent and if they met a *costagarda* they would have to fight. Lacking honest men Rogers manned the *Buck* and the *Samuel* with ex-pirates, filled the holds with goods for barter and hoped that the gamble would succeed. Captain Brisk of the *Buck* was pessimistic. In seaworthy vessels with few law-abiding seamen to oppose them he predicted that the crews would mutiny.

Yet as they sailed from New Providence, setting their sails southwards towards Hispaniola, there was no unease. In those peaceable waters with light winds and a clear sky it was good to be at sea, passing little islands, most of them barren with rock-littered hills but some brightly green, thickly wooded above the bleachingly white beaches that encircled them. With breezes against them the hands were busy and the ships reached Hispaniola safely, anchoring offshore, unloading the cargo, waiting for the inhabitants to creep down to the trees where the goods were hidden. While some of the men hurried casks and bundles across the sand others pretended to be filling water-barrels to fool any *costagarda* that might appear before nightfall. But it was not the Spaniards that ruined the enterprise.

Led by Howel Davis, Walter Kennedy, William Magness and Christopher Moody, the pirates waited until Brisk and his men were asleep and then overpowered them. There was no struggle, no killing, just a change of command that gave the mutineers two fine sloops. After some half-hearted threats to murder Brisk the pirates settled down to enjoy their regained freedom.[7]

Most were English or Welsh. It was said that there were British, French and Spanish pirates but never a Dutchman because Holland supplied fisheries where unemployed men could work whereas in England men begged. It was a fact that pirates were always reluctant to attack a Dutch ship because of their reputation for fierce and prolonged resistance.

Next day the sloops followed the coast, close to the shore, until they came upon a creek in which a ship, French from her lines, lay at anchor. The pirates fired a shot across her and as the sloops closed on her the crew scrambled into a jolly-boat and rowed frantically to the beach. It was a relief. With only six light guns the pirates could fight no large merchantman but this vessel, taken so simply, was an ideal capture. Soon a working-party was aboard and the three ships were under way, hugging the northern shore.

Only the southern side of Hispaniola had settlements. The north had nothing but forbidding forests and wild cattle, an excellent, uninhabited coastline for pirates. Nearby was the

Windward Passage between the island and Cuba. Through it ships passed using the prevailing winds to Jamaica, returning the same way, battling against the contrary winds on the journey to the American colonies and Britain. A pirate could lie in wait, picking off vessels as he chose with only the peril of a *costagarda* to deter him.

The ships sailed in to Privateer Bay, named from the tortuous channel that led to a concealed anchorage behind the hills, almost invisible from the sea and a traditional hiding place for pirates. In its protection the mutineers looted their prize. Putting guards over their prisoners they lolled on the decks with bottles and flagons. It was time to elect a captain.

They wanted a man who, in their own words, was pistol-proof and not afraid to look a cannon in the mouth, one who knew the sea, not boastful or vainglorious, who would keep his promises and, most important of all, one who was lucky. In Howel Davis, a short, dark-haired Welshman, they had their man, already respected for his daring and his cunning. Without dissent he was declared their leader.

Captain Brisk, his two mates, the boatswain of the *Buck* and two unfit seamen were put into Captain Porter's *Samuel* sloop. Porter who appeared to be a truly reformed pirate was also released. But of his crew of thirty-six only seventeen with families in New Providence were freed. The rest were compelled to stay. Men were needed to sail the ships. Amongst them was Archibald Murray, a young surgeon.

Surgeons were always wanted. Although it was rare for such men to be trained doctors they could set bones, staunch wounds, extract bullets, treat venereal disease. So valued were they that they were given larger shares of plunder. Some were actually paid for each voyage that a ship made.

The *Samuel* departed. Those left behind could only hope that Brisk would remember their names and that they had been forced to join the pirates. If they were captured only his testimony would save them. Every pirate on trial for his life swore that he had been forced, that he had never volunteered. Cynical judges demanded proof.

Davis steered to Cuba where they took a vessel from Philadelphia before cruising back to Hispaniola, lingering around Cape Franbarway where it was usual for many traders to pass.[8] This time only a few ships were captured. From one of them came Richard Jones, a seaman who was loth to quit an honest life. Tiring of his repeated refusals the pirate gunner slashed Jones' leg with his cutlass. Then with a rope tied around his waist he was slung into the sea and hauled into the *Buck* by jeering pirates.[9]

Day by day there were grumbles at the lack of prizes and Davis decided to try his luck on the African coast. An unlucky captain could be as swiftly deposed as he had been elected. Indeed, Charles Vane was replaced by Jack Rackam, his quartermaster, because of the captain's sensible refusal to attack a strongly-armed French man-of-war. The following March he was arrested and hanged at Port Royal. Davis needed to be more fortunate.[10]

Before setting across the Atlantic he had the ship careened, its bottom cleaned of marine life. In those warm waters teredo worms burrowed into the timbers. molluscs laying countless eggs, growing to a voracious six inches (15 cm) in length. Without regular treatment planking became riddled, rotten and leaky and the vessel sailed sluggishly as its keel accumulated trailing weeds and encrustations of shells. Careening was usually a simple, quite pleasant task but this time, lacking a proper carpenter, a trained craftsman responsible for the maintenance of the hull, it was a labour that no one welcomed.

Finding a bay where trees came down to the water's edge tackles and ropes were passed from their trunks and around the mast so that the sloop could be hauled onto her side. Below the waterline she was thickly matted with shellfish, tangles of oily undergrowth and pitted with wormholes. Jones and other forced men scraped off the accretions. Others daubed the bottom with sulphur and brimstone to kill the worms, smearing on protective tallow before the *Buck* was tilted onto her other side. Leafy shelters were put up on shore as an escape from the ship which already had a stench that was never to leave it. Built for fifteen men she was now carrying over sixty.

Food was prepared for the long voyage. Strips of raw meat from wild cattle were hung on a wooden frame above a fire until they were tough as leather but well-preserved, something learned from the native Caribs who called the frame a 'boucan'. It was from this that the term 'boucanier' came, given to those European sailors who, because they fought against the Spanish, dared not approach a port for fresh supplies.

In the evenings, away from the reek of the sloop and the sulphur, behind crude earthworks, the pirates relaxed, betting on lizard races, singing, telling stories of the sea, drinking in the somnolence of night, taking food without restraint. 'They eat in a very disorderly manner, more like a kennel of hounds than like men, snatching and catching the victuals from one another . . . It seemed one of their chief diversions and, they said, looked martial-like.'

Eventually they left, tacking through the Windward Passage, keeping a lookout for prizes and *costagardas*, sailing along the coast of Florida until, in the latitude of the Bermudas, they turned eastwards. It was a long, tedious journey. In the evenings pirates came to the captain's cabin for conversation, discussing plans, dreaming of rich takings. With Davis were his 'Lords', men of courage and steadfastness, John Taylor the quartermaster, Walter Kennedy, cruel, conceited but light-hearted, Henry Dennis the gunner, quick-tempered but able. These were long-experienced pirates, feared for their bravery and arrogance, men who counselled the captain and who were allowed privileges such as being allowed on the quarterdeck and free to go ashore as they pleased. It was these men who decided to make for the Cape Verde islands off the West African coast, Portuguese possessions whose easy-going inhabitants welcomed all ships.

They anchored at Sao Nicolau, one of the westward isles, where a town stood above a small and ruinous fort of twelve guns. The pirates knew that they could get fresh food and water from the tiny native huts and cabins and Davis decided to visit the governor taking a few men as a bodyguard. In the boat pulling away from the dingy sloop sat Davis in a maroon coat of velvet, a lace cravat, silver-buckled shoes, his companions in more sober dress but of good cloth and cut. It was an impressive boatload of dandies whose garments were the takings from a dozen ships.

The governor gave them permission to land men for provisions and trade. There was a cloth factory on the island producing a blue and white striped material very popular with the natives of Guinea but it did not interest the pirates. At sea they could get all the cloth they wanted.

His leg now recovered Richard Jones attempted to get away. Sent ashore to fetch water he rushed into the coconut groves around the spring, not knowing where to go but hoping to hide until the *Buck* sailed. Unluckily he was seen by one of the 'Lords', Taylor, whose rôle as quartermaster was to be the go-between between captain and crew.

Despite the dense undergrowth and the palms Taylor did not lose Jones. He had a smattering of Portuguese and whenever the fugitive disappeared Taylor obtained directions from the natives and mulattoes. After desperate hours of evasion Jones was caught, hustled back to the sloop, hands bound behind his back.

One of the governor's officers saw the pair. It did not help Jones. Davis had already lied that they were a man-of-war searching for pirates and Taylor glibly explained why his captive's hands were tied. The wretch was one of the soldiers being taken to Guinea to man the forts there but who had deserted. Now he would be returned to the ship,[11] Speaking no Portuguese Jones was helpless. His treatment was predictable. Pirates dreaded betrayal. Jones was strapped to the mast, his shirt ripped from his back and he was whip-lashed by every man of the crew.

Having provisioned the pirates left quickly. Davis had been told that there were many vessels at the nearby Isle of May and he was hoping for some profitable gains.

Until now the *Buck* had known only small ships whose captains and crews dared not resist. The mate of the first vessel taken at the island was different. It was early in February, 1719, that the *Loyal Merchant* was sighted half a league away. The pirates were at anchor but soon they were off the bows of the merchantman, black flag at the masthead, threats shouted, guns sending chainshot whirling and slicing into the rigging, sails, wounding men, crippling the ship. Her mate was ordered to come aboard. Kennedy questioned him about the sailing qualities of his ship. With so many men the *Buck* was too small and had become slow. A better vessel was needed.

Foolishly the man refused to answer. He was dragged back to the *Loyal Merchant* bleeding from cuts in his shoulder and thigh, his face bruised, the fingers of his left hand blackened and bloody where Kennedy had stamped on them. Then, when he had told them all they wished to know, the pirates took his silver watch. This was not enough for them. After the ship was ransacked of money, clothes and goods they returned to the half-conscious mate. Putting a noose around his neck the end of the rope was thrown over the yardarm and he was yanked up, feet off the deck, left hanging, dancing the gallows' dance, fingers scrabbling feebly at his throat until, contemptuously, the rope was released and he crashed down.

Even this cruelty did not content the pirates. Men such as Kennedy and Dennis felt no pity for someone who had defied them. A loop of thin cord was wound round the mate's head above the eyebrows and twisted tighter and tighter, pirates laughing at his screams, and it was not until he fainted that he was thrown onto the *Buck* where he would be forced to stay and work once he had recovered.[12]

Over the next month more ships were taken. One had chests of firearms, bales of India goods, welcome casks of rum, the sailor's favoured drink, and eight heavy guns for the already overladen sloop. Davis took them because he intended to change vessels and he chanced upon one from Liverpool, large enough to mount twenty-six cannon, a versatile two-masted brigantine that sailed well because its fore-and-aft and square rigging could be changed about according to the winds.[13] The filthy *Buck* was given in exchange.

Davis felt secure. He looked along the length of the maindeck to the bows and the bowsprit that pitched and tossed as they sailed towards the African coast. The craft was named the *Royal James*.

By February 23 they were in Gambia off a port known in turn as Gallassee then Bathurst and today Banjul, a harbour built so uneasily on two low sandbanks that it suffered yearly floods and was to be described as 'a waterlogged sponge, floating in a sea of its own excreta'. Davis had already proved himself successful. Gallassee was to prove the beginning of a period of outstanding piracy that endured for four triumphant years.

With merchant flags at the mastheads to deceive the traders at the Royal African Company's fort they went up the Gambia river. The Company had many forts along the coast, some strong, others tumbledown places that one cannonball would reduce. The Company had received a charter to trade in Africa but found French and Portuguese competition so intense that it built the forts for protection only to suffer the folly of its short-sighted, avaricious shareholders who withheld adequate funds for their upkeep. The forts cost £20,000 a year to maintain but with dividends of some seven per cent most of the Company's stockholders were not willing to forego a penny of their interest. The forts were neglected.[14] The mistake was expensive. At Gallassee, however, there was an active agent who was having the fort rebuilt. During the reconstruction he and his staff conducted their business from a ship, the *Royal Ann*. A second vessel lay nearby.

Davis went to see the agent, Orfeur, introducing himself as a trader who had run into a storm and now required wood and water. Orfeur said little, eyeing Davis' resplendent clothes, wondering how it was that a common merchant captain could dress like a gentleman. Davis looked about him, nothing the *Royal Ann*'s armament and men, the condition of the nearby fort.

That night the pirates made ready. Below decks the gunner and his mate went about checking pistols, testing the sharpness of the daggers and cutlasses, inspecting the great guns aligned upon the fort. Boats were quietly lowered.

They did not surprise Orfeur. Having served on a man-of-war he knew what arrangements to make against attack. As the pirates approached they rowed into crossfire from darkened portholes. For a while the shooting continued but the sixty pirates Davis had with him and the broadsides from his cannon were too much. Orfeur surrendered. Some of his men were upriver trading and when the agent was hit and fell those with him laid down their arms.

By morning the fort was ablaze, the *Royal Ann* plundered, the other ship taken, all at the expense of two pirates injured.[15] The loot was carried to the *Royal James*. For two joyous nights the pirates drank and celebrated in the ruins of the fort.

One morning a sloop came up the river, moving slowly through the misty waters towards the *Royal James*, promising more unresisting booty. The pirates had abundant arms. Even Jones had a cutlass. Since the destruction of the fort he had shared in the plunder and was now a willing pirate.

Nearer and nearer came the sloop, her mast puzzlingly lacking flag or pennant. Davis readied his gunners to send a shot across the sloop. But, suddenly, unexpectedly, the sloop fired on them and raised a black flag. Startled, Davis had his own hoisted.

The sight of the Jolly Roger with its ominous skull brought cheers from the sloop. She was commanded by a French pirate, Olivier le Vasseur, also known as la Bouche or la Buse, 'the buzzard', who laughingly apologised.[16] Together the two vessels lingered in the river for over a week but no ships arrived. It was time to leave.

Not all the African Company's servants were as loyal as Orfeur who lay bedridden in the *Royal Ann*. Of his fourteen men half volunteered to become pirates. It was not unusual. The Company treated its 'servants' almost as slaves, providing them with poor shelter, thin food and thinner wages. Most would die of malnutrition or tropical disease long before their employment was due to end. With the pirates they could expect danger, perhaps execution, but also money, luxuries and pleasures that otherwise they would never know.

On March 7 the ships went down river taking the merchant vessel's captain to guide them through the channels.[17] Behind came his own ship manned by pirates. La Bouche's sloop followed.

Next morning there was haze at the river's mouth. Warned by their experience with la Bouche a keen lookout was kept and the incoming brig with its black flag did not alarm them. It belonged to Edward England, a pirate who had scavenged the West African shores for some months and would later become notorious for his exploits around Madagascar. Unlike la Bouche he declined any form of partnership and sailed on. Too many allies reduced a man's share. Yet a year later la Bouche was to join him.

That was in the future. For the present the French pirate wanted a better ship. The captured merchant vessel was big and stoutly built but she was slow and clumsy. A pirate should have either a small, swift craft that could wriggle through narrows or a proud ship like the *Royal James*, fitted with guns, swivels and mortars so powerful that honest captains shuddered to see her. La Bouche's sloop had been agile but was sluggish now and leaky.

The pirates released the merchantman and its captain but deprived him of his second mate, his carpenter, his boatswain and five men, some happy to be taken, others resentful. Two tried to get away, believing that by hiding in the forests they could eventually return to the fort where some incoming ship could take them home. They had no understanding of the dangers of wild animals or wilder natives. Nor did they realise that the next vessel to arrive would belong to Edward England.

None of this mattered. Taylor bribed some negroes to find the runaways who were brutally treated when found, cut and beaten by the quartermaster, whipped on the *Royal James* by mocking pirates and locked in the stinking darkness of the hold until, if ever, they were well enough to work. Almost at the same time as these events but far across the Atlantic another pirate had died. And in England 'Robinson Crusoe' joined the Navy.

In North America Edward Teach, or possibly Edward Drummond of Bristol, the infamous Blackbeard, strong-bodied, of maniacal appearance with his long braid-and-tasselled beard, was killed on 22 November 1718, in a skirmish at Ocracoke Bay, North Carolina.[18] To prove his death his head was taken back to Virginia and centuries later in 1949, the skull, lined with silver, was sold to a private bidder.

This 'courageous Brute' is best remembered for the legend of his buried treasure, hidden, so it is said, somewhere in the Isles of Shoals north of Boston. 'No Body but himself', bragged Teach, 'and the Devil, know where it was, and the longest Liver should take all'. But like the popular illusion that pirates made their victims walk the plank the 'fortune' is probably no more fool's gold.[19]

He is also reputed to be the source of Robert Louis Stevenson's verse in *Treasure Island*,

> 'Fifteen men on the dead man's chest,
> Yo-ho-ho and a bottle of rum!
> Drink and the Devil had done for the rest,
> Yo-ho-ho and a bottle of rum!'.

Finding some of his crew mutinous he marooned them on a tiny and barren rock off Tortola in the Virgin Islands. It was known as the Dead Man's Chest because of its utter sterility and its swarms of lizards, mosquitoes and snakes. He gave each man a cutlass and a bottle of rum hoping that they would kill each other but when he returned next month fifteen were still alive.

His was a raving, despotic, hellbent life. 'Such a day, rum all out', he wrote in his journal, 'our company somewhat sober, a damned confusion amongst us; rogues a-plotting . . . so I look'd sharp for a prize'. Fearless but sadistic, he was also sexually perverted. Married to a young girl, his fourteenth wife so Johnson recorded, 'with whom after he had lain all Night, it was his Custom to invite five or six of his brutish Companions to come ashore, and he would force her to prostitute herself to them all, one after another, before his Face'. Johnson thought 'His Behaviour in this State, was something extraordinary'.[20]

In 1999 underwater archaeology located the remains of a former vessel of his, the awesome 40-gun *Queen Anne's Revenge*, once the French slave-ship *Concorde*. In his captured ship on 10 June, 1718, Blackbeard had run aground on a shallow sandbank at the mouth of Beaufort Islet, North Carolina. Attempts to re-float it through the use of ropes and a kedge anchor failed and Blackbeard stripped it of vegetables and departed in a smaller vessel.

Almost three centuries later after several frustrating years the wreckage was found in an extensive survey of the sea-bed. Work was slow. A succession of hurricanes had covered everything under layers of sand. Once disturbed the silt eliminated visibility.

Despite this the search was successful. Every article found could be dated to near but never later than 1718: early eighteenth century pewter platters; a lead syringe for injecting mercury to cure VD; a Spanish bell of 1709; a glass wine bottle of *c.* 1712; some grains of gold. The *Concorde* had carried 20lbs of gold dust.

Most convincing of all was the armament, cannons of varying sizes and power, plundered from ships. One stamped IEC came from a late seventeenth century Swedish cannonry.

the trunnion of a light culverin was dated 1713. They had all belonged to Blackbeard's *Queen Anne's Revenge.*

A few days after the end of the excavation ended, a fourth hurricane in that notorious 'graveyard of the Atlantic' howled across the waters as though the sea was resisting any attempt to reveal its piratical secrets.[21]

There was little romantic or attractive about pirates whether Blackbeard's or Howel Davis' men. Philip Ashton, a seaman who was captured by the pirate Edward Low in 1722, was sickened by the uncouth manners, having to live 'with such a vile crew of miscreants, to whom it was a sport to do mischief, where prodigious drinking, monstrous cursing and swearing, hideous blasphemies, and open defiance of Heaven, and contempt of Hell itself, was the constant employment, unless when sleep something abated the noise and revelling'.

Far from Blackbeard's villainies and debaucheries and just as far from Howel Davis Alexander Selkirk was working in H.M.S. *Enterprise.* Having returned to England with Woodes Rogers in 1711 he was awarded a considerable share or prize money but was already missing the isolated pleasures of his marooned island. 'I am now worth eight hundred pounds', he told Sir Richard Steele, 'but shall never be so happy as when I was not worth a farthing'.

He was discontented, easily provoked. In 1713 he was accused of assaulting a shipwright in Bristol. In 1714 he went back to his family home in Largo, Fifeshire, but even there lived as a recluse, choosing to occupy a makeshift 'cave' at the end of the garden. He fought with his brothers. Then he eloped to London with a local girl, Sophia Bruce. In 1717 he made a will bequeathing everything to her. But almost immediately he abandoned her to enlist in the Navy. In 1718 he went back to Sophia only to desert her again, preferring the humdrum sea business of carrying navy stores to ports along the English Channel. It was an unromantic occupation for one who was to become a celebrity the following year with the publication of *Robinson Crusoe*. The tedium of naval peace was not to last however. On 7 December 1718, England declared war on Spain for the second time in the century. Men-of-war would be needed in the Mediterranean.[22]

None of this was known to Howel Davis as he headed southwards on the five hundred mile voyage to the Royal African Company's fort at Sierra Leone. With luck there would be a fortune of ships at that busy and lucrative place. Then there would be plunder and wealth when the accumulated luxuries of diamonds, dollars, daggers of Toledo steel, gold-dust, lace-embroidered doublets and other delicacies of clothing, everything valuable, would be shared out, stored and locked in personal sea-chests to be taken out by their owners, gloated over, gambled with, wasted and enjoyed at every sanctuary they reached.

For his fresh eagerness and because of his understanding of the intricacies of a ship's rigging Richard Jones was elected boatswain.[23]

2

The Raid at Sierra Leone

March 1719

> 'The pirates have met with such recognition there in
> Africa that it is become a place of rendezvous there being
> so many rascals on shore that assist them with boats and
> canoes to bring their goods on shore'.
>
> *Letters sent from Africa*, 1714–1719. (PRO T70/6)

March, 1719. There was no mistaking 'Lion Mountain',
Sierra Leone. Amongst the forested highlands behind the
settlement was a tree much larger than the rest. In the wide
estuary, its banks broken and jagged with creeks and inlets, the
pirates could hear the roaring of the waterfalls thundering
amongst the wooded ravines. Some said the place was called
Sierra Leone because the landscaped looked like a lion
squatting behind the town, others that the grumbling waters
sounded like the growling of the jungle king. The pirates were
more interested in the warmth and the plunder.

Men who had been lounging about the deck, half-naked in
the sun, now attended to their weapons, sharpening cutlasses,
cleaning pistols, taking their places beside the guns. La
Bouche's sloop lay alongside. Easy pickings were expected.
Well-stocked trading ships came here for slaves and ivory and
the only fort was small and weakly defended.

It was no pleasure to find another pirate already there with two captured vessels, a black flag hanging at his masthead. The commander of the *Mourroon* galley was Thomas Cocklyn who had once sailed in the same ship as la Bouche.[1] When he learned that la Bouche was with Davis he at once invited both of them aboard. Hardly had Davis arrived than a seaman rushed up begging him to save innocent men from being murdered as William Hall had been.

Hall had been in the *Edward and Steed* taken the day before by Cocklyn. After the ship had been plundered its mate was ordered by the pirate boatswain to send a sailor up into the shrouds to release the foretop-sailsheet, a sail high above the forecastle. Being by nature a slow-moving man Hall had taken too long for the pirate's liking. Thinking that he was being insolent the boatswain shot at Hall with a carbine. Though hit Hall was not killed. The boatswain clambered into the shrouds after the wounded man, not to help him but to hack him to death with a cutlass, letting the body drop into the sea. Since then the crew of the *Edward and Steed* feared that they too might be slaughtered at the casual whim of some pirate.[2]

Davis swore. He damned Cocklyn for a fool and as he shouted for the rest of his men edged around the two. Cocklyn's men stood nearby fingering weapons. The forced men also watched, some hopeful, most indifferent because whichever pirate won there was no hope of release. They would remain prisoners.

Davis harshly reminded Cocklyn of the difference between punishing those who would not surrender and those who gave in without a struggle. So bitingly did he accuse the pirate and his ruffians of stupidity and cowardice that there would have been a fight had not la Bouche intervened. Chattering gaily, arms around their shoulders, he led them to Cocklyn's cabin. Soon all three were laughing. They agreed to attack the fort upriver where half a dozen ships had fled from Cocklyn.

La Bouche and Cocklyn had once been in a ship commanded

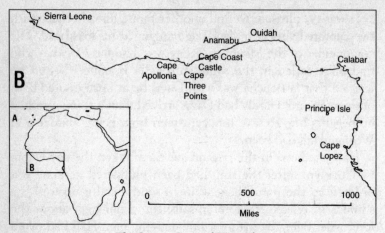

The Guinea Coast of West Africa

by Christopher Moody, whose red flag, the 'jolie rouge' or 'Jolly Roger', bore an hourglass and a hand brandishing a cutlass over a skull and crossbones. Moody sickened of Cocklyn's senseless brutality. Suspecting a plot to depose him he put Cocklyn and other discontents in a leaky galley, the *Rising Sun*, expecting that it would capsize.[3] Cocklyn renamed the vessel the *Mourroon* and in it he reached Sierra Leone. Meanwhile Moody's remaining crew, finding that he was cheating them of their shares, marooned him and elected la Bouche as their leader. Moody eventually reached New Providence where he joined Davis' mutiny in the *Buck*. Now Cocklyn, la Bouche and Moody were reunited, partners in suspicion, in a strong company of pirates.

Cocklyn suggested that Davis and la Bouche should blockade the trading ships at the fort while he took the second of his prizes, the *Two Friends*, to sea to find whether she sailed better than his present ship.[4] At the fort the six merchantmen huddled together at anchor but at the sight of the pirates they slipped their cables hoping to escape. Davis did not hurry. Broad though the river was it narrowed rapidly a few miles upstream. No ship could sail far. He lay just out of range of the fort's guns, calmly waiting for Cocklyn's return. Suddenly two cannon shots exploded.

A pirate chuckled in relief. Their 'attacker' was an old man, John Leadstine, a character known as 'Crackers', a private trader who saluted every pirate that came in knowing that they would bring him cheap goods.[5] Other traders waved from the shore. In the sullen heat the merchant captains watched helplessly. Yardarms creaked as men furled the sails. Wooden blocks clattered together as a breeze caught the rigging. A smell of tar came from the deck. The sun was almost overhead.

It was a hostile land. Over the shabby town scavenging birds dived down onto the muckheaps. Around the ships' masts tiny birds of scarlet circled in the quivering air, gliding with others whose long tails seemed too heavy for their bodies. In the waters were sharks guided by bright pilot-fish. Carnivorous angel-fish flickered in search of crabs and barnacles. Up river in the mangrove swamps were crocodiles twice the length of a man. Beyond the rocky shore, almost without earth, was a thick forest of palms and spiky-leaved cotton trees. Further inland the hills were dense with jungle, steaming with humidity. It was a vivid spectacle, the town, the trees, birds, a sky white with warmth, and ancient 'Crackers' welcoming from the shore with the smoke from his polished brass cannon lingering in the air.

In mid-river on Bence Island was the fort, in miserable condition though strong when contrasted with some of the other so-called 'castles' that the Royal African Company had on the coast. The Company was struggling. Since its inauguration in Elizabethan times it had imposed a total monopoly unlike other chartered companies that permitted private merchants to trade for a fee. Instead, it discouraged them by demanding an exorbitant ten percent charge on all freight. It had once been forty per cent until the West Indian planters had furiously protested because slave-traders passed the extra cost directly onto them.[6]

The African Company had forts and trading posts, 'factories' they were called, all along the West African coast intermixing with other strongholds belonging to Portugal, France and Denmark. To the factories natives brought ivory, dyewood, slaves and gold. These were profitable goods and many ships came for them. It was a rewarding coastline for pirates. At Sierra Leone the local traders waited until they could come to haggle over the plunder.

In the fort the Company's agent was an honest man, Plunket, poorly paid, living in neglect but known for his courage and determination to resist attack. Such African Company servants were known as 'white negroes'. They were completely in the control of the governor to the east at Cape Coast Castle. They could be punished by imprisonment, whipping, fined some of their derisory pay for trivialities such as swearing. Those like Plunket who lived in one of the outer forts might make a little money through personal trade. Nearer Cape Coast Castle the agents were given foul lodging and short provisions, and their wages, paid in local Company money unacceptable to ordinary traders and merchants, was so meagre that with the strict system of fines they often ran into debt. This trapped them in the Company's service until their accounts were settled. Isolated between the sea and an impenetrable jungle they had no life, only existence. Sodden with cheap rum, ill-fed, diseased, the majority died young. They had no choice. Servitude in Africa was the only honest living they could find.[7]

The private traders lived better. 'They all', noted Atkins, 'keep gromettas, negro servants, . . . the women keep house and are obedient to any prostitution their masters command'. Each trader had his own shack in the cooler shadows of the trees. 'Crackers' was easily picked out by its two cannon. Like the others it stood amongst a cluster of sturdy wooden cages. These were for slaves captured by negro raiding parties who brought them in chained three or four together. By an ironical inversion of history this slaving-post became known as Freetown in 1787 when British abolitionists sent emancipated slaves to settle there. But in 1719 Africa was a bitter, savage land of wars and slaves, of a greedy Company and underpaid servants, and of merchant ships with human cargoes. For pirates it was a paradise.

Next morning when Cocklyn had still not arrived la Bouche impatiently decided to attack the fort. Davis refused. Without Cocklyn they were not strong enough against so many ships and the fort. Impulsively and alone the Frenchman's sloop sailed boldly towards the merchantmen. A shot tore through its mainsail. Another shot fell just short of the bows and as the ship hastily veered away a third ball sent water spraying over its decks. The crew of the *Royal James* applauded mockingly.

When Cocklyn finally appeared he came not only with the *Two Friends* but with another, the one taken earlier by Davis at Gambia. Knowing how thoroughly she had been looted Davis wondered why Cocklyn had bothered to bring her with him. Because, Cocklyn replied pretentiously, he wanted both a store- and a hospital-ship.

The three pirate vessels advanced. Seeing that la Bouche was now accompanied by the *Mourroon* galley and the great *Royal James* the captains immediately abandoned their vessels and rushed to the fort. At Cocklyn's mast flew the black flag with a skeleton painted on it. The other side bore a skull and crossbones against an hourglass. At his bows was a second black flag with a man's arm holding a dagger, a skull on the reverse. As though this were not daunting enough his ensign was a St. George's Cross with four balls in the quarter.[8] The *Royal James* and la Bouche's sloop also carried black flags.

Such flags were designed to scare. Death was their message. Many had skeletons or skulls or dried bones painted on them, upturned hour-glasses to remind any seamen thinking of resistance that life was a transient thing. Others had the same warning in the form of weapons. Across the Atlantic, indolently plundering around the Jamaican coast, 'Calico Jack'

Rackam, so called from his fondness for brightly-coloured cotton clothing, had a black flag beneath whose skull were two crossed, upturned cutlasses.[9]

Despite superseding Vane and having a heavily-armed brigantine he was not an active commander. Preference for drink and an easy existence limited his ambition. What made him noteworthy were the two young women in his crew, the twenty-seven year old Mary Read, and Rackam's mistress, Anne Bonny, nineteen years of age. Both of them were as ferocious and ruthless fighters as any of his men. Murderous with their weapons the women were terrifying. Sailors who had been attacked by Rackam remembered them well.

They 'were very active on Board and willing to do any Thing; that Ann Bonny . . . handed Gun-Powder to the Men, That when they saw any Vessel, gave Chase or Attacked, they wore Men's Cloathes; and, at other Times, they wore Women's Clothes; That they did not seem to be kept or detained by Force, but of their own Free-Will and Consent'.[10] Another witness from the captured *Mary & Sarah* remembered that 'Ann Bonny . . . had a Gun in her Hand, That [the women] were both very profligate, cursing and swearing much, and very willing to do any Thing on Board'.[11]

The sight of these screeching amazons chopping, slicing and smashing at any opposition with their yard-long cutlasses and heavy bone-splitting marlin-spikes, the blasting of the pirate guns, the black flag with its threat of death quickly diluted any thought of defence. It was no different at Sierra Leone. The flags, the yelling of the pirates, the booming of cannon aimed at the fleeing boats were enough to scare any honest seaman. When the merchantmen were reached there was no one left in them.

It was a good haul. Cocklyn already had the two prizes down river. To these were now added; the *Robert & Jane* brig; Captain Bennet from Antigua; the *Parnel* snow, Captain Morris from Bristol; the *Nightingale* from the same city; the *Queen Elizabeth*,

Captain Creighton, the *Jacob & Jael*, Captain Thompson, and the *Society*, both from London.[12] There was ivory, cloth, provisions, rum, wines, spirits. The pirate boatswains removed all the undamaged rigging, sails, tallow, pitch, necessaries for sailing. The gunners took powder, matches and firearms. The quartermasters rummaged for valuables to be divided amongst the crews. What they did not find was money.

The merchant captains had optimistically taken the gold and cash with them but the pirates quickly obtained it by demanding a ransom for each ship. Four of the captains agreed to barter for them. Thompson and Bennet refused.

Cocklyn, Davis and la Bouche did not hesitate. The fort had to be overpowered. There would probably be a lot of Company's money in it. Pirates boarded the two unredeemed ships. Holes were smashed in the sides. Palm leaves smeared with tar, pitch and brimstone were flung about the decks. Gunpowder kegs were set in the holds. From their boats the pirates threw flaming torches into the primed vessels. Both were soon ablaze. One exploded, heeled over and sank. The other smouldered into the night.

With nightfall came the assault. Armed with flintlocks, carbines and cutlasses boatloads of pirates rowed quietly towards the fort. At dawn, close to the ruined walls, they began firing. Their three ships had rounded the island to bombard the fort. There was sporadic return fire but many of the fort's greater guns had rusted in the moist climate and were unfit for use. By mid-morning one of the walls had been smashed down. Davis sent the agent an impudent note asking whether he could spare any gold, gunpowder or cannonballs. Plunket an Irishman, retorted that he had no gold to spare but powder and ball in plenty if Davis cared to collect it.

The attack continued until smoke and flames almost hid the fort. No shots came from it. Plunket had used all his ammunition. Realising he could resist no longer he took his men in boats along the back channel of the island onto another islet. They were seen and captured.[13]

In fury Cocklyn shouted and threatened Plunket, shaking his pistol at the captive's head because he had dared resist them. He cursed the agent for his Irish insolence. But Plunket swore back even more foully, damning Cocklyn for a villain and a cut-throat whose mother was even now searching the back-streets of the slums in the hope of recognising his father.[14]

The bellowing, the oaths, the insults, the retorts became so loud and so many that even Cocklyn began laughing. All the pirates were in good moods. The ships and the fort were theirs. Under the directions of the three quartermasters the warehouses were ransacked and everything stowed in Cocklyn's storeship. Division of the loot would come later. Some of Plunket's men received one-sided invitations to join the pirates, one-sided because if they refused they were forced and then given the worst tasks to do, were allowed no firearms nor any freedom to go ashore except under supervision.

'Crackers' and his fellows came to bargain only to be told that until the quartermasters had appraised the goods nothing could be done but that the following evening there would be a celebration in which it was hoped that the traders would participate. Anxious to do business with such easy-going pedlars the men promised to provide whatever they could for the feast.

In the aftermath of the fight some pirates harpooned turtles. Others fished. Some dragged wood for the fire. Casks of rum, cider, brandy, pipes of wine were rowed ashore. Crackers brought scrawny cattle and stringy hens. Negroes watched, the men in loincloths, the women bare-breasted, garbed in a loose skirt hanging from their hips to halfway down their thighs. Pirates looked in anticipation.

The fire was lit. Around it were smaller hearths over which bowls of punch simmered as the wines, milk, limejuice, sugar and spices mingled. Turtles baked succulently in their shells as pirates came ashore bright with earrings, fine stolen silks and suits, silver buckles, jewels, brooches, sparkling chains. It was a life no honest sailor would know.

In the following days three more ships came into the river, one of them, the *Sarah*, coveted by Cocklyn[15] but few more could be expected. Eleven merchantmen had now been captured at Sierra Leone and news of their disappearance would warn others to keep away. The only unsuspecting vessels would be those coming directly from Britain or the Americas. The traders continued to make bids for the loot. Plunket was allowed to return to the wrecked fort. And one of the forced men on the *Mourroon* galley ran off with a friend into the woods.

For a day the pirates searched for them. The refugees knew too much to be allowed to go free. But they could not be found. Davis was untroubled. Leave them to their fate, he advised. The undergrowth, thick, thorny and impassable within a few strides except by hacked-out paths, was so wild, the animals and savages so numerous that no man could reach the next trading-post. Nor could anyone live off the land. He would be slaughtered by beasts, murdered by negroes or would starve.

He was right. After three days Henry Thixton returned. He was half-conscious from lack of food, his clothes were in tatters where he had hidden himself in the thorny undergrowth. His friend was dead. Davis took him on board the *Royal James*. Cocklyn would have killed him, but being a skilled carpenter Thixton was too valuable to be executed.[16]

In Britain from 1718 to 1720 Alexander Selkirk remained on HMS *Enterprise* commuting boringly but honestly from naval dockyard to dockyard, Sheerness to Portsmouth, Woolwich to Plymouth. His fame as the real-life Robinson Crusoe had brought him no reward.

3

The Capture of Captain Snelgrave

'By letters from Cape Coast Castle of the 17 October we have advice that the gang of pirates that are now upon that coast are a new gang'.

Weekly Journal or British Gazetteer, 16 April 1720.

The pirates were ready to leave Sierra Leone. Cocklyn had decided that the *Sarah* was the ship he needed to replace the decaying *Mourroon* and with Davis' and la Bouche's permission he prepared to refit her. But the spoils, still on his storeship, had to be divided. It could not be left until they sailed. Once at sea Cocklyn might slip away at night.

Then the large, well-armed *Bird* galley from London came in.[1] A lookout spied her in the distance and rather than undertaking what could become a long chase at sea the pirates withdrew their vessels out of sight up river. In their haste they forgot to extinguish their camp fires.

The *Bird* dropped anchor late in the dusk and its captain, Snelgrave, sent a pinnace to investigate the cause of the smoke. But night fell rapidly in the tropics and the search-party returned saying that it was hopeless looking for anything in the dark. Not satisfied but unable to see anything Snelgrave went to his cabin for supper. Before he had finished his meal the officer of the watch reported sounds of rowing.

Two boatloads of Cocklyn's men, twelve altogether, were

approaching the vessel. Even though armed with pistols, cutlasses and grenades such a small band had little chance of taking a ship as defensively armed as the *Bird*. The pirates had become so accustomed to instant capitulation that they expected no resistance.

It was not only the fear of reprisals that caused the lack of fight by the crews of merchant ships. Theirs was a hard life. They were often treated inhumanly, their food was sickening and their quarters not fit for cattle. They owned no shares in their vessel. Their pay was small. Except for wartime seamen's wages remained almost unchanged between 1700 and 1750.[2] A merchant captain received between £5 and £6 monthly. First mates and surgeons, necessary specialists, £3 to £4. Boatswains, carpenters, cooks about £2. Ordinary seamen were given no more than £1.10.0 [£1.50] and even this was often stopped when at anchor. Long stays in ports could result in mutiny by unpaid crews.

As Bartholomew Roberts was later cynically to observe that although he had at first shed 'crocodile tears' when forced to join the pirates he soon changed his mind. 'In an honest service, there is thin commons, low wages, and hard labour; in this [piracy], plenty and satiety, pleasure and ease, liberty and power. And who would not balance creditor on this side, when all the hazard that is run for it, at worst, is only a sour look or two at choking. No, a merry life and a short one shall be my motto'.[3] It was a philosophy shared by many pirates who had been near-slaves on honest ships.

In squalor they had laboured in heat and storm for months, voyaging thousands of miles, earning a pittance while the cargoes they carried made the bark's owner rich. There was no reason for them to risk injury or death. Nor were their numbers sufficient or their firearms powerful enough to withstand pirates. A captain with some sixteen reluctant men and no more than six puny cannon could not hope to hold off scores of vicious attackers whose own sloop carried twenty or more great guns as well as raking swivels and the dreadful pateraroes or pedreros loaded with stones, nails and broken iron. Promises of compensation were no inducement for honest men to resist.[4]

Ignorant of the *Bird's* sixteen cannon Cocklyn left to bring the *Mourroon* down the river while his men overcame the merchantman. For half an hour there was silence. Then there was the sound of pistols being fired from the *Bird*. From midriver came the roar of the *Mourroon's* guns. Then silence again.

Suspecting pirates Snelgrave had dropped anchor not wishing to imperil his fully-laden cargo. With a ship of so many guns and with forty-five men he could repel an attack unless taken by surprise. The report of the sound of oars brought him to the deck. With a seaman he lit the ship's lanterns and ordered his mate to rouse the sleeping crew, issue them with arms and send twenty of them to him on the quarterdeck.

He hailed the boats that were now alongside, asking why they were so close at that time of night. A voice replied that they were from the *Two Friends*, Captain Elliott, of Barbados. Snelgrave's defenders had still not appeared when, without warning, shots were fired at him. The captain shouted for his men to shoot from the steerage portholes. Nothing happened. Then an officer ran up. The seamen refused to arm themselves.

Snelgrave rushed below. As he did so the pirates boarded. Hardly had he emerged with the two or three men who were willing to help than the pirates fired again, killing one of them. As Snelgrave started to retreat a grenade exploded on the forecastle. At this his frightened crew begged him to surrender. He had no choice. He had no firearms, the pirates were pressing closer and the lanterns were lighting the deck too well for him to hide. The pirate quartermaster raised a pistol asking why Snelgrave had ordered his men to resist.

The captain replied that it was his duty to the ship's owners and even as he pushed the pistol aside the pirate fired, the bullet grazing Snelgrave's arm. He turned to run but was struck bleedingly on the head by the pistol butt. Dazed, on his knees, he scrambled to the quarterdeck only to be stopped by the pirate boatswain with the words, 'No quarter shall be given to any captain that offers to defend his ship'. He lashed at Snelgrave with his cutlass, just missing his head and cutting into the deck's rail so savagely that the blade snapped.

One of Snelgrave's crew pushed through a bunch of pirates and pleaded for the captain's life to be spared. 'For God's sake, don't kill our captain', he begged, 'for we were never with a better man'. Others joined in and the babbled importunities so infuriated the boatswain and his mates that they lashed out brutally with pistols and cutlasses. Someone would have been killed had the pirates not been distracted by their quartermaster emerging from the hold where he had been inspecting the freight.[5] Ordering the seamen to be tied up he bellowed that there was a treasure-house below: weapons, cloths, pans, bowls, copper bars, provisions, rum, spirits and wine. And there was money. Each pirate in the attack could take a shift of clothes and the lookout that had seen the *Bird* could choose a brace of pistols.

Carbines were fired in the air at such providence. This caused Cocklyn in the *Mourroon* to think that the *Bird* was fighting back and impulsively he ordered all the starboard guns to be fired. The shots shrieked across the *Bird*'s flush decks, smashing into masts and sails and it was only by providence that no one, pirate or honest man, was hurt by the broadside.

Snelgrave was taken to the *Mourroon* where Cocklyn questioned him about the galley's performance even though the pirate had already been given the *Sarah*. Snelgrave's provocatively non-committal answers would have led to more violence had not the quartermaster entered with two documents. One was a General Pardon for all pirates who surrendered before 1 July. Cocklyn jeered. The other was a report of the declaration of war by the British, French, Dutch and Austrians against Spain who had invaded Sicily trying to regain territories she had recently lost in Italy. At the news many pirates, Davis' men amongst them, half-wished they were still honest seamen, not for any thought of patriotism but because it was both safer and more profitable to be a legitimate privateer. In England naval seamen such as Alexander Selkirk welcomed the prospect of war after the monotonous months of peace.

The *Bird* became part of the pirate fleet. Once more the traders came out to buy the plundered goods, one of them, Hogbin, rowing laden boatload after boatload of cloth and material back to his house. The rest of the cargo was transferred to the storeship from which it would be split amongst the ships. Anything not wanted was jettisoned by pirates laughing at the fountains of water and the boxes and bundles bobbing and swirling towards the sea.

Meanwhile Davis and la Bouche had come aboard the *Mourroon* to meet the captain who had brought them such wealth. Henry Glynn, one of the less dishonest traders, was at their side, an old friend of Snelgrave's who was horrified when he saw how the captain had been treated.

But it was time for the rewards. Under the sharp supervision of Cocklyn's quartermaster the cargo was divided. By custom the goods were considered common property. Other than those men who had taken part in the attack, no man, were he captain, quartermaster or ordinary sailor could take anything. Each of the boarding-party picked a complete set of clothes. The lookout who had sighted the *Bird* had his choice of pistols. Everything else was untouched until the three quartermasters valued it together.

This was tradition. It prevented suspicions of cheating for it stopped someone from hiding money or jewellery above his fair share. If found guilty of theft a man would be tried by his shipmates and suffer whatever they felt justified.[6] Cocklyn's men were murderous. One of Davis' crew tried to break open a chest. Cocklyn's quartermaster asked what he was doing. Impudently the eighteen-year-old answered that they were all pirates together. The quartermaster swung at him with his broadsword, missed, and the frightened thief raced into the Great Cabin where Davis sat drinking with Cocklyn. The quartermaster rushed after him. In the cramped space he thrust at the youth, cut him on the thumb but also wounded Davis on the hand.

With a bloodstained kerchief Davis stormed out vowing vengeance. Even if his man was in the wrong Davis should have been told first, no one else had the right to punish a member of his ship, this was not the first insult he had received from Cocklyn, now the *Mourroon* should taste the power of a real pirate vessel instead of skulking like a timid girl behind her escort. On board the *Royal James* the guns were run out. A boat rowed frantically from the *Bird*. Cocklyn had decided peace was better than death. His quartermaster grovelled an apology to Davis.

The quarrel over the three captains discussed their future. Before leaving Sierra Leone Cocklyn and la Bouche wanted to change their ships. La Bouche's sloop was ruinous with teredo worm. It was also very small, ideal for the West Indies where the many creeks and inlets demanded a shallow draught and quick manoeuvrability but off Africa a more seaworthy craft was preferred. Cocklyn's *Mourroon* was leaky with neglect. Two more ships would be selected from the prizes. Cocklyn had been allotted the *Sarah* and la Bouche opted to have the *Bird*. Both were galleys well-fitted for action at sea.

Such galleys were not like those of the Mediterranean rowed by slaves of the Barbary pirates. The Atlantic was too rough for a ship dependent on its oars. The *Bird* and the *Sarah* did have holes between the gunports for oars but they also had the sails of any small merchantman. They were solidly-built craft, wide in the beam with a deck flush from bow to stern like the more powerful *Royal James* brigantine.

Cocklyn and la Bouche set their carpenters to work. The bulkheads dividing the cabins and holds below deck were pulled down so that one could see from end to end with only timber uprights interrupting the view. A clear ship was essential. Narrow gangways or hatches impeded movement. Pirate vessels were overcrowded, sometimes threefold, and extra room was needed.

The lower decks became spacious and threatening. Extra gunports gaped in the sides, extra guns were transferred from vessels that were to be left behind. The *Sarah*, renamed the *Speakwell* by Cocklyn, carried thirty guns, as many as the *Royal James*. La Bouche's *Bird* became the *Wyndham Galley* and had an armament of twenty-four assorted cannon and swivels. The vessel had been transformed into a warship powerful enough to intimidate most merchantmen.

The refitting was almost done. The keels had been scraped and cleaned. The carpenters had only to raise the gunwales breast-high for protection against bullets, and to cut down obstructive deckhouses and hatch-covers. Then all three leaders had ships well-suited to piracy, swift, protected and heavily armed. The ransacked hulks squatted vacantly with their grumbling captains on board. The fort was a smoke-smeared ruin. It was time to share the spoils, a simple matter had it all been in coin. But with provisions, clothes, firearms, jewellery it was the job of the quartermasters to satisfy everyone.

The romantic vision of a pirate captain is of a grand commander giving orders, living in a luxurious, tapestry-draped cabin with soft rugs from Persia and India, a chamber where golden candleholders glittered on exquisite Venetian glassware and decanters filled with rare wines, shining on treasure chests in which rubies, diamonds and emeralds coruscated, a room full of riches for a despot. Such a captain might shoot a man, maroon a man, do as he wished. The truth was different.

Pirate captains were not unchallengeable. Howel Davis had power only when pursuing a prize or deciding which place was to be plundered next. In reality his position was less than that of a quartermaster because pirate ships were manned by sailors who had suffered under the autocracy of merchant captains and Naval commanders. They had no intention of being bullied again. No pirate officer held his command any longer than the majority wished.

It was not Davis or Cocklyn or la Bouche who apportioned the loot but the quartermasters. It was they who protected the crew from the domination of a captain. They decided the punishment for minor offences. They commanded the ship when not in action. They supervised any duel. They were the first to board a prize and to go on any desperate mission.

Once on a captured vessel the quartermaster decided what was to be taken. He would ask the boatswain what stores, sails or rigging were needed. He allowed the gunner to choose weapons. But it was he, and he alone, that made the final decisions. He chose what to take. Gold, silver, jewellery and coins were obligatory. All else rested with the quartermaster's decision. And he supervised the distribution of plunder.

Finding Cocklyn's storeship too cramped the three quartermasters ordered everything taken to the *Wyndham Galley* with its newly-cleared upper deck. There they sorted the booty into three piles taking care that each was equal in value because they did not know which was to be theirs. Only when the last item was added did they draw lots for which stack they would receive.

The share given to Taylor was taken to the *Royal James*. Already there were grumbles. The three heaps were equitable but Davis' crew was much bigger than either of the others so that its hundred and fifty men would each get less than the other pirates, just what had been feared when Cocklyn's ship had been seen in the river.

The sight of the vast plunder minimised the criticisms. Pirates habitually lived in small groups with friends keeping together, cooking their own meals and sleeping in the same quarters. Taylor, the *Royal James'* quartermaster, found it easiest to allocate quantities of the spoil to these messes, leaving it to the men to decide who was to have what. By the time a man took his possessions they had been handled three times: once by the quartermasters for their ships; then by Taylor for the messes; and finally by the mess itself. Davis as captain took two shares, Taylor had a share and a half. The other officers were given one share and a quarter.

Men chattered as they examined their gifts. Fingers were bright with rings. Tankards and medallions were polished. Delicately-chased swords were compared with ivory-handled pistols and pairs of finely-balanced knives. There were rolls of satin and silk and taffeta; and coats and candlesticks, watches and waistcoats and a hundred other articles scattered on a deck resembling a hurricane-blown shop floor. One man plucked at his pear-shaped cittern of smooth Spanish wood while his mates sang. Others were already dicing and gambling away their winnings.

Davis and Taylor discussed the supplies of gunpowder and weapons with Dennis, the ship's gunner. It was time to leave. Since the *Bird* only one ship had entered the river and it had instantly brought trouble upon itself because of its obstructive French captain. Cocklyn's men repaid his discourtesy by their usual method of putting a rope around his neck and hauling him up and down from the yardarm. La Bouche resented the torture of his countryman and Cocklyn had to pacify him by placing both the captain and his ship in la Bouche's care.

Since then almost a fortnight had passed. From Snelgrave it was learned that Edward England was still plundering at Gambia. News moved quickly on the African coast. No merchantman would come near either Sierra Leone or Gambia until some freed victim announced that the pirates had gone.

Incidents broke the tedium. Cocklyn's quartermaster fell sick of a fever and died in a babble of repentance and blasphemy, 'cursing his Maker in a shocking Manner'.[7] Then Davis, Cocklyn and la Bouche decided that they would visit the ladies on shore but that, being captains, they would go in the finest clothes they could find. Without permission they took three of

Snelgrave's embroidered coats. Their crews resented such presumption. The coats were stripped from the captains and auctioned. Williams, la Bouche's quartermaster, blamed Snelgrave and would have killed him had not the captain apologised and with sugary flattery addressed him as 'captain'. This so pleased Williams that he gave Snelgrave a keg of wine.

A final party was given in the *Royal James* to which everyone, pirates, traders, Snelgrave, was invited. Into a huge iron cauldron from the *Wyndham Galley* food went indiscriminately: turkeys, ducks, headless but unplucked chickens from which only the indigestable wing feathers had been removed; Westphalian ham; and a large, unskinned sow. While music played the captains had their supper in the Great Cabin. For them, with table, plate and wine-glasses, it was a feast. For their crew it was a drunken celebration. So drunken that it was nearly their last.

Some pirates staggered below for more rum from the stores and dropped a lamp. The burning oil ignited straw and wood, starting a blaze that was likely to consume the entire ship. When a negro screamed a warning there was hardly a man sober enough to understand the danger. Luckily Snelgrave and the gunner's mate, Goulding, somehow organised a gang to work the pump and make a chain of unsteady buckets down to the hold. When, at last, the fire was extinguished it was discovered that the *Royal James* contained over eighteen tons of gunpowder.

Ironically, his decisiveness nearly cost Snelgrave his freedom. The pirates were so impressed by his ability that they demanded that he be taken with them. Snelgrave, one man persisted, was an excellent pilot. Tiring of the fellow's incessant arguments Davis cudgelled him off the quarterdeck saying they needed no pilot. Instead, Snelgrave was 'rewarded' by the gift of la Bouche's sloop for his homeward voyage. Davis even offered him some left-over goods to be sold along the coast. Snelgrave refused.

Davis was elected commander-in-chief of the three pirate ships. Cocklyn's storeship and the captured *Guinea Hen* were to accompany them. Before they sailed a mate of one of the rifled merchantmen asked Davis for provisions. He had no money, he explained, and its lack was likely to lead to starvation amongst the crew. Davis instead generously offered him a place in the *Royal James*. He had a wife, the man replied in alarm, and was not free to join the pirates. He trusted Davis was gentleman enough not to force him. Davis answered, quite untruthfully, that he had no forced men with him, and gave the mate provisions.

The pirates left Sierra Leone towards the end of April 1719, heading southwards with steady currents and moderate winds, keeping a few miles off the coast, always in sight of its low, tree-thickened shore. There was hardly a bay or inlet, just a rushing surf that made a landing in a ship's boat almost impossible. But it was good to be at sea again with the fresher air and a cool breeze in the shadow of the sails.

Soon Cocklyn let the *Guinea Hen* go[8] because she sailed more slowly than the others. Her captain veered happily westwards towards the trade winds and by morning was out of sight. The fleet sailed on, seeing no vessel, rounding Cape Palmas, on to the Ivory Coast and beyond towards the Gold Coast and the forts of the Royal African Company at Dixcove, Queen Anne's Point, Cape Coast Castle and Anamabu where ships carried money to buy slaves.

In the hot weather the drinking water was quickly consumed. Davis ordered men ashore to fill the casks but the breaking waves and rollers were too hazardous and the pirates waited for the assistance of native fishermen. Such inhabitants were infamous for their treachery. Cruel and suspicious by nature the raids of slave-traders had filled them with hatred of white men. Some, however, could be bribed and because the shortage of water was crucial Davis gave the paddlers some trinkets and old firearms in return for taking men ashore to the springs. Long hours passed.

As daylight faded canoes left the beach. There were no pirates in them, only negroes. Their leader jabbered to Taylor that the white men had run off as soon as they reached the trees. It was unbelievable. One man had been with Davis since the mutiny on the *Buck*. It was unlikely he would want to desert and certain that he was not lunatic enough to escape at that forbidding spot where the nearest trading-post was miles away through unknown jungle. More probably he and his fellows had been murdered for their weapons. But water was still wanted. Only the natives could bring it.

Using Taylor as interpreter Davis informed the leader that he would send a second party. Then, in English, Taylor was told to ensure that the group was so fully armed that it could force the negroes to return to the *Royal James*.

There was haggling. The sea was perilous and more presents would have to be given. Davis accepted. The pirates, he said, would die without water.

Men went to the gunner for firearms. Casks were lowered into the canoes. The negro paddlers held the craft steady as the sweeping breakers rushed them to the beach. Pirates jumped out and pointed guns at the natives as they began to disembark. One was forced to lead other pirates to a stream where the barrels were filled. Once back on the *Royal James* the negroes were asked again what had happened to the missing men. They did not answer.

Taylor had them put in irons. In the morning they were dragged from the hold and Taylor demanded to learn where the missing men were. Their chief insisted that they had run away. No one believed him. Some pirates shouted that the murderers should be flogged, others that they be hanged but Taylor proposed that target-practice would be more entertaining.

Two negroes were pressed to the deck by pirates kneeling on their arms and legs while their chains were released and long ropes tied around their ankles. Men ran up to the shrouds of the mainmast taking the rope-ends with them, passing them over the yardarm and dropping them down to the deck. Waiting pirates hauled at the lines. Their condemned men, one on either side of the mast, were swung upwards, hanging head-first, arms flailing high above the deck. Taylor took aim. He would have the first shot at the swaying, wriggling target then the crew would divide into parties, one for each mark. Rum would be given to the team who killed fastest. Taylor fired. The negro jerked and screamed. It was the beginning of a vicious hour, the pirates boasting at each success until the last victim was shot and thrown into the sea.[9]

Davis was quiet. He suspected that Taylor was plotting against him. With pirates a captain could swiftly be deposed and to be sure Davis had to take a rich prize. He had no luck. Two days after the slaughter of the natives he captured a ship but its cargo was a poor one, hardly worth sharing between the three crews.[10] A malcontent claimed that Davis was a poor leader. Taylor would be more successful. Within minutes the quartermaster was elected captain and, by some irony, Davis took his place.[11]

The *Royal James* was not a happy ship. Taylor was too similar to Cocklyn. Davis had not been a bully although stern enough when discipline was required. Taylor believed in the rope's end as a cure for dissatisfaction and roared his orders from the poopdeck like the Royal Navy captain of a first-rate man-of-war. Within a few days many of the crew were sick of him. Once again there was a meeting and Davis was reappointed captain. Taylor refused to accept this act of instant democracy and went over to Cocklyn's vessel. Several pirates departed with him. Those who stayed, Walter Kennedy being elected quartermaster, were likely to remain loyal to Davis.

The fleet sailed on. La Bouche renamed his galley the *Duke of Ormond* in honour of the Civil War soldier. Changing a ship's name so casually was an unlucky thing to do and superstitious pirates vowed never to board such an ill-starred vessel.

Soon a ship was lost. The *Two Friends*, Cocklyn's storeship, sailed off one night when the others were some distance away.[12]

Towards the end of May the discontented trio took another merchantman. From her came some sails, negroes, money, jewellery, and a few seamen who were persuaded that the life of a pirate was a more pleasant one than their own.[13]

It was the last vessel that the pirates took together. At a meeting in the *Royal James* the captains could not agree. Davis wished to go down the coast to Principe but Cocklyn and la Bouche did not want to travel so far east. The wine and their hot tempers were leading to a quarrel but Davis controlled himself sufficiently to say, 'Hark ye, Cocklyn and la Bouche. I find by strengthening you, I have put a rod into your hands to whip myself. But I'm still able to deal with you both. But since we met in love, let us part in love. For I find that three of a trade can never agree'.[14] Cocklyn and la Bouche left the cabin. Taylor went with them.[15]

Three years later la Bouche and Taylor were still together but on the far side of Africa, marauding around Madagascar. There are reports that la Bouche, having been shipwrecked, renewed his lucrative piratical career and retired in affluence, settling on the remote islet of Bel Ombre near Mahé in the Seychelles, expecting to be safe there. He was apprehended and hanged in Mahé on 17 July 1730. Taylor, still 'a Fellow of a most barbarous Nature', sailed with Edward England, became a commander in his own right and finally took an improbable commission with the Spanish navy. It is said that he died peacefully in Cuba. Cocklyn vanished from history.[16]

Davis sailed on alone. With his enemies gone he was left in a strong ship of thirty guns on a coast where there was promise of plunder. He dressed in clean clothes each day, a white shirt tucked into his breeches and a scarlet sash around his waist. The men were kept busy by Kennedy who, though only a few years past twenty, had a reputation for roughness.

At anchor off Cape Three Points was a vessel from Ostend. The *Marquis del Campo* was a well-manned, great ship of thirty guns. Davis hesitated. Dutchmen were renowned for defending even the most paltry of cargoes. Few Dutch sailors ever turned pirate but they could and would fight against them. Had Davis not been deposed so short a while ago he would have sailed past. Now he dared not risk being thought a coward.

As his ship came alongside the Dutchman fired a broadside. Several shots hit the pirate vessel at the level of the gundeck, shattering the side. The *Royal James*'s own cannon roared back. It was noon on a sweltering day in late May and some of the forced men were experiencing their first engagement. Young William Minty was ordered to fight, given a gun, refused it and received a cutlass-lash as he screamed that he did not know how to use firearms. Another man, Green, also rejected a flintlock and was later whipped at the mast. The battle continued into nightfall.

The gunner and Goulding, his mate, rushed from long culverin to culverin, checking that the powder charge and its wad were rammed firmly home and properly set under the touch hole, the 18-lb cannon-ball tamped hard down the barrel. Priming powder was ignited by a slow-burning match. Men stood clear. The 3-ton cannon recoiled, held from careering wildly across the deck by its thick breeching rope, the ship juddering, the air thickly black with the explosions. Good gunners could fire a shot in just over a minute but it was a rate that could not be maintained in the chaos of battle as the cannon became searingly hot. Davis shouted commands. Kennedy ordered pistolmen into the rigging to fire down on the exposed deck of the adversary. Flaring-muzzled swivel-guns, or 'murtherers', sprayed smallshot, rusted nails and broken glass across the *Marquis*. Jagged splinters of gunwhale, heavy as stones and deadly as spears, were ripped out of the timbers, flailing across the decks. It was a hell of reeking sulphur, smoke, endless crashes, screams, jabbing flames from glowing guns, in the darkness, occasional pauses, then another bombardment. The conflict endured into the morning when the scraping of swords and distant shouting told that the pirates had grappled and boarded the *Marquis* whose wearied, wounded crew surrendered. It had not been a clean victory. The first broadside had killed nine pirates, others had fallen since and more would die.[17]

Davis, a romantic Welshman filled with Arthurian chivalry, had sworn that he would never shame or hurt a gallant opponent. And the men of the *Royal James* were too exhausted and relieved to torture anyone. Not one of the Dutchmen was harmed. Pirates took charge of the *Marquis* and the captured vessel was refitted in a nearby bay. She had better lines than the *Royal James* with three tall masts, square-rigged, bows like the upturned beak of a bird of prey, a waist whose five steps led up to the poopdeck above a magnificent cabin, a highly ornamented stern. For armament she had thirty-two guns and twenty-seven swivels. She was as strong as many naval frigates. Davis renamed her the *Royal Rover*. Her crew were kept in the holds until they could be put on board some other craft.

Wounded men, many with little hope of recovery, were sheltered under makeshift awnings on the shore, tended by the young surgeon, Archibald Murray. When the last to die was buried the two great ships set out to sea.

The pirates passed Cape Coast Castle with its thick brick walls, keeping well out of range of its powerful guns.[18] Davis' men felt themselves veterans of the sea, standard pirates who could withstand anything. Forced men who previously had cringed and whined now strutted. Davis had proved himself a valiant captain.

Between Cape Coast Castle and Accra was Anamabu with a very small fort of nine rusting guns. The fort was in such disrepair that hardly anything other than its outer walls stood. Being only fifteen miles from Cape Coast Castle, the centre of the Royal African Company's trade, the outpost was not important. Its only function was to have an expensive stock of supplies for any private vessel that was anxious for more goods or slaves before quitting the African coast. At Anamabu desperate captains would pay £28, sometimes even £32 for a strong male slave, far above the common price.

Huge numbers of slaves were needed in the West Indies because of the brutal clearance of land on the sugar plantations where a strong negro's working life was no more than ten years. It was reckoned that plantation owners had to replace ten per cent of their labour-force annually in the British West Indies alone: 4,000 slaves for Barbados, 6,000 for the Leeward Isles, 10,000 for Jamaica. And slaves were expensive.

In 1721 a merchant captain's bill of lading for slaves bought from traders such as 'Crackers' listed the sums of 8 guns, a wicker bottle, 2 cases of spirits and 28 sheets for a man, 9 gallons of brandy, 6 iron bars, 2 pistols, a bag of powder and 2 strings of beads for a woman, and 7 large kettles, a length of cotton, an iron bar and 5 lengths of blue and white cloth for a boy. If slaves were purchased from the Royal African Company a merchant would pay around £15 for a man, £12 for a woman. The price would be quadrupled in the West Indies to allow for the 25 per cent of deaths to be expected on board a slaveship. By 1820 when there were detailed bills of sale the profits were almost unbelievable. 'A captive bought on the Guinea coast for $30 (or if the traders were even more fortunate, for a bandanna or a few beads), would sell in America for anything up to $700. Yankee skippers were said to make a million dollars from each voyage'.[19] Even in the early 18th century so great was the demand and so inadequate the supply, the Royal African Company exporting only some 18,000 slaves each year, private traders, 75,000, that often a slave could be sold there for £40 or £50. Hence the steep prices at the market of last resort at Anamabu.[20]

The pirates had no fear of the derelict fort. The three vessels at anchor in the harbour, the *Morris*, the *Royal Hynde* and the *Princess of London* did not fire a shot. Their captains were busy ashore bartering for slaves and their crews had no heart to fight against such a battery of guns. Some canoes at the side of the *Morris* scurried to the quayside. It was June 6, 1719.[21]

A few shots came from the fort but the range was too great for the weak ordnance. Davis had his black flags raised and returned fire. There was silence from the fort. The *Royal Rover* came alongside the *Princess of London* and nervously Stephenson, her second mate, asked what it was the pirate wanted him to do. His captain, Plumb and the first mate were absent. Davis told him and his men to come aboard. The mate was followed by a chirpy little fellow, John Eastwell, a carpenter, and six others: James Bradshaw, William Gittius, a gunner, John Jessup, John Owen and Thomas Rogers.[22] The sixth and last man was the third mate of the *Princess of London*. He was tall, older than most, in his late thirties, broad-shouldered, dark-haired, with a swarthy, stern face brown from years at sea.[23]

His name was Bartholomew Roberts.

PART TWO

The Great Days of the Pirates

June 1719–February 1722

4

Captain Bartholomew Roberts

June 6–August 1719

'The Account of Roberts runs into a greater Length, than that of any other Pyrate . . . because he ravaged the Seas longer than the rest . . . having made more Noise in the World than some others'.
                    Charles Johnson, *A General History . . .* 1724, 6.

'He stood there with the others, saying nothing, waiting, a tall black (of dark complexion) man, near forty years of age.' According to Johnson in his *General History of the Pyrates* Roberts was Welsh, born in the Pembrokeshire [Dyfed] village of Newydd Bach or Little Newcastle ('Newey-bagh' wrote the un-Celtic Johnson) just west of the Preselis and only six miles from the sea at Fishguard Bay. His original name seems to have been John Robert. How, why it was changed is unknown. But the Pembrokeshire Hearth Tax of 1670 lists his probable father as George Robert.[1]

The parish records go no further back than 1813 and there is no direct evidence of the pirate's birthplace but Johnson had spoken to John Atkins who met many of Roberts' crew at their trial. They knew that Roberts came from Wales. A claim that in 1720 a ship was taken by two pirate vessels 'both commanded by Captain Thomas Roberts . . . the aforesaid Captain Roberts was born in Bridgewater in Somerset'[2]

55

only means that the reporter was misled by a victim of the pirates who had confused the captain with Thomas Anstis, one of the 'Lords' who had escaped with Davis in the *Buck* from New Providence.

When Bartholomew Roberts was forced to become a pirate he was already an experienced mariner, in the prime of life, accustomed to the capricious sea, used to giving orders, of an audacious, inventive mind.

The seven men rowed back to the *Princess* in silence having been warned by Davis that some of them would be forced if there were insufficient volunteers. Only Eastwell happily changed sides. The others looked gloomily at the black flags flying at the masts of the two pirate vessels. They saw the looting party on board their own ship. They saw a boat hurriedly leaving the landing-stage of the fort with the three merchant captains in it.

Fearful of wanton damage Captains Plumb, Hall and Fenn chose to accommodate the pirates in whatever they wanted. Opposition could result in the entire crew being forced to join the pirates leaving the captain without men to work his ship. Then he would be compelled to give excessive wages for any hands that would help him return home. Conversely, a captain who resisted might have his ship burnt leaving its crew with no means of returning to Britain. In despair it was known for seamen to work for nothing in return for being taken back to their own country.

'There is an account that the pyrates have done so much mischief on the coast of Guinea by plundering and destroying of ships that the Company's forts are crowded with seamen who will be glad to go on board ships without wages that will give them passage for England'.[3] The depredations of Cocklyn, Taylor and la Bouche were to blame. They had joined forces with Edward England. Having taken some ships near Cape Coast Castle they went on to the Portuguese fort of Ouidah about a hundred miles, some thirty leagues, to the west. There they captured an English merchantman, the *Heroine*, and two French and two Portuguese craft. Later in the year the three pirate ships departed for Madagascar.[4]

By the time that Plumb reached the *Princess* the scavenging was almost done. What Kennedy missed Eastwell discovered. The little man had hurled himself into piracy like a dog at a bear-baiting and was seeking out all possible hiding-places with eagerness. He stole two of Stephenson's hats, stuffed a bunch of ribbons into one, took money from the mate's chest, rummaged amongst what was left in Plumb's cabin and threatened to shoot Stephenson if the mate did not tell him where forty ounces of gold dust was concealed. He was a man with a new and congenial vocation.[5]

With the grudging compliance of the captains the *Royal Hynde* and the *Morris* were stripped of everything, even some negroes. It was usual for them to be taken. They would receive no shares but would be made to do the work that ordinary pirates found too arduous and menial.

By evening it was over. Celebration followed with wines and spirits spilling over the pirate decks. During the orgy two of the crew, Rogers and Owen, of the *Princess* tried to escape by hoisting the sails to run inshore under the protection of the fort's guns. It was a doomed venture. The pirates could have pounded the fort into dust but there was no need. The men were detected and brought to Davis who so admired their initiative that he promptly forced them to join him.[6]

Next morning when the booty had been stored away Davis took stock. With two great ships he needed larger crews and except for Eastwell no one had enlisted. Davis called the captains to him. They had been obliging, he said, and for that he would taken no more men than was essential. Fenn protested.

Cocklyn would have killed him. Davis was different. Though a martinet with a true Welsh spirit he punished Fenn simply but decisively by taking not some but all his men except for one who was crippled and then gave Fenn's *Morris* to the thirty

imprisoned seamen of the *Marquis del Campo* who were
released. Only a Scotsman, John Stewart, was kept because of
his British nationality.[7]

He was not the only exceptional person to be forced. The
same year, off New Providence in the West Indies, 'Calico Jack'
Rackam captured a merchantman and took the only English
seaman, 'a handsome young Fellow' to whom Anne Bonny took
a passionate liking. It was only when her importunities became
too insistent that her would-be lover revealed her very
feminine breasts. She was Mary Read.

In her mid-twenties she had been travelling to the West
Indies to make a new life after her Flemish husband, keeper of a
tavern, the 'Three Horseshoes' in Breda, had died. Before
boarding ship she disguised herself as a man 'for her modesty
according to her notions of virtue'. She became such a ardent
pirate that she and Anne Bonny, equally notorious, had
doggerel verse composed in their honour:

> 'With pitch and tar her hands were hard
> Though once like velvet soft,
> She weighed the anchor, heav'd the lead,
> And boldly went aloft'.[8]

No women were among the men that Davis forced from the
Morris, and from the *Royal Hynde*. The least willing was James
Sail who sneaked back to his old ship only to be discovered and
returned to the *Royal James*. Undeterred he managed to slip
away to the *Princess of London*. Along with some equally
reluctant conscripts he was ferreted out, tied to the pirates'
mainmast and whipped. A final batch came from the *Princess*.[9]
Among them were Bradshaw, Stephenson and Jessup, very
downcast and loud in their protests that they had no wish to
become pirates. With them was Bartholomew Roberts.

The pirates sailed taking the *Royal Hynde* and the *Morris*
with them. Within a few days they took a Dutch galley that

characteristically defied them and only surrendered after a long chase that would have worked badly for its crew had not the vessel been richly laden with £15,000 of money and goods. Davis was so pleased with this bounty that he let the *Royal Hynde* go with Fenn on board. The *Morris* was given permission to depart towards Accra, taking with it all the goods for which Davis had no use. Contrary to a newspaper report Captain Plumb was not hanged.[10] Instead, he reached Cape Coast Castle with Fenn and bartered for fifty slaves, rueing the day that he had gone to Anamabu.[11]

Davis still wished to go to Principe, a Portuguese island six hundred miles ESE of Anamabu and reputedly of great wealth. He took to consulting with Roberts on matters of seamanship. Roberts though despondent had accepted his new life with a seaman's fatalism and willingly advised Davis about the rig of the sails and of the best course to take along these coasts. Few pirates resented this. Roberts had been at sea much longer than the majority of them and had a good working knowledge of Africa and the Americas with his years of sailing the Triangular Route from Britain to Africa to the West Indies and North America before bringing rich cargoes of goods and money back home.

These were voyages that demanded seamanship. Storms had to be recognised before they came, the brewing of the West Indian hurricanes, the gales of the westerlies in the latitude of the Forties. The prevailing Trade Winds had to be found before a ship was becalmed in the monotony of the windless Doldrums. Roberts had an understanding of the oceans and winds from many struggles with them. His learning was not scientific. In times when it was not yet possible to determine a line of longitude navigation depended very much on anticipation and experience. These qualities Roberts possessed.

The *Royal Rover* and the *Royal James* sailed down the coast. The ships were well-manned, their holds were filled with plunder, lookouts at the mastheads scanned the horizon for prey but the days were empty of everything save the sunshine and the distant, forested shore. Then, one morning, at dawn, the *Royal James* was seen lagging nearly a mile behind. Davis feared that Kennedy was deserting him with enough plunder to entice his crew.

It was not treachery. As the *Royal Rover* took in her sails to let the other come up the pirates could see that Kennedy's vessel was listing and that men were working a pump. A bad leak had been discovered. Worms had eaten into the rotting timbers. Now the vessel would have to be careened. Roberts suggested Cameroon Bay where wood and water could be taken in during the repairs.

It was noon when the two ships reached the African mainland. Before them thickly-forested mountains towered above the sea with their shadow darkening half the straits between the coast and island of Fernando Po. The pirates expected to stay here for just a few days while the *Royal James* was cleaned but when the keel was exposed a dockyard seemed more necessary than a sandy beach. The bottom and sides were not so much damaged as devoured. There were more holes than woodwork. The *Royal James* had to be abandoned.

She was emptied of her cargo, men and best guns. Eastwell and the other carpenters took her soundest rigging and tackle. Then the *Royal Rover* turned southwards towards Principe. Pairs of large fish gambolled in the waters behind the vessel, curving, diving, shining in her wake. As the pirates sighted the island birds soared from the rocks above it. Davis had the flags of a British man-of-war hoisted.

Both Kennedy and Jones despised any sort of stratagem and favoured a direct assault on the fort but Roberts, who knew the place, said that there was a battery of twelve guns guarding the mouth of the long harbour. Even if they sailed safely by the unsuspecting guns they would be unable to leave once an alarm was sounded.

A tiny sloop came out and a Portuguese officer demanded their business. Davis answered they were a man-of-war in search of pirates that had been stealing and sacking along the coast of Guinea over the past months. He wondered whether any had been here. No, was the reply, but a merchantman had recently reported that three pirates had raided Sierra Leone.

Davis asked to be allowed to enter the harbour. His men had been a long time at sea and provisions were needed. Permission was given. The *Royal Rover* followed the sloop a short distance before the waters became too shallow. A pinnace was lowered. In his smartest maroon coat Davis climbed down followed by nine men neatly dressed in white linen shirts and dark breeches. At the landing-place a file of musketeers waited at attention to escort Davis to the governor.

In his finery Davis aroused no suspicion. The governor offered all the amenities and advantages of Principe whereupon Davis assured him that any expense incurred would be reimbursed by His Majesty, King George. The governor was not overjoyed at the prospect of becoming a creditor to a foreign power but raised no objections.

The *Royal Rover* remained at anchor near the harbour's mouth. A French ship found the passage blocked and as she lost way three boatloads of pirates under Kennedy swarmed about with pistols prominent. There was little plunder. It was only a small vessel but one that the pirates would find useful. Davis explained to the governor that the Frenchman had been trading with pirates and that he had seized it for the King. The governor commended him and his officers for his diligence. A fortnight idled by.[12] Davis planned to inveigle the governor and his officers into a trap. Patience was needed. Hearing rumours of available women ashore the Lords decided to investigate.

'A few Days after, Mr Davis, with fourteen more, went privately ashore, and walk'd up the Country towards a Village, where the Governor and the other chief Men of the Island kept their Wives, intending, as we may suppose, to supply their Husbands' places with them; but being discover'd the Women fled to a neighbouring Wood, and Davis and the rest retreated to their Ship, without effecting their Design: The Thing made some Noise, but as no one knew them, it passed over'.[13]

Deciding that the time was right Davis invited the governor to lunch in the *Royal Rover*, intending to hold his guests hostage so that the well-defended fort could be taken without bloodshed. The governor gladly accepted. As Captain Davis had to send boats for his guests he was asked to take a glass of wine with the governor at the fort on its steep hill. Davis accepted. The governor was providing the pirate with a free reconnaissance of the stronghold.

The captain took Kennedy and nine others as officers of the man-of-war. Roberts was left in command of one boat, Jones of the second, waiting at the landing for Davis to return with the governor and his colleagues. At the quayside there was a negro. The governor was at the fort. The negro would run ahead to warn his Excellency of their arrival.

Cheerfully the party walked up the narrow track through the trees and were halfway up the hill when they were ambushed. Guns fired from the bushes. Davis fell, shot in the stomach. Half-stunned he raised himself, a pistol in each hand, firing as he died, 'thus like a game Cock, giving a dying Blow, that he might not fall unrevenged'.

Negroes with blow-pipes appeared sending poisoned darts at the bewildered group. Kennedy turned and rushed down the path towards the waiting boats. Another pirate hurled himself into the bushes, raced towards the top of the cliff and jumped from it into the sea. By great luck the *Royal Rover*'s longboat was coming back from a fishing expedition and picked him up. He would have perished otherwise. Sharks abounded in those waters. Only he and Kennedy survived of the confident party, tricked by the governor who had learned of the intended rape of his wife.[14]

The pirates were divided. Some wished to leave, others to avenge the death of their captain. They had no choice said Roberts. The fort's guns still protected the exit from the harbour. But they did not overlook the harbour itself and from there the *Royal Rover* could bombard the fort without retaliation. The governor would expect them to flee. His guns would be primed, loaded and trained on the harbour-roads. It would take a long time for the defence to be reorganised and by then the fort would be in ruins.

The *Royal Rover* was swung round so that a broadside could be directed accurately on their target. Dennis, the gunner, calculated the distance and elevation. Unlike the defenders at Sierra Leone the Portuguese soldiers did not fight. Whether it was the surprise at being attacked when instead they had anticipated sinking the pirate vessel or whether it was cowardice the first crashes of the ship's cannon sent them scuttling out of the fort and into the woods. Sheltered by the bombardment Kennedy and thirty volunteers landed, set fire to the fort and pushed the harbour guns one by one cartwheeling into the sea.

The pirates wanted to destroy the town but the shoals were not deep enough for the *Royal Rover*. Instead, the French sloop was lightened of everything but her armament of a nine-pounder, two four-pounders and a pair of swivels. Then the vessel was steered through reefs and channels until a short hundred metres from the shore she grounded on a sandbank. The cannon were aimed at the houses. From them and from the tinier swivels a barrage erupted on the settlement. Dry thatched roofs caught fire, wooden walls tumbled and even among the stouter, stone-built dwellings two were demolished.[15]

When the *Royal Rover* left Principe she left destruction behind her, a fort devastated, the town a blazing shambles, the French sloop burning in the shallows, and two Portuguese ships that had sailed in plundered and sunk. It was retribution for Howel Davis.

That night as they sailed towards Cape Lopez the men assembled on deck. A new captain was needed. A steaming cauldron of strong punch was carried to the mainmast. Closest to it sat the 'Lords': Anstis, Ashplant, Dennis, Kennedy,

Moody, Phillips, Sutton. It was they who would suggest the best man. It was the crew who would make the decision.

Kennedy's name was proposed. Others mentioned Henry Dennis or Thomas Anstis. Then Dennis himself spoke. It was not, he said, of any great significance who was dignified with the title of captain for the pirates always had the final power to vote in or depose as suited their interests.

'We are the original of this claim and should a captain be so saucy as to exceed Prescription at any time, why, down with him! It will be a caution after he is dead to his Successors, of what fatal Consequence any sort of assuming may be. However, it is my Advice, that, while we are sober, we pitch upon a Man of Courage, and skil'd in Navigation, one, who by his Counsel and Bravery seems best able to defend this Commonwealth, and ward us from the Dangers and Tempests of an instable Element, and the fatal Consequences of Anarchy; and such a one I take Roberts to be. A Fellow! I think, in all Respects, worthy of your Esteem and Favour'.

There was a roar of agreement. The pirates remembered Roberts advising them about the attack on the fort and how Dennis himself had often referred to him. Only Sutton who had been ambitious for the captaincy demurred. He did not care who the captain was, he snarled sullenly, as long as it was not a Catholic. He hated them ever since his father had suffered at the hands of Monmouth's peasants before the rebellion of 1685.

He staggered off swearing. Roberts took his place. He had been with the pirates no more than six weeks and was now their captain. His speech was not the most diplomatic. 'He accepted of the Honour, saying, that since he had dipp'd his Hands in Muddy Water, and must be a Pyrate, it was better being a Commander than a common Man'.[16] It was the second week in July, 1719.

Near Cape Lopez and all along that coast are inlets and promontories that cast light and shadows onto the water in lovely nuances of sunlight and shade. The pirates lay at rest, reorganising themselves and their ship while Roberts debated his best action. The refitting at Cape Lopez was completed without incident except that the forced man, Rogers, tried to escape, was caught, clapped in irons for several days, finally whipped and threatened with shooting. The pirates sailed out and almost immediately, on 27 July, Roberts took his first prize when a merchantman, the *Experiment* appeared two leagues off the Cape. Accidental it may have been but its capture heartened the pirates. Like most seamen they believed in omens and nothing was more important to freebooters than to have a fortunate captain who, without design, fell upon a rich prey.

Roberts lay about half a mile to windward of the *Experiment* but a couple of shots across her bows brought the merchant round. As she came within hailing distance the black flag was hauled up and Kennedy told the captain to come aboard. A yawl brought the ship's sailing-master, Thomas Grant.

Whether the rowers were too slow or whether Kennedy was still smarting at not being elected captain, whether he was reminding Roberts of the powers of a quartermaster, cannot be known but he was in a foul temper by the time Grant climbed on deck. No sooner had he reached Kennedy than the pirate shouted at him, demanding to know where the money was.

Startled, Grant replied that all the valuables were still on board the *Experiment* and that his captain, Cornet, would hand them over. A pirate took the yawl, a jolly boat of a few oars, to the merchantman while others, including the once-reluctant Bradshaw, crossed in their own launch. For no reason other than malicious and mindless vandalism the yawl was sunk.

Back on the *Royal Rover* Kennedy took Grant to the Great Cabin. 'Damn you', he swore, 'I know you and will sacrifice you' and hit him on the mouth. Grant fell, blood streaming from his lips, scared that Kennedy was about to kill him. The raving quartermaster might have done so had not other pirates restrained him and told Grant to get out.

Not satisfied that the *Experiment* had been thoroughly ransacked Kennedy and his mate went to the ship next day. Altogether the vessel contained fifty ounces of gold, a purseful of Portuguese moidores and ten guineas as well as commonplace goods. Roberts had the ship examined to see whether she was worth keeping as a storeship. Kennedy, however, was against it and the vessel was set on fire. Her crew, including Grant, were kept on board the *Royal Rover* from which Grant was unable to escape for another six months.[17]

Roberts' luck held. Next day they took a Portuguese trader with a small cargo and two days later, sailing westwards, they overpowered the *Temperance*. Its British cargo of pots, pans and metalware was almost intact because the captain, Sharman, had been unable to barter it for an adequate supply of slaves. Roberts kept the ship, giving Sharman the Portuguese craft in exchange.[18]

The pirate captain assembled his leading men to discuss their next move. With Edward England and the other pirates believed still to be on the African coast competition for prizes would be severe and other regions might be better. Some pirates suggested Madagascar but Roberts preferred to cross to Brazil and the easy pickings of Portuguese traders there. So, late in August, they went to the island of St. Thome and laid in provisions and fresh water for the long voyage. They were heading for a New World which was already growing old, to the creaking, cautious colonies of Spain, towards the lusty, undisciplined islands of the West Indies, and towards a brief but bloody footnote in history.

5

The Treasure Ship of Bahia

August–December 1719

'By our letters from the West Indies we have an account that the pirates continue to be very numerous there, and do incredible damage to trade by taking, plundering and destroying the ships of all nations without distinction that come in their way'.

Weekly Journal, 2 January 1720

From the bows of the *Royal Rover* they could see the sky lowering before them, clouds swirling and massing from the north with the wind driving the storm to them while they tacked cumbersomely towards it, catching as much wind as possible, then veering in a long approach to the land once more before repeating the tack over and over, always moving towards the brutal sky. Gusts caught them, setting the tackle and rigging cracking, creaking against the stiffness of the masts. Round them the sea buckled in twisted waves, that every moment grew whiter as the crests rolled and rose. Thunder rumbled. Brilliant streaks of lightning lit the stormy mists into which they were sailing.

Roberts knew the signs. Anyone who had been on the Triangular Route expected these sudden autumn tornadoes off the African coast. Sometimes they occurred twice in a day lashing the sea into angry destruction for a few hours before dying away into heat and calm. He knew that there was no hope of reaching the northern trade winds in this weather however strongly built his ship was. One prolonged howl of wind while they were on a shoreward tack would drive them aground, helpless before the great seas that would wreck the vessel beyond repair. They would have to turn about.

Before long the hurricane would reach them. Already the sky was blackening, the thunder more frequent. Men hurried across the vibrating, pitching deck as the ship staggered on. Two pirates heaved at the whipstaff that jerked savagely as the waves crashed against the high, exposed rudder. In the rigging, masts swaying in accelerating arcs, men strained at the sails as the *Royal Rover* sluggishly came round, her starboard exposed to the towering breakers sweeping onto it. Spray lashed across the open deck. What sail had been left unfurled billowed and stretched, and then, in one last reeling judder, the running seas were at her stern and the ship spanked along with the shrieking wind pushing and dropping behind her. Like a skeleton she drove before the storm southwards through the Gulf of Guinea, her hatches and holds barred against the waves that smashed onto her tall cupid- and dolphin-decorated stern.

It would be a long ocean voyage and long voyages were wretched because of the wooden ship. Even in calm weather water oozed between the planking. Timber-built vessels were always damp. In rough seas they were awash. Waves splashed across the deck, leaking beneath the hatch covers, slopping over the sleeping-quarters below as the ship rolled and pitched. The sides were tacky with salt from the incessant brine. The bilges stank.

Such conditions were normal. Clothes and blankets were never dry, the only light below deck was the dim yellow glow of a tallow lantern. Accidents were frequent, slipping on the greasy boards, falling from the high rigging as hands lost their grip on the wet yardarms and lines. Drunken quarrels, inevitable in a bored, overcrowded ship, brought other injuries. Fire was the worst peril. No smoking was allowed below deck unless the pipe had a cap to it. Unprotected candles brought a flogging.

Attempts were made at cleanliness. Decks were scrubbed with vinegar and salt water. Holds were fumigated with smoking brimstone. But there were always beetles, cockroaches, rats, always maggots in the mouldering biscuits and rancid meat. Larger craft had wooden latrines in the least public part of the upper deck. Otherwise a man urinated and defecated by squatting precariously on the forechains below the ship's bows, the 'heads'.

Fine weather brought idleness, monotony and arguments. Bad weather brought danger and exhaustion. The only compensations for a long voyage were the shore pleasures of wine and women. 'Slaves for forty-six weeks', it was said, 'lords for six'.[1]

Roberts watched the sky. Tornadoes rarely lasted longer than two or three hours. Being ensnared in the doldrums was the greater fear on their present course, becalmed for days, even weeks in the still, dead air around the equator with drinking water diminishing, food crumbling into inedibility, men lying on dry, baking decks, too tired and weak to row the boats that could pull them into the areas of wind.

The first raindrops fell. The black sky parted into dark, bloated clouds. Blue sky appeared. Before long a breeze was carrying them towards the Southern Trades that would take them to Brazil. They were lucky. The wind held and in just over a week they changed course westwards. Men lounged in the warmth of the tropics. Sentimental songs were sung, old stories retold of Kidd and Blackbeard, reminiscences of the golden girls of Madagascar and the darker girls of New Providence. In the Great Cabin Roberts sat with the Lords debating where they should go, to Portuguese Brazil, the Spanish West Indies of the plantations of North America.[2] Brazil was chosen.

Spain held much of the Americas with many colonies around the Caribbean Sea and Mexico where the land was richest in minerals. These she guarded. Foreigners were forbidden to settle, even to trade there. Her treasure-fleets were in convoy. Intruders she punished fiercely. The English, French and Dutch settled the more northerly territories along the coastlines of Carolina, Maryland, as far north as Canada, occasionally usurping some less well-protected Spanish possession. The West Indian islands were particularly vulnerable because of their distance from the mainland.

There was always tension in the seas around Central America. Spain had insufficient men but was determined to keep everything. The English and French were uneasy partners against Spain, their common foe. Sometimes the Dutch intervened.

There had been two hundred years of conflict. Buccaneers, one time hunters in the West Indies, had been ruthlessly evicted by the Spaniards. In turn they took revenge, ransacking Spanish ships. Their successors were even more ambitious and were often supported by governments who realised how useful such a unpaid force could be. Men like Sir Henry Morgan led raids on rich strongholds such as Cartagena and Panama. They weakened Spain, enabling islands such as Jamaica to be captured but costing the British and French governments nothing. By 1670 a weary Spain signed a treaty with Britain permitting her some trading rights. In Jamaica, as British soldiers arrived, buccaneers left their rendezvous at Port Royal, going to other islands where they accepted commissions as privateers to attack French vessels during the wars with Louis XIV. Their prizes had to be taken to the colonies where they were valued by Vice-Admiralty Courts. Although this led to abuse both by the privateers and colonial governors who filled their deep pockets with illicit loot from neutral shipping it was at least quasi-legal. Similarly the French had their own corsairs known as Sallee Rovers who scavenged the European seas. They were not always successful.

'We have an account from Portsmouth that the *Mary and*

Martha, a ship of 12 guns, is arrived there from Malaga. and that being becalmed in her passage she was attacked by 3 Sallee Rovers. Upon which the captain ordered some barrels of gunpowder to be placed in his cabin. and as soon as the Moors to the no. of 50 boarded him he sprung his mine and blew up above half of them: the crew at the same time laid about them most manfully with their cutlasses so that the rest were cut to pieces. the Captain killing 4 with his own hands'.[3]

The war ended and the commissions were withdrawn. Rebuffed by their governments and appalled at the prospect of hard work, reinforced by the hundreds of transportees and indentured servants on the plantations who laboured without hope in near-slavery, enticed by the weakly defended coasts and the plentiful islands to which to retreat the privateers turned pirates, against all men, all ships and all governments.

They established a base on New Providence, some even living openly in colonies as Blackbeard did in South Carolina. But in 1718 Woodes Rogers had taken New Providence and in the same year South Carolina began to hunt down pirates. Bartholomew Roberts had to find secretive places for relaxation.

Each day the *Royal Rover* drew steadily nearer to Brazil, her sails full with the unfailing wind blowing westwards across the sea. Within three weeks the Atlantic had been crossed and the South America coast sighted almost exactly where Roberts had predicted. He had been certain of the latitude for that was easily determined by use of the cross-staff by day and, on occasion, by the backstaff or quadrant by night when stars were visible. Longitude was different. No way had yet been discovered of calculating it.[4] Roberts had to rely on his knowledge of the ship's course and a reckoning of the distance travelled using a logline in conjunction with an hourglass to check their speed. The methods were widely known but still susceptible to huge errors. Less capable captains preferred to head towards some great land-mass and then turn towards their destination even though this could make the voyage longer.

The pirates understood these difficulties. Most of them had sailed as merchant seamen and they shared Roberts' satisfaction. Already they thought of him as a lucky captain. Now they respected him for his navigation.

They dropped anchor at the island of Fernandino just off the Brazilian coast, conveniently uninhabited and out of sight of the mainland. Supplies and equipment were checked while the carpenters boot-topped the *Royal Rover*, a process like careening but quicker because instead of unloading the vessel completely and hauling her over by tackles from the mast they merely shifted all her guns and heavy cargo to one side in shallow water giving her a pronounced list. At that angle it was possible to remove most encrustation, sufficient to ensure that she sailed trimly if not at her best.

Then, with the guns runs out and the weapons cleaned, loaded and sharpened, they waited. The days passed. No vessel appeared. A week went by. And another. After a fortnight they cautiously patrolled out at sea. Still the lookouts saw nothing. And week after week they lingered with not one sail to be found. Murmurs of dissatisfaction, aggravated by the tedium, would have swelled into the demand for a new captain were it not for the plunder in the holds and the plentiful stock of drink and provisions.

They were unaware that the Portuguese did little trade with Africa at any time, being generally indolent, and virtually none at all at this time of year. Nor did they know that recently there had been other pirates there.

'Letters . . . tell us that . . . a pirate ship of 14 guns in company of a sloop of 8 guns had done a great deal of mischief upon the coast of Brazil: and that in the height of their undertakings a Portuguese man-of-war which was an excellent sailor came a very unwelcome guest among them and gave them chase. The ship got off but the sloop being closely followed and giving herself over for lost, ran ashore.

There were 70 men on board, 12 of which were killed and all the rest taken prisoners of whom the Portuguese hanged 38 englishmen, 3 dutchmen, 2 frenchmen, and one of their own nation'.

Weekly Journal, 2 January 1720.

The pirates knew only that their captain's fortune had deserted him. Rum casks were broached. Men gathered in groups to complain while Roberts debated with the Lords whether to try their luck in the West Indies where the hurricane season still prevailed. The Lords wanted to quit Brazil. Roberts argued that they should stay longer. It was his judgement that had brought them there and to leave empty-handed would be to admit his error. Pride did not allow him to say he had been wrong but matters were desperate. For nine weeks they had loitered in vain. November was almost gone. In the West Indies traders were loading their ships in readiness for the customary voyage to the North American colonies and then England. If he was to catch them Roberts had to sail northwards immediately. Irritated at his failure he left.

It was late one evening that they drew level with the town of Bahia in the Bay of All Saints, the Portuguese Bahia De Los Santos. In the dusk the pirates could see the lights of a flotilla of ships anchored in orderly lines in the harbour-roads. Two Portuguese men-of-war lay by them, ships of seventy guns with their upper gunports open. They were the guardships of the Lisbon Fleet, an armada transporting the year's accumulation of gold, riches, sugar and tobacco. It was unimaginable wealth. But unattainable. The harbour-wall stretched far out to sea. At its far end stood a small fort from whose ramparts cannon were trained over the harbour. Another fort, seemingly unfinished, lay opposite.

The treasure was out of reach. As the night came on hiding the ships and their armament the pirates resigned themselves to departure. The odds were impossible. There were two forts, two men-of-war, thirty-two other well-armed ships, over five hundred cannon, more than a thousand men, an overwhelming host against one ship and twenty guns. The *Royal Rover* would have to sneak away.

Roberts said they would attack.

The Lords stared in disbelief. Men shook their heads in bewilderment and dismay. Roberts reassured them. He told them about a French buccaneer, Pierre le Grand, called 'the Great' because of his incredible capture of a vessel ten times the size of his own. Early in the seventeenth century Le Grand had been lurking unsuccessfully off Hispaniola, now Dominica and Haiti, in a tiny, almost unseaworthy barque. They had taken nothing. His twenty-eight men were short of food, weak with thirst, almost mutinous. Then, unexpectedly, they sighted a vast treasure fleet in which one enormous galleon straggled far behind the others. Roberts described what happened.

That night, barefoot, armed with only pistols and cutlasses, the buccaneers silently boarded the ship, killed the helmsman, shot or stabbed any resistance, surprised the Vice-Admiral and his officers at cards, and in the darkness made off with a fortune in cargo. By an irony, that very day the captain had been warned that the tiny craft in the distance might be a pirate but had scoffed at so trivial a vessel. Le Grand sold his share of the booty and retired a wealthy man to his home in Dieppe.[5] If one feeble French scavenger could do that to the Spaniards, said Roberts, the pirates could certainly overcome the Portuguese.

What he did not mention was that they had been so near to starvation and death that le Grand ordered holes to be bored in the barque so that there could be no faint-hearted withdrawal. His was a venture born of desperation. Roberts' decision was one of calculated audacity based on contempt for Portuguese courage. He had a plan. It depended on the pirates to fulfil it.

There was no moon and the few stars shone like reflections of the ships' lights. The wide lanes between the ships were black with night. Unlit the *Royal Rover* slid between them, the noise she made indistinguishable from the lappings of water of the other craft as they swung at anchor.

Roberts stood at the bows. Kennedy was at the whipstaff keeping the ship steady as she floated past the merchantmen. Dennis inspected each cannon with its three men for ramrod, tinder and powder-carrier. By them were pistols and grenades and grappling irons with rope neatly coiled where hands could reach it quickly. Other pirates waited with buckets and brushes for the continual swabbing of the deck so that no gunpowder was left drying on it. More pirates crouched beneath the breastworks, each with pistol and cutlass. There was no sound.

Very slowly, quietly, the *Royal Rover* moved on towards the town. The harbour fort was far behind them. On every side were merchantmen. Hardly half a mile off was one of the men-of-war. Roberts whispered orders to Anstis.

The *Royal Rover* drifted round in a wide circle to come alongside a merchant ship. The lights of Bahia disappeared behind them and the merchantman seemed to be creeping up on the starboard beam, the rippling river almost inaudible, until the water between the vessels vanished. There was a dull bump by the thick rope fenders that had been hung over the *Royal Rover*'s bulwarks to soften the impact.

Anstis with a group of pirates clambered onto the merchant's deck even as other pirates flung out the grappling-irons that clattered breath-takingly as they gripped the Portuguese ship. There was a scuffling, a suppressed yell, another crash, the slither of cutlasses, the sound of an anchor being cautiously raised.

Some figures climbed onto the *Royal Rover*. For the first time there was a grin on the face of Anstis. The captain of the merchantman stood fearfully by him. Roberts asked which of the fleet held the richest cargo. The captain stammered that it was the *Sagrada Familia* near the harbour-mouth.[6] Behind him his crew were being led below.

The *Sagrada* was a big ship of forty guns. Her vast stern jutted from the water high above the *Royal Rover*. The Portuguese prisoner was told to call for the captain. A figure appeared asking what was wanted of his commander at that time of night. An urgent message had to be given him from the captain of the tobacco ship. There was a long, nervous wait. Then there was the faint sound of men moving quickly about the *Sagrada Familia*. Without hesitation Roberts shouted for Dennis to open fire.

The *Royal Rover*'s guns exploded in the night with a detonation that rocked the harbour. The *Sagrada* reeled with the shock even though every shot had struck her high above the waterline. Amid the screams and shouts following the broadside the pirates threw out their grappling-irons dragging the ships together.

Swivels swept the open decks of the Portuguese. Instantly pirates leapt aboard her hacking at anyone in their way. Behind them swarmed others brawling, howling cursing as they swung from the rigging and jumped down the hatches in search of defenders. A towline was fastened to the *Sagrada*.

Lights sparkled on the man-of-war. More lights flashed on other ships near them. From the *Sagrada Familia* came a half-hearted volley as resistance ended. The *Royal Rover* moved forward. From the Portuguese ship Jones shouted that what seamen were still alive had been imprisoned below. The man-of-war was now sailing forward but still some distance off.

It was early dawn. The sails of the *Royal Rover* filled and she drove forward, shuddering as she took the strain of the towline. Around them merchantmen were firing their small guns as a signal to the man-of-war. Top-gallants had been hoisted, the little sails that on an otherwise unsheeted vessel warned of an emergency.

The man-of-war was only a few hundred metres behind them with cannon snubbing out from its upper and lower gunports. She was gaining. The *Sagrada* was slowing the pirates. Deeply laden she dragged sluggishly on the towline even with all sails spread. It was a time either to turn on the man-of-war whose superior armament should swiftly end the fight or to cut their prize loose and run away through the barrage of the harbour guns.

Roberts did not weigh the gamble. He gave orders for the gunners to make ready, told Kennedy to hold their course out to sea, and his guns fired almost point-blank into their pursuer.

Eastwell screeched nervously from the mainmast-top. He pointed to the man-of-war. Roberts stared. The huge warship had heaved to and as he looked in amazement the reason was clear. She was waiting for the other man-of-war. That vessel was far away between the lines of merchantmen. One blast from the *Royal Rover*'s cannon had terrified the Portuguese. In fifteen minutes Roberts was beyond the fort with his rich, brave haul.[7]

From *The Weekly Journal or British Gazetteer*, 6 February 1720.

'The Lisbon Fleet from the Bay of All Saints, Brazil, has arrived. But one vessel of thirty-six guns was taken by a pyrate ship (formerly an English hog-boat) and two others plundered'.

On 13 February 1720, the other *Weekly Journal* excelled itself.

'The Pyrates off Brazil, of the number of 2,000 or so, propose to make a base in Madagascar'. It was not sufficient news to disturb the East India Company but Roberts would have been amused to learn of the presumed size of his crew and of their intended destination. The *Daily Courant* of 6 February 1720 was more sober and gave an estimated inventory of the wealth carried by the Portuguese merchantmen.

Lisbon. 27 January. On the 21st inst. the Brazil Fleet arrived, consisting of thirty-two sail.

1 man-of-war that conveyed them.
3 ships from the West Indies.
3 ships from Fernambuco.
25 from Bahia.

Their cargo was:-

7,794 chests of sugar	957 quarter-chests of sugar.
128 baskets of sugar in cake.	11,238 rolls of tobacco.
21,751 hides.	205 raw hides.
92 barrels of honey.	104 slaves.

Large quantities of planks and East Indies goods. Gold in specie and dust not yet declared. For private people, 759,128 octaves of gold dust and 164,161 moedas of gold. For the King, 10,270 of the same.

By any reckoning Roberts had made his name as a pirate.

Two thousand miles they sailed, north and then north-west, always out of sight of land, past the estuary of the Amazon and beyond to the archipelago of the Iles du Salut off Surinam, anchoring at the tiny islet of the Ile du Diable, later to become notorious as the penal colony of Devil's Island. It was time for celebration.

On the long voyage they counted their losses and gains. Only two pirates had been killed in the fight against the *Sagrada Familia*[8] although several others had been wounded and were still recovering under the care of Murray. The Portuguese dead had been buried at sea. Those that had survived were kept below decks.

The plunder was magnificent. The pirates had already possessed the loot from Howel Davis's depredations from Principe, from the ships that Roberts had taken, and now there were chests of sugar that could be sold profitably, skins, hides, rolls of tobacco, chains, trinkets, and 40,000 moidores, *moeda do'oura* or 'money of gold'. Most superb of all was a large golden cross, beautifully designed and encrusted with diamonds. The

Portuguese captain said it had been made for the King. No one disbelieved him.[9]

Merrily the ships sailed on. Roberts had two musicians, a fiddler and a trumpeter, playing through the day. Nearing Surinam they captured a Rhode Island sloop whose captain, Cane, made no protest when he saw the strength of the pirates. Roberts was so elated that he renamed the sloop the *Fortune* in honour of Bahia and to the sound of music and with all flags flying the fleet came to Devil's Island where the governor, delighted at the present of the golden cross, welcomed such profligate guests.[10] News of their exploits was spreading before them to the West Indies where the man-of-war, *Seaford*, was patrolling. None of this was known to the pirates. Nor would they have cared. Enjoyment obsessed them. For weeks they caroused. Money and wine were plentiful. The pirates swarmed through the streets, brawled and roistered in the taverns, slumbered in linen sheets, carefree in their spending of the enormous fortune.

Less richly the petty pirate, Rackam, continued his lack-lustre marauding of fishing-vessels in the Americas. His mistress, Anne Bonny, had a baby in Cuba then rejoined the men. At New Providence, armed with sword and pistol, she terrified the two seamen of a small but very fast and desirable sloop into surrender by swearing 'that if they pretended to resist, or make a Noise, she would blow out their Brains (that was the Term she used)'. Learning of the sloop's theft the governor issued a list of Rackam's crew including 'two women, Ann Fulford, alias Bonny, and Mary Read', confusing Bonny with Anne Fulworth [sic] her alleged mother.[11]

Elsewhere, in different manner, women were both instant delights and ultimate disasters. Infected by men they infected other men. Venereal disease, gonorrhea and syphilis, was widespread amongst pirates whose surgeons always endeavoured to keep a stock of mercurial compounds as painful cures to cauterise the ulcers.

Blackbeard was once so desperate for medicines that he held a prominent citizen of Charleston hostage until the town's governor complied with the demand for supplies. Two chests worth between £200 and £300 were sent out but sunk in a squall and Blackbeard left without them. Other pirates were luckier. After a blood-soaked battle at the Comoros Islands off Madagascar in 1720 Edward England with Taylor and la Bouche overcame the stoutly-built Indiaman *Cassandra* whose freight was valued at £75,000. Yet 'no part of the cargo was so much valued by the robbers as the doctor's chest, for they were all poxed to a great degree'. The promiscuous men of Robert's crew were probably no different. John Atkins, naval surgeon on H.M. *Swallow* that was to pursue Roberts, wrote 'a neat Pocket Volume, *The Navy Surgeon*, price 3/- [15p], to which is added, a Treatise on the Venereal Disease, its Causes, Symptoms, and Method of Cure by Mercury'.[12] Pox was the scourge of seamen.

While their festivities continued Roberts sent the *Royal Rover* to a nearby island for careening while he checked the marine stores with the boatswain. They were in need of provisions and equipment if they were to sail the hundreds of miles to the West Indies. It had been known for pirates to be captured in hostile parts because of enforced landings for sustenance. Forethought overcame these mishaps. A few looted vessels solved the problem. Roberts had lookouts posted on high ground and was about to return to the pleasures of Devil's Island when he was told that men were planning a mass desertion, hoping to reach the protection of a French colony. It was the forced men that were dissatisfied and Roberts resolved never to compel anyone to join him unless he was an indispensable sea-artist such as a carpenter or a surgeon. Common seamen were nothing but nurseries of discontent.

The escaping longboat was soon brought back and the thirty deserters questioned. Eastwell, Hews an the incorrigible Rogers were the ringleaders. Eastwell, previously so eager, had realised at Bahia that a pirate's life was not all easy pickings and that death in battle was possible.

Ashplant suggested marooning the runaways, the statutory punishment for their crime. The majority of the company voted for flogging except for the leaders who were to be more severely treated.[13] Eastwell was condemned to be shot. Later this was commuted to a cruel whipping by Kennedy, before being cut down half dead, fettered and locked in the dripping blackness of the hold. Hews and Rogers were sadistically lashed. The remainder were whipped and guarded. With three ships Roberts dared risk no shortage of hands.

The celebrations continued. Desires became sated. Quarrels started. Roberts welcomed the news that a brig had been sighted to the east of Surinam and decided to chase her himself in the *Fortune* taking only reliable men with him. Kennedy was left in charge of the *Royal Rover* and *Sagrada*, all the prisoners securely confined.

It was a strong company that Roberts took: Dennis, Moody, Ashplant, Anstis and a score of others, setting out in pursuit of the brig now barely in sight on the skyline.[14] Hours later Moody discovered that they were very low in food and water. The *Fortune* had not been restocked since her capture and all that she held were biscuits writhing with weevils and some little water-barrels that reeked when their tops were removed.[15]

At first there was no concern. They expected to catch the brig before nightfall. But at dusk they were no nearer their prey. Next day they were caught by contrary winds and currents for eight unavailing days, ending almost a hundred miles away from their base with no food to sustain them, weak from deprivation. Even though Moody rationed everything there was too little. Anxiously they steered towards an island but could find no creek to enter. They dropped anchor wearily a quarter of a mile from the shore.

There were insufficient provisions for them all to return to Surinam. Moody and five others left in the sloop's boat to reach

Kennedy and bring the *Royal Rover* to the rescue. Roberts and the rest waited for the cool of evening to row to the land where there would be fresh water and fruit. Ashplant mumbled of similar plights when starving men had eaten their shipmates. Roberts slouched by the gunwales looking down at the limitless, undrinkable seawater that gurgled and rippled a few feet away. Suddenly Dennis cursed. In their panic to send for Kennedy they had also given their only chance of life. Moody had taken the boat. There was no other.

At desperate times commanders prove themselves. Roberts ordered a raft to be improvised. They ripped up planking and lashed them together. Fortunately the sloop lay so low in the water that the makeshift lifeboat could be lowered into the water without damage. Carefully they paddled to the island, beaching the raft, searching for water.

Three days later Moody returned in a deeply-laden boat. He brought bad news. The *Royal Rover* and the *Sagrada Familia* were not at Devil's Island. Kennedy had deserted.[16]

6

Trials in Virginia, Edinburgh and London[1]

December 1719–July 1721

'Edinburgh, 9 January. Four more of those condemned for piracy were executed at Leith on the 4th Instant, they all went to death affirming they had been pressed into that wicked Course of Life, and that they returned to Britain resolving to forsake it'.

Caledonian Mercury, 9 January, 1721

The piracies of Bartholomew Roberts became widely reported. Gradually more information becomes available for the biographer. Dates are more exactly quoted. Events are more fully described. Pirates who had been captured gave evidence at their trials and many of their statements can be corroborated. The testimony recorded at courts in Virginia and Edinburgh in 1720 and London in 1721 contains details of many minor episodes.

When Moody reached Devil's Island in the *Fortune*'s boat only to discover that the *Royal Rover* and *Sagrada Familia* had gone leaving no message it was natural for him to assume that Kennedy had deserted with the wealth of plunder in the two pirate ships. Roberts would have believed this.

Kennedy, however, had not abandoned his captain. He had seen Roberts depart to chase the brig and supposed that the pursuit would last no longer than a few hours. By the following evening he was worried. He had a great responsibility for a young man. He was hardly twenty-four.

His two ships contained the opulent booty from six or seven ships. Below decks were Portuguese prisoners that he dare not release. Eastwell and his mutinous companions lay in irons. Other faint-hearted pirates who would desert at the first opportunity wandered about resentful of their whippings. Worse, by his arrogance Kennedy had alienated even the hardened criminals who were the core of his crews.

Days passed. There was no sign of the *Fortune.* Roberts must have been lost at sea in a storm. By the ninth day with no news the demands of the men to leave the island were too much for Kennedy. Two days later the *Royal Rover* sailed for the West Indies. Kennedy was elected captain because he was ruthless enough to give his men some hope of survival. But his crew remained rank with dissatisfaction.

The pirates let the *Sagrada Familia* go. There were too few men for both ships. The plunder was transferred to the *Royal Rover* and with the liberality of owners whose generosity cost them nothing they gave the *Sagrada* to Captain Cane whose own sloop they believed now lay somewhere on the bed of the North Atlantic Ocean. Cane sailed to the British island of Antigua where he gave the prize to Governor Hamilton of the Leeward Islands who wrote to the Secretary of the Commissioners of Trade and Plantations in London.

Governor Hamilton to Mr Popple.
16 February 1720.
'We have of late heard of several pirates that rove in these considerable seas, particularly one of about 30 guns that had been for a considerable time upon the coast of Guinea where she had done a great deal of damage, afterwards took a Portuguese ship upon the coast of Brazil, which he brought to the island of Cayon, a French islet

lying off of Surinam; and there plundered her of a vast booty, mostly in moidores, not valuing the rest of the Cargo (which consisted of sugar, tobacco and Brazil plank) would have set the ship on fire but meeting a Rhode Island sloop which they took and fitted out for their use, they gave the Portuguese ship to the master of the R.I. sloop who with the Portuguese that were left on board brought her into Antigua where I have ordered a merchant to take care of her, and what remaining on board for use of the owner or owners'.[12]

Hamilton knew little about Roberts but trusted that the pirate would not bother him. He was comforted by the knowledge that the man-of-war *Seaford* cruised off his shores and that the naval sloops *Rose* and *Shark* were on their way. The age of piracy, he hoped, was in decline. He was to be disillusioned.

Kennedy in the *Royal Rover* sailed off the West Indian islands. On 15 December 1719, he took his first ship, a snow, the The *Sea Nymph*, whose captain, Bloodworth, had left New York at the end of November on a voyage to Barbados. Nearing his destination he was seen by the pirates and he was caught after a chase lasting seven hours. His was not a sensational cargo. Little of it was of value to the pirates and although a snow was the largest of two-masted vessels the *Sea Nymph* would not make a good exchange for the *Royal Rover* despite that ship's poor condition.

The *Sea Nymph* was taken northwards with the *Royal Rover*. The desultory plundering continued. Bloodworth's men were penned in the pirate ship while the snow was ransacked. Eight days later, Kennedy who had futilely attempted to conceal his name under the alias of Miller allowed Bloodworth to return to his ship with a gift of several negroes and other unwanted goods.[3]

Sixteen men were allowed to go with him because the pirates said they 'were pressed men and desirous to leave them'. One was Archibald Murray, the young surgeon who had been forced to stay with Howel Davis when Woodes Rogers' *Buck* sloop had been taken over by mutinous pirates in 1718. Bloodworth reached Barbados on Christmas Day, 1719, and after a stern examination the forced men were freed. Eleven months later Murray was to testify at the trial of Kennedy's pirates in Edinburgh.

Having parted from Bloodworth the aimless and luckless Kennedy took the *Royal Rover* to Virginia, found nothing, wandered back to the West Indies and in January, 1720, met Captain Knot. In the same month a financial catastrophe was originating in London.

The South Sea Company had been founded in 1711 to sell slaves to Spain's American colonies. Two years later the Spanish government granted the Company the privilege of an *Assiento*, or concession, to import 4,800 slaves annually for thirty years. Incredible fortunes loomed.

By January, 1720, the directors of the Company were so sure that their profits would swell endlessly that they offered to take over Britain's crippling National Debt in return for some trading rights. Share-holders in the National Debt would convert their shares into South Sea Company stock with its guarantee of higher rates of interest. As an additional inducement the Company would pay the British government £7,500,000. The government accepted. Several ministers had been lavishly bribed. Speculators were attracted by the boldness of the scheme and the assurance of vast gains.[4]

None of this was known to Kennedy or to Captain Knot, a Quaker against all violence even in defence. He had no armament, not a pistol or a cutlass, an admirable victim because yet more pirates in the *Royal Rover* wanted to quit. If they went with Knot he could not hurt them and he would make an ideal host for the journey to Virginia. To make his complicity doubly sure they gave him ten chests of sugar, ten rolls of tobacco, thirty moidores and some gold dust, a small fortune of some £250. Any impoverished seaman would be seduced into discreet silence.[5]

There had never been such repeated and unopposed desertion from a pirate ship and it revealed how undisciplined, disheartened, even indifferent to their fate, the pirates had become. The depleted *Royal Rover* sailed off. Knot resumed his voyage to Virginia with his eight optimistic-ex-freebooters. Their anticipation of liberty was short-lived.

Weekly Journal or British Gazetteer, 30 July, 1720.
Philadelphia. 17 May.

'Last month Captain Knot in a ship of 150 tons and 12 men arrived in the Capes of Virginia from London; he reported that within 20 leagues of these Capes he was taken by a pyrate ship manned with 148 bold fellows who took from him some provisions but restored the ship and the cargo. The captain of the pyrates obliged Captain Knot to take 8 of his men on board and to give an obligation under his hand that he had shipped them as passengers from London to Virginia. The Captain of the pyrates gave these men a boat which Captain Knot was obliged to let any of them have when they required to go from his ship. The pyrates put also two Portuguese prisoners on board (which had been taken on the coast of Brazil) to be set on shore in Virginia. When the Captain was within the Capes, the wind turning easterly, he came to an anchor, and 4 of the pyrates required leave to hoist their boat out which Captain Knot complied with, upon which these 4 pyrates put off the boat designing to go up the Bay, but being soon weary of rowing they put into Back River. As soon as they came ashore their first care was to find out a tavern and ease themselves of some of their golden luggage. and they quickly found out a place to their minds: where for some time they profusely treated all that came into their company, and there being in the house some English women servants they so pleased these picaroons that they set them free, giving their master £30 demanded for their time. This extravagant way of living soon discovered that they were not passengers from London as they pretended but rather pyrates. Accordingly they were seized and committed.

The other 4, not hearing of the fate of their companions, landed at Hampton in James River, where pursuing the same courses, were likewise apprehended and imprisoned.

The 2 Portuguese being set on shore found, by chance, the master of an English ship that could talk Portuguese to whom they related that they had been taken by a pyrate ship on the coast of Brazil and that the 8 men in the gaol were some of the crew that took them. The master immediately waited on the governor with these 2 men, and declared to him on oath as before, he being the interpreter. Upon this information the 8 pyrates were tried and condemned. 7 of them were English, the other a mulatto. Soon after, 2 were reprieved and 6 executed and hanged in chains. When they came to the place of execution one of them called for a bottle of wine and taking a glass of it drank, 'Damnation to the governor and confusion to the Colony', which the rest pledged'.

And, reported another sheet, 'were turned off just after'.

The Quaker, Captain Knot, surrendered his unlawful presents.

The *Royal Rover* drifted purposelessly about the sea with her crew split into irreconcileable factions. Some wished to return to an honest life. Others wanted to enjoy the remains of their plunder. A very few wanted to continue as pirates. Had Kennedy been a more congenial character he might have won the support of one of these groups. But he was hated by all, harsh and dictatorial, patronising because he had some education, and worst of all, unlucky. Had there been any lingering aspiration for command in his crew he would have been deposed.

Early in February, 1720, they took Captain McIntosh's New York snow, the *Eagle*,[6] and it was with the capture of this prize that the pirate company, first commanded by Howel Davis, briefly in Taylor, and then by Bartholomew Roberts, finally dissolved in argument, treachery and desertion. Those who longed to abandon piracy were sneeringly informed that there was no current Act of Pardon and that if they were caught they would hang. The would-be deserters retorted that if they did not leave they would be committed to even more piracy until it would be impossible for them to prove their innocence. The hardened pirates shrugged and proceeded to get drunk.

Taking their chance the forced men desperately plugged the *Royal Rover*'s cannon, threw all the firearms they could find overboard, crossed to the *Eagle*, hoisted the sails and resolved either to surrender to any man-of-war they met or to land unobtrusively in England and make their way home.

Their reaction when they discovered that Kennedy had sneaked aboard the *Eagle* was aggressive.[7] Some were for throwing him overboard fearing, justifiably, that being so self-centred he would betray them all if ever he was apprehended. Kennedy, self-assured and imperious, said that the forty-seven men needed him as navigator if they were to reach the British Isles.

In the *Royal Rover* next morning there was panic. Twenty-five pirates, all with hangovers, discovered their captain, the larger part of the crew, all their plunder and most of their weaponry gone. The vessel was too big for them. Its description was known to every merchant and naval captain in the West Indies and its size made it difficult to conceal. She was a floating death-trap and would have to be taken to some welcoming foreign island such as St. Thomas or St. Barthélemy. Devil's Island was too far away.

They sailed to St. Thomas in the Virgin Islands, anchoring

well out of range of the fort's guns. The pirates rowed uneasily ashore, unsure of their reception. An unknown alliance with Britain might cause the Danish governor to imprison them as an act of good faith. The governor was neither pleased nor displeased. His was a poor settlement that could not afford to reject affluent pirates. Moneyless they did not interest him. The pirates offered to sell the *Royal Rover* in exchange for a smaller sloop. Bartering commenced. The governor was in no hurry. The more moidores were frittered away in the taverns the better bargain he could make.

What both he and the pirates overlooked was that lying as she did beyond the fort's cannon the *Royal Rover* was in plain view from the sea. Major Richard Holmes and Mr Thomas Ottley from Nevis saw her and deduced from her raised gunwales and clear deck that she had been converted for piracy.

Prize money was always desirable. With no more than a skeleton crew apparent in the *Royal Rover* Holmes and Ottley decided to tow her away and claim the reward. There was no resistance. Not a shot was fired. The few pirates abandoned the vessel. Holmes and Ottley took the vessel only to find that their capture was unlikely to be lucrative. With few cannon, firearms or plunder the ship was little more than a hulk, worn by her long voyages, battered from the battle at Bahia, neglected. The wretched cargo were fifteen negroes, three barrels of flour, and derisory amounts of sugar, tobacco, bars of iron, steel and a miscellany of trivia.

At sea she sailed so badly that there was no hope of bringing her to Nevis almost two hundred miles to the south-east. Apprehensively they towed the *Royal Rover* to St. Croix forty miles to the south.[8] From there they sent a message to Governor Hamilton who added a postscript to Mr Popple.

Nevis. 16 February 1720
'I was told that last Sunday morning on the way to St. Eustatius and St. Thomas that a pirate ship lay under the

isle of St. Thomas, most of the pirates being on shore. Major Richard Holmes of Colonel Richard Lucas's Regiment and Mr. Thomas Ottley went to the ship at anchor. She was well-armed with several pirate colours on board. As they were not able to bring her to any of my inhabited isles they took her to Santa Cruis Isle where they left her in charge of officers of the Regiment till the Major could tell me. So I sent Captain John Rose of the *Seaford* to bring her back. He sailed on 15 February'.[9]

In a subsequent despatch he was less complacent. On 28 March he complained that he still had not received the *Royal Rover* and was unlikely ever to do so. Captain Rose, having inspected the pirate ship, took her in calm weather to Basseterre on St. Kitts, a harbour twelve miles from Charlestown on Nevis. The captain reported in person to Hamilton that the vessel could have borne thirty guns and was reputed to have had two hundred men aboard her at St. Thomas.

Hamilton commented that St. Thomas was known as a place 'that harbours all villains and vagabonds . . . it's long been suspected that the Danes give too much encouragement to that vermin', pirates. He requested Rose to bring the *Royal Rover* to Charlestown but on St. Kitts the captain found Ottley and Holmes in pugnacious moods fearing that once the *Royal Rover* reached Nevis they would lose their share of the capture. To avoid this they dismantled the ship leaving her unfit for sea. Giving up hope of her and hearing of a sloop plaguing the seas off Barbados Hamilton sent the agreeable captain of the *Seaford* in pursuit. The *Royal Rover* never reached Nevis. The history of Bartholomew Roberts' first ship had ended in anti-climax.

For more than piracy 1720 was an unquiet year. There was a major epidemic of plague in Europe. In France John Law's over-optimistic financial forecasts of the profits of the French Mississippi Company left the proposed citadel of New Orleans nothing more than a miserable collection of wooden shacks and reduced France to national bankruptcy. And by mid-year commercial piracy flourished on dry land in London.

Dealings in South Sea Company shares developed into madness. With the Company's stock valued ever more highly and with its share issue limited the only way to acquire the £100 bonds was to purchase them from a previous investor. Prices rose. People stampeded for the precious scrip. £200 was offered, £300, ever upwards like the promised dividends. Sensible people used their savings, never questioning that today's £500 would be tomorrow's £800. At the peak of the frenzy £1050 was being paid.

Like bloodsuckers on the feverish body unscrupulous directors of illegal, uncharted companies offered - and sold - shares in schemes better described as swindles. The gullible subscribed to plans to drain the bogs of Ireland; to transmute mercury into silver; to an invention that would create a wheel of perpetual motion; to an alchemical method of extracting silver from lead; even 'for building ships against pirates'. Cash had no meaning. Only shares were wealth. But unlike the democracy of piratical plunder the London shares were over-priced. By September, while Kennedy and the *Eagle* were crossing the Atlantic, stories spread that the South Seas Company's trade in slaves was proving less profitable than predicted. Share prices slowed, dropped, collapsed to £135. Thousands, including the poet Alexander Pope and the playwright, John Gay, were ruined. By November the South Sea 'Bubble' had burst.[10] The following March, John Aislabie, Chancellor of the Exchequer, suspected of fraudulent dealings in it, was sent to the Tower.

The deserters in the *Eagle* had reached England having robbed a last ship for provisions. Kennedy, despite his promise, was no navigator nor were his men competent. Beyond Ireland a storm drove them helplessly northwards to the treacherous coastline of the Mull of Kintyre in Argyll where the ship was badly holed.[11]

At Craignish Point they sent two men inland to ask for a magistrate but were told there were no officers of the law for miles. Kennedy and some others decided to make for Ireland where the Irishman had friends. From there they could eventually reach England. The majority preferred to wander southwards by land. Like their former comrades in Virginia every tavern was a fatal temptation.

'The main Gang alarm'd the Country where-ever they came, drinking and roaring at such a Rate, that the People shut themselves up in their Houses, in some Places, not daring to venture out among so many mad Fellows: In other Villages, they treated the whole Town, squandering their Money away, as if, like Aesop, they wanted to lighten their Burthens: This expensive Manner of Living procured two of their drunken Stragglers to be knocked on the Head, they being found murdered in the Road, and their Money taken from them: All the rest, to the Number of seventeen, as they drew nigh to Edinburgh, were arrested and thrown into Gaol upon Suspicion, of what they knew not; however, the Magistrates were not long at a Loss for proper Accusations, for two of the Gang offering themselves for Evidences, were accepted of; and the others were brought to a speedy Tryal'.

Extract from the *Caledonian Mercury*. Tuesday, 8 November, 1720.

Edinburgh.

'On Friday last compeard [appeared] before the Lord Judge Admiral: Roger Hews, John Clark, Richard Johns [Jones], John Eshwell [Eastwell], William Fenton, Hymen Saturly, William Minty. William Green, John Gerrel, Thomas Dowden, John Stewart, James Sail, Richard Luntly, Thomas Rogers, Nicholas Kerny, Dennis Toppen [Topping], Henry Thixton, late sailors aboard the ship called the *Eagle*-snow, after having received their Indictment for piracy. His Majesty's Advocate, His Majesty's Solicitor and the Procurator Fiscal of the High Court of Admiralty appeared against them. Nine lawyers were allowed to plead for them. After the Pleadings were over the lawyers on both sides were appointed to give in to the Admiralty Office their respective Informations, and the further Tryals of the Pannels [accused] was adjourned to Tuesday the 15th Instant. The Witnesses adduced against them are Nicholas Simmonds, William Savage, John Owen, James Nawlor, lately sailors aboard the ship called the *Eagle*-snow. John Johns, lately Midship-man Extraordinary aboard the *Worcester* Man of War commanded by Captain Boyle. Duncan Daw, Mate to Duncan Glasfoord in Borrowstounness. Archibald Murray, Chirurgion [surgeon] to the deceast Murray of Deuchar. Peter Cheap, Supercargo on Board the Ship the *Loyalty of Glasgow*. John Daniel, Couper on board the said ship the Loyalty. Thomas Brewer, Boatswain of the said ship the Loyalty, James Campbell of Stonefield.[12]

The court agreed to accept Owen's statement that he had been forced and deem him innocent so that he could turn King's evidence against his shipmates. With him was Archiblad Murray, for so long the pirates' doctor.

Robert Dundass, His Majesty's Advocate, reviewed the history of the pirates from the time they had mutinied on Woodes Rogers' two trading craft until their landing in Scotland. Such a comprehensive survey, however sketchy, allowed all manner of accusations against the prisoners. In reply the defence lawyers argued that the prosecution was too vague in its omission of ships' names; that a man's mere presence at an act of piracy did not make him a pirate as he may well have been forced to remain with the true pirates. They pointed to the attempt to escape at Devil's Island, the desertion of the *Eagle*, and the effort to find a magistrate in Scotland.

His Majesty's Advocate was unconvinced. Forcing was not an adequate plea unless there had been continual protest by the forced men. Three of the accused, Hews, Clark and Jones had been with the pirates since New Providence. Their protestations were an impertinence to the court. Had they not agreed to sign the pirates' Articles they would have been confined at the ship and made to work with the negroes. Instead, they had been at one act of piracy after another. They must therefore have signed the Articles and willingly foregone all possibility of innocence.

They could, moreover, have escaped somewhere had they been determined. Other men had got away but the accused had stayed. Some even held positions of authority. They had voted at elections, taken their share of plunder, a fact that had doomed them through their wanton spending of the loot in alehouses. Even their 'escape' in the *Eagle* had been illegal. The snow had been stolen. It was obvious that their departure from Roberts had been by mutual consent.

When apprehended they did not admit being former pirates but had pretended to be shipwrecked mariners from Newfoundland. They had not given themselves up. They had been arrested. Indeed, it was believed that some others had managed to evade the officers of the law and were now in England. As for the particular plea that Nicholas Kerny was continually ill and could not have participated in piracy this was unbelievable. He was certainly active in the taking of the *Eagle*.

The defence tried another approach. Some of the accused had asked to be tried first so that, if found innocent, they could testify for the others. The Advocate was indignant. Such wretches would swear anything. Oaths meant nothing. And those that would be tried first were the very rogues who had joined the pirates last and whose testimony would be of the least value. As for the Articles that the defence claimed were never signed these had long since been lost and could not be used in proof.

The prisoners were brought to the bar. The defence council prepared to speak although he prefaced his argument by stating that like any honest man he abhorred piracy. After which he repeated that the indictment was too unspecific in matters of dates, names and places. Whereas nothing could be proved to the discredit of the accused it was a verifiable fact that they had returned to Britain thus proving their honesty. As for the taking of the *Eagle* the snow had already been captured by hardened pirates. That the accused should use it to escape was praiseworthy, not a crime.

The prisoners testified individually, explaining how they had hated piracy and how they had plotted together to get away. But the witnesses that followed swore of seeing misdeeds, of the accused participating in attacks and accepting their shares of plunder. The verdict was inevitable. The charges were proved against all the defendants but the Court did find the defence of forcing, fear of death and sickness exculpated seven of the accused: Dowden, Eastwell, Gerrel, Kerny, Rogers, Thixton and Topping. Eastwell almost capered in delight. With all that he had done condemnation had seemed certain.

The remainder of the pirates were sentenced to death. Only for young Hymen Saturly was there a hope. 'The Assize . . . desired the Judge to recommend Hymen Saturly in respect of his age to His Majestie for His Gracious Pardon, the Judge declared he had accordingly recommended him to his Majestie's mercy'. There were no more reprieves.[13]

17 December, 1720.

'The said Roger Hews and John Clark to be taken to the Sands of Leeth within the floodmark upon the second Wednesday of December next being the 14th of the said month between the hours of two and four o'clock in the afternoon and there to be hanged by the neck upon a gibbet till they be dead'.

Seven more would follow them. On 4 January, 1721, James Dougal, wrote from Edinburgh, 'There were four pirates hanged at Leith today . . . very hardened. They were a melancholy sight, and there is three to be hanged next Wednesday'.

One of them was Richard Luntly, a carpenter, who had vowed his innocence, stating that because of his intended desertion he had been marooned 'upon a desolate island' from which he had providentially been rescued by the *Eagle*. 'Forced men', he swore, 'were compelled by the force of arms to do things that our conscience thought to be unlawful'. Being a skilled carpenter and just the kind of sea-artist that pirates needed he was probably telling the truth. Vainlessly. He was hanged on 11 January. [14]

The pirates died 'within the floodmark', *infra fluxum ac refluxum*, because piracy was theft at sea and thus a crime against the Admiralty whose jurisdiction extended to the low tide mark. This writ extended throughout Britain. Whereas in London highwaymen and other criminals were hanged at Tyburn in the centre of the city pirates were executed at Wapping Old Stairs alongside the Thames. It was there that Captain Kidd was put to death in 1701.

Symbolism attended Admiralty executions. After death the corpse was taken from the scaffold and chained to a post until it had been washed over by three high tides. It was then hung in chains and left to rot further down river. Even in Africa the rule applied. At Cape Coast Castle pirates were sentenced to he hanged 'within the floodmarks' after which their bodies were taken in chains to be suspended from gibbets on nearby hills as dreadful warnings to those who might be tempted to live outside the law.

Far from the Edinburgh executions Kennedy and his companions were finally in England. Most went to the slums of London where thieves abounded. In the maze of East End alleys a man could hide for ever. It was said that Kennedy opened a brothel on the Deptford Road near the docks which, if true, was rash. Any honest seamen visiting it might recognise the ex-pirate.

It was rumoured that he became a footpad robbing travellers on Blackheath. Just as believable is the tale that early in 1721 he was arrested for stealing from one of his whores.[15] Under guard he was taken to the Justice of the Peace at Rotherhithe. The group passed a tavern where a man asked what the commotion was about. Being told that a man accused of robbery was going by he went to look. Seeing Kennedy he accompanied the prisoner and escort to the Justice where he testified against the pirate. He had no doubt. He was Thomas Grant of the *Experiment* whom Kennedy had struck and threatened just after the raid on Principe.[16]

Kennedy was committed to a Bridewell gaol and then to Newgate prison to await his trial at the Old Bailey. Hoping to save himself by turning King's Evidence he gave the names of ten comrades, five of whom he believed were still in London. Only one of them was arrested. Bradshaw was indicted by a Middlesex magistrate on 19 March 1721. Both pirates were to be tried at the next Admiralty Sessions on 3 July.

Kennedy realised that the evidence of Grant would condemn him and he denied nothing, admitting his piracy with bravado, 'behaving', wrote the *London Gazette* on 8 August, 'with so much impudence in Court as if he desired Mercy no more than he deserved it'. He was of good education, said Kennedy. His father had been an anchor-smith at Wapping but Kennedy, having fought at sea during the French wars, decided that the pleasures of piracy were better than the drudgery of hard work in London and had the effrontery to sail with Woodes Rogers for New Providence with that intention. He described the events at Principe and Bahia without any attempt at deceit. Then the Clerk read out the list of friends he had betrayed.[17]

Thomas Lamburn whose father and mother lived in Robin Hood's Alley in Suffolk Lane in the Mint; James Bradshaw at the Cock, a public house in Cock Lane in Spitalfields. He kept the house; John Cherry who lived at the White Lion, a public house, in Wheeler Street in Spitalfields; Thomas Jenkins (true name, Francis Channock) to be heard of at the Sign of the Yorkshire Grey or the Golden Bull, Rotherhithe; Charles Radford, a lodger at a musician's in Brook Street; and also Thomas Burnaby; John Williams and George Carlisle whose addresses Kennedy did not know.

Grant's evidence was damning. He told of the *Experiment's* capture and Kennedy's treatment of him, mistakenly calling the pirate the boatswain's mate. He described the attack at Bahia and the attempt to escape at Devil's Island. Nor did he spare Bradshaw who had pleaded forcing. That man, said Grant, was active in the pirate ship and on at least two occasions had accepted a share of the plunder. At that moment a surprise witness for Bradshaw appeared. It was Eastwell, joyfully back from Scotland, who affirmed that Bradshaw had assuredly been forced, that he had never done anything willingly, and that he had tried to escape at every opportunity.

Grant retorted that, if anything, Eastwell had been a worse pirate than Bradshaw. He had been the carpenter on the *Royal Rover* and when Grant had been captured had told the mate that he would force him to join the pirates. Eastwell, said Grant, was easy, active and took his share of loot at every prize that was taken.[18]

Eastwell complacently informed the judges that he had already been tried and exonerated of such charges in Scotland and could not be tried again. Sceptically the Court sent him to prison until a certificate could be produced of his acquittal. Bradshaw and Kennedy were found guilty and returned to the care of William Pitt, the keeper of Newgate. Eastwell's certificate arrived eventually and his now-acceptable evidence secured Bradshaw an unlikely and probably undeserved remission.[19]

On 21 July, 1721, in a tumbril preceded by the traditional silver oar of the Admiralty, Walter Kennedy was taken to

Execution Dock, Wapping Old Stairs, where he fainted at the sight of the gallows. Recovering, he called for a drink and then spoke to the crowd. 'Though it is a common thing for us when at sea', he said, 'to acquire vast quantities both of that metal which goes before me, and of gold, yet such is the justice of Providence that few or none of us preserve enough to maintain us; but as you see in me, when we go to death, we have not wherewith to purchase a coffin to bury us'.

He was turned off and slowly choked to death.[20]

There were no more executions of the men who had returned in the *Eagle*. Those who had left Bartholomew Roberts were either dead or living in furtive freedom.

On 29 July, 1721, there was a note in the *London Gazette*. 'Our merchants are in no little pain for the Brazil Fleet; being apprehensive of the famous pirate Roberts who has of late done so much damage in the West Indies'.

7

The Articles of the Pirates

December 1719–February 1720

'By a ship arrived this week from Barbados we have an account that the pirates continue upon that coast and few or no ships escape them; that some they plunder, others they carry off which together is an incredible detriment to the trade.'

Daily Post, May 7, 1720

The *Fortune* sloop lay off the coast of Brazil. On board carpenters worked repairing the deck from whose planking the makeshift raft had been improvised. Bartholomew Roberts watched them.

Since Kennedy's disappearance his attitude had changed. He no longer discussed every problem with his Lords. Although of little formal education he was an intelligent man and he understood that most pirates were lazy, dissolute and thoughtless bullies, taking to the life because it offered them luxuries without labour. It was not dare-devilry that encouraged them to run the perils of being maimed, killed or hanged but a stupid refusal to think of those matters. Theirs was pleasure without contemplation. Content to loaf and live easily they often acted violently, even sadistically, when over-running honest ships because of an irrational resentment that anyone should own more than they. Embittered by the aristocracy and the wealthy merchants who exploited the poor, galled by the living conditions in Britain where poverty was treated as a crime, their hatred reached out to anyone prosperous. Piracy, in their minds, was a justified means of obtaining those benefits that an unfair world had denied them.

Roberts comprehended this and as his life was knitted with theirs he considered how best he could safeguard his crew. The position was simple. He had the beginnings of a reputation but lacked the instruments to increase that notoriety. His ship was small and without adequate armament. His crew were toughened and experienced criminals but few in numbers. His provisions were low, his plunder non-existent. There was not a single base in the West Indies, the Americas or Africa that would welcome an impoverished pirate. He had to capture prizes with one wretched and weakly-armed little sloop. This exposed him to far more risk than there had been in the mighty *Royal Rover* with her thirty guns. For success his hardened crew needed more discipline, something that had to be created at their own wish.

New Articles were needed, a code of conduct to which everyone must assent and, whatever his reservations about consultation, for this Roberts would certainly need the agreement of the Lords. The old Articles had gone with the *Royal Rover*. The new ones would be more precisely drafted.[1]

It has been asked why pirates, many of them illiterate, wanted such dangerous documents that could be used against them in a trial. This, paradoxically, was their purpose. Just as forced seamen anxiously guarded the certificates given by their captains at the time of their capture, proving their unwillingness to join the pirates, so signing or putting one's mark to the Articles bound the novice pirate to his mates. He had put his name to a death warrant. Only those dedicated to piracy would do that.

Articles had been drawn up by the buccaneers, then by privateers. Pirates inherited the tradition of their forebears. The

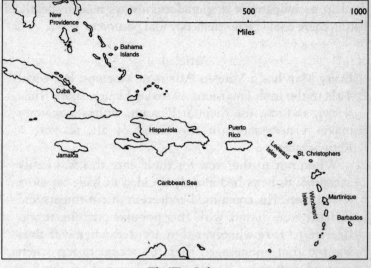

The West Indies

Articles laid down a simple pattern of behaviour. In essence, they were a fair set of rules. Everyone's share of plunder was specified. Punishments were itemised for different offences. The pirates had achieved an agreeable form of democracy. Without Articles and a jury to legislate upon them a pirate crew would have fallen into anarchy, parting company, dissenting, weakened, easily seized.

Roberts talked over his suggestions with his Lords. The Articles that they decided on were later quoted by Johnson. 'The following, is the Substance of the Articles, as taken from the Pyrates' own Information'. The list is so similar to those of other pirates such as Lowther and Philips that it is likely to be accurate. It contained eleven sections, some offering inducements and rewards, others condign punishments for transgressions. In the confined space of a ship there was no latitude for disharmony caused by cheating, fighting or theft.

And in a company of desperadoes, always near to death in battle, there could be no clemency for cowardice.

Article I

Every Man has a Vote in Affairs of Moment; has equal Title to the fresh Provisions, or strong Liquor, at any Time seized, and may use them at Pleasure, unless a Scarcity make it necessary, for the Good of all, to vote a Retrenchment.

When put to the crew for their vote this was easily accepted. Roberts had already decided to have no more forced men. His committed collection of cut-throats and ruffians were happy with this popular Article. It was licence to take whatever they wanted whenever they wanted that encouraged them to accept orders when demanded. It was a licence for freedom and equality but not for anarchy. It was parity between comrades. Article Two protected each man from another's dishonesty.

Article II

Every Man to be called fairly in Turn, by List, on board of Prizes, because (over and above their proper Share) they were on these Occasions allowed a Shift of Cloaths: But if they defrauded the Company to the Value of a Dollar, in Plate, Jewels or Money, MAROONING was their Punishment.

If the Robbery was only betwixt one another, they contented themselves with slitting the Ears and Nose of him that was Guilty and set him on Shore, not in an uninhabited Place, but somewhere, where he was sure to encounter Hardships.

The Article was both a bribe and a threat. To reward courage and audacity there were gifts. But to steal from plunder was an abomination. Savage punishments, disfigurement, abandonment on a treeless island, were inflicted without mercy for the filching of one trivial coin such as the dollar or 'piece of eight'.

Danish ducats, French deniers and *Louis d'Or*, English guineas, Spanish doubloons, the *onza* or double doubloons, were current coinage but the most common was Spain's piece of eight. Worth four pesetas or eight reales it had an 8 stamped on one side, an R on the other and was usually written as 8, the origin of the United States $ sign. In 1720 5000 were worth about £1,000, and one about four shillings [20p].[2] At a time when an ordinary seaman was paid a pittance of a shilling a day, to rob one's comrades of an article worth just four of such paltry days' wages could result in vicious mutilation, perhaps death. Democracy was never more sharply enforced.

The pirate captain, George Lowther, a contemporary of Bartholomew Roberts, was even more specific in his Article 4, imposing a time-limit on theft. Anything 'to the Value of a Piece of Eight, and the Finder do not deliver it to the Quarter-Master in the space of 24 hours [he] shall suffer what Punishment the Captain and Majority shall think fit'.[3]

There is an engaging if imaginative sketch of Lowther standing proudly in the opulence of a victorious commander. Trimly moustached, debonair from tricorn hat to buckled shoes, sash across his fashionable jacket, knee-length breeches, silk stockings, a model of luxury, Lowther's only difference from a London beau was in his basket-handled sword, long musket and the pair of flintlock pistols in his waistband.

His war sartorial splendour but it did not last. Trapped on an island off the coast of Venezuela he fled into the bleak wilderness, alone and without sustenance. Starving, hopeless, he killed himself. Days later his body was found 'dead, and a Pistol burst by his Side'.[4]

Roberts' Article III
No Person to Game at Cards or Dice for Money.

was very similar to another of Lowther's which condemned any crew member 'found Guilty of Gaming, or Defrauding Another to the Value of a Shilling', but both Articles were probably unenforceable. Gambling was exciting and it was addictive. However sensible and well-intentioned the Articles there was little chance of their being obeyed by bored and easily-tempted seamen. Roberts could only hope against mischance as he had to with his next Article.

Article IV

The Lights and Candles to be put out at eight a-Clock at Night: If any of the Crew, after that Hour, still remained enclined for Drinking, they were to do it on the open Deck.

Fire at sea was the dread of all mariners. Those pirates who remembered how close they had been to an explosion aboard the *Royal James* at Sierra Leone did not hesitate to agree with the Article. There were too many risks. Long, easily-broken clay pipes, smouldering dottle, an upset oil-lantern, candles, all were hazards in a wooden ship. Sun-dried decks, inflammable pitch and tallow, gunpowder, made the vessel a floating bonfire waiting for a match. Anyone ignoring the Article, even when drunk, would be flogged.

Article V

To keep their Piece, Pistols, and Cutlash clean, and fit for Service.

It was hardly needed. Pride in their weaponry and simple self-preservation caused most pirates to be meticulous in their care of pistols, daggers and cutlass, polishing, cleaning, sharpening, practising swordplay and markmanship. At auction a man might bid £30 or £40 for a brace of flintlocks. Two were needed. Loaded as soon as a prize was sighted the powder was ramrodded down the barrel, more powder sifted into the priming pan, pan cover snapped shut and, when action was near, the cock pulled back ready to be triggered. It took time and time was unavailable once fighting began. Firing one pistol as he boarded, a pirate would have the second primed and his knives and cutlass at hand.

Confused by the cacaphony of trumpets and drums from the pirate ship, intimidated by the bellowing, firing, slashing human arsenals that rushed at them few honest men resisted. Pirates knew very well what effect their weapons had. They tended them. It is surprising that John Phillips, another pirate captain, thought it necessary to have an Article, 'That Man that shall not keep his Arms clean, fit for an Engagement, or neglect his Business, Shall be cut off from his Share, and suffer such other Punishment that the Captain and the Company shall think fit'.[5] It is probable that this was an order directed only against reluctant forced men.

Fire at sea, cowardice, were not the only problem for captains like Roberts. Sex was another. Youthful and full-blooded pirates, starved of women for weeks, perhaps months, constantly looked for ways of slaking their frustration. Lust was perilous. Roberts and his Lords knew this.

Article VI
No Boy or Woman to be allowed amongst them. If any Man were found seducing any of the latter Sex, and carry'd her to Sea, disguised, he was to suffer Death.

There is no statistical evidence for 18th century homosexuality at sea but it is likely to have been widespread in the dull confines of a ship. An estimate has been offered that as many as one in two pirates engaged in acts of fellatio and sodomy.[6] Cabin-boys and powder-monkeys were always targets although for them their masters were frequently amongst the skilled officers whose occupations set them apart from the commonalty of the crew. One reads of 'the carpenter's boy', 'the cook's boy', 'the fiddler's lad'.[7]

Boys were unavoidable members of a ship. Women were not. Unlike Rackam the majority of pirate captains took great care to have no female on board. There were exceptions. Thomas Cobham persuaded Maria, a Plymouth prostitute, to marry him and go to sea. She prospered and became rich enough to buy an estate in Normandy. Mary Ann Talbot accompanied her guardian, Captain Essex Bowen, who compelled her to wear men's clothing 'to protect herself from seamen' but sexually abused her himself. She died of wounds at the age of thirty.[8]

Women such as Cobham and Talbot, Anne Bonny, Mary Read, Hannah Snell, were unwanted by most pirate captains. 'Blackbeard was known to strangle captured women and pitch their bodies overboard'.[9] Murderous but, in his mind, preferable to incipient mutiny. In the one-for-all and all-for-one philosophy of egalitarian-minded pirates it is likely that if a pirate brought a woman on board his fellows would demand their fair share.

When any woman, wrote Johnson, 'fell into their Hands . . . they put a Centinel immediately over her to prevent ill Consequences from so dangerous an Instrument of Division and Quarrel; but then here lyes the Roguery; they contend who shall be Centinel, which happens generally to be one of the greatest Bullies, who, to secure the Lady's Virtue, will let none lye with her but himself'.[10]

This is the cynical contrast to an Article of Phillips that decreed, 'If at any Time we meet with a prudent Woman, that Man that offers to meddle with her, without her Consent, shall suffer present Death'. Similarly, a rule of William Betagh in 1719 ordained that 'Every Man aboard a Prize found drunk, or in any indecent Act with a white or black Woman, to be Punished according to the Nature of his Offence'. Conversely, when pirates overran a merchantman in the Indian Ocean they killed all the men but neither protected nor raped the one woman they discovered. Like Blackbeard, they simply threw her overboard to avoid any troublesome disagreement.[11]

The treatment of a woman in a ship taken by Bartholomew Roberts is described in a later chapter.

Article VII
To Desert the Ship, or their Quarters in Battle, was punished with Death or Marooning.

To be marooned was the cruellest of penalties. Execution by shooting was a mercy in comparison. Few expelled men were treated as leniently as Alexander Selkirk, given clothing, tools and weapons and left on the island that had water and vegetation. For the coward there were no blessings. If lucky, he was given one bottle of powder, one bottle of water, one small-arm, one bullet and abandoned on an islet far from land with no hope of survival. For the luckiest the sandspit became submerged at high tide and death came quickly. More wretchedly for others there were the long and increasing agonies of thirst and starvation. Their skeletons were sometimes found on lonely islands.[12]

Article VIII
No striking one another on board, but every Man's Quarrels to be ended on Shore, at Sword and Pistol.

An Article of Phillips offered a less stringent condition. 'The Man that shall strike Another whilst these Articles are in Force, shall receive Moses's Law (that is 40 lashes lacking one) on the bare Back'. This was retribution enough for a blow struck in sudden anger but when lives were threatened in a violent quarrel, a duel settled the dispute. Johnson elaborated on Roberts' Article:

'The Quarter-Master of the Ship, when the Parties will not come to any Reconciliation, accompanies them on Shore with what Assistance he thinks proper, and turns the Disputants Back to Back, at so many Paces Distance: At the Word of Command, they turn and fire immediately (or else the Piece is knock'd out of their Hands:) If both miss, they come to their Cutlashes, and then he is declared Victor who draws the first Blood'.

The most famous of these hand-to-hand battles was fought by a woman, Mary Read. When her lover quarrelled with another of Rackam's crew and the inevitable duel was arranged, fearful that her man would lose, she instantly insulted his opponent and 'fought him at Sword and Pistol, and killed him upon the Spot' in a hacking, chopping, lunging brawl doubtlessly watched, enjoyed and betted on by their shipmates.[13]

In their next Article Roberts and his Lords anticipated National Insurance and the Social Services by over two centuries.

Article IX

No Man to talk of breaking up their Way of Living, till each had shared £1000. If in order to do this, any Man should lose a Limb, or become a Cripple in their Service, he was to have 800 Dollars, out of the publick Stock, and for lesser Hurts, proportionably.

Such protection was normal amongst pirates who were keenly aware of the dangers of being crippled and incapacitated. Lowther promised £150 for the loss of a limb, and wrote that anyone disabled could remain with the company for as long as he desired. At a time when an injured merchant seaman was entirely dependent upon the unguaranteed generosity of the ship's owner pirates were more considerate to their fellows.

Late 17th century buccaneers had made even nicer distinctions about the practical value of different limbs. In pieces of eight the rates were:

Loss of	Right	Left
Arm	600	500
Leg	500	400
Eye or finger	100.[14]	

Bartholomew Roberts and the Lords then drafted the proportions of plunder that each man was to be allotted.

Article X

The Captain and Quarter-Master to receive two Shares of a Prize; the Master, Boatswain, and Gunner, one Share and a half, and other Officers one and a Quarter.

Comparable rates were accepted throughout the pirate world and to sign the Articles was known as 'going on the account'. There were no wages for a pirate. Nor did his length of service count. Having signed the Articles he received a share of loot equal to that of his mates. It was like belonging to a stock company whose members were offered no salary, only dividends when a ship was taken, their worth determined by the value of the plunder.

Article XI

The Musicians to have Rest on the Sabbath Day, but the other six Days and Nights, none without special Favour.

It has been suggested that this Article was included because Roberts was a strict sabbatarian but it was more probably simple consideration for the fiddlers and hornpipers from whom a tune could be demanded at any time by any pirate. Musicians were plentiful. There were players of high-pitched, double-reeded hautboys, piping ocarinas, fluting recorders, drummers to beat a rhythm. Music was part of a sailor's life: work-songs, shanties, bawdy ditties, dances and reels. Without rest a musician would have died of exhaustion. Over the months Roberts, a lover of music, assembled a small orchestra to play the popular airs and tunes of the day.

The Articles were agreed and each man signed or put a cross to them, his left hand on the ship's Bible. Phillips' crew did not have the book and used the improbable substitute of an axe.

Aboard the *Fortune* there must have been anxious debating about the proportion of the shares, not grumbles about them for most men considered them fair but pirates would wonder about the likelihood of rich prizes in the West Indies where so many merchant ships were small. It would take a long time for a man to accumulate a thousand pounds unless the captain intended to live dangerously and repeat the terror of Bahia again and again. A short life and a merry one they speculated, with music to play them to their deaths. Or sun-drying on the gibbet. Better to dream of wenches and wine, to dress in satins and silks and lord it over some honest captain who would have dealt with them harshly had they served under him. A short life and a merry one with their sloop rolling easily in the sea.

But there were more immediate matters. With the departure of Kennedy many of the former officers were gone. New ones were needed. Thomas Anstis was voted quarter-master. Jones was re-elected boatswain. Henry Dennis remained the gunner. Christopher Moody, a long-serving Lord, became sailing master responsible for navigation, for steering, for the set of the sails, even though he was not an expert seaman. He would have to do until a more experienced man could be engaged – or forced.

The *Fortune* was repaired. The Articles had been accepted. Now booty was needed. Roberts sailed northwards past Trinidad and on to Tobago. The island was not a large one even amongst the broken bits of land that rose from the sea in the West Indies. It was not thirty miles long and was always hot in spite of the sea-breezes. In 1682 title to it had been transferred to a group of London merchants and since then desultory trading had gone on along its sparsely-peopled shores.

The sloop *Philippa* was at anchor in the Laquary Roads. Her captain Daniel Greaves, lay below suffering from gout and his small crew took their orders from the elderly mate, John Wransford. He was on deck just after dawn on 10 January, 1720. What he saw sent him rushing below for pistols and other firearms. A canoe was approaching he told the captain. Fire on them, shouted Greaves. He wanted no scoundrels around his vessel.

Wransford returned to the deck with some crew. When the canoe was close he had shots fired and called for the paddlers to come no nearer. A contemptuous voice bellowed that they were going to board and if there were any more firing no quarter would be given. They were English pirates who expected no resistance. If any were offered it would go badly for the merchant because there was a well-armed pirate vessel at the mouth of the small harbour. No one would escape.

The pirates clambered up. Anstis swaggeringly informed Greaves that his sloop was impounded. The anchor was weighed and soon the vessel was at Sandy Point alongside the *Fortune*. She was no better than his own, decided Roberts. just worth her plunder. Dennis removed two ship's guns because of their good carriages, Jones commandeered an anchor, cable and some tackles. From the run-of-the-mill cargo Anstis took 300 lbs of sugar, bread, clothes, a sixty-gallon cask of rum and some muskets and pistols. Greaves was presented with an indian and negro taken from a French ship but as the pirates confiscated six negroes for menial, unpleasant tasks it was no favour. Three seamen volunteered to join the pirates. Simpson, a very big man known as 'Little David', was to remain with them for a long time.[15]

Conditions were perfect for pirates. To the north the American colonies were in turmoil over the renewed war with Spain. On New Providence Woodes Rogers feared an unchallenged invasion by a Spanish Fleet with so few British men-of-war patrolling the thousands of miles of coastline. It was a convenient time for a pirate to arrive.

Governors of islands and colonies rarely worried about minor acts of piracy. Many colonists welcomed pirates with their cheap wares. The blame lay with the British Navigation Acts, especially that of 1696 which was intended to safeguard British traders from Dutch competition. Fearing that their own traders would be underbid the Act ordered that the colonies could import only those goods that arrived in ships belonging to Britons or to inhabitants of British colonies. Three-quarters, moreover, of their crews had to be British.[16]

Inevitably, what had been intended as protection ended as exploitation. With no competition British merchants greedily increased their prices. Equally inevitably, the less expensive goods of Dutch interlopers and of pirates were preferred by the settlers. Few governors were prepared to act against the wishes of the wealthy and influential planters in their domains. England was a long way off. Nor did she offer considerable help. In wartime she pleaded a shortage of men and ships to protect her distant lands. In peacetime a shortage of money was the excuse.

Only where outgoing trade was the chief source of income did the colonists make a determined effort to suppress pirates. Four islands in particular acted vigorously: Barbados, governor Walter Hamilton; Jamaica, Sir Nicholas Lawes; Virginia, the Earl of Orkney; and Maryland, John Hart. The first two grew sugar, the others tobacco, produce that had to be exported to bring in revenue. The return of Daniel Greaves to Barbados with his news of the pirates brought alarm. Without exports the merchants would suffer. With the Spanish War in progress they could expect no naval aid except what presently existed and whose captains were notoriously unenthusiastic about hunting pirates.

While the merchants debated their best defence Bartholomew Roberts sailed northwards. It had been an unprofitable voyage, a couple of sloops, some goods, a little gold, everything easy, nothing worthwhile. Roberts would gamble for better things as long as his men remained loyal.

Barbados is perhaps the healthiest island in the West Indies because of the Trade Winds that continually blow gently across it. Made of coral it is surrounded by treacherous reefs, some extending three miles out to sea with only flecks of foam to warn the mariner. Even so, it was a popular place for shipping. The Trades carried vessels towards the island from Africa and Europe. The salubrious climate attracted planters who were eager to do business, particularly if a trader carried slaves. The sugar plantations needed strong men. Off those shores Roberts lingered and looted and his activities caused Governor Hamilton to send the man-of-war *Seaford* to Barbados to search for him. Captain Rose did not find Roberts.

The record of the Royal Navy against piracy was poor. The most obvious reason was the shortage of vessels to control so long a stretch of coast. Complaints about piracy in the Americas as early as 1717 were so unceasing that an Admiralty list was made of the men-of-war out there.

Whitehall, 15 September, 1717

Station	Ship	Guns	Whereabouts
1 Jamaica	*Adventure*	40	On station.
2 Jamaica	*Diamond*	40	Left England in August.
3 Jamaica	*Ludlow Castle*	40	On roving patrol.
4 Jamaica	*Swift* sloop	8	On station.
5 Jamaica	*Winchelsea*	20	On station.
6 Barbados	*Scarborough*	30	On station.
7 Leeward Isles	*Seaford*	?	On station.
8 Leeward Isles	*Trial* sloop	?	On station.
9 Leeward Isles	*Lime*	20	On station.
10 Virginia	*Shoreham*	30	Sailing to England.
11 Virginia	*Pearl*	40	Left England in August.
12 New York	*Phoenix*	30	On station.
13 New York	*Squirrel*	20	On station.
14 New York	*Rose*	20	Sailing to England.

'Those at Jamaica, Barbados, and the Leeward Islands, are to join upon Occaasion, for annoying the Pyrates, and the Security of the Trade: And those at New-England, Virginia and New-York, are to do the like'.[17]

Superficially the list was impressive but the realities were that with vessels immobilised in harbour because of sickness and desertion there would never be more than six or seven ships at sea, searching a million square miles in a vast triangle of ocean from Newfoundland at the north down to Barbados at the south with the Gulf of Mexico at the western apex. Pirates lurked out of sight in the inlets and creeks of a thousand islands. The odds were at least five hundred to one against any pirate being sighted.

Yet even this did not explain the almost complete failure to apprehend pirates. More pertinent was the self-interest of naval captains who were more concerned with enriching themselves. A related factor was the treatment given to their own seamen. Many had been press-ganged, kept aboard in port to prevent desertion, subject to severe discipline, poorly paid, living in cramped quarters that encouraged disease. In the West Indies several men-of-war were in harbour for three-quarters of the year because of under-manning, so many men had died or had run away.

An order from the Admiralty Office of 8 January 1719, stated that 'The Lords Commission of the Admiralty strictly charge and require all such men as belong to H.M. Ships the *Ipswich* and *Portsmouth* and *York* at Chatham who have absented themselves therefrom, immediately to repair to their duty on board the said ships, as they will answer to the contrary at their peril and forfeit the wages due to them'. It had no effect. The situation was worse in the West Indies with so many more chances of escape.

Frequently, when a man was press-ganged he was not immediately enlisted but transferred from ship to ship as an unpaid supernumerary until some vessel, desperate for men, engaged him. It was only then that he was entitled to wages. When signed on he was given a ticket bearing the date from which he was to be paid. If the ticket were lost he automatically forfeited a fifth of his money. Even with the chit it could be months, sometimes a year or more before any money was received. In despair men would sell the precious tickets for a pittance to money-lenders in Portsmouth and other naval ports.

Theirs was a dilemma that did not bother the government. When the Treasury had to choose between paying off debts and settling seamen's wages it was the seamen that went penniless. A Member of Parliament observed that 'Their growing wages is a deposit which detains them, it is a bank which they do not forget, which keeps them cheerfully together'.[18] It was a neatly circular argument. Because they were unpaid men wished to desert but they would not desert because they wanted the money due to them.

But they did desert. Merchant captains were sometimes so short of crew that they were willing to pay as much as £45 a man for one voyage home. There were also instances when a naval seaman would desert to a trader for as little as £10 and ten gallons of rum, conditions were so bad in his ship.

Desertion and the sickness in the dirt and crowding below decks left naval vessels short-handed. With no volunteers forthcoming the answer lay in press-ganging merchant crews, not those of ships sailing from Britain as this could damage foreign trade but of men taken when the trader's voyage was almost done. In the West Indies there was a simple rule of thumb. An ordinary merchant captain might lose one in five of his men as the remainder were needed to sail the ship across the turbulent Atlantic. But a slave ship could have one in three taken because of the easier voyage to Africa.[19] Amidst this mismanagement and dishonesty pirates profited. So did the Navy.

It was not unknown for a man-of-war to escort vessels lucratively through dangerous waters. Captain Dorrell convoyed the Salt Fleet to Tertuda.[20] Frequently, a naval captain transported the cargo himself. At a price. It was against naval rules and regulations but the commanders were unworried. Britain was remote, unlikely to be informed of the misconduct and even less likely to investigate.

In consequence many captains were casual in seeking pirates who were indirectly providing them with enhanced incomes. Woodes Rogers complained about the practice. 'Every capture made by the pirates', he wrote to Sir Richard Steele, 'aggravates the inclination of the commanders of our men-of-war who have openly avowed that the greater number of pirates makes their suitable advantage in trade; for the merchants of necessity are forced to send their effects in the King's bottoms, when they from every part hear of the ravages committed by the pirates'. In such a situation it is not surprising that Captain Rose failed to encounter Bartholomew Roberts.

By 12 February, 1720, Roberts had taken more vessels, none of them valuable. On that day he captured the *Benjamin* from Liverpool, whose young commander was in such a panic that he later testified that Anstis, the quartermaster, was the pirate captain, calling him Thomas Hanse. There was little aboard, just some bacon and dry goods, and after keeping the ship for three days to prevent an alarm being raised Roberts let it go.[21]

On the 18th they took the unremarkable *Joseph* sloop. There was no resistance. Nor was the cargo rich. The event was only noteworthy because four years later the sloop's captain, Bonaventure Jelfes, was murdered by a mutineer, Michael Moore, who was later condemned and then pardoned at the Old Bailey. With with pirates, *costagardas*, the Navy, storms and mutiny a sea-captain was safe from nothing.[22]

Roberts was disatisfied and impatient. There was no true wealth to be accumulated from the trivialities of insignificant merchantmen on the trade routes around the islands. Such pickings were welcome to unambitious predators like Rackam making sporadic sallies a few leagues out to sea, ransacking some ill-armed brig and then returning to base for a week's idle festivity but it brought no fortunes. Roberts wanted more.

It was a day or two after taking the *Joseph* that Montigny la Palisse joined their company.[23] Sighting a little sloop the *Fortune* hoisted the black flag but instead of fleeing the sloop turned towards the pirates. There was a black flag at her own mast. La Palisse was the kind of pirate that Roberts despised, a snatcher of scraps of booty, but two sloops were better than the weak *Fortune* by itself and Roberts agreed to accept the French ship as a partner. Eventually it might be possible to have even more ships at his command, a strong fleet that could withstand the power of a man-of-war. In the meantime, he had to decide where he might look for better gains. Although La Palisse knew the islands almost creek by creek he was unable to persuade Roberts that Martinique or St. Christophers would be more profitable than the seas of Barbados.

Something different was required, somewhere that could be surprised, somewhere where Roberts could strike and gather worthwhile plunder. By nature he was an attacker, taking the initiative, not waiting for something to happen. He would institute the action.

Meanwhile, at Port Royal in Jamaica, Captain Whitney was ordered to take His Majesty's ships *Rose* and *Shark* to the Leeward Isles to assist Governor Hamilton. Whitney replied that at present his ship's company was very sick but that he hoped to be able to sail for Antigua in eight days' time.[24]

8

A Fight at Sea

26 February–June 1720

'From Portsmouth in N. Hampshire they tell us that a brig arrived here from Barbados in 22 days and reported that a Bristol galley and a sloop were fitted out to take a pirate sloop of 12 guns that lay to windward of the island; they came up and engaged her but the pirate having a great number of men on board gave them such a warm reception that they were obliged to go back to Barbados without her. In this engagement many men were lost on both sides'.

Weekly Journal, 25 June 1720.

While Captain Whitney waited in Jamaica for his crew to recover from their fevers; while Captain Rose drifted about the Leeward Isles in a desultory search for Bartholomew Roberts; while Roberts himself with Montigny la Palisse looted insignificant sloops off the shores of Barbados; while Jolly Jack Rackam and his assorted crew marauded further north; while the merchants of the Royal African Company agonised as they read the lists of ships and factories ransacked on the Guinea coast; during these times the traders and citizens of Barbados decided they would have to get rid of the troublesome pirates by themselves.

They could expect no help from the Navy and they had already implored Governor Lowther for assistance without result. They must either resign themselves to ruin or retaliate. On February 19, 1720, they petitioned the governor for permission to fortify two strong ships. Stating their need for protection the merchants wrote, 'that a certain pirate sloop carrying twelve guns and manned with seventy men hath lately taken several vessels to windward of this island and still lyeth there to intercept the trade'.

They proposed to equip two merchant ships at their own expense, properly armed and manned, 'both warrlike vessels', the *Summersett* galley, commanded by Owen Rogers, and the *Philippa*, Daniel Greaves. Greaves must have spoken pugnaciously on his return from Tobago after being robbed by Roberts, convincing his would-be employers that he did not fear the pirates. The *Summersett* would carry sixteen guns and one hundred and thirty men, the *Philippa* sloop six guns and sixty men. Ignorant that Roberts had been joined by la Palisse the merchants believed that they had put the odds in their favour with two ships, twenty-two guns and almost two hundred men against one small sloop, twelve guns and seventy pirates. Battles, however, are not joined on sporting chances but on the probability of winning.[1]

Two guarantees of good behaviour were demanded in case the possession of two strongly-equipped ships should lure their crews into piracy themselves. Rogers was ordered to fight any pirate but not to attack any of His Majesty's allies. It would be embarrassing if he should plunder a French or Dutch vessel. Any captured pirate ship was to be brought back to port. He was to keep a fair journal. He was not to take any person from an island without that governor's consent; and he was to provide a list of the men on board to the Secretary of Barbados before sailing. All of these men he was to bring back, 'death and the dangers of the sea only excepted'.

The merchants were aware of the temptations that might beset Rogers once he was at sea in a ship more heavily gunned than any of the trading vessels around him and he was instructed not to attack vessels sailing in and out of Barbados. He was to fly no jack or flag except that of His Majesty's shipping with the distinction of a white escutcheon at its centre. He was not to go to any island other than Tobago unless in distress. On his return he was to hand over his remaining weapons, powder, ammunition and stores.

Being both dishonest and devious Lowther dared not refuse the petition despite his probable reluctance. There were rumours that he had dealt with pirates privately. He had been recalled to England in 1714 to answer charges of corruption. In 1715 he was reinstated as governor but only four years later he was charged with taking bribes. By October of 1720, on trial in London, he was found guilty of misappropriating £28,000 of Barbadian funds and of illegally allowing a Spanish ship to trade in defiance of the Navigation Acts. He was also accused of imprisoning two naval captains who had been chasing pirates.[2]

With such a reputation the governor had no choice. The petition was granted. On Sunday, 21 February, the *Summersett* and the *Philippa* sailed down the harbour and anchored where they could see Needham's fort on their bows a mile away. Next day, firing eleven guns in salute to the fort, they reached out into the vastness of the sea. Somewhere beyond the immediate horizon was the pirate sloop. For two days they sailed and by the Wednesday were off Martinique. They had seen nothing.

The seas were choppy on the Thursday morning. In the afternoon the lookout sighted a sail. They chased it. It was a tiny pink, a vessel with a narrow rounded stern, whose mizzen mast and a third of her mainmast had been cut down by pirates. Her French captain told Rogers that there were two pirate sloops, one of twelve guns, the other, from Virginia, smaller.

The morning of Friday, 26 February, had blue skies and strong winds. Rogers expected to find the pirates that day.[3] When he told Greaves his colleague showed no elation. Since learning that there were two pirates he had been silent. Rogers took no notice. He prepared the *Summersett* for action. He had portable bulwarks brought up from the hold and placed on the quarterdeck. Made of elm they would not splinter if pierced by a cannonball but would leave only a little hole that would slowly contract.

Hammocks were strung together in the masts to make a breastwork behind which marksmen could shelter as they fired down on the enemy. Netting was suspended from the shrouds to impede boarding parties that could be cut down as they tried to hack their way through the nets with heavy boarding hatchets.[4] There were no signs of similar preparations in the *Philippa*. Greaves had been full of violent oaths in Barbados. Now he was docile. Rogers ordered him to ready his ship and to follow the *Summersett* when the pirates were sighted. Nothing was done.

It was mid-morning when two sloops came into view, changing course towards the merchantmen. Greaves swung to Rogers' port bow, away from the approaching ships. The slower *Summersett* hoisted all sails as though to run. The bigger of the sloops fired twice and sailed within musketshot of Rogers' starboard, intending to come alongside and give a broadside. From the other sloop a black flag flew with a skull at its centre. A long black pennant, also bearing a skull, blew in the wind from the masthead of the *Fortune*.

Rogers turned to starboard even though the manoeuvre would expose the *Summersett* to the pirates' guns as the galley slowly pulled round. Greaves kept the *Philippa* on the far side with Rogers between him and the pirates who were shouting for the ships to strike their colours. Rogers decided to suffer the cannonade and pass by the *Fortune* in a move which would leave Greaves perfectly positioned to deliver his own salvo before the pirates could reload.

Roger's men crouched behind their breastworks as the first broadside struck them. There was a blasting of wood and a roaring sound of wrenching timbers and cascading water as the *Summersett* shuddered and reeled under the shock. Pistols and muskets were firing. Bullets thudded against the bulwarks, then a sudden silence against the ominous beating of a single drum from the *Fortune*.

One more gun fired, its cannonball striking jarringly against the galley, then silence again. La Palisse's *Sea King* had fired and instantly was cramming all sail towards the south and safety. Taking no notice of the cowardice the *Fortune* turned some distance away towards the stern of the *Summersett* to come in again to the attack. It was a classical tactic. Few guns could be brought to bear upon the sloop and Roberts would wait until his bows over-reached the galley's stern when pirates could hurl bombs of combustible tar and sulphur from the rigging, suffocating the *Summersett* in clouds of dense, choking smoke, shots would be fired from the yardarms, swivels would spray their nails and glass and leadweights across the decks and in the confusion the galley would be boarded and over-run. Faint-heartedly, Greaves moved, not to attack the pirate but to shelter on the far side of the galley, protected but impotent.

Bartholomew Roberts was bringing the sloop towards Rogers and the drum-roll grew louder as the ships closed. Greaves was rapidly falling behind the *Summersett*. Roberts no longer had the *Philippa* between him and Rogers but was able to come up almost within jumping distance of the galley. Rogers glimpsed the glitter of cutlasses before hurling himself behind a bulwark as a second broadside smashed into his ship. The men readied themselves for the swarm of boarding-pirates but whether it was the sight of the nets and the barricades or the flight of la Palisse that deterred Roberts but he veered sharply away. There was still the monotonous beating of the drum.

The *Fortune*'s stern was raked by the *Summersett*'s two decks of guns but it was too small a target for great damage. Behind the sloop trailed a boat whose occupants had intended to scramble into the galley. In an irregular crackle of pistols one of the pirates tried to climb up the rope towing the boat but as he grasped it he was hit and tumbled into the sea. Another fell. Up on the *Fortune*'s roundhouse the drummer fell forward, rolled and slithered from the cabin deck.

Rogers turned onto the new course of the pirate realising that the vacillating Greaves could be relied on for nothing. The *Summersett* would have to fight alone. A further cannonade damaged the pirate below the waterline and several men scrambled down the ship's sides to effect some repairs but when the *Fortune* tacked again two lost their footing on the wet sides and were washed away. It was an unequal contest. Even with the irresolute Greaves refusing to endanger himself the pirates in their small sloop were outgunned in numbers of men, cannon and weight of shot. The ocean rumbled with gunfire. Lumberingly the *Summersett* drew alongside the pirate sloop. Greaves was hiding well out of range. Rogers ignored him. One more broadside from the galley and the *Fortune* could be boarded. But even as he gave the command Greaves came up between him and the pirate himself. For a moment Rogers thought the man intended to board the pirate himself. Instead he kept his station, preventing any further shots being fired into the enemy's sides.

On the *Fortune* every sail was hoisted and the ship turned to the south-east away from the two Barbadian vessels, jettisoning an 'abundance of broad chests' and sawing down the heavy gunwhales to lighten herself. There was no doubting the courage or determination of Roberts. But to battle against such odds would have been suicidal.[5]

Rogers watched helplessly. In his cumbersome galley there was no possibility of catching the faster-sailing sloop and it was evident that Greaves had no intention of doing anything heroic. Bartholomew Roberts had escaped. By seven in the evening he was almost out of sight and once dark came there was no chance of discovering him in the creeks and shallows of the numerous islands.

Greaves was slightly apologetic. He blamed his helmsman who had misunderstood his instructions. Greaves had not fired because he was not a well-armed vessel and he did not want to attract a devastating attack from the pirate. He had intended to board but his helmsman had turned to port instead of starboard and it was that mistake that had thwarted Rogers. He had not given chase because he lacked the necessary sails, no topsail, no spritsail or even jib halliards. It was regrettable.

Far away the *Fortune* sailed north-westwards. Never a smart ship now she listed heavily from her bombardment. Everywhere was wreckage. Splinters of wood from the mast and ruined gunwhales lay in grotesque chaos. The door of Roberts' Great Cabin was shattered and bloodstained. Smoke drifted from the forecastle where a fire had burned. The deck was scored and ravaged with bullets. A cannonball had ricouchetted from the foot of the mast, scratching and scraping deeper along the planking in a torn, jagged path until it had ripped a hole through the side of the lower deck. A sail had been slashed from its furlings and hung tattered and stained black from powder burns. Everywhere reeked of gunsmoke, devastation and charred wood, a ship scarred and soiled from defeat.

The night hid much of the ruin and repairs could be made at the first well-wooded island where they would find sanctuary. But on those battle-doomed decks lay the wounded and the dying, tended by their companions, and their groans and screams were intensified by the silent darkness around them. Blood was everywhere. Blood from a bullet-smashed arm. Blood from the mouth of a man whose lungs had been lanced by flying wood. Blood from the stumps of a man whose legs had been obliterated by the velocity of a heavy cannonball. Blood from the horror of a body torn apart at point-blank range by the spreading blast of a swivel-gun.

Twenty or thirty there were, almost half the ship's company, some jesting at the compensation for loss of a finger or foot, others numbed as their friends staunched wounds with fierce, experienced pressure to stop the bleeding. And there were the seriously wounded and dying for whom there was not the benefit of a surgeon since Archibald Murray had departed with Kennedy. The more fortunate lay stupefied with rum. Others writhed in agony, hindering the attempts to bandage bodies that would die as gangrene set in.

Nearly two hundred miles they sailed, passing out of sight of the inhabited islands of St. Lucia and Martinique where they dared not land, patching up the sloop, casting corpses into the sea to the traditional volleys of muskets, no one laughing as they watched the growing infection and fever of the dying, fever that could spread to the entire ship's complement if a place to land was not soon discovered.

Twenty men perished before they weighed anchor at Dominica. More would die. It had not been possible to sail quickly in a crippled vessel that had to avoid other shipping. Roberts swore an oath of vengeance on the inhabitants of Barbados that had reduced him to this. He was a beaten man in a useless ship. All Irishmen, he vowed, all Irishmen like Kennedy, and all Barbadians would feel his revenge.

Dominica was an island of magnificent hills, rivers, lakes and sulphur springs with a great mountain. Morne Diablotin, rising high above the others. It was a lovely place but dangerous. Everything needed by the pirates to refit and recuperate was here: wood, water, sunshine, few people, but not far to the south was Martinique whose French governor would quickly send ships to capture the pirates once he knew of their presence.

They could take only what was most urgently required before leaving for a smaller, safer island. Hurried parties of men bartered with the natives for provisions while carpenters took in stocks of wood for temporary repairs. In two days they were ready to depart. Lookouts had been posted to watch for vessels. It was not a ship but a group of men that one of them noticed.

There were thirteen of them. Naked. Their spokesman, Robert Botson, explained that they had been marooned from the *Revenge* sloop of Antigua, left there without clothing, guns or any equipment by a Spanish *costagarda* about three weeks before. They had despaired of ever seeing a ship but now they were saved and could get away from the island.[6] Anstis told them that they were welcome. Men were needed. But he and his mates were 'men of the sea', meaning that they were pirates. It was not a threat. Roberts would not force them to join.

Botson did not hesitate. Nor did his companions. Better to be a pirate than to endure the hardships of life on an island to which no other ship might come for months. Articles were signed and within a hour the sloop limped out, sailing southwards towards the scattered islands of the Grenadines. Their fears of pursuit were justified. Next morning two heavily-armed sloops arrived at Dominica from Martinique. After questioning the natives their officers set sail southwards, barely half a day behind the *Fortune*.

Bartholomew Roberts who had voyaged for years in those waters chose to hide in the Windward Islands at Carriacou with its natural harbours and fine beaches.[7] The *Fortune* was hidden from the sea on all sides by high land. The only nearby settlement of any size was Grenada and that was twenty miles to the south. It was unlikely that anyone there would know of the pirates' arrival. The carpenters went about their repairs. The sloop's keel was cleaned. Its damaged sides were mended. Out of the poisonous atmosphere of the ship the less badly-wounded slowly recovered in the shadows of tall palms, tended by their friends, comforted by the fine-tasting sap of wine-palms and the baked meat of land tortoises.

As the days passed spirits lifted as relaxation and time eroded the shock of their defeat. Roberts called his Lords to him. He had new plans. It was a waste to attack ships at sea, waiting for them to appear only to discover a worthless cargo of trinkets and logwood. Why not repeat Gambia, Sierra Leone, Principe, not waiting for the ships to come to them but go to the ships at anchor and the laden depots and the money in the forts? Any ship met at sea could be taken but the real riches were in the harbours. There were chandlers there with all the ship's goods that were wanted. There were taverns. There was money in the purses of merchants, planters and the agents of Companies. And once the place was taken there would be no one present to oppose them.

The choice was straightforward. They could stay in the sloop, lurking in the islands, scurrying in and out, yapping at the heels of the trade, or they could dwell in a tall ship, invading ports with all the risks of being overpowered but with all the prospects of rich pickings. Greed overcame fear. The Lords voted for the strategy. From being a daring pirate and a fighting pirate Bartholomew Roberts was about to become 'that Great Pyrate'.

The stay at Carriacou lasted barely a week, the pirates being restless 'as they had the impudence to own, for the want of wine and women'.[8] Doubtlessly this was true but there was a more urgent consideration. On the seventh day lookouts spied the sloops from Martinique exploring island after island searching for the pirates.[9] Barbados, Martinique, thought Roberts. He would hang their governors. And he would advertise the intention. He would have a black flag made, a large one, and on it would be his figure, feet astride, sword held aloft. Under each foot would be a skull. Beneath one would be the letters ABH, under the other AMH, signifying 'A Barbadian's Head' and 'A Martinician's Head'.[10] One day he would settle his scores.

That night they left the lagoon. It was the beginning of March, 1720. They sailed north past Puerto Rica and Cuba, past the Bahamas, past the North American colonies of Carolina and Virginia, past New York and Maine, ever northwards to Newfoundland, the heart of the fishing industry, an active region but unaccustomed to piracy, an area of small shipping, too far north for men-of-war to patrol unless there was news of trouble.

It was a promising place. By the middle of June Roberts had captured several ships and had raided the minor harbour of

Ferryland on the east coast where he took the largest ship, the admiral's, and burned it at its moorings as a warning to the townsfolk not to interfere. It was a good beginning. His men were cheerful. There was no resistence from the dozen vessels they captured nor from Ferryland itself.[11]

Bartholomew Roberts once more dressed in fine clothes and listened to the music of his conscripted orchestra as he sipped his favourite blend of tea, 'for He was a sober man'. His appreciative men often gave him presents of fine crockery and chinaware because 'it may be noted that Roberts drank his Tea constantly'. Such an abstemious idiosyncrasy must both have amused and bemused the drunken toss-pots of his crew.[12] He was ready. The *Fortune* would sail south into Trepassy just down the coast, one of Newfoundland's main harbours. If that could be taken there would be wealth and the debauched revelries of success.

Before then, on 25 May, 1720, thousands of miles away on the far side of Africa, Captain George Shelvocke, quarrelsome and drunken captain of the *Speedwell*, was wrecked on the Juan Fernandez islands where Alexander Selkirk had been marooned. His crew superstititiously blamed the disaster on the mate, Simon Hatley, who after several shots had killed a 'disconsolate black albatross' that had followed the ship for several days during stormy weather off Cape Horn. The misfortune inspired Coleridge's *The Rime of the Ancient Mariner*.[13]

In June, Governor Hamilton of Nevis, in the Leeward Islands reported to the Secretary of the Colonies that His Majesty's ships, the *Rose* and the *Shark* had at last completed the long easterly voyage from Jamaica to replace the *Seaford* but both had been so battered by the seasonal gales that neither was presently seaworthy.[14]

9

Pickings in Newfoundland

June–July 1720

'Two light men-of-war are ordered for Newfoundland in quest of Roberts and other pirates who continue to commit great depredations on our merchant ship that way'.
Applebee's Original Weekly Journal, 28 January, 1721.

It was not only the hope of better takings and a wish to evade capture that sent Bartholomew Roberts so far north. It was the weather. Years at sea told him that in the West Indies the hurricane season was coming, months of such sudden and calamitous storms that no ship was secure.

August and September, often a day or two before the full moon at the Autumnal equinox, were the worst times, and most captains, unless compelled to sail, remained in port. Roberts knew very well that his light, hastily-mended sloop could not withstand the tempests that it might meet. He was prescient.

That very year, 1720, on 12 June, a fleet of ships left Jamaica for England escorted, probably at an agreed but undocumented price, by His Majesty's man-of-war, *Milford*. Three days later off Cuba the hurricane hit them. Sailors would have recognised the omens, a day or two of disturbed seas, the sullen swell of muscular waves, then, after a false lull, a sharp dimming of the sky. Lightning came almost in a second and the tornado built into a madness of thunder with the shrieking wind transforming the seas into a fury that few ships could survive.

In August the *Post Boy* reported the disaster.[1] Of the flotilla the *Milford* was sunk with all its hands except for the purser and thirty men. The *Prouse* frigate foundered but its crew were saved. The *James* galley and its crew went to the bottom. So did the *Africa* sloop and the *Sunderland*. From the *Diamond* galley only two men were rescued. Together, from the *Prince George*, the *Hannah*, the *Grand Lewis*, the *Dragon*, *Asia* and *Tilldasee*, all of which were lost, a mere dozen men lived. The rest were drowned including a child from the *Dragon*, swept overboard and never seen again. In the fleet were two sloops from New York. One man was recovered.

Fourteen vessels sank and at least two hundred men were killed in this 'local storm'. How many other lonely ships, trapped far out to sea, went down in the Caribbean was unknown. Nothing was left to record their fate.

Far to the north Roberts escaped the tragedy. When the hurricane struck he was creating a fearsome name for mercilessness amongst Newfoundland fishermen. He had not hurried to Trepassy. Having taken Ferryland and the two ships there he almost sauntered around the Banks plundering the shipping. He sent a message to Trepassy informing its inhabitants that he was to visit them. The bravado could have been fateful for it was more than two days later that he came to the harbour which could, by then, have been put in a state of defence. But Roberts had anticipated what effects his letter would have.

Because of the swarming shoals of fish off the Newfoundland Banks hundreds of boats sailed there each year manned by fishermen from western England. Impoverished and desperate men travelled in another man's vessel. The work was hard and the wages meagre. Such paupers might fish in the owner's boat for long hours and little pay or engage in the drudgery of splitting cod on shore. The fish was hung to dry on long wooden racks that lined the harbour, giving off a stench that never left the place, and when dried was split, cleaned and salted ready for despatch to Europe. For the workers it was long hours for little cash, far too small for much saving because, when finished, they had to pay for the voyage home.[2]

Of relaxation there was none except for the drinking of the vile Blackstrap, a toxic mixture of strong rum, molasses and chowder beer, a concoction brewed from black spruce twigs soaked in water. The only benefit obtained from drinking it was rapid unconsciousness.[3] It is not surprising that wearying of such slavery many of the men turned to piracy.

In Trepassy there was both apathy and panic.[4] Since Roberts' warning some were inclined to scoff, saying that no pirate would dare invade the harbour where there were so many ships and guns. Others went to those guns to ensure that they were primed and loaded. Among them was Admiral Babidge, a fat poltroon, who possessed the greatest, strongest ship and who was one of the richest men in Newfoundland.

The majority of the captains loitered in the taverns. Where pirates were concerned it was better to do nothing because those that resisted and were beaten were liable to lose ship, money, possibly even life. By Tuesday, 21 June, just nine days after the fated convoy left Jamaica, a manmade hurricane was about to sweep across Trepassy. Resolute men would have removed cannon from some ships and mounted them at the harbour mouth. Determined men would have grouped their vessels together to concentrate their firepower against the foe. Yet only a few vessels had their guns prepared or a flag of defiance flying when the frail *Fortune* bore down on Trepassy.

She sailed in past the empty defences, black flags flying, the drummer beating out a staccato rhythm, trumpeters blowing brazen notes of triumph as though returning from some notable victory, pirates leaning over the bulwarks yelling and jeering, firing pistols at anyone scurrying along the shore. Roberts ordered the helmsman to steer towards Admiral Babidge's ship,

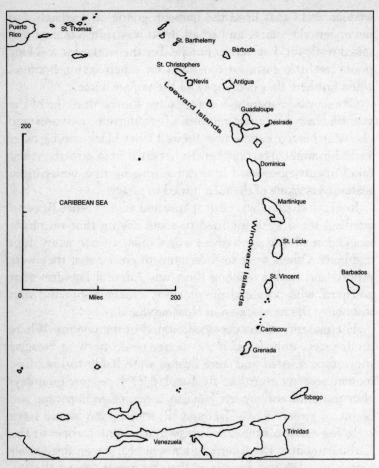

West Indies, the Leeward and Windward Islands

the *Bideford*. At the sight of the incoming pirate and the blasting of its cannon Babidge and his entire crew scuttled across the quay into the improbable shelter of wooden houses.

Anstis and a band of men whose names were next on the list of boarders entered the *Bideford*, hauling down the Admiral's jack, pendent and ensigns. Those guns that faced landwards

were fired at Babidge's refuge, bursting it into flame. In all this
the only other sounds was the rolling drum and the trumpeting.
Not one shot had been fired at the *Fortune*.

Roberts looked at the harbour with a score of ships anchored
at its landing-piers and crowds of minute fishing shallops
leaning on their sides along the strand. There was no sign of
anyone. The docksides were empty. The ships were abandoned.
Had it not been for the abrupt flight of Babidge and his men
Trepassy might have been a deserted town. The pirates had
taken twenty-two sound sea-going vessels without a single
gesture of resistance.

Roberts laughed. For two days they had been at sea and
during that time they had captured a dozen vessels with
nothing worth taking in their holds. Now they had control of a
whole settlement. It was a tribute to audacity. Paradoxically, it
did not please the stern Welshman. There was a grimmer,
crueller side to his nature. He loathed timidity, especially from
merchant captains who would show no kindness to their own
men. He would punish the inhabitants for their cowardice. The
lily-livered caitiffs could have blasted the *Fortune* to bits had
they acted together. They would regret their failure. On 26
November, five months later, *The Weekly Journal or British
Gazetteer* informed its readers of the episode:

'St. Lawrence. 28 June. A pirate in a small sloop of 12
guns and 160 men entered Trepassy on Tuesday the 21st
inst, and made himself master of the said harbour and of
all the ships there, being 22 sail and 250 shallops. He
made the masters all prisoners and beat some of them
heartily for their cowardice for not making any resistance.
The Admiral, one Babidge, in the *Bideford Merchant*,
suffered most because he and all his hands left their ship
with jack, ensign and pendent flying, his guns all loaden,
in order to defend themselves but the pirate was close
alongside him, struck his colours, hoisted their own, and

fired all his guns. They cut his masts and several others close by the deck. He cut all the other ships' cables in junks and their shrouds. He seized one Copleston's ship for himself, and set all the ships carpenters to work to fit her for his purpose. He threatened to burn all the rest and to hang one of the masters at least for their incivility in not waiting upon him to make him welcome at his entrance. He destroyed about 30 sail, French and English, on the Banks'.

Roberts commanded all the captains, Babidge included, to come to the *Fortune* and to their horror they realised that the pirate had not been joking. He really had expected to be welcomed as a distinguished visitor. Indignant at this omission and despising them for their feeble abandonment of a score of ships, more than a hundred guns with a thousand men to use them he had several of the commanders lashed by Anstis. As a particular example Babidge was tied to the mast, his wrists strung high above his head and his expensive shirt ripped from his back. He was ruthlessly flogged.

Next day at the sounding of Roberts' morning gun, the captains came aboard for their orders. They were to assemble every morning as soon as the gun was fired. Anyone absenting himself would have his ship burned. No chest was to be locked. Nothing was to be removed from the vessels without permission.

The ransacking began. Systematically Anstis took parties of pirates from ship to ship accompanied by their captains who were made to reveal any concealed gold and coin. It went hard with anyone denying the existence of money. Except for Copleston's brig every ship was disabled to prevent escape. The two-masted, square-rigged vessel from Bristol was an impressive improvement on the shabby *Fortune* and Roberts requisitioned her. Carpenters were put to work and in a fortnight she was ready for sea. She carried sixteen good guns.[5]

The pirates had not wanted for enjoyment. Each day forty or

fifty of them went ashore to the taverns. They had no need of money. Everything was free, food, drink, women. The entire harbour had been taken and there was no need to pay for anything. Bartholomew Roberts never left his ship but stayed aboard supervising the working groups, and indulging in the pleasure of trying on new coats, shirts, cravats and breeches, enjoying tea from fragile bone china.

Every day the great gun sounded. Every day the resentful but acquiescent captains rowed out to Roberts' new ship where their possessions were stored in readiness for the share-out and the auction. Roberts greeted the men affably. His vessel had plenty of provisions, plunder was bountiful, he had a worthy ship. Sometimes he discussed his plans with his guests, informing them that he intended to sail to St. Mary's where he heard that a Mr Hall had a fine ship. The captains said nothing. Around them were their vessels, some like skeletons bared of sails, rigging and goods, some with rough stumps of chopped masts, all of them with tattered shrouds. From the shore came laughter, squeals, a festive pistol-shot.

The captains waited for the nightmare to end when they might salvage something from the ruin. For most of them that time never came. By late June Roberts was ready to leave, unforgiving as ever. On the day that he departed every ship was set on fire, over twenty of them burning brightly in the chilly air, many shallops destroyed, smouldering fishracks, with the smoke swirling so high above the harbour that it could be seen from Cape Pine thirteen miles away.

The news of the pirates' departure spread quickly. Merchant shipping carried it to the North American colonies, to Virginia whose Governor Spottiswood scorned the inhabitants of Trepassy for the 'want of courage in this heedless multitude', and to New England where Governor Shute, after deploring the incident, added of Roberts that 'one cannot with-hold admiration for his bravery and courage'. He was already notorious.

On 3 July a secretary at Placentia, not far from Trepassy, grumbled at the islanders' lack of foresight and industry.

'There are many ships drove in here by the pirates who infest our coast and in one of our next ports they have burnt and destroyed twenty-six ships with a great number of fishing craft. Those pirates have now destroyed near 150 boats and 26 ships at Trepassy and St. Mary's which, if a communication had been cut overland, had not been above a 2 days' march to have rescued these harbours where the pirates have been repairing their ships for 14 days past, nor could any vessel sail from hence to reprive 'em if we had any ships of force'.[6]

Roberts knew nothing of this. He was concentrating on the shipping on its way to or from England. These were good days. Booty mounted and his satisfaction was marred only by the stupidity of a man who tried to steal a length of cloth before the loot had been shared out. Months ago the captain and the Lords might have overlooked the matter but Kennedy's defection made them determined that no one should undermine their authority. In front of the crew the thief was sentenced to a whipping by Anstis, a flogging of thirty-nine-strokes administered unsparingly by the quartermaster. Had the culprit purloined coin or jewellery he would have been marooned which would have meant certain death in those cold waters.

At sea lookouts were posted. Roberts had decided on a policy of attacking ships once any harbour behind him was powerless. Rapidly he took nine or ten French ships, one of which so attracted him with her square-rigging, vertical stern and strong lines that he commandeered the vessel, strengthening her with twenty-six cannon. He named her the *Good Fortune*.[7] He felt a match for anything he met. Again he had a well-armed ship instead of the puny sloop in which he had entered Trepassy. Though it lacked the manoeuvrability of the *Fortune* the *Good*

Fortune had speed and strength. In one short but imaginatively daring month he had transformed weakness into power, poverty into wealth. And he had regained the confidence of his crew.

In the *Good Fortune* he had no difficulty persuading merchant captains to surrender. They were unable to oppose such an arsenal, particularly as Montigny la Palisse had rejoined the menacing flotilla in his fast-sailing, ten-gun sloop, full of apologies for his flight at Barbados.[8] The *Richard* pink was taken by them and its boatswain, Thomas Wills, went through the farce of being 'forced', being secretly willing to change his loyalties. He was a good seaman but unusual being always reading good books. Then the *Willing Mind* of Poole; and the *Expectation* of Topsham; and a Dutch ship near Cape Broyle that they would have burned for its resistance had not its crew pleaded to a benevolent Roberts. On the 16 of July the pirates captured the *Little York* from Virginia, the *Sudbury* sloop, and Captain Thomas's *Love* brig of Liverpool. Next day they took the *Phoenix* from Bristol. Richard Harris was 'forced' as was John Walden of the *Blessing* of Leamington. 'No man was forced on these occasions', he said at his trial two years later.[9]

Thee were many other 'conscripts', skilled and not unwilling and the *Good Fortune*'s company became awash with seamen and sea-artists of every maritime trade. The pirates had never known such days. Plunder fell to them from every point of the compass. Day after day vessels appeared, hove to, were ransacked without bloodshed and released after yielding a few more precious trinkets, barrels, coins and provisions. The Newfoundland coast was a garden of plenty.

Reports of Roberts' depredations poured into the London news-sheets telling of the attack on Trepassy and of his robbing of ships at sea. Even biographical details were given. The *Weekly Journal* called him Thomas Roberts, an amalgam of Thomas Anstis and Bartholomew Roberts, of quartermaster and captain, the article stating 'the aforesaid Captain Roberts was born at Bridgewater in Somerset', which would have offended

the captain's Welsh pride but went well with Anstis' south-west
country accent.[10]

Of all the vessels captured during this lucrative period from
July to August, 1720, the time in London when speculation in
South Sea Company stock was at its most reckless, one ship
that was frequently mentioned was the *Samuel* whose captain,
Samuel Cary, talked at length to the reporter of the *Boston
News Letter*.[11] On 13 July he had been eleven weeks out from
London. Off the Banks of Newfoundland he noticed the
approach of two vessels. Having been at sea so long and
meeting no ship it did not occur to him that these might be
pirates. It was farther north than their customary haunts and
the first inklings he had of trouble were the warning shots and
the black flag.

There were hours of daylight left and Cary was of no mind to
argue matters with a powerful brig and a sloop of ten guns. He
waited for the pirates to board. Much practice over the weeks
had made the pirates fast and efficient in their selection of what
was worth taking. They gathered together the crew and
passengers on the upper deck, stripped them of the clothes they
wore and of their belongings below. Charles Johnson in his
History . . . wrote vividly of the action.

'The *Samuel* was a rich ship, and had several Passengers on
board who were used very roughly, in order to make them
discover their Money, threatening them every Moment
with Death, if they did not resign every Thing up to them.
They tore up the Hatches and entered the Hold like a
Parcel of Furies, and with Axes and Cutlashes, cut and
broke open all the Bales, Cases and Boxes, they could lay
their Hands on; and when any Goods came on Deck, that
they did not like to carry aboard, instead of tossing them
into the Hold again, threw them over-board into the Sea;
all this was done with incessant Cursing and Swearing,
more like Fiends than Men. They carried with them Sails,

Guns, Powder, Cordage, and £8 or £9,000 worth of the choicest Goods; and told Captain Cary that they should accept no Act of Grace; that the King and Parliament might be damned with their Acts of Grace for them; neither would they go to Hope-Point to be hang'd up a Sun drying as Kid's [William Kidd the privateer, executed in 1701] and Braddish's [a Massachussetts pirate hanged with Kidd] Company were; but that if they should ever be overpower'd they would set Fire to the Powder with a Pistol, and go all merrily to Hell together'.[12]

The crew of the *Samuel* were made to transfer over forty barrels of gunpowder to the *Good Fortune*. Two of the heaviest cannon were removed. Bartholomew Roberts came aboard dressed in the finery of a damask coat, sash, dress-sword, hands scintillating with jewelled rings. He invited Cary's seamen to join him. In a pretence of intimidation pirates levelled pistols at the *Samuel*'s crew several of whom crossed to Roberts, imploring Cary to witness that they had been compelled. The mate of the *Samuel*, Harry Gillespie, hid in the hold but was discovered by Anstis who dragged him roughly to the side and shoved him into the sea. Hauled aboard and threatened for his disobedience the northerner was perhaps the one man from the ship genuinely to be forced.[13]

The *Good Fortune* and la Palisse's *Sea King* continued to raid along the shores of Newfoundland while in England rumours of them increased. The *Daily Post* told its readers that a French man-of-war had destroyed a pirate sloop off the Banks. It was believed that it was the same sloop that had caused so much damage in those parts.[14] It was not. La Palisse had stayed with Roberts.

Then, in October, *Applebee's Original Weekly Journal* wrote that two light men-of-war had been ordered to Newfoundland to intercept the pirates 'who continue to commit great depredations on our merchant ships that way'. In the same issue but clearly from another source was the news that the two men-of-war were the *Rose* and the *Shark* which, having been repaired, had sailed to Nantasket for 'the pirates who infest the coast there'.[15]

Two months later the *London Journal* commented on the result of the expedition. 'On the twenty-fifth past arrived the *Jeykel* galley, Captain Hart, from Barbados in seven weeks. The master says that a pirate of thirty-six guns and twenty men [sic] having taken twenty-two sail of vessel the *Rose* and the *Shark* went in pursuit of him; but the said pirate having fitted out one of the said prizes, the former thought fit not to attack them'.[16] Captain Whitney of the *Rose* was no more zealous than he had been with Woodes Rogers.

In England there were negotiations between the Royal African Company and the Admiralty.[17] The Company's forts had suffered badly from the raids of Howel Davis, Cocklyn, la Bouche and England. Before them, in 1718, the directors agreed that they wanted no unprejudiced body like the Admiralty looking into their business practices and sending reports about their affairs to Britain. Questioned by the Board of Trade & Plantations three of them, Higham, Harris and Morrice, declared there was no necessity for His Majesty's ships to patrol the African coast. There had never been any insult or disturbance from a foreign nation, uttering a direct lie about the ugly rivalry between the British, Dutch and Portuguese Companies. Morrice thought that naval ships could assist the Company only in the carrying of stores and provisions.

That was in 1718. By June, 1720 after piratical depredations had cost so much money the Company's attitude changed. The directors attended the Lords Justices who after hearing their case ordered two men-of-war to escort the Royal African Company ships that were being loaded in the London docks. The cost would be borne by the Company. The men-of-war were intended to be the *Swallow* and the *Experiment* but the latter was impossibly undermanned and was replaced by the *Enterprise*.[18]

The directors also agreed that a settled allowance should be given to employees of the Company wounded in an attack and similar allowances granted to the widows and children of any man 'killed in defence of any of the Company's Factorys or ships which shall be attacked by pirates or any other enemies'.[19]

For almost two months nothing had been heard of Bartholomew Roberts. Then he reappeared in the West Indies.

10

Fortunes in the West Indies

August–November 1720

'They write from St. Christopher that Captain Roberts who is the most desperate pirate of all who range these seas now calls himself Admiral of the Leeward Isles'.

[*Applebee's Original Weekly Journal*, July 1, 1721]

Since leaving the Grenadian island of Carriacou six months earlier Bartholomew Roberts had grown in prestige and infamy in the honest world. Letters and despatches about him reached government secretaries in England who noted his name as one more worry with which they were expected to cope from a distance of three thousand miles. Colonial governors looked to their shore defences not wishing their territories to be ravaged like Trepassy. The men-of-war *Rose* and *Shark* ostensibly searched for the pirate but in reality were disinclined to engage his great guns.

When, suddenly, news of him ceased speculation spread across the islands. He had gone to Africa. To Madagascar. A hurricane had sunk him. A foreign man-of-war had sent him down. A thousand whispers and guesses spread and echoed from island to island and colony to colony.[1]

Affairs like Trepassy could upset three months' trading and it alarmed the London merchants. A successful pirate was as effective as an enemy blockade. He could bring want and hunger to islands, could ruin small businesses and, worst of all, could cause American colonists to question ever more angrily the wisdom of being governed by a European country that could not or would not protect her own possessions.

When the navy became a laughing-stock the pirates had won a victory. When colonists preferred to barter with smugglers and pirates the British government had suffered a defeat. It lost the justification for the demanding taxation it extracted from the colonies because some of those levies were to pay for safeguarding the colonies. A ravenous marauder like Roberts created concern in Whitehall.

No accident had befallen him. With his holds crammed with booty and with merchant ships sheltering in the ports Roberts realised that his station at Newfoundland was no longer worth maintaining. His crews were restless to enjoy themselves and he set sail southwards towards the warmth and welcome of the West Indian islands.

He discovered that Gillespie was an excellent sailing-master, sullen, reluctant, but a mariner far superior to anyone the pirates had. He was a typical northerner, dour and taciturn but an outspoken craftsman when he saw idle seamanship. It was he who had the sails of the *Good Fortune* adjusted, even to having a spar lowered to use a topsail to better advantage. Under his advice Roberts' flagship for all its size and weight became almost as fast as la Palisse's scudding sloop. Gillespie's intimate knowledge of the currents, the coasts and the winds that blew off them saved the pirates days as they voyaged past the American colonies.

Roberts drank his tea complacently in his Great Cabin that was fitted out luxuriously with embroidered drapes at the leaded windows. A carved oak table stood on a carpet whose pile would have been the envy of an eastern potentate. In a veneered dresser were goblets and tankards of pewter, bronze and silver that gleamed as brightly as the golden snuff-box against which the captain's long lace cuffs rested.[2]

Roberts himself was as resplendent. Now that the ship was capably ordered by Anstis and skilfully navigated by Gillespie their captain indulged in a glorious wardrobe whose silks, satins and velvets crowded together, breeches and waistcoats, three-quarter length coats, shirts ruffled and pleated, buckled shoes, fine hose, hats, wigs, sashes, thinly supple swords, engraved pistols whose loss had cost their previous owners half a year's income.

Days passed. Roberts preened himself, sometimes strolling around the balconied sternwalk outside his cabin, sometimes standing on the quarterdeck with his Lords, glancing down at the multitude of pirates who sprawled on the maindeck below him. Each day some of them would visit him in his cabin for he had no power to forbid them and they would open bottles of wine and remember Bahia or Trepassy and the almost century of vessels they had captured. Roberts promised them a thousand. They would roar with laughter, some scratching their chests or running dirty fingers through dirtier hair as they thought in bewilderment of the fortune each of them had already.

Occasionally on their long voyage the ships would berth at nightfall in a deserted bay or wide rivermouth where they could anchor safely and go ashore to light warming fires. It was noticeable that Gillespie talked with no one except Valentine Ashplant, the loudest and coarsest of all the Lords, not a northerner like the sailing-master but a Londoner from the Minories. To Roberts Gillespie would speak politely but briefly. To Anstis he said nothing except to acknowledge his commands. Everyone else he ignored apart from some forced men to whom he was sympathetic.

Once, one of the pirates, offended by Gillespie's indifference, hit him so hard and unexpectedly, that the sailor fell half-stunned to the deck. Ashplant leapt at the aggressor and ferociously grabbed his throat, determinedly strangling him until others dragged him off. After that, despite his aloofness, no one harmed Gillespie. A strongly-muscled, hot-tempered brawler Ashplant was not a man to argue with.

So leisurely was the southwards journey that it was not until late August that they were off the coast of South Carolina. There they encountered Captain Wallace Fensilon who was soon deprived of eight hogsheads of rum, a tierce of sugar, his best cable, all his clothes, bedding and instruments, some for the surgeon, some for Gillespie who had not requested them but accepted them in silence, and every drop of fresh water save for one barrel that the pirates left in response to Fensilon's entreaty that his crew should not die of thirst. Roberts persuaded the mate, the carpenter and one of the seamen to enlist.[3]

Stripped of crew, provisions and equipment Fensilon had to land for food and water many times before eventually reaching Virginia, at the end of September. Bitterly he complained that having been ransacked by Roberts he had then been taken by another pirate, 'Calico Jack' Rackam.

Rackam had become such a nuisance that the governor of Jamaica, Sir Nicholas Lawes asked the naval commodore, Edward Vernon, for the loan of a sloop to drive the pirate away.[4] The Commodore offered one excuse after another until, in desperation, on September 5 the governor commissioned a sloop in his own name to pursue the pirates. He listed the names of Rackam's crew including the two women, Anne Bonny and Mary Read.

Rackham was little more than a thief of trifles. On 1 October he looted Dorothy Thomas's canoe of her pathetic provisions: four pigs, six chickens, rice, yams, sugar, salt, pork and beef. Thomas remembered the women.

They 'wore men's jackets, and long trousers, and handkerchiefs tied about their heads: and . . . each of them had a machete and pistol in their hands and cursed and swore at the men, to murder her; and that they should kill her to prevent her coming against them'. Thomas added that she knew them to be women 'by the largeness of their breasts'.[5]

In the same month of October, frustrated at the failure of the first mission Lawes sent out a second sloop with twelve guns and fifty-four men under the command of Jonathan Barnet, offering a reward of £200 for the capture of Rackam. Barnet collected it.[6]

'They write from Bristol of the 9th . . . that the pirates were very busy in these parts and that the governor had sent out two sloops from Jamaica with 100 hands in each to cruise upon them, one of which had brought in a pirate sloop commanded by Rackam of Jamaica having on board fourteen men, all condemned, which will soon be hanged'.[7]

Taken by surprise at Port Negril in Jamaica, with all his crew intoxicated, Rackam was quickly defeated. Cowering in the hold he was shamed by the maledictions of Bonny and Read who were firing and battling like wildcats, shrieking for him to 'Come up and fight like a man!'. No one came. The pirates were handed over to Major Richard James, a militia officer and his guard. Manacled, they were taken to Spanish Town gaol.

At their trial on 16 November at St Jago de la Vega, Jamaica, Bonny and Read were condemned. 'You . . . are to go from hence to the place from whence you came, and from thence to the place of execution: where you shall be severally hanged by the neck till you are severally dead. And God of his infinite mercy be merciful to both your souls'.[8] It was at this dramatic point that the women made their historic defence, 'Milords, we plead our bellies'. The hearing was postponed for them to be examined. Death sentences were pronounced for Rackam and eight others. Next day the captain and four pirates were hanged

A GENERAL
HISTORY
OF THE
Robberies and Murders
Of the moſt notorious
PYRATES,
AND ALSO
Their *Policies*, *Diſcipline* and *Government*,

From their firſt RISE and SETTLEMENT in the Iſland of *Providence*, in 1717, to the preſent Year 1724.

WITH

The remarkable ACTIONS and ADVENTURES of the two Female Pyrates, *Mary Read* and *Anne Bonny*.

To which is prefix'd

An ACCOUNT of the famous Captain *Avery* and his Companions; with the Manner of his Death in *England*.

The Whole digeſted into the following CHAPTERS;

To which is added,

A ſhort ABSTRACT of the Statute and Civil Law, in Relation to PYRACY.

By Captain CHARLES JOHNSON.

LONDON, Printed for *Ch. Rivington* at the *Bible* and *Crown* in St. *Paul's Church-Yard*, *J. Lacy* at the *Ship* near the *Temple-Gate*, and *J. Stone* next the *Crown* Coffee-houſe the back of *Greys-Inn*, 1724.

FACSIMILE OF THE TITLE-PAGE OF THE FIRST EDITION

Title page of the General History . . .

Howel Davis

Blackbeard

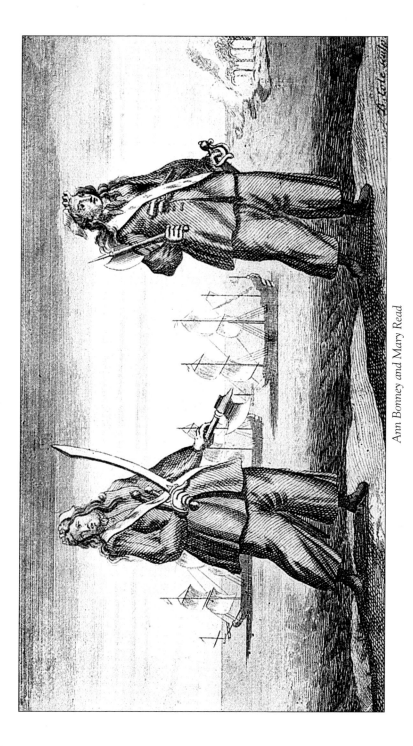

Ann Bonney and Mary Read

'Calico Jack' Rackam

Mary Read

Bartholomew Roberts

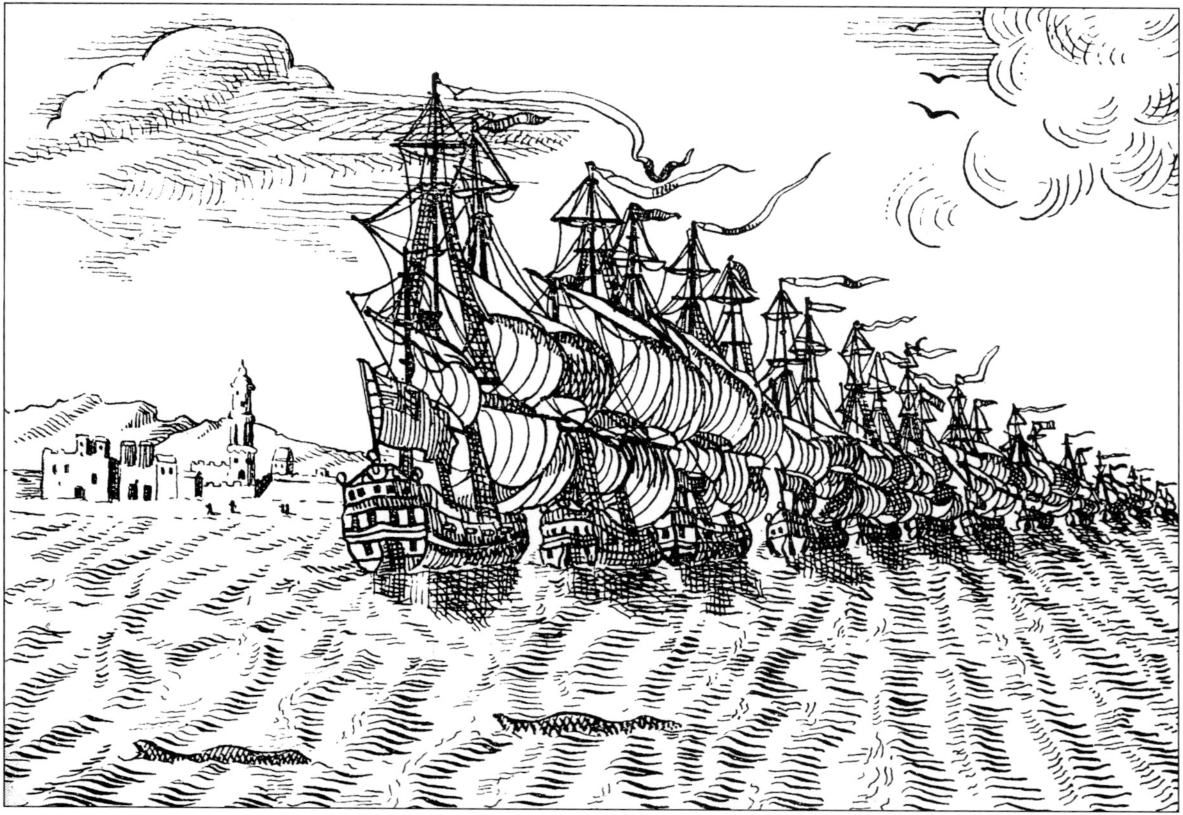

Portuguese fleet at Bahia

A boarding-party

Blackbeard

Execution of Stede Bonnet

Execution Dock, Wapping (Kennedy)

Captain George Lowther

Roberts' flags

A View of a Stage & also of y^e manner of Fishing for, Curing & Drying Cod at NEW FOUND LAND.

A. The Habit of y^e Fishermen. B. The Line. C. The manner of Fishing. D. The Dressers of y^e Fish. E. The Trough into which they throw ye Cod when Dressed. F. Salt Boxes. G. The manner of Carrying y^e Cod. H. The Cleansing y^e Cod. I. A Press to extract y^e Oyl from y^e Cod Livers. K. Casks to receive y^e Water & Blood that comes from y^e Livers. L. Another Cask to receive the Oyl. M. The manner of Drying y^e Cod.

Ann Bonney

THE
TRYALS
OF
Captain John Rackam,
AND OTHER
PIRATES, *Viz.*

Geroge Fetherſton,	Noah Harwood,
Richard Corner,	James Dobbins,
John Davies,	Patrick Carty,
John Howell,	Thomas Earl,
Tho. Bourn, *alias* Brown,	John Fenwick, *at* Fenis

Who were all Condemn'd for PIRACY, *at the Town of* St. Jago de
La Vega, *in the Iſland of* JAMAICA, *on* Wedneſday *and* Thurſday
the Sixteenth and Seventeenth Days of November 1720.

AS ALSO, THE

TRYALS *of* Mary Read *and* Anne Bonny,
alias Bonn, *on Monday the* 28th *Day of the*
ſaid Month of November, *at* St. Jago
. de la Vega aforeſaid.

And of ſeveral Others, who were alſo condemn'd for PIRACY.

ALSO,

A True Copy of the Act of Parliament made for the more effectual ſuppreſſion of Piracy.

Pamphlet of Rackam's Trial

Pirates carousing

3rd-rate man-of-war

Captain
Bartholomew Roberts

Captain Chaloner Ogle

at Gallows Point, Port Royal. A day later four more were hanged at Kingston.

Rackam's body was suspended in chains at Plumb Point. It is said that Bonny visited him in jail, still scornful of his weakness, saying that she was 'Sorry to see him there, but if he had fought like a man, he need not have been hanged like a dog'.

On 28 November, because of their pregnancies, the women were reprieved from execution but imprisoned. Bonny's freedom was supposedly purchased by her rich father and there is a story that she later married and moved to North America. On 28 April, 1721, Mary Read died of fever in prison.[9]

> 'Tis o'er. That voice for ever now is still;
> But ah, in those waned eyes what vision stands
> That is not of the sea, or sun, or sands,
> While Death halts o'er the summit of the hill'.
> 'The Death Jest', *Buccaneer Ballads*, 1910. 23.

The belief that both Read and Bonny had concealed their sex from everyone save their chosen lovers is romantic but unreasonable. The fact that they wore women's clothes proves this. Nor could their bodily functions have been kept secret. Some larger naval vessels did have wooden latrines in secluded parts of the ship but smaller craft had only the forechains exposed to the open air. Neither woman could have avoided their use.

An experienced sailor, Course, who had gone to sea at the age of fifteen, ridiculed the notion of privacy. 'As one who served in sailing ships and knows the lay-out of those old pirate ships, I am positive that no such opportunity would occur before it was too late. There were no cubicles or small rooms allocated for this and no doors could be locked or secured in any way. The 'heads', the open space on each side of the bow, where the bowsprit passes into the foc'sle head, was the open space used as a lavatory. One had to climb over a rail to get there and it was open to the view of anyone standing on the foc'sle head above. The other places used were the scuppers, the gutterways running along the full length on each side of the ship, just inside the bulwarks. They were used in the same way as a trough is used in a men's public lavatory on shore'. The women were bound to be discovered.[10]

So far from being unsuspected, monogramous mistresses it is feasible that the favours of Read and Bonny were shared by others. Only their physical ferocity may have safeguarded them from unwelcome promiscuity. Fables and facts are restless bedfellows.

Eight months before Read's death and a thousand miles east of Jamaica Bartholomew Roberts intended to go to the island of Désirade off Guadaloupe hoping to meet smugglers who often landed there under the pretext of being African traders. They would pay well for his stolen goods.

It was a fine September day when the islands came into view through the early sea-mist, rich, harshly brilliant in their colouring with the blue of the sea blending into a translucent green near the shores, the starker greens of trees beyond them, a polychromatic glare accentuated by the dazzling white sands and powdery blue of the sky. Men could see patches of red and purple and yellow where flowers grew wild and thick. Down the hillsides silver pendants of waterfalls glittered like wavering bars.

Each island changed as they approached, first the greyness of the mountains lightening into mauve as the lowlands came into sight and then a vivid spectrum as the ships passed the empty shores. A gentle breeze carried the fragrance of blossoms into the stink of the *Good Fortune*. Gillespie glanced at the helmsman who held the whipstaff on a steady course. Quietly he ordered the topsails taken in and a heavy cannon dragged to the whipstaff. Despite the calmness of the sea a hurricane was coming.

Wind caught the flapping mainsail. Another blast heeled the ship over momentarily as the mainsail billowed and sagged. Overhead the sky darkened. Gillespie shouted for the sails to be shortened and the gun to be lashed firmly to the whipstaff. The wind strengthened, began to whistle through the rigging. A small, glowing meteor hissed into the sea. A seabird was hurled against the masthead. Lightning forked down through the blackening clouds.

Gust followed gust until the wind's shrieking died to a distant roar. The whipstaff heaved against the dead weight of the gun as thunderous waves broke on the bows, breaking over the forecastle in explosions that sent spray bursting and spreading in washes of foam across the decks.

Like toys the ships fell and rose and the sky lowered behind them in a backcloth of swirling clouds that became darker as the wind screamed across the sea. The *Good Fortune* climbed a wave, hovered, slid from its crest, paused deep in the trough beneath a clutching wall of breakers that curled and grasped the vessel before squeezing it out leaving the ship lurching from the heaviness of the waves plunging over it. The brutal tugging of the whipstaff lifted the cannon from the deck, dropped it in a splinter of planking. A streak of lightening seemed to split the sea. There was an enormous rumbling and seconds later thousands of leaves and fragments of bark swept across the *Good Fortune*.

It was a confusion of wind, lightning, thunder and sweeping, surging waves. For more than an hour the pirates battled against the storm and then, almost as instantly as it had erupted, it went, leaving the same blue sky, the same colourful islands, the same placid waters. Of la Palisse's sloop there was no sign. Incredibly, except for one or two strained spars, a stretch of smashed gunwhale and ragged sails the ship was undamaged. Jones had replacements for everything. Roberts continued towards Désiderade.

The coral island was deserted. Remains of fires and marks of ships' boats high on the sand showed that traders had been there but with no knowledge of when they might return it was useless to wait. Provisions were needed. Disappointed, Roberts chose to continue to Carriacou where he could careen without fear of prying *costagardas*. That evening Montigny la Palisse's sloop appeared. He had driven before the hurricane and was relieved to find that his strong companion also was safe.

On the fourth of September, 1720, they sailed into Carriacou lagoon where they found Captain Robert Dunn of the *Relief* sloop turtling. The big, clumsy amphibians could be eaten in a salivating variety of ways and the pirates welcomed the captain warmly. Within hours succulent aromas drifted amongst the trees, smells of turtle soup being stirred in the cauldron and of turtles being baked in their shells for deliciously appetising meat. One man chuckled over a violet landcrab that he had caught. His comrades watched dubiously as he munched. A surfeit could result in blindness.

Other pirates prepared a drink of rumfustian. Eggs kindly provided by the acquiescent Dunn were broken over a large bowl and mixed liberally with beer, gin and sherry. When the concoction was creamy cinnamon and nutmeg were added for flavouring and the bowl was set over a small fire to simmer while brown sugar was poured in until Ashplant was content with the tangy strength and warmth of the drink.[11]

Days followed agreeably. Dunn's small sloop was loaded with goods not wanted by the pirates. The captain did not own his sloop and was eager to sell his contraband at St. Christophers and then sail out to the pirates to give Roberts his share before returning to the island with even more stolen goods. It was an easy way for an impoverished seaman to make money.[12] When at last the *Good Fortune* was cleaned and repaired the merchant captain sailed away promising to meet Roberts off St. Christophers on the 26th. The pirates remained at the lagoon. There was no hurry. It was better carousing on the quiet island

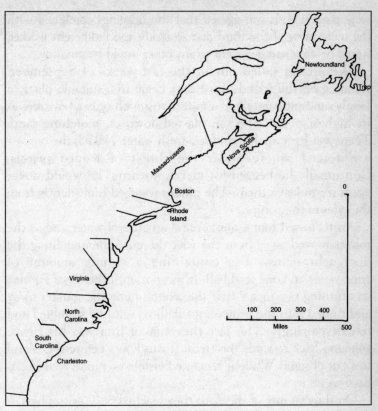

Eastern North America

than sailing the sea-routes. Because of his triumph at Trepassy Roberts, mindless of the sailor's superstition that ill-luck would follow the changing of a ship's name, decided to rechristen his vessel the *Royal Fortune*. La Palisse's sloop became the new *Good Fortune*.

Then, when everything had been prepared for their departure, three men attempted to escape. It was stupidity. Carriacou was a small island, precipitous and unfriendly and a day later the fugitives were marched back. After a whipping two were pardoned. It was agreed that the floggings combined with the marooning of the third man, a sickly and indifferent worker, would be sufficient deterrent to any other would-be runaway.

The pirates sailed out in the last weeks of September, standing off the islands until they came to a suitable place, a lonely sandspit barely half a mile across with only a few trees at its highest point. The sun blasted down on scorching sand. There was little shelter and less fresh water. Naked, the outcast was forced ashore under the threat of loaded pistols. Continually he begged for mercy, swearing he would never again try to leave them. The pirates watched him silently from the sides of their ships.

Anstis tossed him a musket and a bottle of water and as the rowers moved away from the islet the quartermaster flung the distraught man a bag containing a minute amount of gunpowder and one lead ball. It was not until the *Royal Fortune* was turning out to sea that the wretch flung the musket away and rushed into the water, arms flailing, until he stumbled and fell despairingly. The last they saw of him was his figure trudging back towards the trees. It was hours before the island was out of sight. While it remained visible no pirate could keep his eyes off it.

On the evening of the 25th they reached St. Christophers, a mountainous, well-wooded island whose chief town, Basseterre, lay by a riverside in a bay. Nevis rose close by, separated by a strait called the Narrows in which there was a small rock called Booby Island from the flocks of seabirds on it.

The pirates waited all day for Dunn. Roberts suspected treachery. It would be easy for the captain to land the plunder and keep the profits rather than handing half to the pirates even though Roberts had told him that if that happened he would set fire to the settlements. When he noticed soldiers moving cannon on the forts lining the bay he assumed that Dunn had betrayed them. He decided to attack. After Trepassy he was ambitious to test a stronger town. Fort Smith stood on the right of the bay's mouth. To the left of the entrance was a second fortification, Bluff Point. Basseterre should have been hard to take.

Roberts was only half correct. Lieutenant-General Mathew, the governor, knew that the pirates were to attack and was frantically trying to overcome the sloth and neglect of years by issuing orders that despatched militia to every part of the island.[13] Lieutenant McKenzie marched to Charles Fort with a sub-officer and thirty men. Lt-Colonel Payne was sent to raise two armed companies at Sandy Point settlement. Captain Nathaniel Payne, his brother and an equally important plantation owner, was to do the same at the Old Road. So was Major Willet at Palmeto Point. As though these levies were insufficient the governor commanded the gunners at the four most strategic positions on the island, the forts, to be on the alert.

In Basseterre the unexpected bustle caused more confusion that had been known since the time when the war against Spain had been at its most dangerous. Militiamen scuttled everywhere. Ladies rushed to their houses gathering up children and slaves. Gentlemen took down their flintlocks.

When the *Royal Fortune* sailed into the harbour, black flags flying, the pennant with the Barbadian and Martinician skulls at the masthead, drummers beating, trumpeters fanfaring, Basseterre should have been at arms. It was not. The only reception was a ship's boat that rowed out to enquire who had entered the bay so flamboyantly. The two sailors in it found a dozen pistols pointing at them. A voice ordered them aboard. Anstis asked who they were. One was Bridstock Weaver, mate of the *Mary & Martha*. The other was George Smith, the boatswain. Being sea-artists they were taken to the Great Cabin and made to sign the Articles.[14]

Meeting no opposition Roberts sailed towards the five vessels lying in the roads. Boarding parties entered them. Captain Wilcox of the *Mary & Martha* foolishly argued. After being ransacked his ship was burnt. The same fate met the *Greyhound*

of Bristol whose captain, Cox was never to know that this was because another sea-captain, Owen Rogers, had also come from Bristol. His mate, James Skyrme, became an important officer of Roberts.

Roberts contemplated keeping M. Pomier's French sloop and towed it out. Captain Hingstone's vessel was also much admired and examined for the presence of the footings for a new-fangled steering-wheel in place of the customary whipstaff. Frustratingly, the captain was ashore and had taken the wheel with him. The captain of the third craft, Henry Fowle, realised that co-operation was likely to be more advantageous than blustering. Learning that Roberts was in need of fresh meat, he offered to write a letter asking for beasts to be brought to the quayside. Roberts agreed. The town was his and it was better to finish the plundering before his pirates went ashore for the traditional drunken festivities and became incapable.

The compliant Fowle penned his note:

'To Mr James Parsons 27.9.1720.

I shall forever be in your favour if on the morning tide you would send some sheep and some goats out to the pirates you may see here. I am treated very civilly and promised to have my ship and cargo again and desire Captain Henksome to send his wheel that he steers his ship with, or it may be the worse for him.

Henry Fowle.

As evening was coming on Roberts decided it was prudent to move out of range of the forts' guns. The *Royal Fortune* and the *Good Fortune* put out to sea taking Pomier's and Hingstone's vessels with him. Behind them the bulks of the two merchantmen still burned.

In Basseterre there was panic. The governor discovered that the shore batteries that had been designed to defend the town had no gunpowder or ramrods for the cannonballs. Only two guns were fit for use. Through long neglect the rest were corroded beyond repair. In desperation Mathew requisitioned seven and a half barrels of powder, that these might keep the pirates at a distance. But the shot was too large for the barrels and the gunners were so out of practice that not one of the few rounds they fired fell anywhere near their targets.

From Fowle Roberts discovered that it was not Dunn's bad faith that had alerted the governor. Two nights previously the captain of the little sloop had been unloading a canoe when he had been taken unawares by a gunner from Fort William. The stolen contents of the canoe and the sloop condemned Dunn. In fear of hanging he informed the governor that the pirates would attack unless he were released at once. Lt-General Mathew had more fibre than the admiral of Trepassy. He put Dunn in gaol.

That night the carcases of the sheep and goats were taken to the pirates. But Hingstone refused to surrender his wheel and his vessel was sent blazing into Basseterre Bay where the fire was put out only after the ship had been badly damaged.

Thirteen great guns arrived from neighbouring forts, including one of 24-lb balls, and they were disposed about the harbour in readiness for the return of Roberts. Some were fired at the distant pirates without success. Shortly afterwards some seamen from Hingstone's disabled ship rowed ashore bringing two letters with them. One was addressed to the Governor of Nevis stating that Roberts intended to visit his island next and burn his town for hanging some pirates. Mathew supposed that this referred to the men from the *Royal Rover* that had been executed months before. The other message was for Mathew, dictated by Roberts by a rare literate member of his crew who wrote it in a fine clerical hand.

'Bartholomew Roberts the pirate to Lieutenant-General Mathew. *Royal Fortune.* September 27, 1720

This comes expressly from me to lett you know that had you come off as you ought to a done and drank a glass of

wine with me and my company I should not have harmed
the least vessel in your harbour. Farther it is not your
gunns you fired that affrighted me or hindred our coming
on shore but the wind not proving to our expectation that
hindered it. The *Royal Rover* you have already burnt and
barbarously used some of our men but we have now a new
ship as good as her and for revenge you may assure
yourselves here and hereafter not to expect anything from
our hands but what belongs a pirate and farther gentlemen
that poor fellow you now have in prison is entirely
ignorant and what he hath was gave him and so make
conscience for once let me begg you and use that man as
an honest man and not as a C if we hear any otherwise
you may expect not to have any of your island yours.

Signed Bartholomew Roberts.

There is no record of Mathew replying to this impudence.
Nor is it known what happened to Dunn but as he had been
smuggling he was probably hanged.

At nine the next morning the *Royal Fortune* re-entered the
harbour to set Fowle and two of his men ashore. The pirates
would have kept one until they were told that he suffered from
fits. At eleven Roberts returned to pick up Fowle but by then
Mathew had his guns ready and fired two rounds from every
cannon available. Seven shots hit the *Royal Fortune*, ripping
her jib and her mainsail halliards. Roberts did not reply but
swung out to sea. His chance had gone. Basseterre was too
strongly defended for him to storm.

He kept his word and released Fowle. To compensate Wilcox
whose *Mary & Martha* was little more than charcoal he gave
him Pomier's sloop. Then the pirates headed towards Nevis to
avenge the men of the *Royal Rover* but the wind was against
them and eventually Roberts sailed westwards past Basseterre
and then south as though intending to go to Antigua and its
neighbouring islands.

Pleased with his rather lucky relief from invasion Mathew went to bring in Fowle's ship. On the companion way a wag had scrawled:

'For our word's sake we let thee go
But to Creoles we are a foe'.

Another couplet was discovered in the blackened timbers of Hingstone's craft.

'In thee I find
Content of mind',

presumably referring to the cargo of wines and spirts.

After the fiasco of Dunn's trading expedition and the absence of smugglers on Désirade Roberts needed cash. One of the pirates suggested that they call on the French governor of St. Barthélemy who was so destitute of amenities that he could afford to rebuff no one.

There was little fresh water on the hilly island and ships ignored it leaving its inhabitants for ever short of supplies. The governor was delighted to see the two pirate vessels. He was too poor to discriminate. France did not bother with him. The British had not helped him when his islanders had been starving. On eight square miles of rocky poverty he needed equipment, anything that would raise his existence from that of an exiled slave. St. Barthélemy was a pictorial glory of palms and tropical plants but its scrub-thick vegetation was useless as food and its people lived in deprivation.[15]

At the sound of the trumpets the townsfolk rushed to the quay. After courteous words with the governor Roberts had the holds of his vessels unloaded of the plunder amassed from Trepassy, the Banks of Newfoundland, the ships captured on their voyage south to the West Indies and the looting at St. Christophers. Joyfully the islanders carried everything to a warehouse where the haggling would begin. Even more joyfully they discovered that the pirates were generous businessmen. At job-lot prices the first piles were disposed of. For his collaboration the governor was presented with a jewelled chain of gold worth more than his whole year's salary. Merchants were given rings and brooches as earnests of the pirates' appreciation. In response, the townsfolk hugged the dirty, unshaven criminals, fawning over them as their minds tallied the profits they were making.

The crews of the *Royal Fortune* and *Good Fortune* did not wait for the cargoes to be translated into coin. Their own shares were readily acceptable to tavern-keepers and broad-minded ladies. The two meagre inns overflowed. Pistol-shots celebrated freedom from the sea. Windows were shattered by tankards flung over roistering shoulders. Complacent husbands waited for enriched wives.

For three weeks the pirates stayed on the island. Little work was done. It was drink, delight and debauchery. The only precaution taken by Roberts was to leave a detachment of men aboard the ships each night to prevent desertion during the jovial, inebriated festivities. At the end of the third week they sailed away, going to mountainous Tortola in the Virgin Islands.

There was little there except for a brig of twenty-two guns that pleased Roberts so much that after making some hurried alterations he exchanged his ship for it. The old *Royal Fortune* had served him well since leaving Newfoundland but needed to be thoroughly cleaned and mended. Unsuspected after the hurricane planking, spars and yards had gradually loosened. Leaks were springing below decks.

A rapid boot-topping at Carriacou instead of a thorough careening had not been adequate. In the shallow lagoon the guns and cargo had been shifted to one side to tilt the vessel and expose the upper part of the starboard below the waterline. Once scraped clean the port side was similarly treated. But the keel was untouched. Without complete careening at least three times a year in the tropics a vessel became sluggish and steadily decayed. The *Royal Fortune*, for all her size, had become a burden. Her replacement was ideal. The pirates departed leaving a fuming merchant captain with only a filthy, rotting craft to compensate him for the loss of his cargo.

By the twenty-fifth of October Roberts was at St. Lucia a few miles south of Martinique, planning a swift raid on the shipping before slipping away. His luck held. The sight of the heavily-gunned brig and the sloop disheartened the two vessels in the harbour. The English brig was stripped of its contents and the sloop of M. Courtel was commandeered to become a storeship.[16]

Dominica was less than a hundred miles to the north. With his three ships Roberts felt safe. He was confident that the black flags, drums and trumpets would frighten everyone. He was wrong. It was known that Dutch interlopers, so called because they were forbidden by the Navigation Acts to trade at British islands, would always resist. The one at Dominica was no exception.

She was a large vessel of forty-two guns, far stronger than the *Royal Fortune* and the *Good Fortune* combined. Roberts was not deterred. A man who had attacked at Bahia when most would have sneaked away, the audacious plunderer of Trepassy, the aggressor that only contrary winds had thwarted at Basseterre, was not daunted by an excess of enemy guns. The interloper was bound to contain a treasury of gold and goods.

For hours they fought, the *Good Fortune* and La Palisse's sloop darting at the sides of the Dutchman, worrying at her unprotected stern while the *Royal Fortune* and the interloper cannonaded and blasted in a choking, blinding reek of gunpowder. Then they grappled and pirates swept over the Dutchman's sides mercilessly slaughtering the crew because of their resistance. When the vessel was finally subdued and la Palisse was rounding up the fifteen frightened vessels in the harbour Roberts' crew exacted their revenge, hanging prisoners from the yardarms, whipping the bloodily wealed backs of others, slicing off the captain's ears as a reward for his gallantry. It was savagely vindictive. Too many friends had been wounded, maimed, killed, and their comrades were ruthless. Torture and butchery mixed in a madness of vengeance that did not cease until the last Dutchman had been dragged out and mutilated. Roberts did nothing to prevent them. The punishment would be broadcast around the islands as a warning not to defy his ships.[17]

Once more the holds were crammed with booty. The Dutch vessel with its great armament became the third *Royal Fortune*. At her stern fluttered the gigantic black flag with its emblems of Martinique and Barbados. La Palisse kept his battered sloop, satisfied with the protection that Roberts provided.

The fifteen ships were rifled of every valuable. Depending on the attitude of their captains some were set free, other burned. From one of them came a promising volunteer. John Mansfield, a deserter from the naval vessel *Rose*, who having once been a highwayman, or so he claimed, looked a likely prospect. To the contrary, he was so frequently drunk that the only benefit the pirates gained was his intoxicated absence from the share-outs.

Bartholomew Roberts, Admiral of the Leeward Isles, sailed away with his fleet of the powerful *Royal Fortune*, the brig from Tortola, the sloop from St Lucia and la Palisse's *Good Fortune*. He was mightier than any man-of-war in the West Indies and he feared nothing.

The few little guns and timorous crew of a merchantman were of no consequence when confronted with Roberts' 180 pirates and 48 negroes. He commanded a dreadful battery of ordnance. Seven 2lb and 3lb guns threatened from the bows. Eight 4lb minions lined the sides. Between them lay a dozen falconets, half a ton each, firing 6lb shot. Eighteen fearsome brass demiculverins, 3m long, slender, loaded with 8lb balls jutted from the gunwales. The armament was complemented by four huge 12lb cannon that by themselves were capable of sinking any small craft that opposed them.[18]

The ship was an arsenal of gunpowder, roundshot, poundshot, grapeshot, handshells, deckshells, doubleheaded shot and the miscellany of smallshot, pellets, broken bottles and nails for the raking swivels that could ravish a living body into a carcass of disentangulated flesh and scarecrowed bone. To any vessel other than a great man-of-war the pirates were irresistible.

The governor of Martinique wrote despatch after despatch to the British governor of Nevis, first about the assaults on Tortola and St. Lucia, later about Dominica, asking for the support of Captain Whitney and the *Rose*. Whitney did not oblige even when promised that two more vessels would be equipped in Martinique to support him. Months later the governor was still writing and Captain Whitney was still unco-operative.

A sloop passing Dominica at the time of Roberts' attack reported its escape from the pirates. Its captain remembered both the Dutch ship and its guns and, in particular, Roberts' flag, 'one with a picture on each side and infamous inscriptions written in French on them; the said pictures and their inscriptions are representations of the General of Martinique and Barbados'.[19]

Everywhere, before sailing away, the pirates told their prisoners they would sail to St. Eustatia where they had heard of another interloper. In fact they lingered around the east coast of Dominica. It had been in Roberts' mind that it would be wise to return to Africa from which they had been absent for so long. Raiding would grow more difficult for them in the West Indies as the governors united in their search for the predators. On 6 January 1721, the *London Journal* reported, 'We are in expectations of hearing of a bloody action with the pirates in the W. Indies, three of H.M. ships well manned being gone from the Barbadoes in quest of them upon information of the place of their rendezvous'.

More germane than that almost empty threat was that merchant ships had become rarer as news of the pirates circulated. Fewer traders put to sea. Every harbour would be on guard. A voyage to Africa would offer an unprotected coast, a hospitable base at Sierra Leone and a welcome diversion before either a return to the Americas or an excursion to the area of the Red Sea whee the opulent East Indiamen sailed.

The ships anchored in an inconspicuous bay on Dominica. Roberts was arrogantly confident that to land on the very island he had just pillaged was an insurance against surprise, especially as they were well hidden from view by the gorge in which they camped. Dominica had a succession of ravines, each with a stream at the foot of the valley. Fish abounded. At night the pirates drank around their fires, reminiscing about St. Barthélemy to which everyone vowed to return. Stories were told of ghost ships, of cannibals whose heads were planted in their chests. Dominica had its own mystery.

High in the mountains there was a lake in the mouth of an extinct volcano. It was always silent and whatever the season it was always cold. Natives believed that it was bottomless and that anything thrown into it would sink for ever until the goddess who had given birth to the world received the gift to her bosom.

Others thought that the lake was joined by an underground tunnel to an inlet on the coast called the Abyss. It was rumoured that a few years earlier a traveller had climbed to the lips of the volcano to look at the still waters below. At the very centre of the lake he saw a monstrous serpent with a sparkling jewel between its eyes that illuminated everything around it. The traveller stared aghast, unable to move. Slowly the beast raised its head, looked venomously around it and sank without sound into the depths.[20] There were no volunteers amongst the pirates to test the truth of the story.

Two days later as Roberts sat in his even more richly furnished Great Cabin Gillespie and two men tried to get away and were caught. A trial was agreed. The entire crew assembled in the *Royal Fortune*'s steerage. Judges were selected and the charges against the sailing-master and the two men with him were read out. No one held much hope for Gillespie. He denied nothing but stood before the judges with their punchbowl and pipes as the accusations against him were confirmed. The fugitives had been captured as they climbed the hills hoping to reach the towns on the other side of the island. That would have led to vessels sailing out to trap the pirates. It was desertion.

The judges whispered together. 'Maroon' was heard. 'Shooting'. Suddenly Ashplant jumped up, flinging his pipe to the deck where it broke in a crack of splintering clay. 'By God, Gillespie shall not die. Damn me if he shall'. The judges surrounded him, arguing fiercely. Ashplant ignored them.

'God damn you, gentlemen', he swore, 'I am as good a man as the best of you, damn my soul if I ever turned my back to any man in my life, or ever will, by God. Gillespie is an honest fellow, notwithstanding this misfortune, and I love him, Devil damn me if I don't. I hope he'll live and repent of what he has done, but damn me, if he must die, I will die with him'.

Charles Johnson described the sequel. 'And thereupon, he pulled out a pair of Pistols, and presented them to some of the learned Judges on the Bench; who perceiving his Argument so well supported, thought it reasonable that Glasby should be acquitted; and so they came over to his Opinion, and allowed it to be Law'. His companions were shot.[21]

Gillespie was led below. He would never again be allowed ashore unless under guard. He would enjoy no secret confidence of Roberts but would be given orders until he became resigned to the life of piracy.

Through the days and nights the squadron sailed northwards towards the area of winds that would bear them eastwards to Africa. The brig became leaky and was abandoned. The second sloop was cast adrift because there was insufficient plunder to fill her. Near the latitude of the Bermudas they turned towards the African coast. It was mid-November, 1720.

In London His Majesty's men-of-war *Enterprise* and *Swallow* having fitted out at Portsmouth went to Spithead to await the arrival of the Royal African Company's fleet. The *Enterprise* was found to be unseaworthy and the two ships returned to Portsmouth. After more delay the *Weymouth*, Captain Mungo Herdman, was chosen as a substitute. On board as her mate was the real-life Robinson Crusoe, Alexander Selkirk. Having abandoned his 'wife', Sophia Bruce a year earlier, on 12 December 1720, he married Frances Candis, an attractive widow with a public house in Oreston, Plymouth. Selkirk made a new will leaving everything to her.

Idly the *Swallow* waited as the *Weymouth* careened and stored provisions of corned beef, beef, pork, pease, oatmeal, butter, cheese and water.[22]

On 25 March 1721 *Applebee's Original Weekly Journal* reported:

'A pirate of 40 guns and 2 smaller ships cause havoc on the coast of Carthegena and St. Martha (West Indies). They have taken several rich French ships from Petit-Guaves and 2 Dutch and about 5 English ships and sloops. But we hear since that the pirates have left for Cuba and design to go from there to Martinico. They take any nation's ships. What exploits our men of war have done against them we hear but little'.

11

Misfortunes for the Navy

November 1720–April 1721

'Our merchants have advice that H.M. sloop the *Shark* of 10 guns and 90 men having lately sailed from Antegoa in quest of the pyrates on the Coast of St. Christophers had the bad luck to be taken by them'.

Weekly Journal, 3 February, 1722.

The movements of the *Swallow* and the *Weymouth* were unknown to the pirates. Nor would they have worried them. They had become accustomed to the tales of naval ships that were always about to chase them yet never seemed to stir from harbour.

Captain Whitney continued to ignore requests to pursue Roberts and returned to Massachusetts for repairs. He added that it was not only repairs that were needed. He had lost twenty-five men through sickness and desertion and would be forced to find replacements as the Leeward Isles were infested with pirates. Probably he press-ganged a crew from a merchantman because the *Rose* came back to Nevis and Governor Hamilton a few months later.[1]

He would not have found the pirates. They were off to Africa with a full cargo to splurge in the delights of Sierra Leone. The massive *Royal Fortune* and la Palisse's sloop sailed casually northwards on the weather side of the Leeward Isles with only anticipation of the revelry ahead.

About thirty leagues east of the Bermudas they bore down on a vessel. There was so much eagerness to be in the boarding-party and win a fresh set of clothes that Anstis was compelled to draw up a rota for volunteers so that each man should have a chance. There was no fear of hurt. so confident were they that any ship would fall without risk that its capture seemed a feat no more difficult than walking into a shop whose proprietor was giving his stock away. The *Thomas Emmanuel* was no exception. At the first shot Captain Thomas Bennett hauled down his flag and waited impotently for the plundering. All his crew save himself and one fellow who had protested at the theft of his possessions and had his arm broken for his ignorance were taken aboard the *Royal Fortune*. Bennett's ship was towed behind it.[2]

Just after midnight they set sail south-westwards before the unreliable winds that would bear them to Africa. The sea rose in a steady, nasty swell. An hour later with the weather worsening Bennett realised that his lightened vessel was in danger of sinking. Roberts had wanted the brig as a storeship but the weather was defeating him just as the poor condition of his previous ship had. A launch brought Bennett and his seamen to the *Royal Fortune*, the towrope was cut and the *Thomas Emmanuel* was freed to the roaring waves that would engulf her.

The pirate fleet voyaged on before the high winds, their sails reefed, their masts void of flags. Ahead of them, thousands of miles away, were the Cape Verde islands where they would water before heading for Sierra Leone. The storm sped them along. Within three weeks they were close to the islands and had they not sighted some ships they would have landed within the day.

The pirates turned towards the two merchantmen before noticing that they were escorted by a pair of Portuguese men-of-war of gigantic size, one of forty guns, the other a colossus of eighty ship-blasting cannon. Together they outgunned the pirates three to one. But Roberts remembered Bahia. He attacked. La Palisse was hesitant. The *Royal Fortune*'s crew were not. They were not mistaken. Hardly had Dennis run out his guns than the Portuguese moved off with all sails spread leaving the merchantmen defenceless.

The attack had taken the pirates farther to leeward than they anticipated. In that latitude the winds blew constantly off the African shores and unless navigation was precise a ship would be unable to reach the coast. Roberts cursed the impetuosity that had caused him to chase two insignificant traders. He had been moving gently towards the Cape Verde islands. Now, lying so far to the south-west, it would require nice judgement to bring them to land. He decided to head towards Brava, the southernmost of the islands. Jones reckoned their latitude with a quarterstaff. Roberts calculated their longitude as best he could.

In the afternoon of the following day as the winds blew steadily across the deck away from the land an island came into view to port. The pirates began the long tack that would take them ashore if they were lucky. By evening it was clear that they had failed. The island was still three or four leagues away and being left behind.

Gillespie tried to swing the *Royal Fortune* about for another run towards land but skilful as he was they ended farther away than ever with night closing rapidly. The sea was too deep for anchoring. By morning they were alone in the uninterrupted ocean under an unceasing wind travelling south-westwards towards the Americas. It was then discovered that there was just one barrel of water for the entire complement with their nearest harbour in Surinam six weeks away.

A frantic search found nothing but empty casks with which they had been so liberal. The thoughts of Sierra Leone had made them forgetful of the dangers of the sea. Now they were being driven farther and farther from land with scarcely a week's supply of water between them.

Next day they rationed the water to a cupful a day. Some said that inhaling the sea-wind would quench their thirst but those that tried ended with a fierce dryness in their throats next morning. Men slumped in the shade, eating too much, brooding angrily at the sea around them.[3]

Within a week they were out in the Atlantic deeps. Roberts and Gillespie agreed to try for South America. Days passed and the water was rationed to a mouthful a day. Anstis guarded the dwindling barrel. Lookouts were posted in case some ship should appear but the sea was empty and the days dragged agonisingly on. The weak-willed drank seawater, found their thirst greater than before, drank more and died screaming in madness. Their bodies were dropped over the side leaving more water for the survivors. Others drank their own urine and for a while improved. But as the days continued their water darkened and as they drank it again and again they returned to their bodies the poison that finally killed them.

In such straits crews had been known to drain corpses of their blood, something to be done within two hours of death before coagulation. The heart also could be eaten though the rest of the body was too bitter even for starving men. In the *Royal Fortune* those who still lived moistened their lips with brine to prevent them glueing together. Around them lay the dying, feverish, moaning, begging in thickened voices for water. Those who almost starved themselves fared best. A mouthful of bread each day was enough to keep them alive and reduced their thirst. Others ate much and perished.

When there was rain they trapped it in canvas canopies, dribbling it into buckets, pails, containers. One precious night when a rare fog surrounded the ship they hung up linens and cottons that the mist dampened. The great cask that Anstis guarded was almost dry.

Then the food was gone. In the water-barrel there were still some greenish, thickening dregs but every mouthful of bread and rancid meat had been eaten and the only sustenance was the occasional fish caught on lines hanging over the sides baited with hard leather from a dead man's shoe.

The sun rose over them. Wispy clouds evaporated. The wind still filled the sails but no one cared. The fishlines hung unattended. Through the heat of noon and the afternoon's haze they sailed onwards with the whipstaff lashed down because there was no one strong enough to hold it. Shadows of sunset outlined the decks like the ribs of skeletons. Squawking birds overhead seemed to mock them in the evening light.

Half-conscious pirates stared at the gulls as they circled and swooped around the mastheads. Birds were never far from land. Somewhere there could be an island, a coastline, some source of water that by morning could be far behind them as they passed it unseen in the night.

By next morning there was land in sight and they sailed towards it suddenly strong with the strength of men saved from death. They sent a barrel-laden boat and it returned with clear spring water that only will-power prevented them from gulping. There was sufficient for all of them and for la Palisse's sloop but there was no food. They had landed near the mouth of the Maroni river in Surinam, a wild place with no township nearby and nowhere where meat could be found. They were untroubled. They would live. As one of them said, 'Providence which gave them Drink would, no doubt, bring them Meat also if they would use but an honest Endeavour'.[4]

The last days of 1720 saw the great *Royal Fortune* and the *Good Fortune* sloop taking in water and provisions at the island of Tobago where they learned of the two sloops that the governor of Martinique had long ago sent after them at Carriacou. Roberts still swore revenge. He was hardened in his role of a pirate captain. What the years of honest seafaring had given him in experience the months of piracy had added in caution and suspicion. He rarely asked advice except from Gillespie. He accepted the carelessness, sloth and brutality of men who accepted discipline only because of the booty he provided. He could never escape them. There was no chance of his amassing a fortune and retiring to Wales or settling in the Americas.

Early in January they were off Barbados. It was not a shore to dawdle by after their experience of Rogers and the *Summersett*. There was no prospect of plunder and they sailed on to Pigeon Island, a small piece of land about a mile north-west of St. Lucia. On the morning of 13 January Richard Simes of the *Fisher* brig was anchored in a small cove shared with Benjamin Norton's Rhode Island sloop when Roberts and la Palisse entered. Guns were taken from Simes' vessel. Norton's sloop which had run ashore was on fire.

Its captain, closeted with Roberts, suggested that he could dispose of any plunder on behalf of the pirates easily and profitably in Rhode Island. Provisions and supplies were always needed there, particularly at prices undercutting those of traders, even of Dutch interlopers. Roberts was interested but non-committal. Robert Dunn had made a similar proposal at St. Christophers only to be captured, probably at the cost of his life and certainly at a considerable loss to the pirates.

For a fortnight the pirates hovered around St. Lucia, gobbling up small craft like John Rogers' *St. Anthony* sloop, forcing some men, putting others ashore, compelling a surgeon to join them, giving captured vessels to favoured prisoners. Roberts entertained his captives, cynically observing over their glasses of wine that 'there is none of you but will hang me, I know, whenever you can clinch me within your power'. When his huge Dutch ship and the brig sailed out, the old *Good Fortune* sloop having been burned as useless, they left the coast littered with stranded seamen and ruined ships. Simes sailed in the opposite direction. He had been one of the lucky ones and was now the possessor of Pomier's sloop. With him he took Captain Bennett who had endured the privations of the Atlantic nightmare.[5]

Roberts was still considering Norton's proposal when they

came to Dominica and sighted yet another interloper. Once again the Dutch fought. The battle did not last long. Roberts now sailed in a ship as big as his prey's and soon the *El Puerto del Principe* from Flushing was being towed out of the harbour.

The captains of two puny pirate ships, Porter and Tuckerman, joined, flattering Roberts, 'having heard of his Fame and Atchievments, they had put in there to learn his Art and Wisdom in the Business of pyrating, being Vessels on the same honourable Design'.[6] They also made it plain that they had no intention of staying long. They had business enough already but they could help for a short while, especially if they were provided with some powder for their guns.

By the end of January the guns of the Basseterre forts on Guadaloupe were vainly thundering out on a fleet that sailed impudently by them with no flags flying except on the brig whose French colours streamed briefly before they were hauled down. The brig entered the harbour, fired several times at a flyboat too far from the shore for safety, boarded it, cut its lines and took it out beyond the range of the forts. Luckily for the flyboat's crew they had fled ashore as their danger was realised.[7] One who escaped was Richard Halliard. Six days later at Martinique he met Charles Elliott just in from St. Thomas. Elliott had hardly left port than he had been chased back again by the same pirates that had scared Halliard.

For once the Navy had not been absent and it may have been an awareness of its unusual victory that sent Roberts to Hispaniola to career and carouse. Whereas the recalcitrant Whitney was almost an ally of the pirates Durrell of the *Seahorse* was a formidable opponent, patrolling the coasts of Barbados and Martinique. Three months before at Boston the Council of Massachusetts suggested that he go southwards to protect the West Indian colonies. Within a fortnight he was at sea. Three weeks later he was at Barbados just a few days behind Roberts. Unfortunately the wind was blowing steadily from the north-east and even though he knew that the pirates were plaguing shipping around Martinique Durrell was unable to reach that island until February. He had already sent a despatch to Massachusetts stating that he needed ninety more men and some ammunition.[8]

By 2 February, the month that the *Swallow* and *Weymouth* left for Africa, he had cajoled and press-ganged eighty-six men from Barbados and the unusual weather had abated. Yet hardly had he set out than the winds returned and he struggled against a strong north-westerly sea. Four days out and he met a Martinician sloop and learned that the pirates had been there but gone to leeward. Realising that his quarry might be anywhere and discouraged by the pounding, antagonistic seas Durrell returned to Barbados. Three weeks later Bartholomew Roberts was over seven hundred miles away.

He had intended to careen on Mona Island west of Puerto Rico but finding the sea running too high he went a hundred miles north-west to Hispaniola and the lovely Bay of Samana with its many coral reefs and calmer currents. Porter and Tuckerman departed for their homes in Jamaica where they assumed the roles of honest merchants. They promised to return as soon as they might. Roberts was not impatient. After the long and ruinous voyage from Africa both his men and his ships needed a rest. He had adequate supplies of wine, spirits and food.

A week passed jovially with recently forced men cleaning and mending the vessels under the supervision of the carpenters. Old hands lolled under the palms, retold stories, drank, gambled on lizard races. To add to their cheer there was rumfustian and its demon brother, rumbullion.

For that catastrophic brew two huge vats were rowed ashore and filled with molasses, skimmings of overripe fruit, a minimum of water and a liberal splashing of sulphuric acid. The liquid fermented for eight days while a still was constructed. A complicated system of pipes arranged vertically in a trough of water led from a capacious copper vessel over a fire to a spiral tube under a cooling waterfall that continually dribbled over it. A pewter tankard was set under the spiral and drop by paralytic drop the rumbullion filled it. Only the most foolhardy of the pirates drank more than one mug.

Norton continued to cajole Roberts. Porter and Tuckerman came back but they were not to enjoy freedom for long. Already they were suspected in Port Royal. Porter was doubted because he had been on New Providence when Woodes Rogers had arrived with his Pardon. Porter took it and promptly sailed out with his brother and other veteran pirates, excused of all past crimes but intent on committing new ones.

Tuckerman was known to associate with pirates, having helped one, Stede Bonnet, to escape from prison, a man who had turned to piracy to get away from a nagging wife. Tuckerman was jailed until Bonnet was recaptured.[9] In Jamaica it was believed that he worked with Porter and had signed an agreement to share spoils taken by him. It was not piracy, however, but the misguided patriotism of Tuckerman's friends that led to his downfall.

H.M. ship *Mary* lay at anchor in Port Royal, Jamaica. At two o'clock in the afternoon of 10 June the silence was broken by five shots from the *Adventure* galley alongside the wharf. Five more shots rang out. Irritated, Captain Vernou ordered Lieutenant Swale to learn the reason for the noise. Tuckerman was at the house of Mr Pendigrass with other guests having dinner with Colonel James who had ordered that five shots were to be fired from the *Adventure* each time he waved a handkerchief. Swale forbade any more firing.

Thirty minutes later there were further shots. Swale took an armed boat to the *Adventure* where he was told that James had countermanded Swale's instructions. The lieutenant promptly took the diners to the man-of-war where Vernou questioned them asking James why he had ignored Swale's orders.[10] When the colonel impertinently replied that he had only been merrymaking he was reminded that 10 June happened to be the birthday of James Stuart, the Old Pretender, whose rebellion, the first Jacobite Rising, had failed in 1715. He had fled to France early in 1716, exactly five years ago. Five years. Five shots. The unwarranted salutes could well be misconstrued as treason to His Hanoverian Majesty, George I.

James was released with a stern warning but Tuckerman was detained on suspicion of 'notorious crimes'. He and other prisoners from the Jamaican gaols were sent to England and by September he was standing trial in London on a charge of piracy. His fate is unknown.

Months before that, on Hispaniola, Gillespie and ten others ran away early one morning while other pirates were asleep. Avoiding a marsh too treacherous to cross they headed towards a forested barrier of hills. They had only one small pocket compass and before long they were lost in the wilderness. Their aimless turnings and zigzaggings brought them back to the waterside and the pirates.

Gillespie insisted that he had not tried to escape. His companions backed him. One pointed out that he had always been active on board. Another reminded their accusers that he had been first to board several prizes. A third asked how it was that if they deserted they had come back to the ships. In the end their protestations of innocence saved them from death.

The cargo of the interloper was examined and found full of valuables and easily tradeable goods. Roberts summoned Norton. Commodities such as cocoa, flour and other foodstuffs were useless to the pirates but to Norton they were exactly the items he could smuggle without fear. Jewellery and money were incriminating. Buckets, bundles of cotton and tools were not. He was given the *El Puerto*, a skeleton crew of his own men who were unlikely to confess to the Rhode Island authorities and a hold filled with food, ironmongery and cloths that could be sold untraceably. Having disposed of the plunder he was to meet Roberts off the South Carolina coast within six or seven weeks. There would be more for him.

Roberts realised that an intermediary like Norton could save him much inconvenience. As long as the pirates replenished Norton's cargo they would receive cash. They would no longer have to discard unwanted articles and jettison worthless crates at sea. Instead, they could make a few short trips, keep everything they took, wait for Norton and then sail off to St. Bartholomew or St. Thomas or some other welcoming haven where every amenity desirable to pirates was provided.

It was a simple scheme. Norton would not betray them because the trader would gain from every voyage. With two ships the pirates had space enough to load Norton's brig to the full. All they had to find was the plunder and recent experiences had given Roberts the solution. There was no need to lurk for small merchantmen scuttling from island to island with a few miserable bales and barrels. There were ports to be attacked with whole flotillas of traders waiting for capture. There were Dutch interlopers with bulging lower decks. Roberts was the only pirate bold enough to overcome such adversaries but so much the better. And there was the governor of Martinique who had not yet been punished for sending two armed ships after them.

On 18 February the harbour on St Lucia again reverberated to the booming of guns as the pirates attacked the interloper lying in the roads.[11] Townspeople watched fascinated as Roberts closed on the Dutch vessel, attempted to board her, was repulsed as the defenders threw out booms and fenders to prevent the *Royal Fortune* coming alongside. Roberts stood off and bombarded the interloper with a shattering cannonade while la Palisse slid around his victim, pounding at her stern, raking her open decks with swivel-shot. When the Dutch guns were stilled pirates swarmed in, leaping onto the rigging, swinging across on lines, clambering up the sides, yelling, shouting, waving their cutlasses as they slithered on the greasy planking and smashed open the hatches where the survivors crouched. The inhabitants of St. Lucia heard pistol shots, saw bodies flung into the water, noticed the pirate quartermaster with a yellow kerchief about his heard ordering cables to be passed from the captured vessel to the large pirate ship. The interloper was towed away. As she left the harbour a wounded survivor jumped from its side and tried to swim to shore. Moments later he disappeared.

Bartholomew Roberts was ready for vengeance. The damaged interloper was repaired to be a decoy. When the carpenters were done he, Anstis, Jones and other seasoned pirates boarded her. The *Royal Fortune* and the *Good Fortune* voyaged southwards. Roberts sailed to Martinique for retribution.

At dawn the interloper was off the Martinician coast. Her Dutch flags signalled to the islanders that there were negro slaves for sale. Past Vauclin she sailed, and Sainte Marie, Morrain and St. Pierre, Schoelcher and the Fort de France, at every place lingering so that her message should be seen. Then she went to the bay of St. Luce at the south of the island, an accepted centre for illegal transactions.[12]

Within two or three days little sloops were pouring out of Martinique carrying gold with them. The captain of the first outdistanced his rivals and scrambled up the ladder only to find a pistol at his head. The bag of coins was snatched from him and he was thrown heavily down a hatchway. One by one the other sloops fell into the trap. By evening there were fourteen of them side by side under cover of the interloper's great guns. Their captains and crews were secure below deck. Their money filled a chest. Roberts was ready to exact justice.

It was vindictive, unjustified and cruel to innocent men. They were beaten, whipped, some men shot or cutlassed. Thirteen sloops burned to their waterlines and sank. Only when the last wretch was cut down did the pirates stop. He was thrown into the remaining sloop where his thrashed fellows cringed. The interloper swung out of the bay. The tiny sloop with torn sails and injured seamen crept back to Martinique to tell of Bartholomew Roberts' revenge. 'He said he hoped we should always meet with such a Dutch trade as this was', the horrified governor was told.

Despaches and letters were sent between Martinique and Antigua where Governor Hamilton still tried to persuade Whitney to chase Roberts. The naval captain appeared willing to comply. 'I do not mind whether I water at St. Christophers or Guadaloupe', he wrote on 20 February. 'Just let me know where the pirates are'.[13] As Whitney was at Antigua Hamilton was able immediately to order him to Martinique. Whitney left. By the first of March he wrote to Hamilton triumphantly. 'Martinique's governor knows nothing of the pirates. They were probably just smugglers'. Two days later in a squall off the Bay of Biscay Alexander Clark, a seaman in the *Weymouth*, fell from the topsail and drowned. 1721 was not a good year for the Navy.

On 13 March the governor of Martinique wrote two despatches. The first to Whitney said that the pirates had left Dominica. The other to Hamilton stated that the pirates had definitely gone and that he was no longer fitting out vessels to pursue them. Two frigates were coming from France and their captains would be given what information he had. He sent Hamilton two barrels of red wine.

Whitney told Hamilton that he was going to St. Christophers for water and was ordered to consult Governor Mathew who had a deposition about the pirates. Whitney responded, 'You cannot order me but I serve my King's good'. At this defiant reminder of the constant conflict between the Navy and colonial governors Hamilton sent another despatch. 'I enclose a copy of my instructions which give me power to suspend commanders of His Majesty's ships who neglect their duties. Do not disobey orders. I shall still write them to you'. Whitney answered. 'I shall take no notice of that. Captain Pomeroy had seized two French sloops that may be pirates'. With that non-sequiter Whitney left Antigua on 6 April.

'I am sailing', he told Hamilton, 'because of the deposition John Lamb has given to Lieutenant-General Mathew that there are pirates in St. Lucia. I have ordered the *Shark* to Antigua to consult with you'. He then sailed not to St. Lucia but to St. Christophers. It made no difference. Roberts had been gone for a month and was roistering on St. Barthélmy a mere eighty miles from the unenterprising captain. Indeed, while Hamilton and Whitney squabbled he had captured the *Lloyd* galley of twelve guns and eighteen men almost within sight of Antigua.

On 24 June *The Weekly Journal or British Gazetteer* printed an extract from Captain Andrew Kingston's letter to his employers. He had left London in February bound for Jamaica.

From St. Christophers. 24 April, 1721.

'I am sorry to give you this account of my great misfortune in my voyage. On the 26th of March I made the island of Desirade about eleven o'clock of noon and soon after I saw two sail standing the same course as I did. I made the best of my way from them but about eight at night they came alongside me. I was then about four leagues from Antigua. They fired at me, being pirates, one a ship of thirty-six guns and two hundred and fifty men and fifty negroes; the other a brig of eighteen guns, forty-six men and twenty negroes; these I could not withstand. They had been but two days upon that station before they saw me, and are both under the command of Captain John Roberts. They carried me into Bermuda, there kept me five days, and what of the cargo was not fit for their purpose they threw overboard. They took away most of my rigging and sails, all my anchors, blocks, provisions, powder, small arms etc. and twelve of my men, and then carried me to the northward that I might not come into these islands to give an account of them; and the first of this instant they left me in latitude 30°N in a very sad condition'.

Next day the doubly-unlucky Kingston was overcome by a Spanish pirate and marooned. He was saved by a passing ship and reached St. Christophers where Whitney was told of his mishaps. The *Rose* put to sea, found nothing in a feeble search and returned to port. Kingston's letter continued:

'I hope the ships bound from London to Jamaica soon after me may escape the said Roberts: for he designed to keep the station and destroy all the ships that come to these islands which may fall into his hands. They left me without any manner of clothing; and Roberts brought my brother (the chief mate) to the gears and whipped him within an inch of his life by reason he had concealed two gold rings in his pocket. This is the dismal account I am to give of this voyage.

A. Kingston'.

As a resigned postscript he added. 'The pirates captured at Santa Cruz are in prison here but may not be hanged'.

Kingston had not meant Bermuda but Barbuda, an island not far north of Antigua, and he neglected to itemise what the pirates had spurned: coppers, stills, saddles and bales of dry goods.

He was not responsible for the rumour that Roberts now commanded a French ship seized on its way from Martinique to France, the island's governor on board being hanged from the yardarm. According to *The Weekly Journal or British Gazetteer* of 29 July 1721, Walter Kennedy repeated the story at his trial, saying 'that Roberts could have no peace of mind if only for murdering the French governor'. If true, Roberts must have revelled at the sight of his enemy's execution.[14] He had had his revenge. The pirates had enjoyed themselves on St. Barthélmy and went northwards to meet Norton.

On their way they chased a vessel into New Providence where, once in the harbour, it felt safe. But at night three longboats filled with pirates crept towards it before being accidentally sighted by a man-of-war's six-oared pinnace which, having given the alarm, fled before a fusillade of bullets. The terrified merchantman hoisted every sail and retreated into the depths of the port.

In the darkness the man-of-war did not feel capable of seeking the pirates. Alone, helped by no one, Joseph Slinger, a forced man on board the *Royal Fortune*, jumped from her side crying, 'I shall be drowned' and optimistic that the pirates would not search for him swam all night until the tide washed him ashore.[15]

There were hysterical reports of a large pirate vessel off the coast of Maryland, or off Virginia, or off Brazil lying in wait for the Portuguese Fleet that in 1721 had only one man-of-war to protect it which 'considering the pusillanimity of their defenders . . . will be put little security against the bold, desperate attacks of these hardy knaves, the Pyrates'.[16]

Another report said that Roberts was going to Virginia to avenge the pirates executed there, a reference to Kennedy's deserters who had taken ship with the quaker, Captain Knot, a year before. Governor Spotswood bullied his Council into having batteries of guns erected at the mouths of the James River, York and Rappannahock, to have fifty-four cannon ready to repel any piratical invasion. He also wrote to London repeating that a man-of-war of at least forty or fifty guns was necessary to patrol the coast.

Roberts waited for Norton but his accomplice did not appear. Impatient, la Palisse returned to the West Indies taking a captured sloop with him. His *Good Fortune* was given to Anstis who grumbled because the ship was being used to store Norton's second load of cargo. Roberts was irritated by Norton's continuing absence.[17]

In Antigua matters worsened between Hamilton and Whitney. At the end of April the naval captain wrote that he was searching for a French ship, actually Kingston's, reputedly taken by Roberts to Barbuda and then captured by a French, actually Spanish, pirate named Nicholaus. This garbled account did not impress Hamilton who retorted that if Whitney had obeyed orders he would probably have met the pirates. Whitney was to explore the seas around Desirade and then take Hamilton to the Leeward Isles.[18]

By the middle of May the governor's patience was exhausted and he wrote to London complaining about Whitney's inactivity. The governor of Martinique had suggested how the pirates might be taken and Hamilton had given details to the captain on 19 February. He then called a meeting of the Council on 21 February asking Whitney to attend but despite waiting until noon the man did not come. Hamilton sent a letter to the *Rose* asking for an explanation. Whitney said he was doing his accounts. He also needed water. Nevertheless he would do his best to catch the pirates.

He was reminded that Hamilton had to go to the Leeward Islands with letters from the Secretary of State and would be ready to leave with five or six days of the messages arriving from England. Whitney, however, sailed the day after the ship came in and did not return until 26 April. He thought Roberts was cruising off Desirade.

There was still no sign of Norton. He was not coming. Since leaving Hispaniola he had sailed the *El Puerto* to Naushon in the Elizabeth Isles, left it there and went on to Rhode Island where he told Joseph Whippole and other comrades of his lucrative arrangements with Roberts. Greedily his friends prepared their sloops while he went back to Naushon. Things went wrong. On his way from Roberts Norton had not resisted bragging of his pact to Samuel Phips, master of a small ship that he met off the Shoals of Nantucket. Phips told this to the first sheriff he found in New England.

Just as foolishly Norton's friends invited other acquaintances to Naushon and inevitably Governor Cranstone of Rhode Island heard of it. Lieutenant Hamilton of the Royal Navy was sent to investigate. As a result, while Norton was distributing plundered sugar, cocoa and other goods to the sloops of

Whippole and comrades in Tarpaulin Bay, the law was converging on him from two directions. Hamilton was the first.

Defiantly Norton refused to allow him on board. The lieutenant returned to Rhode Island for instructions. Whippole, Almy, Pease and others scuttled off. Norton continued selling his wares to merchants who had come from the mainland. Then the sheriff of Bristol County, Massachusetts appeared. Norton followed his erstwhile accomplices.

Hamilton sailed back to Naushon to apprehend Norton but found that the sheriff had anticipated him. The *El Puerto* was impounded. So was Mr Draper's sloop because it was crammed with loot. Norton's ship was taken to Rhode Island. By July the Admiralty had news of the affair which dragged on until August, 1722, when the governor and Council of Rhode Island were told to deliver the proceeds of the sale of the ship and its contents to the Judge of the Vice-Admiralty Court of New England. A brisk reminder followed in September. Of Norton there was no mention. Even as late as January, 1724, Mr Richard Partridge, the agent for Rhode Island, was indignantly refuting the suggestion that his island had a reputation for encouraging piracy. It was not his island's fault that the *Porto Prince* of Flushing had been given to a Rhode Islander named Benjamin Norton by the pirates.[19]

The pirates knew only that there was no sign of Norton. They were out at sea with stores running low, no prizes or plunder for a fortnight, no prospect of celebration, the ship stinking and rotting, overcrowded, all because Roberts had become so arrogant and dismissive that he would listen to no reason. Anstis, the best quartermaster ever, was stuck on a storeship and had been replaced by the unpopular Simpson. The food was disgusting, the drink not much better, and even when Roberts decided that he had waited long enough tempers did not improve. Had he deigned to explain why he had delayed things could have been different. He did not.

When 'Roberts saw there was no managing of such a

Company of ungovernable Brutes, by gentle Means, nor to keep them from drinking to Excess, the Cause of all their Disturbances, he put on a rougher Deportment, and a more magisterial Carriage, correcting whom he thought fit; and if any seemed to resent his Usage, he told them, they might go ashore, and take Satisfaction of him, if they thought fit, at Sword and Pistol, for he neither valued or feared any of them'.[20] It was undiplomatic and it increased the dissatisfaction.

Men performed tasks sullenly. Even taking in water was a chore and it was not surprising when a badly fastened barrel fell and injured a man in the boat below. Roberts cursed the culprit who swore back and spat at the captain who instantly reached for his pistols and killed him. It was a disaster. His victim had been the close friend of Thomas Jones, a pirate of long-standing. There was trouble when Jones returned from shore.

The bereaved Jones was in no mood for conciliation. He looked at the body of his friend and swung round on Roberts, shouting that the captain deserved the same treatment. In fury Roberts 'ran to him with a Sword, and ran him into the Body'. Wounded, Jones reached for a knife in his belt lashing out at the captain who ducked, stumbled off balance and was flung back against a ship's gun. His assailant hit him again and again. Trapped by the man's body Roberts could only ward off the blows until Jones was dragged away amidst a crowd of shouting pirates.[21] A few weeks before they would have been supporting Roberts. Now there was disorder. It was Simpson, the new quartermaster, who ordained that Jones should be whipped for his insult to their commander. It was agreed but without enthusiasm.

Roberts needed action and success. The *Royal Fortune* and the *Good Fortune* scoured the seas of everything they met. Early in April they overpowered a French ship of twenty-six guns after a brief engagement that left them infuriated. The ship they kept, naming her the *Sea King*, but those of her crew that still lived were marooned on the most desolate island they could find.[22] A few days later they took a Virginiaman who must have been aghast at the sight of three ships bearing down on her with their black flags guttering in the sharp Atlantic winds. She was stripped of everything including men that were needed for the pirates' extra vessel.

One night in the middle of April just as the three ships set course for Africa the *Good Fortune*, Captain Thomas Anstis, deserted with Thomas Jones and other disaffected mutineers.[23] There was nothing Roberts could do. It was better that those who were against him should leave rather than have traitors plotting on board. As long as he continued to gather in pickings for his two remaining crews he would be unchallenged.

So they plundered a Dutch ship and a little snow and sailed eastwards towards the coast of Guinea. By October Captain Whitney, now resting at Port Royal, was able to write, 'There has not been any account of the pirates lately, but believe they have gone over to the Cape d'Verde islands'.[24] In the Cape Verde islands there was no doubt. Already the *Norman* galley had been ransacked, a minor event notable only for the fact that Benjamin Jeffrys who had been forced told his captors 'that none who could get their bread in an honest way would be in such an account' and received six lashes from each dishonest man for his effrontery.[25]

Earlier, on 5 February, the *Swallow* and the *Weymouth* left Britain, escorting eleven Royal African Company ships to Africa: the *Royal Africa*, *Martha*, *Widaw* and sloop, *Gambia Castle* and sloop, *Cape Coast Castle* and sloop, *Greyhound* sloop, *Congo* sloop and *Accra* sloop.[26] In spite of poor weather they passed the Madeiras and by the end of March came to the Cape Verde islands a few weeks before Roberts. The *Weymouth* went to the Gambia river while the *Swallow* took the merchantmen to Sierra Leone. On 7 April the agent, Plunket, wrote from his repaired fort on Bence Island that the *Swallow* had arrived.

Mishap had still blighted the Navy. On 31 March at St. Mary Island at the mouth of the River Gambia the *Weymouth* ran aground on a sandbank and could not be refloated for four days. At Sierra Leone the *Swallow* was overlight in the river and Captain Chaloner Ogle had her bottom unplugged to let in water and restore her balance. Forgetfully the plug was only replaced when nearly two metres of water had flooded the bilges.[27]

Happy to be away from the Americas Bartholomew Roberts finished his business at the Cape Verde islands and decided to work his way down the coast to Sierra Leone where his crews would be safe to celebrate. Prey and hunters were converging.

12

Deserters and Disasters

April 1721–May 1724

'On 11 May, 1723, Captain Orm of H.M. *Winchelsea* brought 9 pyrates to Antegoa. Two had been forced so gave evidence against the rest. Captain Finn, once with the infamous pyrate Roberts was commander of the brig *Good Fortune*. Four others were executed with him on 20 May, 1723. As one was about to be hanged it was found he had been forced so was reprieved at the foot of the gallows'.

CO 239/1. St. Christopher. No. 28.

Anstis and Jones had no wish to go to Africa. Anstis, a slow-thinking man, could not understand why the pirates had to leave the West Indies when those islands provided so much wealth. Conceited because of his physical strength he believed he could be as successful a commander as Roberts.[1]

Supported by the embittered Jones he voted to return to the Americas. With Bartholomew Roberts thousands of miles away across the Atlantic and with the smaller crew of the deserters' *Good Fortune* plunder would go farther.

Anstis was the worst type of pirate, attacking only when peril was at its least but in victory vicious. It was characteristic of him that once free of Roberts he devised no tactics of his own but blundered from island to island always hoping, never planning.

His first prize, the day after his desertion, was the *Inwen*. From her a carpenter, John Phillips, was forced. Then followed the little *Two Sisters* whose captain, Richards, suffered no harm probably because Anstis was elated at his cleverness in catching her.[2] The *Two Sisters* was not a rich vessel and the *Good Fortune* turned southwards towards the West Indies where trade would be more widespread.

Anstis sailed towards Martinique and ignorant of the proximity of the two French men-of-war floundered into them off Montserrat. Managing to get away after a brief fight his men went on to commit one of their vilest acts. The *Weekly Journal* of 13 January 1722, reported it.

'Our merchants have received the following advice from St. Christophers dated 15 October 1721, that they were in daily expectation of the arrival of the new governor, with some men-of-war along with him which they very much wanted. That the *Hector* man-of-war, Captain Brand, having buried most of her crew could then do but little service.[3] That several pirate ships infested the coast where one carrying thirty guns and four hundred men some days before had engaged two French men-of-war. She carried a black flag at her topmasthead. The action took place off Montserrat but she got away from them and bore away from Antegoa. That five men were newly come in there that did belong to the *Inwen*, Captain Ross, from Cork in Ireland having on board six hundred barrels of beef besides other provisions which ship was taken off Martinico by a pirate sloop well mounted with guns and one hundred and forty men. That Colonel Doyly of Montserrat with his family was on board the said vessel and was very much cut and wounded by the pirates. That twenty-one of these brutes had forced a

189

woman passenger one after another and afterwards broke her back and flung her into the sea'.

The Colonel had been attacked when he went to the assistance of the woman being raped.

Charles Johnson was open-minded about Anstis' involvement in this outrage. 'I will not be positive it was Anstis's crew that enacted this unheard of Violence, and Curelty, tho' the Circumstances of the Place, the Time, the Force of the Vessel, and the Number of Men, do all concur, and I can place the Villainy no where else'.[4]

Shortly afterwards, between Jamaica and Hispaniola, Anstis took Captain Marston[5] robbing him of liquor, provisions, clothes and five men. He then captured the *Hamilton* on June 22.[6] That ship was taken to Mohair Key where the pirates lay for several weeks indolently enjoying their spoils. Thirteen men had been forced. Among them were John Finn and John Phillips, the carpenter from the *Inwen*. They joined Anstis, Jones and Roberts' former partner, Montigny la Palisse. Phillips and Finn were to become dominant.[7]

In September the *Hamilton* was returned to Smith and with a reduced crew he gladly quitted the pirates who took to the seas again heading towards the Bay of Campechy in the Gulf of Mexico over a thousand miles from Jamaica. Of the two Spanish ships they encountered one was burned and the other driven ashore. The miserable loot amounted to no more than ten pounds in coin and some silver buttons and cups, a share for each man of less than three pounds.

Disgruntled they set out next morning only to come upon the *Hamilton* yet again. Once more Smith had been unlucky. He had been taken by a Spanish privateer and his ship was being escorted to Cuba in the hope of prize money. It did not materialise. Like its compatriot off Campechy the privateer was driven aground. Jones mockingly asked Smith if he had returned to look for empty bottles. The thrice-unlucky captain was put in an open boat with what was left of his crew. The *Hamilton* was set on fire.

Anstis had not lived up to his promises of quick and rich takings. All he had achieved in the six months since his desertion was the capture of a few impoverished merchantmen. It was an uneasy record. Men muttered that an extra ship was needed to strengthen them. Anstis knew that if he did not soon meet a well-laden vessel he would be deposed.

The *Don Carlos* provided the needed plunder.[8] Taken near Hispaniola on 21 October she carried £3000 in goods as well as a protesting surgeon. Two of her men were killed and five more forced. Her lines were unsuitable for conversion to piracy but the *Morning Star*, taken a week later, was better.[9] There had been some demur about attacking her because she was big and sturdy but there was no fight. For all her size she had little armament and the pirates towed her to a convenient island where thirty-two of her guns were transferred after her ballast had been jettisoned to compensate for the extra weight. John Finn, a one-handed villain, was elected her captain.

There were conflicting newspaper reports about the episode. On 13 January, 1722, the *Daily Post* was vague but accurate. 'Our merchants have advice that the *Morning Star* belonging to Bristol going from Guinea to Carolina and a ship from Barbados to New York have lately been taken by the pirates'. Differently the *Weekly Journal or Saturday Post* of April 7 was more specific and entirely mistaken with, 'Pirate Shemineau in a sloop of eight guns, sixteen pateroes and ninety men in the West Indies has captured the *Morning Star*, Captain Chacot, a Bristol brig'.

In December the two pirate vessels returned to sea and ransacked the *Portland* of Captain Lubbock, a poor craft hardly worth their efforts, before drifting to Tobago without seeing another sail. Anstis had still not understood what Roberts had swiftly realised, that easy pickings would be where ships were most concentrated and where the risks were higher. It had been at Bahia and Trepassy and St. Christophers and Martinique that

Roberts had won the greater part of his takings, regarding ships at sea as no more than useful supplements to his major income. Anstis relied on those ships.

After the ravaging of one or two more traders the *Good Fortune* and the *Morning Star* idled southwards through the islands and beyond the Lesser Antilles to the desolate speck of Tortuga off the north coast of Venezuela. There at anchor was the *Nightingale*. They kept its captain, Ellwood, under lock and key while his cargo was inspected. It was April, 1722.

For seven weeks they stayed on the island, casually careening their ships while the sun burned down on the palms and the rocks. It was a dreary place only visited by ships in distress. Unorganised, with little to do, grumbling and dissension grew, some pirates wishing to return to sea, others wanting to go to England and an honest life, more arguing that such a dream was unrealistic. The only sensible thing would be to beg for a Pardon. Anstis was helpless. When he tried to persuade the men to return to sea he was reminded of his pathetic plunder. Men turned to Finn for advice. Anstis took to carrying a naked cutlass in his sash in case of mutiny.

Some forced men conspired to steal the *Good Fortune* and run her to the nearest port. An informer betrayed them and from that time both ships were closely guarded. When Anstis raged at them for such cowardice he was deposed as captain of the *Good Fortune*. Bridstock Weaver was elected in his place. In return for a promise that his ship and cargo would be unmolested Captain Ellwood of the *Nightingale* agreed to take a petition to Governor Lawes of Jamaica and bring back the answer.[10]

To His Most Gracious Majesty, by the Grace of God, Of Great Britain France and Ireland Defender of the Faith.

The Humble PETITION of the Company, now belonging to the Ship *Morning Star* and Brigantine *Good Fortune*, lying under the ignominious Name and Denomination of Pyrates, Humbly sheweth:

That we your Majesty's most loyal Subjects have, at sundry Times, been taken by Bartholomew Roberts, the then Captain of the aforesaid Vessels and Company, together with another Ship, in which we left him, and have been forced by him and his wicked Accomplices, to enter into, and serve, in the said Company, as Pyrates, much contrary to our Wills and Inclinations: and we, your loyal Subjects utterly abhorring and detesting that impious Way of Living, did, with a unanimous Consent, and contrary to the Knowledge of the said Roberts or his Accomplices, on, or about, the eighteenth Day of April, 1721, leave, and ran away with the aforesaid Ship *Morning Star* and Brigantine *Good Fortune* with no other Intent and Meaning than the Hopes of obtaining your Majesty's most gracious Pardon. And, that we, your Majesty's most loyal Subjects, may with more Safety return to our native Country and serve the Nation, unto which we belong, in our respective Capacities, without Fear of being prosecuted by the Injured, whose Estates have suffered by the said Roberts and his Accomplices, during our forcible Detainment, by the said Company. We most humbly implore your Majesty's most royal Assent, to this our humble Petition.

And your Petitioners shall ever pray etc.

It was signed and given to Ellwood. The three ships left Tortuga together. The *Nightingale* was released off Newfoundland where the pirates were safe. With her went the Petition and some pirates including Thomas Jones, who had thrashed Bartholomew Roberts, and John Phillips, the forced carpenter who felt confident of a reprieve. Most pirates stayed with Finn who had arranged to meet Ellwood off Cuba in August.

Hardly was the *Nightingale* out of sight than Finn and Weaver turned southwards. They concluded that it would be wise to lie low on Cuba until Ellwood's return. Their petition contained so many lies that further piracy might swiftly bring out the truth as merchant after merchant added his deposition to those already in front of bewildered authorities.

In Jamaica Governor Nicholas Lawes sent the petition to London with a detailed report that he had received it on 6 July 1722, from John Ellwood of St. Christophers, master of the 106-ton *Nightingale* captured by pirates in April off Tortuga. The pirates' captain was Thomas Anstys. Ellwood had been held for seven weeks but after agreeing to carry their petition he was released off Newfoundland. They were by then commanded by John Pinn and had two ships, one of thirty-two guns, the other a brig of twenty-two. They were a company of a hundred and forty-six men with some Spaniards and negroes.

Ellwood, the petition and some apprehensive pirates reached England. In London the matter was not considered urgent. By November Whitehall recommended that the petition be referred to the Council of Trade & Plantations, advising the Council to consult with London merchants who had interests in the West Indies. The Petition with its two pages of Round Robin signatures was transferred to the Council. Early in December Mr Secretary Popple wrote to Joshua Gee asking what he 'and the other merchants may have to offer upon the pirates' petition?' Three days later Mr Harris replied that his colleagues were of a mind to pardon the petitioners. It was too late. August was long past and the suppliants were back on the account.

Life had been tedious on Cuba. For all the games they played, the mock trials they had held, the relaxation, the pirates were bored. Provisions were low, the liquor had been drunk. They left. Sailing southwards they plundered a ship of its food but were watchful. Life was hazardous. Two British men-of-war, the *Hector* and the *Adventure*, were combing the spits of land and were assisted by French warships and Spanish *costagardas*.

In their anxiety to avoid detection Finn and Weaver crept through shallows where they could not be followed but after capturing a sloop they carelessly ran the *Morning Star* aground on Grand Cayman, the largest and westernmost of a group of islands on the Cayman Ridge. Just as Weaver was bringing the *Good Fortune* to take off the scared and stranded men who were in no state to enjoy the island's elegant pines and abundant lilies and orchids the *Adventure* came into view followed by the *Hector*.

In the panic men were abandoned. Finn managed to reach the *Good Fortune* where he took over from Weaver and crammed on all sail to outdistance the pursuing *Adventure*.[11] Then the wind dropped. The two ships lay motionless a few hundred metres apart. Fortunately the pirates were in a brig with oars and the incentive of survival encouraged even the most listless man to heave and strain and very slowly the *Good Fortune* pulled away.

Their comrades on the island watched in despair. Forty were picked up by the *Hector*. Others like George Bradley scrambled into the woods which were so inhospitable that the hideaways were glad to surrender to the captain of a passing sloop. A few luckier got away in a sloop that they had commandeered in the Bay of Honduras.

Finn had to careen the *Good Fortune*. He captured two or three vessels on his way, making the captain of one, Dursey, come with him. With incredible bravado the captain attempted to take over the pirates' brig while many of its men were on shore taking in water. Being apprehended Dursey hurried to land with five others taking pistols and ammunition with them. Coming upon a canoe they set off in it. Finn sent a party after them but it was repelled by a burst of gunfire. It was a rare occasion when prisoners contrived to get away from their captors.

Finn steered the *Good Fortune* along the Windward Passage between Cuba and Hispaniola, took the *Antelope* sloop and some other ships in the first months of 1723 and finally came to Tobago. Several pirates cajoled him into allowing them to return to England in the *Antelope*. Months later they arrived off the north coast of Devon, sank the sloop and landed at night under the ominously-named Little and Great Hangman cliffs by the fishing village of Combe Martin near Ilfracombe. Whether it was the men's unexpected and unexplained arrival or their rowdy behaviour but they ended in the dock of the Old Bailey. Once there Henry Treehill turned King's evidence, saving himself and condemning the others.

On Tobago Finn set his depleted crew to lighten the *Good Fortune* so that she could be thoroughly cleaned. Anstis refused to take part and retired with his cutlass to the shade of the woods. The lacklustre quartermaster joined him and the unsupervised work made slow progress with no one to organise the few sweating, grumbling men as they heaved at the guns and shifted tackle.

His Majesty's man-of-war *Winchelsea* arrived on 11 May. There on the beach was the pirate brig, sails furled, guns withdrawn, no more than a dozen men aboard who abandoned her when the warship was sighted. Captain Orm sent three boatloads of strongly-armed seamen to bring in the fugitives.[12] Nine pirates were caught in the woods but the *Good Fortune* got away. Because of a contrary wind Orm was unable to follow the brig as she slowly squeezed through a maze of shoals. Anstis had escaped with a score of fellows. But Orm had Finn.

The trial was held in Antigua on 17 May. Two of the nine prisoners offered evidence against the rest. Finn was the first to be examined and once it was shown that he had been an associate of 'the infamous pirate Roberts' he was doomed.[13] Five others were also found guilty. One man was acquitted. On the twentieth the six convicted pirates were taken to the high-water mark. Spectators from St. Johns turned out to watch the executions in the harbour of Rat Island. At the last moment a man was freed after proving that he truly had been forced. For the others there was no respite. With chains securing their bodies they were hanged on the gallows. The sea hissed and surfed beneath their bodes as the tide rose.

Governor Hart wrote a commendation about the captains of the men-of-war. 'It is to the indefatigable care of Captain Brand

and Captain Orm in pursuing the pirates wherever they hear of them that the trade in these parts is so secured from that pest, for which they can't be too much recommended'.

Although Finn had been hanged and Anstis had escaped the latter did not benefit. Once they were safe the crew rebelled against a return to piracy. Anstis, the quartermaster and other resolute criminals were murdered as they slept, half a dozen were tied up and the brig was taken to the Dutch settlement of Curacao in the Lesser Antilles. Those that had mutinied were freed by the authorities, the others executed. It was almost the complete end of those who had deserted from Bartholomew Roberts two years before.

Almost but not quite. John Phillips returned to piracy. He had gone to England in the *Nightingale*, had avoided suspicion and was living quietly in Bristol. Although forced from the *Irwen* he had no faith in British justice and had not surrendered himself in the hope of clemency. When he heard that some comrades in Bristol were in the gaol he did not wait to prove his innocence but ran off to Topsham and took ship to Newfoundland.[14]

There he toiled in the cold misery of fish-splitting at St. Peters not far from Roberts' triumph at Trepassy. Whether he was curious to find what had happened to Finn and other colleagues or whether the menial work was too arduous and penurious a life he conspired with fifteen others to seize William Minott's schooner as it lay in harbour.

Only four of the fifteen turned up. It did not deter the four that did. The schooner was not a difficult craft to handle and a couple of prizes would give them plenty of forced men to sail it comfortably. After a quick scuffle they took possession of the ship and next day, 29 August, formally renamed it the *Revenge*, signed Articles, swearing on a hatchet in the absence of a Bible, and elected their officers in the traditional manner of men setting out on the account. John Phillips was captain; John Nutt, sailing-master; James Sparks, the gunner; Thomas Fern, the carpenter. William White, who had joined them from Minott's men, was given no post although the pirates still lacked a quartermaster.

Phillips had courage. Within a week the *Revenge* had substantial booty from three fishing vessels, a schooner and a French ship from which he took a great gun and the welcome gift of thirteen pipes of wine worth £300. John Fillmore and Edward Cheeseman, a carpenter, were conscripted together with Isaac Lassen, John Parsons and an indian. A well-built rogue, Burrill, joined them voluntarily. He was made boatswain. The best signing was John Rose Archer whose appearance and conduct belied his somewhat angelic name. Tall and hefty, his skill with cutlass and pistol impressed Phillips who proposed him as quartermaster. When it was discovered that Archer had served with Blackbeard his election was assured. Phillips was elated. With Nutt, Burrill and Archer he had a quadrumvirate equal to any for villainy.

The *Revenge* took four more ships in October, vessels bigger and more profitable than previous victims: the *Mary* brigantine which gave them clothes and provisions worth £200; another brig; a Portuguese brigantine with an assorted cargo of thirty-six shirts worth £40, brandy and foodstuffs valued at £30, and a £100 negro called Francisco; and the *Content* sloop with its silver and pewter plate, and its first mate, John Masters who was compelled to join them with three others, James Wood, William Taylor and William Phillips.

Despite these successes John Phillips was worried. He could not rely on the loyalty of his crew. Too many had been forced. He locked up his smallarms. For weeks they careened and feasted on the north-east coast of Barbados. No one would expect them there. Coral reefs made the approach difficult and the towns lay to the south. So they reclined in the sunshine while their trapped conscripts sweltered on a boatless deck until the shortage of food caused the *Revenge* to put out to sea.

Off Martinique they sighted a French sloop. With her twelve

guns and numerous crew she was a dubious prospect but Phillips was more concerned with sustenance than peril. For nearly a day the sloop ran before them. For two hours she fought of all attempts to board her. At last the pirates overcame the resistance and her crew were cut down or swung into the sea where expectant sharks gathered.

Two Frenchmen, one a surgeon, survived the massacre and were kept. The pirates still needed men. Phillips lingered off Barbados in the hope that some of the plantation workers would join him. White men on the plantations were hardly better than slaves, sometimes more badly than the negroes, living a life that promised small chance of liberty. Only the vigilance of their overseers prevented these labourers from running away.

They were of two kinds: transportees and indentured servants. The first, convicted criminals, were usually sent to the tobacco plantations of Maryland or Virginia, sentenced to toil in the colonies rather than rot in a British gaol. The length of their sentence was determined by their crime.[15] A contractor shipped such prisoners out at his own cost, relying on his judgement of their worth to make a profit. Prices varied according to the sex, physical condition and the years of penal servitude the man had been given. Whatever was bid for a prisoner the contractor did not lose. He had paid nothing. That accounted for the sickening conditions the white slaves endured on the long sea voyage when jail fever and gangrenous feet killed many in mid-Atlantic. The system was not popular in the America. With so many indentured servants available the unskilled and slovenly criminal riffraff were liabilities, not assets.

Unlike them indentured men went to the Americas of their own free will, signing for a stipulated time of paid service, usually five or seven years, at the end of which they became free men, often receiving a grant of land. The 'Indenture' was the contract written in duplicated columns down a sheet of paper which was ripped down the centre, one half for the master, one for the servant its unevenly dentated edges proving its authenticity.

Such 'redemptioners' were sometimes duped by unscrupulous sea-captains who tricked them into signing indentures on the understanding that on arrival in the colonies they would be given a fixed number of days to find a master of their choice rather than be foisted on some brutal taskmaster. But the men would be kept on board the vessel when it docked until the agreed period elapsed. The captain then proclaimed the contract void and put their credulous victims up for auction, selling them into lifelong slavery.

Children were not exempt. Those younger than eight were unwanted as they habitually died at sea. Older boys and girls were in danger of being kidnapped in England and sold. One kidnapper or 'spirit' bragged that he had averaged five hundred sales annually for twelve years, another that he had despatched eight hundred and fifty children in one year alone.

Given such conditions Phillips expected volunteers. Although many indentured servants could anticipate freedom and land within a few years and had no incentive to turn pirate there were as many who distrusted the unenforceable contract between them and their wealthy employer. Planters took care to keep negroes alive for these were slaves for life. Their owner wanted as long a bondage as possible out of them. Indentured servants were different. A man with only some months left of his term because less and less valuable. He was often given the hardest, heaviest tasks, the poorest food, the worst accommodation. Hundreds of them died of privation. Others fled to sea. None, however, joined Phillips.

The pirate made for Tobago. On the island a negro told them of Finn's capture and the escape of Anstis. Some pirates had managed to hide but the men-of-war had returned and caught them. Only he was left. Thinking that Tobago would now be left in peace Phillips decided on a rapid boot-topping of the long-neglected *Revenge*. The work had only just been finished when

Burrill shouted that a warship had anchored at the headland less than two miles away. Horrified, the pirates watched as a boatload of seamen landed for water within shooting distance of Phillips' crouching men and for an hour the naval party filled casks and barrels while no pirate dared look up.

Captain Laws' snow was the first to be captured when the pirates left. Phillips, still concerned about his forced sailors, split them, putting James Wood, William Phillips and William Taylor in the snow under the command of Thomas Fern who had long been ambitious for a ship of his own. Faithlessly, one night he steered away from the *Revenge* but was noticed and at dawn was still within range. Several swivels scoured the tiny vessel's decks. Wood was killed outright as he stood by the whipstaff. William Phillip's right leg was shattered at the knee and had been so badly damaged that on Fern's surrender it was amputated by Archer. If gangrene did not appear within a day or two and if the stump knitted properly, as often it did not in that climate, Phillips would recover. Two days later Fern again attempted to escape. Captain John Phillips did not hesitate. When the man was dragged up he drew his pistols and shot him.

Continuing northwards off the coast of North Carolina on 7 February, 1724, the pirates took a large vessel under the command of Captain Huffan then a Portuguese ship and some sloops bound for Jamaica, forcing Harry Gyles, a skilled navigator, to go with them, Charles Ivemay also but releasing John Masters after his insistent begging to be freed as he had a wife and children who would remain penniless as long as he was away.

On 27 March Captain Mortimer's ship fell into their hands. Being a hot-tempered martinet he reacted furiously to the rampaging pirates and stabbed Phillips with a hand-spike badly injuring the commander's shoulder. Philips drew his sword, stabbed Mortimer three times and Nutt and Archer hacked him with their cutlasses as he lay on the deck. Burrill kicked the body and beckoned to Mortimer's crew to throw the corpse overboard.

In the following weeks Phillips took eleven ships including John Salter's sloop and Chadwell's schooner without bloodshed. He relaxed. There was an abundance of plunder, enough for a welcome retirement to a convenient island where the warmth and drink would hearten some of the cowardly impressed men. Captain Andrew Harradine of the *Squirrel* spoiled the dream.

He was captured off Nova Scotia in his new sloop, so new that there were still carpenters' tools lying about the decks. Phillips was attracted to the ship's clean lines and next day, 15 April, his pillaged goods and guns were transferred to the sloop by docile but resentful conscripts. There were almost twenty of them but only eight confirmed pirates.

That night Harradine tested some of the unwilling men about rising against Phillips. To his relief Cheeseman and Fillmore replied that at least half the crew wished to get away. To do anything that night would be foolish. Nutt, the sailing master, was on duty and he would not be frightened by the threats of unarmed men. Any rebellion would have to take place in daylight. Cheeseman offered to attend to Nutt, Fillmore to Burrill and Harradine would have to cope with Phillips who was likely to be in his cabin at noon. The 17th, the day after next, was fixed for the insurrection, giving time for other reliable hands to be warned.

Noon on the 17th blew cold and grey. Cheeseman invited Nutt to stroll the deck with him. Fillmore lounged by the deckrail near a hatchet that carpenters had forgotten. Cheeseman suddenly peered over the side as though noticing something unusual. Nutt leaned over and Cheeseman grabbed him by the waist and hoisted the pirate onto the rail. He was toppled into the sea.

Fillmore swung at Burrill with the hatchet, cutting him deeply in the shoulder and body. The pirate's dying shouts brought Phillips on deck. One glance told him of the danger and he rushed at Harradine. Cheeseman sprang between them, Phillips tripped over a coiled rope and before he could regain his feet Cheeseman hit him again and again with a mallet. Sparks, the gunner, rushed to Phillip's assistance only to be intercepted by Ivemay and another forced man who hauled the pirate to the ship's side where he was hurled overboard.

Archer leapt from a hatchway with pistols blazing. Flinging them away he pulled a cutlass from his belt. A Frenchman jumped on his back. Harradine pinned his arms to the deck. Cheeseman ran up with his mallet, hit Archer two or three heavy blows and would have killed him had not Gyles stopped him. It would be better to preserve the quartermaster as evidence of his opponents' innocence.

A week later the *Squirrel* entered St. Anns harbour, Nova Scotia. Below decks the pirates lay in chains. At the mast's head hung the heads of Phillips and Burrill. Exhilarated, Harradine ordered the swivel-gun fired in salute so that the townsfolk should know of his triumphant return. The forced men were on deck when the insecurely-held gun went off. The French surgeon received its full blast and clawed at the deck in his death-spasms.

Fillmore brought the ship to Boston on 3 May and on the 12th the trial began.[16] As well as the prisoners two gruesome exhibits were brought to the courtroom. Phillips' and Burrill's heads had been pickled in Newfoundland so that they might be preserved for the prosecution's inspection.[17]

It was a short case. Harradine, Tricker and Mills gave evidence against their former shipmates. Fillmore and Cheeseman were tried first and found not guilty. White, the one-legged William Phillips, Taylor, Archer and two others were condemned. The rest were acquitted. After the trial Fillmore, who was the great-grandfather of Millard Fillmore, thirteenth President of the United States, was given Phillips' gun and silver-hilted sword, silver shoe- and knee-buckles, a tobacco-box and two gold rings, the awards of a grateful Court for his services. Cheeseman and Harradine also received presents.

Three pirates were hanged on Bird Island in Boston harbour

after speeches of repentence. Three more were sent to England and executed on 'the Tree' at Execution Dock and in this murderous manner ended the last of those who had deserted Bartholomew Roberts in 1721.

Anstis had started it but despite his brutality had been unsuccessful. Finn had failed after him. Phillips made no name for himself. Times were turning against the unambitious pirate with his snatching of trivial prizes. Governors were more determined on defence. Conscientious naval captains relentlessly searched the seas. The pirates' West Indian playground was changing into an ever-closing death-trap. The coastal roads in the Americas were watched by sheriffs on guard against smugglers. In Africa men-of-war ranged the shipping lanes.

Thomas Jones, old companion of Howel Davis, the man who had fought Roberts, deserter with Anstis, the optimist who had sailed for England in the *Nightingale*, was caught in Bristol in 1723 and sent to London's Marshalsea prison.

13

Pleasures in Africa

April 1721–January 1722

'Tis computed that within the five years past the pyrates have taken one hundred and forty English vessels on the coast of Newfoundland and Africa. The report of the taking of the *Weymouth* man of war by Roberts the pyrate proves groundless'.

The *Weekly Journal*, 24 February, 1722

By May, 1721, a time of heavy rainfall, Roberts had left the Cape Verde Islands and the *Weymouth* had been floated off the sandbank in the Gambia river. At Sierra Leone she rejoined the *Swallow* whose bilges had been pumped dry.

The men-of-war moved along the coast past the River Cess and Cape Palmas, by Jacqueville and Half Assini to Cape Three Points where, through ignorance of local customs, they encountered trouble. Overlooking the Cape was Brandenburg fort, built by the Danes but long since abandoned. John Conny, an autocratic negro with a smattering of English, took it and exacted a tribute of gold from all ships that put into the bay for water. The Dutch heard of this and coveting the fort now that trade was reviving they sent a bomb-vessel and some frigates to demand Conny's evacuation.[1]

Conny demanded to see the receipt of purchase on which

the Dutch based their spurious claim of ownership. The land, he said, was his and the Danes used to pay him rent for it. Holland had no right to the fort unless a document could be produced to prove that Conny had leased the ground to them. 'Even then', he announced, 'I am Lord. The Danes once paid me rent but I do not wish to rent it again'.

Enraged at his insolence the Dutch fired bombs and shells before landing forty men and a lieutenant to take the fort by storm. A horde of Conny's warriors cut them down. Later when the Dutch ships had gone the negro leader used the dead men's skulls to pave the entrance to his palace, hanging their jawbones from a tree in the courtyard.

Conny was secure in his fort with its four bastions, forty guns and high walls. Treacherous currents swirled in the sea below. The surf was so fierce that European traders found it almost impossible to land and instead used 3-metre long cottonwood canoes sent out by Conny. Even that was perilous. The canoe faced seawards, its paddlers standing, while the leading negro judged the speed of the racing breakers. On the highest the canoe was swung round to rush in on the crest of the wave. Often it capsized leaving men drowning in the grasping undercurrents.

None of this was known to the *Swallow* and *Weymouth* and on 7 June heavy boats were launched to bring in fresh water. A negro carrying a long, gold-headed cane engraved with the name of John Conny strolled down to the seamen and demanded gold. When it was refused the sailors were surrounded by armed negroes who took possession of the water-casks and prepared to march their captives back to the fort. A naval officer explained that his men represented Great Britain only to be struck bloodily on the head. Captain Chaloner Ogle had to pay six ounces of gold to redeem his men and water and on 9 June they were freed.

Having been to Cape Coast Castle the *Swallow* and *Weymouth* sailed to Principe Island almost seven hundred miles east of Cape Three Points. Their departure neatly synchronised with Bartholomew Roberts' triumphant entry into Sierra Leone more than eight hundred sea-miles north-west of the Cape and John Conny. Pursuer and pursued could hardly have been farther apart.

Roberts had not been idle. However aloof he may have become he knew that only action combined with plunder would keep his men content. Where there were harbours to attack he would invade them. Where a ship hove into view he would take it. Once the accumulated loot had been distributed there were plenty of places for the pirates to visit for their celebrations. As long as forbidding forts such as Cape Coast Castle were avoided the pirates had the freedom of the coast.

Roberts knew the land well. He knew the ruinous state of the Royal African Company's forts, their walls crumbling through years of niggardly indifference, their guns corroded, knew the poverty of the agents who would welcome the diversion of the pirates' carousing when wine flowed copiously in joyful contrast to the miserable conditions enforced by the Company. For six months, a year, Africa could be a paradise for Roberts' crews. Then, when the fruit was picked, they could journey back to the Americas or try the rich haul of the East Indiamen off Madagascar and the Indian Ocean.

The Dutch *Royal Fortune* had been abandoned at Cape Verde. It was leaky and the guns and loot were transferred to the French *Sea King* which became yet another *Royal Fortune*. She sailed along the coast of Senegal. Two French cruisers on the lookout for Dutch interlopers and other smugglers chased out when the spied the big vessel with no flags sailing serenely by their harbour. Roberts lured them out to sea, putting on all sail as though fleeing until the ships were out of sight of land.

The courage of the French drained away as black flags were hoisted and the snouts of forty guns poked from hitherto empty gun-ports. The great ship swung across their path leaving them either to turn away inviting a broadside or to sail straight into range of a dozen murderous swivels trained intently on them.

They did neither. Their flags were hauled down in surrender and in this manner Roberts took command of two more strong ships, the *Comte de Toulouse* which became the *Ranger* and the other, smaller but suitable as a storeship, the *Little Ranger*. Roberts' men were proud of their success, 'every Man being in his own Imagination a Captain, a Prince or a King'.[2] Officers were elected for the new ships. Few of the older pirates received nominations. It was not the pirate custom to appoint by seniority. The criteria were boldness, ability and popularity. Simpson was demoted from his post as quartermaster because of his bullying manner. Roberts remained overall commander. With him as quartermaster was William Magness. James Phillips was the boatswain, Dennis the gunner. Harry Gillespie, the sailing-master, was not consulted.

On the *Ranger* Thomas Sutton was made captain but did not remain long in that position. William Main became boatswain. James Skyrme was elected captain of the *Little Ranger*. No other officers were deemed necessary although Roberts reminded the complement that they had no surgeon.

The trumpets, fiddles and drums were playing a raucous jig as they sailed into Sierra Leone on 12 June.[3] Old 'Crackers' fired his brass cannon. From his rebuilt fort on Bence Island agent Plunket cursed the *Swallow* for having left six weeks before. Futilely he watched as the traders rowed out: John Leadstine whose cannon had awakened him; Pierce; Glynn; the Presgrove brothers; Lamb; England; Warren; Bonnerman; and others,[4] thirty swindling knaves that knew Plunket was powerless. For two months the pirates stayed. The *Swallow* and *Weymouth* were unlikely to return so soon unless news reached them of the unbridled orgy in the settlement. Strict orders were enforced that any ship that came in should not go out.

William Davis drank his fill. For over twelve months he had mouldered in enforced servitude at Sierra Leone until the pirates arrived. He had deserted from the *Ann* galley after a quarrel with the mate and had settled down in the shanty town taking a negress as wife. When he sold her one jovial night in exchange for rum her relatives demanded redress and even Plunket was unable to prevent Davis from being sentenced to two years' service to a negro landowner, Signor Joseph, who had built a little church at Sierra Leone where some children were taught to read.[5] Now Davis was free.

William Williams tried to escape, was caught and whipped. Two others had got away before him and had evaded capture. It was believed that they had died or been murdered in the deep jungles. The trees, undergrowth, wild animals and savage natives were like prison walls. Except for a watch kept on the ships and their boats nothing was guarded. There was no discipline. Weary musicians were kept on their songs and dances unable to protest when tipsy pirates insisted on them having a drink, knowing that if the alcohol impaired their playing and the melodies scraped out of tune and tempo they were likely to be beaten into sobriety. They longed for Sundays.

June passed. And July. In his fort Plunket completed another despatch and added it to the pile that would be sent when the pirates left. It was not until the beginning of August that the *Royal Fortune* and her flotilla weighed anchor and Sierra Leone returned to the dreary hardship of making money for the Royal African Company.

Plunket gave his reports to the captain of the *Providence*. He submitted the names of the traders who had associated with Roberts; he pointed out that the men-of-war were useless if they did not have a fixed and convenient station which he proposed should be somewhere between Cap de Nord, Cape Mount and Cape Mesurado in Liberia two hundred miles down the coast. Pirates often watered in that region. An additional fort should be built at Sierra Leone to overlook the harbour, probably at Frenchman's Bay. It would protect the settlement and also prevent the pirates building a garrison of their own for wood and water. The fort on Bence Island was only useful for the storing of provisions.

Plunket returned to his ledgers. Soon merchantmen would be coming for slaves, buying negroes to fill those spaces below decks still unoccupied after trading at Cape Coast Castle. With the signing of the Spanish *Assiento* in 1713 England had guaranteed within thirty years to supply 144,000 slaves to the Spanish West Indies. There were also French and British possessions to be satisfied. In some years 20,000 men, women and children were shipped overseas in conditions that would kill one in ten of them before the three-month long voyage was over.

Death also came to the Royal Navy. For Europeans the unhealthy shores of West Africa were rabid with disease and ever since the time of Columbus the Gold Coast had been known as the 'White Man's Grave'. The humid climate, the insects and mosquitoes, ignorance of hygiene and sanitation, created a multitude of infections, malaria, dysentery, black fever, yellow fever, and it was reckoned that one in three white men arriving would be dead within four months. Black humour had it that the Royal African Company had three governors for each of its trading-posts, one that had just died, one acting in his place, and a third on his way out from England.

> 'Beware, and take care of the Bight of Benin,
> For one that comes out there were forty went in'.[6]

By 15 June yellow fever has affected the *Weymouth*. Men collapsed with high temperatures, jaundiced skins, vomiting, briefly seemed to recover then relapsed with internal haemorrhaging and delirium, passing into a coma and death. By 11 July the mosquito-borne epidemic had killed the purser. Three days later the schoolmaster died. By 26 August the man-of-war was anchored at Principe and had hired two houses for its sixteen sick sailors, buying bread for them. Four died that day.[7]

The Dutch *Semm* galley fell to Roberts in that month, an insignificant capture of a few bales but a significant influx of volunteers. A cheerful seaman sprang in front of Magness, the quartermaster, bowed to Roberts who shouted, 'Look you, these fellows would be forced'. Magness gently shoved the 'conscript' to the side of the *Royal Fortune*. The fellow shrieked. As the Dutch captain watched Magness prodded the sailor with his pistol whereupon the man shouted that he was being forced into piracy and begged his captain to add his name, Charles Bunce, to the lists of men made pirates against their wills. Another man who underwent the farce was Robert Armstrong who had deserted the *Swallow* at Cape Three Points eight weeks earlier.

On 8 August at Point Cestos, three hundred miles south-east of Sierra Leone, Roberts found two great ships at anchor, Captain Canning's *Robinson* from Bristol and Captain Gee's frigate *Onslow* transporting soldiers to Cape Coast Castle.[8] Most of their crews were on shore with the water-casks and the only resistance the pirates met came from the *Onslow*'s mate who had his pistol knocked away by enraged attackers who would have cut off his ears for such insolence but were distracted by the prospect of rich plunder.

On board there was a tempting prize. While the rest of his comrades were racing from cabin to cabin and through the holds flinging clothes and firearms and jewellery onto the upper deck for the quartermaster's inspection a pirate, William Mead, kicked in a door and saw a white woman cowering in a storeroom under the poop.

The sound of screams brought another man to the storeroom where Mead was wrenching and tearing the petticoat of the hysterical woman whose skirt already lay ripped on the deck.[9] John Mitchell may have felt that rape did not fall into the category of fair shares or perhaps was mindful of Roberts' punitive Article VI but he smashed Mead on the head with his flintlock and curtly told the woman to get below to the gunroom. When the *Onslow* and *Robinson* had been looted Roberts would be told of her presence.

She crouched in fear as pirates brought money, trinkets, apparel and valuables to Magness. The succession of sun-tanned, unwashed villains, bearded, moustached, scarred, heavily armed with pistols and cutlasses, all looked in amazement and lust at the female before returning even more eagerly to their ransacking in the hope of finding one for themselves.

For two hours the pillaging continued. Everything was sorted into piles, enormous heaps of materials and clothing, coins, rings and necklaces and brooches. In the holds lists were made of the crates and barrels. Then, at last, when the work was completed Magness told the woman, Elizabeth Trengrove, the wife of a Cornish mine-captain, she was going to the *Royal Fortune* where Bartholomew Roberts would decide what was to be done with her.

On the after-deck of the frigate Roberts assembled the crews of his two prizes asking which men wanted to join his company. A band of soldiers pressed forward but were ignored as landlubbers. Roberts wanted no soldiers and 'put them off with Refusals for some Time' until he grudgingly offered them a quarter-share if they volunteered. Even with that insulting gift a lot of them crossed to the pirate ship.[10]

To the seamen Roberts repeated that no man would be forced. Several sailors looked uneasy and disappointed. Picking out the men who appeared most theatrically unwilling the pirates went through the pretence of driving them onto the *Royal Fortune*.

Roberts turned to the clergyman of the *Onslow*, the Reverend Roger Price. Piracy, said Roberts, was a wicked and dissolute life but he did his best to keep his men in order, permitted no evildoing on Sundays, or games or rowdiness, and having a man of the cloth on board might reduce bad behaviour on other days. Price was unenthusiastic. He would never willingly console scoundrels.

But, argued Roberts, the post would be a sinecure. All that would be required of the minister would be to hold services, offer prayers and, now and then, make punch as occasion demanded.

Price answered that his conscience would not allow such an ill combination of duties. Roberts did not press him but contented himself with the theft of three prayer-books and a corkscrew.[11]

The *Onslow*, like a frigate with its high forecastle and poopdeck, looked a better vessel than the French-built *Royal Fortune*. Carpenters pulled down the greater part of the bulwarks and cleared the lower decks. Some cabins were saved. Forty guns were mounted and lashed to their blocks. It was a proper ship, fast, nimble, clean and dangerous. A fortnight later the pirate fleet left Cestos, holds bulging with loot. Roberts was so proud of his floating fortress that she became the fourth *Royal Fortune* despite the superstition that to change the name of a ship was a sure guarantee of disaster. There is a water-colour painting of the ship in Konstam, 30.

Elizabeth Trengrove was confined to a tiny cabin. She was a threat and would not be allowed about the ship. As a safeguard 'Little David' Simpson was appointed her custodian. No one dared challenge him and, according to his testimony, grateful favours were permitted for his protection.

Having given the old *Royal Fortune* to Captain Gee[12] in compensation for the loss of his frigate Roberts sailed eastwards past Jacqueville and Cape Coast Castle seeing few vessels except one in which the pirates mistook the overbearing surgeon for the captain. Into the ship all the unwanted booty was piled. The pirates kept the surgeon, George Willson, assigning him to the *Ranger*. Already they had forced Hamilton from the *Onslow*.

Willson was an enigma. He did not protest but two days later said he had to go to another prize for medicines and instruments. Sutton hesitated. The ship was already moving off. He halted her by firing a shot, lowered a sailing-boat and told Willson to collect his requirements and return speedily. Willson left with two others but instead of steering towards the ship took a straggling course to land. Sutton was helpless. The runaway was too near land. The *Ranger* went after the *Royal Fortune*.

Captured despatches told Roberts that the *Swallow* and *Weymouth* were at Principe over two hundred miles to the south. So far away they were no threat and Roberts decided to attack another port. On 1 October, 1721, his three vessels lay far to the east outside Calabar in Nigeria waiting for a ship to guide them in. At the entrance the water was only five metres deep and, beyond it, a long, intricately winding channel made the town almost unapproachable. Roberts could do nothing until Captain Loane and his *Joceline* brig appeared, Loane being cajoled into piloting them into the port by a convincing blend of cocked pistols and purses of gold.[13]

To his chagrin Roberts discovered that the booty was limited to two ships, the *Mercy* galley and the *Cornwell*, neither of which contained much wealth. Hardly bothering with them Roberts sent ashore for provisions from the negroes who, when they learned their customers were pirates, refused to trade. Robers landed forty men to storm it only to be faced with two thousand armed negroes. Several pirates were killed before the natives retreated taking all their goods and food with them. Their town was set on fire but the landing-party returned empty-handed and with his three new but unprofitable ships Roberts sailed out in an ill temper.[14] From the vessels he obtained some men, James White, a hunch-backed musician, and Peter Scudamore, a surgeon who might have remained free had he not deliberately struck Moody when the pirate would not allow him on the *Royal Fortune*.

Anxious to impress his 'captors' Scudamore went back to the *Cornwell* for medicines, scales, blowpans and surgical knives ignoring the explostulations of his former captain, Rolls, who swore to denounce the surgeon to every authority he met. When the three prizes were released Gillespie secretly gave Loane some golden moidores for the sailing-master's family. Gillespie had agreed to take his share of plunder to allay suspicions of him and to make provision for his wife and children.

At Principe the *Weymouth* was still suffering fatalities from yellow fever. By 21 September so many men had died or were in hospital that twenty negroes were hired to weigh the anchor. The disabled man-of-war and the *Swallow* made for the Gold Coast, parting on 20 October. Three days later the *Weymouth* was at Cape Coast Castle. The governor, worried about reports of two pirate vessels, asked how many fit men the *Weymouth* had. Seventy-two officers and men he was told. By 25 October the number had diminished to fifty-seven. Despite scores of press-ganged seamen to make up the original crew of 240 the man-of-war had '280 dead upon her Books'.

Through November and December the pirates careened and relaxed at Cape Lopez and then at Annabón, a small island sometimes known as Palagula, two hundred miles out from the Cape, an ideal retreat for men needing seclusion.

Nothing disturbed them. A man had deserted at Cape Lopez but there had been so many volunteers that the ships were crowded with cut-throats. No one bothered about John Jessup but they would regret their indifference. The runaway had been with them for years, by the bitterest of ironies having been a shipmate of Bartholomew Roberts when the *Princess of London* had been taken by Howel Davis in June, 1719. As a gunner he had fought bravely against the *Summersett* galley in 1720 but, like John Mansfield, ex-highwayman and naval deserter, he was so frequently drunk that he was usually asleep when the plunder was shared out and he had become disillusioned with the promises of pleasures and rewards that he always seemed to miss.

He sneaked off and struggled miles northwards along the rough coast to Gabon where he was picked up by a Dutch trader. Suspicious of his story that he had been marooned the captain took Jessup to the *Swallow* at Cape Coast Castle. There, chained and in fear for his life, he turned informer.[15]

His defection seemed of no account to the pirates at Annabón. Roberts preened himself in his wardrobe of finery. Ashplant concocted ever more catastrophic potions. Simpson

resentfully regretted the loss of Elizabeth Trengrove who had
been liberated at Calabar. Sutton resigned the captaincy of the
Ranger and was replaced by Skyrme.

Early in January, 1722, the *Elizabeth* was sailing off Jacqueville
on the Ivory Coast. There had been no mention of pirates for
two months but even as she turned for harbour three ships
appeared and a shot hissed across her bows. On board was
George Willson, the missing surgeon. He had not misled Sutton.
He had been unable to prevent his small boat being blown onto
the beach at Cape Mesurado where he had survived miserably
for five months, afflicted by fever and lack of food. Early on his
old ship had put in but Captain Tarlton refused to take the
renegade aboard. After months of privation and illness, a French
ship picked him up. Even then he was unfortunate.
Apprehensive of his fever the captain left him at Cestos.[16]

He was penniless and would have starved had not negro traders
taken him as a bond-servant, a state of back-breaking slavery in
which he have perished. But the *Elizabeth* put into Cestos and his
luck turned. Captain John Sharp kind-heartedly ransomed him
for three pounds five shillings [£3.25] and took him aboard where
Adam Comrie, the surgeon, nursed him back to health.

Now the pirates had returned. Willson borrowed a shirt from
Comrie and in a few minutes was telling the *Royal Fortune*'s
men of his adventures. Together he and Scudamore persuaded
Roberts that Comrie would be a useful addition to the medical
staff. Hamilton, the unwilling surgeon of the *Royal Fortune*,
refused to sign the Articles and would obviously desert if he
could. Comrie might be equally unhappy but two forced
surgeons were better than one.

Then Willson saw Thomas Tarlton, brother of the captain
who had abandoned him at Cape Mesurado. When the pirates
were told they set on the blameless mate and beat him
ruthlessly. His unconscious body was dragged away by fellow
Liverpudlians who hid him under the shelter of a staysail.
There was a desultory search for him that quickly petered away

except for Harper and Moody who continued for an hour with pistols cocked.

While the *Elizabeth* was being scavenged the little *Hannibal* was captured after a struggle during which Richard Hardy broke his cutlass on Captain Ousley's head, causing his death. The ship was later used as a hulk for a rapid boot-topping of the two great pirate vessels.[17]

Once the *Elizabeth* had been voided of all her valuables Sharp prepared to return to the empty ship. Willson asked him if he still had the ransom note. Because of the thoroughness of the looting Sharp could not be certain. Willson shrugged 'It's no matter, Mr Sharp', he said, 'I believe I shall hardly ever come to England to pay it', and with this gratitude he bade farewell to his benefactor.

Comrie was made to sign the Articles and became surgeon of the *Ranger*. Willson wished to have the post on the *Royal Fortune* where Hamilton was still mistrusted but, frustrated as always, he was not elected. On the *Ranger* the pirates so disliked the supercilious Scudamore that they voted en bloc for him to be transferred. Willson received nothing.

On 5 January the *Diligence* was taken and next day a lookout reported a ship at anchor at Cape Apollonia. She surrendered at the first shot. Pirates rowed across calling for the crew to yield when suddenly a pistol was fired. On the *King Solomon* Captain Trahern had ordered his men to support him but their resolution evaporated when Magness bellowed that no quarter would be given if there was more defiance.[18]

This ship was well-sized with a crew of some forty men. Hers was such a fruitful cargo that the pirates were distracted from ill-using the captain who had tried to protect his freight. 'How dared you fire?', he was asked. 'Didn't you see the two ships commanded by the famous Captain Roberts?'

Like termite ants the pirates ravished and destroyed. John Walden hacked at the anchor cable with a hatchet. 'What occasion is there for this needless work of heaving up the anchor when yours will be burned presently?' In mock sympathy he hoped that there would be more anchors in London for the one he had just sent to the bottom of the Gulf of Guinea.

Below decks the boarding-party were quarrelling among themselves about their entitlements. Mansfield found a beautifully patterned glass. Moody seized it. Mansfield shouted. Moody swore. 'I'll blow your brains out if you mutter about this glass', he bawled. Mansfield did not mutter.

Scudamore put aside a set of fine medical equipment, some medicines, salves, and a backgammon table. Behind his back someone took it and Magness had to separate the two men before it became a duelling matter. Scudamore tramped off with the table and later took Trahern's quilt and bolster.

In his anxiety to join the plundering Willson impatiently refused to dress a man's wound. When the pirate complained Roberts turned on the surgeon, telling him that he was a double rogue to be with them for a second time and if ever Willson again forgot his duties he would have his ears cut off. The *King Solomon* was set loose. Phillips, the boatswain, pleaded that he had been forced to sign the Articles because a pistol had been laid on the table in front of him as though to say, 'Sign or Die'.

Later in the afternoon the *Gertrouycht* from Flushing was taken. The cargo was not remarkable and it was the carpenter who benefited most with a maintopmast, a mainyard and the spritsail yard. For once his unenriched colleagues did not care. Having found several yards of sausage in the cook's galley they strung the links around. Captain Gerrit de Haen's neck, cut the heads off some fowls and invited the captain to dinner. Providing themselves with all the liquor available they settled around the table of the great cabin, de Haen in their midst, and opening some Dutch prayer-books began to sing. Most of the songs did not come from the books. On the *Little Ranger* Bunce fired regular salutes in celebration.[19]

News reached the forts and factories that the pirates were on the coast again, and ships moved watchfully from port to port. There were rumours that the *Swallow* had left Principe but nothing was heard of the *Weymouth*. Roberts decided to raid another harbour before retiring to a quiet haven where they could rest. He was tired of continual chases at sea. He ordered the steersman to head towards Ouidah four hundred miles away.[20]

It was a lucrative target. Because of its position on the Bight of Benin, the Slave Coast, it was the wealthiest harbour in West Africa. Ships inevitably called there. Although the prices were high the negro slaves were strong and healthy. The king of Dahomey, a fat and lustful despot, lived with a century of wives in a dirty bamboo palace six miles inland. From there he exacted a toll to the value of twenty slaves from every ship calling at the earthen-walled insanitary town separated from the shore by a lagoon and stinking marshes. Although exorbitant the tax was paid every year by forty or fifty merchantmen grumbling at a ruler so avaricious that he sold the slaves naked having stripped them of their loin-cloths or 'arse-clouts'. In spite of their complaints the traders knew that even after every miserly penny had been extracted they would still get bargains. Ouidah was worth the attention of any pirate.

The *Royal Fortune* and its attendant flotilla sailed in, trumpets fanfaring, drums rolling, a black flag at the mizzenmast bearing the emblem of a skeleton holding an hourglass in one bony hand, crossed bones in the other, a spear at its side, a bleeding heart under the fleshless feet. The eleven ships at anchor instantly struck their colours and the captains hurried ashore with their money hoping that the pirates would be content with the litter of goods and chattels that had been left behind.

The quartermasters reported to Roberts. The ships were virtually empty. Roberts shrugged. Ships that employed every square centimetre of space for the storage of slaves were unlikely to be laden with silks, satins and bulky commodities. The wealth would be in the captains' pockets. The captains would have to come to the pirates. Or their vessels would be burnt.

Orders were sent, always with the same formula. Eight pounds of gold would ransom a ship. The captains or sometimes the supercargoes who acted as intermediaries replied that they did not possess so much. Roberts did not relax. He, not the captains, had the power.

On shore the supercargo of the *Carlton* was aghast to find that almost all his money had been spent on negroes manacled in the very ship he hoped to buy back. Instead of having the demanded one hundred and forty ounces of gold he had no more than forty. In panic he tried to borrow but no one could help him. The other captains had been left almost impoverished. It was only after hard bargaining that Mr Baldwin, agent of the Royal African Company at Ouidah, advanced him the balance. The *Carlton* was released.

So was the *Sandwich* galley and others. The captains entreated Roberts to give them receipts to show their owners on returning to England. Roberts cheerfully agreed and, to prove his sincerity, helpfully added the signature of a honest man to his own. What the London merchants thought of the documents can only be guessed.

'This is to certify whom it may or doth concern that we GENTLEMEN OF FORTUNE have received eight Pounds of Gold-Dust for the Ransom of the *Hardey* [or whatever other vessel], Captain Dittwatt Commander, so that we discharge the said Ship.

Witness our Hands, this

13 January, 1722. Batt. Roberts.
Harry Gillespie.[21]

To captains of some foreign ships the flippant Sutton and Simpson gave similar receipts but signed them Aaron Whifflingpin and Sim. Tugmutton.

Frivolity was everywhere. Deciding to force a seaman to join a pirate picked on Thomas Diggle and told him he was permitted to become a freebooter. Diggle protested. Then, answered the pirate gravely, he should be given a chance. A small circle was drawn on the deck and opposite each other on the circumference two chalks were set, 'Go' written by one, 'Stay' by the other. If Diggle knocked over 'Go' he would be free. If 'Stay' fell he would become a Man of the Sea. The seaman was blindfolded, led into the circle and twirled around several times.

The scared sailor hardly dared move. He hovered, touched a chalk, trembled, dithered, pirates shouted encouragement, roared in laughter, mocked. Diggle hesitated, boggled at making a decision until he felt the cold muzzle of a pistol at his ear. He knocked a chalk over. 'Stay'.

Across the harbour on the *Royal Fortune* Roberts checked the money. Every ship had paid except the *Porcupine*. Captain Fletcher had stoutly replied that he could give nothing as he had no orders from his employers about such an emergency. This may have been the truth, or he may have been a stubborn man, or maybe he did not consider his cargo of slaves worth what Roberts was charging. He sent no cash and pirates, including Harris and Walden, were told to set the negroes ashore and burn the slaveship. What happened was sadistic.

Every slaveship was overcrowded. Below decks the hold, never more than two metres high, was divided halfway up by a platform and on that and on the floor below slaves were chained in pairs by their ankles, lying on bare boards with a space less than 2m long, 0.4m wide and 0.8m high for each man. The ships reeked of excrement and in the open seas could be smelled a mile away. In the foetid stench candles guttered and went out.

Malnourished on a cheap mush of maize and palm oil those who did not contract smallpox often suffered from dysentery, the 'bloody flux' even though the slaves were taken daily into the open air while the decks were hosed down with vinegar and fumigated. Men suffered, died amidst the wailing, shrieks and groans of those around them. Negresses were the playthings of captains, sometimes of crews. Once at sea conditions in the ships were described as 'half bedlam, half brothel'. In 1723 125 slaves out of 339 died on the *Greyhound*. Nearly two-thirds of the 229 slaves in the *Hannibal* perished. It was thought almost indulgent that the Royal African Company should instruct the governor of its Cape Coast Castle, 'Pray lade no more than are necessary to prevent Mortality which often happen'd by crowding the ship with too many Negroes'.[22]

It was not compassion but economics. Black bodies were bulletin and callous black oppressed defenceless black, tribe against tribe. White traders and white captains were the instigators but not the hunters of the human merchandise. It was powerful African chiefs who marauded the villages and trapped the men and women, rulers like the king of Dahomey who would allow no forts or competitors and who sent his spearmen out on regular raids into the interior to depopulate villages of their young men and women. Eighty were chained on board the *Porcupine*.

Walden, sarcastically nicknamed 'Miss Nanny' by his fellows because of his delight in cruelty, ordered the ship's carpenter, Scott, to unshackle the negroes but Captain Fletcher had the key to the locks and the carpenter had to struggle to prise each deeply-embedded bolt free by hand amongst the mass of negroes jostling and writhing in the darkness. Overhead, Harris finished spreading tar over the decks in readiness for the burning of the ship.

Impatiently Walden yelled that they were setting fire to the *Porcupine* in two minutes whether the slaves were released or not. The carpenter climbed from the hold. He had not heard what Walden had said. When told that the pirates were ready to start the flames the man gasped in horror. The negroes were chained, he had no key and it would take him at least an hour to finish his task. Indifferently, Walden struck a spark from his tinder-box, lit the tallow and dropped the burning flax. The tar and resin bubbled into flame.

The pirates scrambled into the boat. After a second's hesitation the carpenter followed. There was nothing he could do in the *Porcupine*. Within a minute the slaveship was a candle. The screams of the imprisoned slaves reached across the harbour. Some, still manacled in pairs, wrenched themselves free from their bolts and leapt into the water only to die as savagely. 'Those who jumped over-board from the Flames, were seized by Sharks, a voracious Fish, in plenty in this Road, and in their Sight, torn Limb from Limb alive. A Cruelty unparallel'd'.

Sharks menaced all along the coast. One bit through a heavy oar of the *Weymouth*'s barge at Sierra Leone. And when that sick man-of-war buried her dead at sea Atkins watched sharks seize the corpse, 'tearing and devouring that, and the Hammock that shrouded it, without suffering it once to sink, tho' a great weight of Ballast in it'.

On the *Royal Fortune* 'Miss Nanny' Walden, sadistically stupid as always, thrashed the carpenter for his slowness, blaming the seaman for the murder of so many negroes. The *Porcupine* settled in the water. Smoke still poured from her but the screaming had stopped.[23]

A despatch from General Phipps to the Royal African Company's agent had been found. It said that the pirates had been sighted to the windward of Cape Three Points. The *Swallow* had been informed and was pursuing them.[24] Roberts knew that the man-of-war would search the intervening ports and it might be weeks before she reached Ouidah. The pirate still chose to leave. 'Brave Fellows cannot be supposed to be frightened at this News, yet . . . it were better to avoid dry Blows, which is the best that can be expected if overtaken', he mused. Two days after their departure the *Swallow* arrived.[25]

The pirates had sailed out on the thirteenth leaving Hamilton behind. With Comrie and Scudamore and Willson they had no need of an obstinate surgeon. The *Royal Fortune* led. Behind her came the *Ranger*, Captain Skyrme. Behind

Skyrme came the *Little Ranger*, Captain Bunce. Behind Bunce came a commandeered French ship. They headed for the pleasant shores and countryside of Cape Lopez. On their way they took the *Wida* sloop, looted it, realised that they dare not let it go when they were so close to the Cape, took its crew aboard and burned the vessel.

By October, 1721, in the *Weymouth* seamen were dying almost daily. Mungo Herdman desperately took in provisions and transferred men from other ships to replace the dead. In December Alexander Selkirk was taken ill. On the thirteenth, on the left side of the ship's Log, the Master wrote, 'Alexr. Selkirk, DD' and on the right, as though knowing that the man was of some importance, 'P.M. Alexr. Selkirk Deceased'. At sea the weather was stormy.[26]

A year later, on 5 December 1723, Selkirk's will was proved in favour of his wife, Frances Candis, who had remarried. As Mrs Frances Hall she collected Selkirk's wages of £40.00 and took possession of the will's contents. Sophia Bruce was excluded. Demanding justice as the true wife she was put on trial, found guilty and fined £500. Unable to pay she was put in prison.[27] Probably in 1725 she wrote a pathetic letter to a clergyman in London saying that she was 'much reduced in want'. Nothing more is known of her.

In 1868 Commander Powell and the officers of H.M. *Topaz* placed a commemorative tablet on the island where Selkirk had been marooned. On it the year given for his death was wrong.[28]

14

The Swallow *meets the* Royal Fortune

October 1721–February 1722

'There is great mortality in the *Swallow* and the *Weymouth*. The pirates sailed to Leeward for Jaquin [Jacqueville] on September 19'

Letters from Africa, 20 October 1721

Since arriving in Africa H.M. 3rd-rate, 50-gun men-of-war the *Swallow* and the *Weymouth* had experienced accident, insult, sickness and frustration. They had stayed at Principe island from July until late September, bleak months when man after man died of the yellow fever. Captain Chaloner Ogle reported that he had buried fifty and had a hundred more ill.[1]

In October the ships returned to Cape Coast Castle where the *Weymouth* lay to with only half her men fit for service. It had been fifteen hundred miles of empty sea, five hundred leagues of being cooped in malodorous vessels with mouldering biscuits, rotting, gristly, unchewable meat for sustenance, and harsh naval discipline.

Ogle, later knighted and made admiral, went to Jacqueville near Grand Bassam east of Cape Three Points. Two hundred wasted miles. Despite rumours the pirates were not there. Evidence of them was. Ports along the Ivory Coast were filled with seamen whose ships had been sunk or burnt. Rather than be stranded on the sickly coast desperate men offered to work their passage back to England without wages. Captain Barlow planned to man his sloop with slaves and other unpaid hands as long as he could get to sea again.

Off Cape Apollonia Captain Bird of the *Mary* passed on the vague news that the pirates were about somewhere, where he did not know. He was surprised that they were still in Africa with two men-of-war hunting them.[2]

The *Swallow* sailed on. At Sekondi by Cape Three Points she was heeled and scrubbed in preparation for a chase. Then Ogle made the short voyage to Dixcove where the *Carlton*'s captain reported that soldiers carried by the *Swallow* to Gambia Fort had mutinied, spiked the guns and gone off pirating in the *Bumper*. There were yet more villains to hunt down.

Backwards and forwards went the *Swallow*, to port after port, hearing rumours that were always unreliable except that everywhere it was said that large numbers of men had volunteered to join Roberts. November passed and December of 1721 and the silence continued. In wearied failure the *Swallow* returned to Cape Coast Castle. The *Weymouth* had sailed to go to Des Minas for goods that the Dutch were holding illegally. For the *Swallow* there were despatches – and news. There was a letter from General Phipps at Axis about the pirates. There was another from Dixcove that three suspicious ships had been seen there. Both letters contained the same name, Ouidah.[3]

Ogle ordered the sails hoisted. His prey was becoming over-confident. After delivering some messages on the way the man-of-war would go to Ouidah where, if Ogle knew anything about pirates, they would be drinking and sleeping and taking no care of tomorrow, certainly not of today. With his armament of 9lb, 18lb and vessel-sinking 32-pound cannon, the heaviest below decks, the *Swallow* was a match for any pirate.

At Accra he had to wait hours, almost a day, for a Royal

African Company ship, the *Margaret* with a woman passenger that an ill-advised joker called 'Miss Betty'. Ogle was unamused. He fumed at the delays over despatches and tardy ships. It was not until 15 January, 1722, that they came to Ouidah. The harbour was silent. There was the charred hulk of the *Porcupine* and there were burnt dwellings. Nothing else. Ogle was told that Roberts had gone two days ago to Jacqueville. The captain was sceptical. It was a story to deceive. More sensibly the pirates would keep out of sight of land now that the *Swallow* was on their track, would raid one or two harbours and then run off to the West Indies or to Madagascar or somewhere where Ogle would never find them.

A letter from Mr Baldwin of the Royal African Company repeated that the *Royal Fortune* was almost certainly at Jaquin [Jacqueville] nearly five hundred miles to the east.[4] Passing Axim near Cape Coast Castle on what he was sure would be a fruitless search Ogle had to tolerate an angry General Phipps irritated that Roberts should have been missed at Ouidah through a few hours delay. Ogle refrained from replying that the 'few hours' had actually been a few days and proceeded to Jacqueville where the seas were as free of Roberts as anywhere else.

Then the naval captain remembered that John Jessup was on board. The pirate had been picked up by a Dutch vessel at Gabon and carried to Cape Coast Castle and the *Swallow*. Gabon might be Roberts' base. Ogle went a thousand pessimistic miles south-east but despite a keen search of the river found nothing. Ogle sent for Jessup. How could the sailor have been at Gabon when it was obvious that no one had been there for months, no signs of fires, rubbish, of the mess and untidy shelters left by a pirate sojourn?

Jessup explained that he had not escaped from the Gabon estuary but had made his way there after getting away from the pirates at Cape Lopez. The Cape was only a hundred miles to the south. Ogle decided to investigate.

Just before dawn on 5 February the officer of the watch heard the sound of a ship's gun. Ogle quickly dressed and came on deck. As the day brightened he could make out Cape Lopez. He and his officers trained their spyglasses on it. A lieutenant claimed he could see three ships. Bartholomew Roberts had been discovered.

To close on him the deeply-laden *Swallow* had to sail into the wind taking repeated soundings amongst the bewilderment of sandbanks. With the coming of daylight Ogle saw that two of the pirate vessels were being boot-topped, the larger still having flags at her mainmast, the King's colours amongst them. Forty guns, Ogle estimated, thirty or more in the French-built ship and perhaps ten in the small vessel behind them. The odds were heavy.

On shore pirates were yawning out of sleep. It was gently cool in the shade of the trees on the low, steep cliff where they relaxed with no fear of danger from the friendly natives or the buffaloes grazing around the waterholes. In the bay was a multitude of fish. On land there were animals to catch. The weather was fine. One could rest in the shadows with the sun burning down on the dazzle of surf-wet sands and watch the work progressing in the ships whose smell of tar and canvas mingled with the salty breeze. There were barrels of rum, bottles of wine, good fellowship. There were dice, backgammon, mock trials, or simple rest letting the warmth sink into comfortable bodies.

Since leaving Sierra Leone six months before the ships had criss-crossed the Gulf of Guinea in three thousand miles of onslaught, bombardment and devilry and had accrued a fortune. Men padlocked their private treasure-chests and fantasised of a rich, anonymous retirement. For the present it was relaxation that they wanted.

On a rocky platform at the cliff's head Bartholomew Roberts with a few well-liked companions sat at a breakfast of small beer and salmagundi, a spiced salad dish of pickled herrings, minced chicken, apples, onions, lettuce, radishes, tomatoes and hard boiled eggs.[5] The approaching ship did not disturb him. A merchantman might put in for water. The distant vessel looked Portuguese from her lines in which case she would contain sugar that the pirates would appreciate for their rum punch. The King's flag at the masthead of the *Royal Fortune* would reassure any doubtful captain worried at the sight of three ships in the bay.

Roberts was taken aback when the oncoming ship turned away, heading out to sea again. Now it would have to be chased. The *Royal Fortune* needed at least another day's work on her keel before she could be righted. The *Little Ranger* was not strong enough. Skyrme got to his feet. The *Ranger* would have to go. It would not take long to lash the guns down, weigh the anchor and raise the sails but the prospect of a long chase was not appealing. Probably a whole day wasted.

In the *Swallow* Ogle was raging at his steersman. The pirates had been easy prey, unprepared, stranded on the beach away from their guns, their ships on their sides, as peaceful a capture as a man-of-war could hope for. But the helmsman had almost grounded the *Swallow* on Frenchman's Bank leaving her for target practice by the pirates. Now Ogle would have to go out to sea again and make yet another long tack before he could run into the bay once more. By that time the enemy would be ready and would fight.

To Ogle's astonishment an officer reported that the French-built vessel was sailing out. The *Swallow*'s last-minute veering away must have deluded the pirates into thinking that the man-of-war was running away, not realising that their prey was a naval ship. Ogle ordered the lower gunports closed and told Lieutenant Sun to simulate the appearance of putting on all sail while in reality moving slowly enough for the pirates to catch him in a few hours. By then both ships would be out of sight and sound of land.

Skyrme urged the *Ranger* on. He wanted to get back. By mid-morning the pirates were close enough to fire four chase-guns in the bows as a signal to the other to heave to. Black flags were hoisted. Fragments of shot pattered against the sides of the *Swallow*. She kept to her course. Cursing with impatience Skyrme shouted that they would have to board the rascal.

Within half an hour the ships were in range of each others's cannon. Slowly the Ranger crept up until her spritsail yard was alongside the *Swallow*. White-shirted pirates balanced on the bulwarks brandishing pistols and cutlasses. The quartermaster yelled for grappling-irons. A discharge from the *Ranger*'s swivels raked across the man-of-war's decks.

Suddenly the *Swallow* changed course, running parallel with the pirate. Her gunports fell open. A broadside of 32-lb guns blasted into the *Ranger*. Walden was flung down from the bulwark on which he had been standing but 'tho' he had lost his Leg in the Action, he would not suffer himself to be dressed, or carry'd off the Deck; but . . . fought upon his Stump'.[6]

As the startled *Ranger* swung away her own guns boomed but aboard there was chaos. Crewmen lay dead or dying. Others ran shrieking that they were trapped. Someone hauled down the black flags. A sterngun fired futilely at the *Swallow* as Ogle took up the pursuit. Skyrme shouted for calm. Ashplant shoved men back to their stations. Behind him came Hynde, his boatswain's silver whistle dangling round his neck, his shirt blackened with powder and grease. They bellowed to the cowards to fight back, told Comrie to see to the wounded, had the black flag raised again.

Gradually the panic subsided. Steering a twisting course the *Ranger* evaded the guns of the *Swallow*. But the aggression had gone. There was desultory firing at long range which did no damage to either vessel. The black flag was joined by the red English ensign, the King's jack and a Dutch pennant giving the *Ranger* a festive appearance not shared by the majority of her crew. Many were for yielding. Others were for running off from the man-of-war to rejoin Roberts. He would know what to do. But in the uncertain winds they could not get away from the *Swallow*.

Some pirates suggested blowing up the powder-room as they had often boasted they would if in peril of being caught. Terrified, a forced man, Lillburn, ran down with a musket determined to resist any attempt to destroy themselves.

About two o'clock in the afternoon the *Ranger* lost way on a long tack and lay becalmed. In fear and frustration the pirates watched the man-of-war closing on them. Another broadside struck them and then another as their own guns fired back sporadically at the relentless foe. The maintopmast collapsed in a splintering crash of spars and canvas onto the *Ranger's* deck. The black flag fluttered feebly across the body of a pirate. Hynde staggered down the hatchway clutching the stump of his arm. Blood and black smoke was everywhere as the bombardment thundered repeatedly. There was no resistance.

By three o'clock the *Ranger* asked for quarter. Ogle ordered the guns to cease. Boats were put out to bring in the survivors. The pirate ship had been so severely damaged that she was likely to sink. From her came the sound of a slight, muffled explosion followed by a brilliant flash. Morris with Ball and Main had pushed Lillburn aside and fired a pistol directly into a barrel of gunpowder. Being damp the keg had not blasted the ship apart but had detonated with only enough force to smash a hole in the ship's side through which the badly-burned Ball was thrown leaving Morris and Main injured and senseless.

On deck Ashplant weighted the pirate flags to throw them into the sea. He was not having them hung mockingly at half-mast in the *Swallow*. Forced men talked excitedly of release. Others who had been with the pirates longer were anxious, realising that they would put on trial where, perhaps, one misguided but remembered deed in the months of enforced piracy might be recalled by a vengeful captain and cause their execution. The hardened pirates hoped they would be taken to Cape Lopez. Roberts would rescue them.

The prisoners were transported to the man-of-war. Ten men had died in the *Ranger*. Another twenty were seriously hurt.

Atkins, the *Swallow*'s surgeon, went round trying to staunch the bleeding. One of the ship's officers saw the powder-burned Main standing apart, a silver whistle on his chest hanging from a silken cord.

'I presume you are the boatswain of this ship', he said. Main stared at him 'Then you presume wrong, for I am boatswain of the *Royal Fortune*, Captain Roberts, commander'. 'Then, Mr Boatswain, you will be hanged, I believe'. Main spat. 'That is as your Honour pleases'. Curious, the officer persisted. He asked Main what had caused the explosion. The boatswain showed more interest. 'By God, they are all mad and bewitched for I have lost a good hat by it'.

The hat had been whisked from his head when Morris had fired into the barrel and it had been blown out to sea. 'But what significance is a hat, my friend?', he was asked. Main grinned wryly as his sash and pistol band were taken from him by naval seamen going from pirate to pirate stripping them. 'Not much', he said.[7]

He was asked about Roberts' crew. Were they of the same calibre as the desperadoes that had been overpowered today? Main sneered. 'There's a hundred and twenty of them, as clever fellows as ever trod shoe-leather. I would I were with them'. 'No doubt on't', said the officer. 'By God, it is the naked truth', answered Main as the last of his clothes were removed.

Ball, who had been flung into the sea by the explosion and had been picked up by the *Swallow*'s boat resisted all attempts to dress his wounds, ripping off bandages, shouting that he would rather die than be attended to by naval dogs. It was not until the pain from his powder-scorched skin caused him to swoon that his injuries could be seen to.

During the night he became delirious. He raved at the top of his voice about Roberts' bravery and cunning. He would soon be released, he yelled. The man-of-war would meet a tartar that would give it hard blows. In the 18th century the navy was not noted for its compassion and understanding. For his insolence

Ball was whipped next morning on the forecastle. He wrenched at the grating to which he was pinioned as the scourge raised weals on his blistered, ravaged back. He was lashed even more violently for his resistance. Through the day he lay in the gloomy corner where he had been thrown, eating nothing, silent, brooding in the darkness until he lapsed into a coma and died early the next day.[8]

Ogle's concern was to secure his prisoners and have time for the man-of-war to return to Cape Lopez before Roberts became alarmed. Urgency was added to anxiety when it was learned that a fortune in plunder lay in the hold of the *Little Ranger*. It had been proposed to burn the *Ranger* at sea because it had been so badly damaged that it did not seem seaworthy. Instead, it was used as a prison-ship. The pirates were incarcerated in it, guarded, and the ship was cautiously steered two hundred miles northwards to Principe. The *Swallow* sailed to the Cape.

The pirates were wondering what was keeping the *Ranger*. The general opinion was that Skyrme had been committed to a long chase and had chosen to ransack his prize at sea. Captain Bunce of the *Little Ranger* said he would give the *Ranger* a 13-gun salute when he returned just as he had celebrated the capture of a pink, the *Neptune*, Captain Hill, a little ship with a cargo awash with liquor, that the *Royal Fortune* had taken that day. No one guessed that it had been a man-of-war that had decoyed the *Ranger*. Now that the *Royal Fortune* was cleaned and trimmed into her best sailing condition Roberts was only waiting for Skyrme's return before voyaging out again.

On the morning of 10 February a ship was sighted entering the bay in the early mist, making slow headway against the gentle offshore wind. Bunce prepared to fire his salute. Roberts went back to breakfast in the Great Cabin where some of his men were already greeting the day with their customary bottles and tankards. Even so shortly after dawn many pirates were drunkenly befuddled on the barrels and bottles from the *Neptune*.

As the incoming vessel neared it was clear that she was not the *Ranger*. Some said it was Portuguese, others that it was a French slaveship putting in for water. It was of small importance. There was a wealth of gold-dust and booty aboard the *Royal Fortune* and the *Little Ranger*. Pirates lolled easily in the sunshine. Three forced men looked at the sleeping bodies of intoxicated ruffians and debated running off in the *Little Ranger* while so many pirates were incapable of preventing them.

Roberts continued his breakfast. With Hill as his guest he was enjoying a variant of 'Solomon Grundy', a fish salmagundi lavishly flavoured with pickled herring, anchovies and olives.[9] Sated, he leisurely stretched his legs in their crimson breeches, brushed a crumb from his starched, white linen suit, sipped his tea. Sunlight filtered through the diamonded windows laying bars of shadow across the cabin.

A pirate rushed in. It was Armstrong, the sailor who had deserted the *Swallow* months before. He had recognised his old ship. Roberts sprang up. The pirates would have to fight. He cursed. Years of easy victims had made him careless. Now he was caught on the hip, he the victor of Bahia, the raider of St. Christophers, caught in a trap that need never have been.

Men sprawled drunkenly. Roberts bawled at them to get ready. The men on shore had to be brought aboard, drunk or sober, the crew of the *Little Ranger* also. Every man was needed. No one moved. Roberts shouted, drew his sword. They stirred. Dennis punched his gunners into near-alertness. Magness strode the decks briskly, snapping at lingerers, roaring at the faint-hearted, kicking at half-awake men fumbling at the ropes.

Roberts put on his coat. To Armstrong he asked questions about the sailing qualities of the *Swallow*, what she did best, what her firing-strength was, how she was trimmed. He had to make a plan.

The man-of-war was on the second of a long tack that would bring her to the *Royal Fortune*. Hampered by the sandbanks her progress was snailike. By half-past ten the *Royal Fortune* had slipped her cables. The *Little Ranger* with its private treasures of chests and coffers of coins, gems and rich delights was abandoned. Ogle prepared for battle. Fenders were slung out to absorb the shock if the two great ships collided. Pirate and H.M. man-of-war bore down on each other in an appalling silence.

His decisions made and orders given Roberts finished dressing. He climbed the steps to the poopdeck, sword in hand, crossing to a place where he could look at the *Swallow* that was now almost within pistol-shot. He was clad in crimson from head to foot, a gold-patterned damask coat to match his breeches, a curling red feather in his hat. Round his neck were loops of a gold chain on which a diamond cross hung. Two pairs of elegant pistols were tucked in the folds of a silk shoulder-strap. To the crew of the *Royal Fortune* he was reassurance, standing there gazing boldly at the enemy, just standing there looking confidently at the *Swallow*.[10] Stephenson was with him, his old shipmate from the *Princess of London*, second and third mate together. Quietly they waited for the gunfire.

Johnson, the helmsman, was not so calm. Roberts had ordered him to sail straight past the man-of-war. As the ships glided by the steersman would be exposed to every gun, musket, pistol, swivel, and grapeshot that the *Swallow* could fire. He shuddered.

Armstrong had said that the naval vessel was at her best when going into the wind, but sluggish when her sails were filled from behind. Knowing this and seeing that what wind there was came from the shore Roberts decided on a stratagem that would bring the pirates to safety if one desperate moment went well. There would be no great fight he told Magness and Dennis. There were too few sober pirates for success against the powerful *Swallow*. Instead, they would let the man-of-war come deep into the bay against the wind and then, at the last moment, the *Royal Fortune* would sail directly past her rather than manoeuvring away. The pirates would have the benefit of the wind and speed enough to get out of the bay while the *Swallow* wallowed on a long turn. Once at sea the pirates' ship after its recent careen would rapidly outdistance Ogle. The naval captain would have one single chance for a broadside and then the danger would be gone.

At eleven o'clock the figureheads of the *Royal Fortune* and the *Swallow* were within twenty metres of each other, creeping together in the light breaths of wind. Chaloner Ogle stared at his opponent as Roberts sailed onwards without firing a shot. The vessels were almost level. A blasting cannonade smashed into the *Royal Fortune* and was returned by a broadside of twenty cannon that Dennis brought to bear. Swivels and smallarms spat and cracked. The pirate ship sailed on away from the *Swallow* as the man-of-war drifted helplessly towards the shore. The pirates' flags fluttered jubilantly. Roberts had escaped.

But he was already doomed. A bullet had embedded itself in the deck by the helmsman's feet. Part of the mizzen topmast had been struck by the *Swallow*'s guns and was sagging over the poop, partly entangled in the rigging of the mainmast directly above Johnson's head. He twitched as the pellets and nails and bits of glass from a long-range swivel spattered harmlessly against the stern of the *Royal Fortune*. In terror and panic the helmsman disobeyed his instructions to keep on a straight course. No sooner had the two ships passed than he swung the ship over to starboard, directly behind the departing *Swallow*'s stern. Only a few small guns could be fired from there. Almost at once the *Royal Fortune* lost way, moving hardly at all when she should have been increasing her distance from the *Swallow* as the man-of-war cumbersomely swung round.

Roberts looked at the sails. Instead of being plump with the following breeze they were limp as though the day were windless. The *Swallow* was a quarter way round the arc that would put her on course to the pirates. By changing direction Johnson had set the ship in line with the man-of-war whose sails had taken every gust and breath of air, absorbing them, becalming the *Royal Fortune*. The battle would have to be fought again, this time with both vessels abreast of each other when it would be almost impossible for either to drawn ahead without suffering devastating damage.

Helplessly Roberts waited. As the *Swallow* with its arsenal of destruction completed her turn the *Royal Fortune*'s sails creaked again but it was too late. With hysteria on the gundeck where Dennis rushed from gun to gun and where Magness bellowed and punched the still-drunken pirates back to their quarters, even as this was happening, while Roberts raged round the poopdeck swearing he would kill the next man who showed cowardice, in those minutes the *Swallow* came alongside and delivered her second broadside.

Above the impacting thunder of her guns the swivels snarled again and again. Grapeshot and whirling chainshot swept across the pirates' decks. Seamen in the *Swallow*'s rigging poured down a fury of shots from pistols and muskets. Stephenson flung himself down on the deck behind the protection of a great gun, its tackles powder-blackened, a pyramid of iron balls unfired at its side. As he picked himself up he saw the helmsman trembling. Stephenson spat at him.

Then he saw Roberts kneeling on the deck, arms outstretched, holding on to the ropes that held a cannon steady, his head bowed as though not daring to rise into another murderous flailing of shot. Stephenson kicked him. 'Stand up and fight like a man', he shouted. Roberts turned. Blood poured from his throat where the grapeshot had struck him. As he slumped forward Stephenson caught him, knocking the captain's sword from his hand with his knee. When Magness arrived Bartholomew Roberts was dead, held by a weeping Stephenson who helped the quartermaster drop the body of their captain over the side as he had often requested if he were slain in action.[11]

For two hours more the conflict roared. The *Swallow*'s huge guns crashed out their uneven bombardment. The *Royal*

Fortune more and more feebly returned fire. Magness hurled men aside so that he could fire the guns himself. Dead and wounded lay around him. Jagged holes were torn through the decks. A fire broke out in the forecastle. The mainmast fell shudderingly in a tangle of sail and lines. Under it, immoveably trapped, lay a black flag. Two or three guns continued to fire. Perhaps a score of pirates were still fighting but the majority huddled in safe places. The *Royal Fortune* quaked as another broadside hit her. The unequal fight continued, the few sober pirates hampered by the drunk, hindered by the cowards, obstructed by the forced men until they were drained of resistance. In exhaustion and futility Magness signalled for quarter before the powder-room was ablaze and blew them all to the devil.

Below, in the magazine as the firing quietened, a demented James Philips struggled with two forced men who were prising a lighted match from his hand. 'To hell together', he screamed, 'we'll blow up and go to hell together'. He struggled until he was knocked unconscious. As boats began rowing out from the *Swallow* Magness threw the Articles overboard. If that document were discovered those who had signed it would, quite literally, be condemned out of hand.

Over the years a folk-story embellished the battle off Cape Lopez with a poetically dramatic tempestuous background of driving rain, 'lightning and thunder and a small tornado'.[12] The truth was less spectacular. The *Swallow*'s officers often reminisced about the shower that had almost immediately followed the engagement with the sound of sharp raindrops like the rat-tatting of thousands of smallarms, of the flash of lightning that had split the mainmast of the *Swallow* and the heavy rains that poured down on the smoking ships followed by an eerily deathlike silence.[13]

The *Royal Fortune* was emptied of pirates and forced men alike. The *Swallow* went back to Cape Lopez on 12 February to pick up the *Little Ranger*. Some £2000 of gold-dust had already been recovered from the *Royal Fortune* and Gillespie informed Ogle that as much again was stored in the *Little Ranger* in gold, money and jewellery.

The *Little Ranger*, however, was bare. Of coins, gold, trinkets, valuables of any kind there was none. Even the pirates' own chests had been broken open. Nor was the *Neptune* in the harbour, Captain HIll having departed before the pirates came back. He also seemed to have recompensed himself for the seizure of his alcoholic freight by helping himself to a fortune. Later, when the British government was enquiring how it was that so much plunder had vanished, Hill admitted that he had commandeered a few goods in repayment for his own losses and in August at Barbados he handed over fifty ounces of gold-dust. The remainder was never recovered.

Rumours that Roberts had concealed the bulk of the treasure on the Ile de Los just north-north-east of Sierra Leone had no substance. Pirates did not hide wealth. They wasted it. 'Your true pirate dissipated his gains with a prodigality based upon the belief that what comes easily should not tarry in the going'. Even Captain Kidd's fabulous cache on Gardiner's Island off New England or Blackbeard's notorious buried treasure on Smuttynose Island, Isle of Shoals, are no more than chimerae.[14]

The *Swallow*, the *Royal Fortune* and the *Little Ranger* went to St. Thomas where the *Royal Fortune* with its naval crew stayed to pick up fresh provisions before following the man-of-war to Cape Coast Castle. Amongst the few pirates still on board the pirate vessel was Scudamore, the surgeon, the officers of the man-of-war thinking it so incredible that he could be guilty of any crime that they allowed him to stay with them and tend to some wounded pirates. So unlikely did they consider it that a skilled, well-paid doctor should voluntarily become a pirate that he was often invited to dine with the officer on the *Royal Fortune*.

Shortsightedly, Scudamore plotted a mutiny, telling one pirate that it would be easy to free the negroes held on board, overcome the unsuspecting naval guards and take the *Royal Fortune* to Angola where a new company could be raised. The wounded man refused. He was hoping for an acquittal at his trial. Scudamore crawled over to Harris, another of the wounded. 'I understand how to navigate a ship, and can soon teach you to steer', Scudamore whispered. 'And is it not better to do this, than to go back to Cape Corso and be hanged and sun dry'd?'.[15] Because of this ridiculous plot he was hanged. His chances of freedom would otherwise have been good. No surgeon had ever been executed for piracy. But when a forced man eavesdropped on the surreptitious conversation and told the officer Scudamore was chained with the others.

The majority of the pirates were in the *Swallow*, men from the *Royal Fortune* and the *Little Ranger*. Stripped, shackled to the bulwarks, manacled together, held in a prison within a prison, their cell being the barricaded gunroom in front of which Captain Ogle had another guardroom constructed, watched over by pistolled, cutlassed officers day and night, the pirates remained rebellious, their restrictions being so different from their previous anarchical freedom that they cursed and swore at everything, vowing that they would get free if there were the slightest opportunity.

Some like Bunce were cheerful. 'They would yet in these Circumstances, be impudently merry, saying, when they viewed their Nakedness, that they had not left them a half-penny to give old Charon to ferry them over Stix: And at their thin Commons, they would observe, that they fell away so fast, that they should not have Weight left to hang them'.[16]

Moody and Ashplant with two or three others planned to escape with the aid of a mulatto boy who brought their food but on the night that they were to make their attempt two unwilling pirates heard the boy whisper the time at which the uprising was to start. Learning of this the officer on duty informed Ogle who had the manacles and shackles inspected. Many had been worked loose. The guard was doubled.

It was a long, dreary, dreadful voyage. Sutton, hater of Catholics, noteworthy for his filthy oaths, was chained alongside a man who did nothing but read fitfully and pray aloud. Swearing scornfully Sutton asked what there was to pray for. 'Heaven, I hope', the man replied. 'Heaven', jeered Sutton, 'You fool, did you ever hear of any pirates going thither? Give me Hell, it's a merrier place. I'll give Roberts a salute of thirteen guns at entrance'.

The man continued his devotions. Sutton shouted for the officer to take away the fellow's prayer-books or shift him. In this way, with jests and imprecations and sighs for their ill-luck that had found them so drunk at the time of their greatest crisis the pirates were transported in the *Swallow* to Cape Coast Castle and their trial.

Bartholomew Roberts was dead. For over three years he had dominated the shipping off Africa, the West Indies and the North American coast. He amassed fortunes, marauded, fought battles, raided harbours, kept a disciplined ship, captured four hundred vessels. He had bluffed, threatened, dared. He was described, simply and properly, as 'that great pyrate, Roberts'.

'That was Roberts' men, that was, and comes of changing names to their ships, *Royal Fortune* and so on'.

[Robert Louis Stevenson, *Treasure Island*, 57.]

PART THREE

The Last Days of the Pirates

February 1722–June 1723

15

Cape Coast Castle

February 1722–June 1723

'The said man-of-war carried the said pyrate ship to St. Thomas, there left the ships and made for Cape Coast Castle where he arrived the same day the beginning of March . . . with the prisoners, in number 170, several having made their escape on shore'.

The *Daily Post*, 6 July, 1722

Built by the Portuguese and later seized by the British the great fortification of Cape Coast Castle with its projecting bastions and turrets was surrounded by forests and low hills on three of which were smaller forts. On the seaward side of the castle was a long rampart mounted with thirteen heavy cannon. Inside the towering brick walls of the quadrangular castle was a parade-ground in which vats were set to catch whatever rainfall there was. Amongst them, quarried deeply into the bedrock, were vaults to which the only access was a small hole in the surface barred by a heavy iron grating. They were for slaves. In 1722 they were also for pirates. The manacled prisoners were lowered into the dark, mouldering stink, one hundred and sixty-nine of them. Four were to die in the subterranean cells before the trial.

Organising the trial was not straightforward for naval officers

in Africa. Being unaccustomed to acting as servants of the
law they had to be doubly meticulous to avoid charges of
injustice against a prisoner who, in England, might have been
reprieved because of some technicality of which the naval
Court was unaware.

For guidance there were various Piracy Acts which
authorised Courts of Admiralty to try cases overseas to avoid
the former expense of sending suspects and witnesses back to
England for examination. By the Piracy Suppression Act of
1701 men thought to be pirates could be tried in any English
island, colony, fort or factory by a Court of seven naval officers
or other official persons such as a governor, lieutenant-governor
or president of a factory. The board had to contain the captain
of a man-of-war. At Cape Coast Castle Captain Mungo
Herdman of the *Weymouth* was elected President. Decisions,
including the death penalty, were to be reached by majority
vote in private. A further Act of 1721 stated that any person
having dealings with pirates would be deemed one himself. The
medieval claim of benefit of clergy by those literate enough to
read and write was denied.

The Court had to appoint a Registrar and a Provost. John
Atkins, surgeon of the *Swallow* was chosen as the Registrar and
was paid thirty shillings [£1.50] a day for the twenty-six days of
the hearing. One-third of this was deducted in England. The
Provost received seven shillings and sixpence [£0.38] daily.[1]

The law was clear. The difficulty lay in interpreting it. To
convict a pirate the time and place of piracy had to be proved.
Those sitting in judgement should 'have no interest directly or
indirectly in the ship, goods etc. for the robbery of which the
party stands accused'. Most members of the Court, however,
were officials of the Royal African Company whose ships,
factories and forts had been plundered by Roberts' crews. It was
known that the pirates had looted and killed elsewhere than
Africa, but there was not a single witness available to testify to
it, and very few in Africa itself except for those ships that had

been taken in the last two months. The Court would be guilty of bias if it tried the prisoners solely on the basis of their African misdeeds.

There was a debate as to whether King's Evidence could be accepted from one of the accused. Henry Dennis had offered to inform upon his fellows. He had been with Roberts from the beginning and it was a tempting solution but there was the likelihood that his would not be an uncontaminated account. There would be untestable prejudice against some shipmates and favourable excuses for others. He was rejected. With subtle logic it was decided to waive every crime of which the prisoners might be guilty except that of having resisted capture by the *Swallow*. Depositions by naval seamen and officers provided the necessary factors of time and place, and the proof of unlawfulness was that one of His Majesty's ships had been attacked. To avoid mass condemnation the accused would be tried individually.

Each man was tried on three counts: that he was a volunteer and not a forced hand; that he had willingly taken part in the plundering of vessels; and that he had accepted a share of the plunder. To be acquitted a prisoner had to be found not guilty of all three charges. The resulting trial at Capt Coast Castle was considered so fair that Charles Johnson felt able to comment that it was 'among other Happinesses, exempted from Lawyers and Law-Books . . . [and] perhaps if there was less Law, there might be more Justice than in some other Courts'.[2]

The Court consisted of the President, Captain Herdman, and six others: the Honourable James Phipps, Esq; Mr Henry Dodson; Mr Francis Boye; Mr Edmund Hyde; Mr John Barnsley; Lieutenant Charles Fanshawe; and Lieutenant John Atkins as Registrar. Transcribing from Atkins' records Johnson mistook some of the names and titles.

Separate indictments were drawn up against the crews of the *Ranger* and the *Royal Fortune*. The charges did include reference to crimes other than the attack on the *Swallow* but did not give details. It was the fight with the man-of-war that was the heart of the prosecution case, something that could be confirmed by naval witnesses. By the inclusion of vague reports of other wrongdoing a prisoner might be able to use them to prove his innocence.

On Monday, 28 March, 1722, in the castle's chapel, a spacious rectangular room, the crew of the *Ranger* were assembled for their trial. It was a Hogarthian scene. Behind a long table at one end of the chapel sat the judges, naval officers in their blue, brass-buttoned uniforms, elegant, three-corner hatted governors, powder-wigged, comfortably seated. Atkins, the Registrar, was at a separate table, quills sharpened, inkwell filled, notepaper neatly arranged.

At the far end of the hall were the pirates. Guarded by scarlet-coated soldiers the men were in rags, filthy from the dungeons, fetters clattering as they shuffled in, unshaven, unwashed, bandaged, all reeking with dirt, unrecognisable from their days of silken glory. The indictment was read.[3]

'Your, James Skyrm, Michael Lemmon, Robert Hartley & etc.

'Ye, and every one of you, are in the Name and by the Authority of our dread Sovereign Lord, George, King of Great Britain, indicted as follows: forasmuch as in open Contempt of the Laws of your Country, ye have all of you been wickedly united and articled together for the annoyance and disturbance of His Majesty's trading subjects by sea. And have in conformity to the most evil and mischievous intentions, been twice down the coast of Africa with two ships, once in the beginning of August and a second time, in January last, sinking, burning or robbing such ships and vessels as then happened in your way.

Particularly, you stand charged at the instance and information of Captain Chaloner Ogle as traitors and pirates for the unlawful opposition you made to His Majesty's ship, the *Swallow*, under his command.

For on the 5 of February last past, upon sight of the aforesaid ship you did immediately weigh anchor from under Cape Lopez on the southern coast of Africa in a French-built ship of 32 guns called the *Ranger* and did pursue and chase the aforesaid King's ship with such despatch and precipitancy as declared you common robbers and pirates.

That about ten of the clock the same morning, drawing within gunshot of His Majesty's aforesaid ship, the *Swallow*, you hoisted a piratical black flag and fired several chase guns to deter, as much as you were able, His Majesty's servants from their duty. That an hour after this, being very nigh to the aforesaid King's ship, you did audaciously continue in a hostile defence and assault for about two hours more in open violation of the laws, and in defiance of the King's colours and commission. And lastly, that in the acting and compassing of all this, you were all, and every one of you, in a wicked combination, voluntarily to exert, and actually did, in your several stations, use your utmost endeavours to distress the said King's ship, and murder His Majesty's good subjects'.

The crew were then asked one by one how they pleaded and all answered, 'Not guilty'. They were escorted back to their dungeons. The crew of the *Royal Fortune* were led in and received a similar indictment to which, having cited the chase and battle against the *Swallow*, was added:

'That this fight and insolent resistance against the King's ship was made, not only without any pretence of authority, more than that of your own depraved will, but was done also under a black flag, flagrantly by that denoting your selves robbers and traitors and violators of the laws'.

The accused pleaded not guilty and the Court adjourned until the following day.

On 29 March the prisoners from the *Ranger* appeared, each being informed of what the Court intended as evidence. If a prisoner refused to plead he would be held to have confessed. Witnesses were to be sworn in. The prisoner would be permitted to cross-examine the President. To testify against the crews of the *Ranger* and the *Royal Fortune*, Lieutenant Sun, Ralph Baldrick, boatswain, and Daniel McLaughlin, seaman, all from the *Swallow*, were selected. Between them they could confirm an accused man had been in one of the pirate ships. The prisoner would then have to prove his innocence.

One of the first to be tried was Stephen Thomas, master of the *Diligence*, who claimed that he had been forced in January that year. He had begged Captain Joseph Trahern of the captured *King Solomon* to ask Roberts for his release. Thomas Castell, who had also been taken from the *Diligence*, was called as a witness. He convinced the Court of Thomas's innocence, the judges thinking it most unlikely that a master of a ship would volunteer to join the pirates when he was earning six pounds a month. Thomas was acquitted.

Then Magness, Main, Ashplant, Bunce and twelve others were accused of attacking and ransacking the *King Solomon*.[4] Captain Trahern and his mate, George Fenn, testified against them. 'Can you shape your memory with any particulars in the seizure and robbery?', the President asked them.

'We know that Magness, quartermaster of the pirate ship, commanded the men in this boat that took us', they replied, 'and assumed the authority of ordering her provisions and stores out, which being of different kinds, we soon found were seized and sent away under more particular directions. Main, as boatswain of the pirate ship, carried away two cables and several coils of rope as what belonged to his province, beating some of our men for not being brisk enough at working the robbery. Petty, as sailmaster, saw to the sails and canvas; Harper, as cooper, to the casks and tools; Griffin to the carpenter's stores; and Oughterlaney, as pilot, having shifted himself with a suit of my clothes, a new tie-wig, and called for a bottle of wine, ordered the ship very arrogantly to be steered under commodore Roberts' stern - I suppose to know what orders there were concerning her. So far, particularly. In the general, sir, they were very outrageous, and emulous in mischief'.

The President enquired how the pirates chose men for the boarding-party to go to the *King Solomon*. The forced seaman, Castell answered that he had been a prisoner of the pirates at the time. Pirates were asked which of them wanted to go. 'And I saw that all that did, did it voluntarily. No compulsion, but rather pressing who should be foremost'.

At this alarming accusation the pirates protested. They had gone because Roberts had made them. 'Roberts commanded us into the boat, and the quartermaster made us rob the ship. We dared refuse neither of them'. Herdman was unimpressed. 'And granting it so', he responded, 'these are still your own acts, since done by orders from officers of your own election. Why would men honestly disposed, give their votes for such a captain and such a quartermaster as were every day commanding them on distasteful services'.

There was a silence. Then William Fernon, the man who had threatened to cut the ears off Comrie, the surgeon, weakly muttered that he had not voted for Magness as quartermaster but for Simpson. 'In truth, I took Magness for too honest a man and unfit for the business'. The Court ignored this irrelevant defence. It had been shown that the accused had all freely offered to board and ransack the *King Solomon* and those two crimes were sufficient to condemn them.

Henry Dennis, the would-be informer, had no credible defence. Too many forced men told of his behaviour, of his organising the ship's armament. He was unable to deny that he was a confirmed scoundrel. He denied nothing but relied on the information he had given to gain him the mercy of the Court. It did not.

When Harry Gillespie, the sailing-master of the *Royal Fortune*, was brought before the judges several conscripted seamen testified that he had always been civil to prisoners, that he appeared a reluctant member of the ship, that he had been beaten and half-drowned when captured because of his refusal to join the pirates. Mrs Trengrove told of a conversation she had had with Magness when the quartermaster said that everyone expected that Gillespie would make more attempts to get away. Gillespie had also offered to give evidence of atrocities committed by the worst pirates and this was in his favour. When information was given of how he had helped to prevent the blowing-up of the *Royal Fortune* at the risk of his own life and of his repeated endeavours to run away the Court was unanimous in its verdict of 'Not Guilty'.[5]

William Guinneys was less deserving. He had been the mate of the *Ranger* and had taken charge of one of the watches when Skyrme had been suffering from an agonising hangover. He was not a prepossessing figure. He admitted that he had supped with Roberts, 'but nobody ever looked on it as a mark of favour or any sort of distinction because everyone came and ate and drank with him as the humour took them'. The Court, not being composed of rigorous English judges, considered him a pathetic human being, a man fit only to be commanded. Astonishingly, they acquitted him. Two naval sailors carried Guinneys, who had swooned in unbelief, from the hall.

James Harris failed. He had accepted a nightgown from Roberts knowing it to be stolen. He was condemned to imprisonment in London's Marshalsea gaol until further witnesses could be discovered. A more fortunate and certainly ingenious seaman was Christopher Grainger, one of the men forced from the *Cornwall* galley at Calabar the previous October.

He persuaded the Court that he had pretended to be Irish because 'it was against the pirates' rules to accept [Irishmen] because they had been formerly cheated by one Kennedy who run away with their money'. The judges believed him.

James White, the crippled musician who had given money to Captain Rolls to have his name entered in the *Gazette* as a forced man was acquitted. So was his shipmate, Nicholas Brattle, a fiddler. One by one the pirates were brought before the Court, some insolent with a resigned bravado while others sobbed and begged for mercy. Some forced men were so scared that they could hardly speak and were nearly sent to the gallows through their failure to plead. Others babbled on unthinkingly until some sentence slipped out that damned them. Willson the surgeon came, his sentence almost a foregone conclusion, so much was known of his eagerness to rejoin the pirates and his obsessive desire to share in the booty. Although the Articles were lost men swore that he had signed them.

The surgeon blandly denied everything.[6] He called on Comrie to defend him, the very man he had persuaded the pirates to force. He reminded him of four things that proved his innocence. Comrie would remember that Willson had asked Roberts why surgeons were compelled to sign the Articles. Secondly, he had told Comrie how glad he was to have been able to escape from the pirates; thirdly, he had only said to Roberts that he welcomed gunfire because it gave him practice in surgery; and, lastly, whenever the pirates released a surgeon Willson had claimed that it was his turn.

Comrie agreed with everything. No questioning from the Court dissuaded him and although the verdict was deferred until the following day Willson was released. It would never have happened in England. But Willson did not live long to enjoy his luck. He died quite suddenly in Africa, probably as a result of the privations he had suffered on that coast.[7]

Isaac Russell, one time boatswain's mate of the *Royal Fortune*, claimed that he had continually feigned sickness to evade the uncongenial duties demanded of him. He had been with the pirates for only a year. As evidence of his honesty he stated that he had been with Lieutenant Maynard when that officer had trapped and killed Blackbeard. It did not save Russell. He was sent for trial at the Marshalsea.

What was remarkable about the Court was its clemency. Of the some hundred and sixty or so that were tried only fifty-two were executed. Batches were brought back to the hall to hear the sentence of death pronounced.

'David Simpson, William Magness, Richard Hardy, Thomas Sutton, Christopher Moody, Valentine Ashplant:

Ye and each of you are adjuged and sentenced to be carried back to the place from whence ye came, from thence to the place of execution without ye gates of this Castle, and there within the Flood Marks to be hanged by the neck till ye are Dead, Dead, Dead,

And the Lord have mercy on your souls.

After this ye and each of you shall be taken down, and your bodies hung in chains'.

It was the largest trial of pirates ever held. Seventy-four men were acquitted. Fifty-four were condemned to be hanged but two were reprieved. Twenty more were sentenced to death but in the ensuing weeks saved their lives by volunteering to become indentured servants of the Royal African Company. Seventeen others were sent to London's Marshalsea prison. Ten pirates in the *Ranger* had been killed at sea, three in the *Royal Fortune*, Bartholomew Roberts among them. Fifteen more had died on the voyage back to Cape Coast Castle and four in the castle dungeons. Excluding seventy-five negroes, later sold as slaves, it was a total of one hundred and ninety-seven men of whom over a third were released.

The twenty successful in petitioning to join the service of

the Royal African Company exchanged an immediate death for a lingering one. Henry Dennis was among them.

'The Humble Petition of Thomas How etc.[8]

Humbly sheweth: that your Petitioners being unhappily and unwarily drawn into that wretched and detestable crime of Piracy, for which they now stand justly condemned, they most humbly pray the clemency of the Court, in the mitigation of their Sentence, that they may be permitted to serve the Royal African Company, in this Country for seven Years, in such a manner as the Court think proper; that by their last Punishment being made sensible of the Error of their former Ways, they will for the Future become faithful Subjects, good Servants, and useful in their Stations, if it please the Almighty to prolong their Lives'.

The five judges remaining at Cape Coast Castle consented to the petition on the basis that it was better to save lives that could perform some useful purpose. By 26 April the indentures were drawn up and the agreements were signed, sealed and exchanged in the presence of the Court.

'This Indenture made the twenty-sixth day of April, *Anno Regni Regis Georgii magnae Britanniae etc. Septimo, Domini, Millessimo, Sepcentissimo, viginti duo*, between Roger Scot, late of the city of Bristol mariner of the one part, and the Royal African Company of England, their Captain-General and Commander in Chief, for the time being, on the other part, witnesseth that the said Roger Scot, doth hereby covenant, and agree to, and with, the said Royal African Company, their Captain-General and Commander in Chief, for the time being, to serve him, or his lawful successors, in any of the Royal African Company's settlements on the coast of Africa, from the day of the date of these presents, to the full term of seven years, from hence next ensuing, fully to be compleat and ended; there to serve in such employment, as the said Captain-General, or his successors shall employ him, according to the custom of the country in like kind.

In Consideration whereof, the said Captain-General and Commander in Chief, doth covenant and agree to, and with, the said Roger Scot, to find and allow him meat, drink, apparel and lodging, according to the custom of the country.

In witness whereof, the Parties aforesaid, to these presents, have interchangeably put their hands and seals, the day and year first written above.

Signed, sealed and delivered, in the presence of us, at Cape-Corso-Castle in Africa, where no stamped paper was to be had.

> Mungo Herdman. President.
> John Atkins, Register. Witnesses.

The volunteers went to the diseased mines of the Gold Coast, now Ghana, then the unhealthiest part of Africa for Europeans. Few survived seven years. Malnutrition, hard labour and fevers would have killed them long before.

Thomas Armstrong who had deserted from the *Swallow* and who had informed Roberts of the man-of-war's sailing qualities was taken to the *Weymouth* to be executed in accordance with naval regulations.[9] After long hours of repentence he was led on deck. A noose dangled over the yardarm, secured to the capstan where a party of seamen waited for the order to turn the wheel and wind up the rope. Armstrong urged the onlookers to lead a good and honest life and they accompanied him in singing the last verses of Psalm 140. A gun was fired. The deserter was hauled up by the neck and executed as the court-martial ordained.

In the castle vaults the condemned pirates waited for their

own deaths with stoicism. Peter Scudamore asked for two or three days' grace as he prepared himself for death. It was granted and he passed his last days reading the Bible and praying. Samuel Fletcher had been promised a reprieve and was alarmed when officers arrived to take the prisoners to the gallows. He had a hurried message sent to the Court. 'I ask the meaning of it', he wrote, 'and humble desire to know whether you design mercy for me or not. If you do, then I am infinitely obliged to you and think the whole service of my life an incompetent return for so great a favour. But if I am to suffer then the sooner the better that I may be out of my pain'.[10]

The Provost returned. The reprieve had been signed. The Court had merely overlooked it in the mass of orders for executions that had to be endorsed.

There were no other remissions. Nor did the pirates behave as though they expected any. Since their convictions they had been damning and cursing the Court for its partiality that had brought them to such a fate while others had been excused. Their warrants were issued.

'Pursuant to the sentence given on Saturday by the Court of Admiralty at Cape Coast Castle against Dav. Simpson, Wm Magness &c

You are hereby directed to carry the aforementioned malefactors to the place of execution, without the gates of this Castle, tomorrow morning at 9 of the clock, and there, within the floodmarks, cause them to be hanged by the neck till they are dead, for which this shall be your warrant.

Given under my hand this 2nd day of April, 1722.

Mungo Herdman.

To Joseph Gordyn, Provost Marshall.

The bodies remove in chains to the Gibbets already erected on the adjacent hillocks.

Soldiers escorted the pirates to the parade ground where their fetters were broken off and they were taken to a large gallows on a rock overlooking the sea. They almost rushed from the castle, ranting, in loud voices. Atkins, surgeon, naval lieutenant, Registrar, and now a voluntary chaplain, noticed that unlike the others Sutton was whispering to himself.[11] Thinking that the man was expressing remorse Atkins asked if he wanted to confess his sins. Sutton swore at him. He was suffering from fever but he was as fit to go to Hell as Atkins would be in another forty years.

When the lieutenant called on other men to repent they laughed and called for drinks as was usual at public executions. Some entreated the soldiers to lend them their caps so that they would look finer on the scaffold. Then they cursed the tribunal again. Hoping to distract them Atkins asked one or two how old they were or what part of Britain they came from. 'What's that to you', shouted Ashplant, 'I shall soon be dead because of the law and I'll give no account of myself but to God'. Simpson saw Elizabeth Trengrove in the large crowd of onlooking sailors, civilians and negroes. 'I've lain with that bitch three times', he hissed, 'and now she's come to see me hanged'.[12] This, like other statements such as the comment that William Williams was 'speechless at execution' quoted in the *General History . . .* by Johnson, is a remark that only Atkins could have known.

At the foot of the scaffold the prisoners' hands were tied behind their backs. Hardy muttered at this breach of custom. 'I've seen many a man hanged', he said, 'but this way of the hands being tied behind 'em I'm a stranger to and never saw before in my life'.

They were turned off. When the corpses were taken down some were dipped in tar and enclosed in a framework of iron bands. Their bodies were carried to the gibbets on nearby hills where they were suspended by chains, washed by the sea, timbers creaking, metal clanking in the morning breezes, hanging there as Bunce, who died bravely, said, 'as a beacon upon a rock to warn erring mariners of danger'.[13]

'You've seen 'em' maybe', wrote Robert Louis Stevenson, 'hanged in chains, birds about 'em, seamen p'inting 'em out as they go down with the tide . . . And you can hear the chains a-jangle as you go about and reach for the other buoy'. They were just one more batch of four to five hundred pirates hanged between 1716 and 1726.[14]

Others slowly perished in unremitting drudgery for the Royal African Company. John Jessup was one. His escape from Cape Lopez and his information about Roberts' whereabouts to Ogle did not help him. As a gunner he had fired at merchant ships and he had bought plundered clothes 'at the mast as was the custom'. There was no mitigation and he was given a death sentence. Only by joining the Royal African Company did he avoid the gallows.

Other pirates decayed in the foul dampness of the Marshalsea cells where jail fever claimed them. A few, a very few, had escaped into the wilderness at Cape Lopez from which it is improbable that they emerged.

In August, 1723, when the trial was over, the *Swallow*, the *Weymouth* and their three prizes crossed the Atlantic to Port Royal in the West Indies, seeing an eclipse of the moon on the way. On the 28th the severest hurricane in memory roared across the island, sinking all but six of the fifty ships anchored there, splintering the *Royal Fortune* and the *Little Ranger* to bits on the rocks. Houses were blown to fragments, the castle was split, the church demolished, two thirds of the town flattened as torrents undermined the foundations. Three or four hundred people were killed or drowned in streets more than a metre deep in raging sea-water in which boats, barrels and lumber slammed and swirled murderously. Atkins took shelter in a brick-built house.[15]

The two men-of-war returned to England in April, 1723, and the crews were paid off in May. The following month Ogle was knighted by George I for his defeat of the pirates. Earlier, in January, the *Ranger* was brought into Rhode Island by H.M. *Greyhound* to be disposed of as a prize.[16] The ship and her effects were appraised at £5364.9s and 9d [£5364.49] and on 4 May this sum was given to Ogle as a reward. From it £280 was deducted for expenses and £1940 was allotted as 'head-money' for the crew of the *Swallow*.

Ogle did not advise his men of the award and it was not until 3 April 1725, that the *London Journal* exposed his silence, explaining the unexpected source of their reporter's information. 'It is remarkable that none of the Officers and Crew of the said Ship knew they were entitled to the said Bounty, till the publishing of a book entitled, *A General History of Pirates*, where the said Proclamation is taken notice of'.

£1940 was a derisory sum, no more than a few pounds for each man. Ogle received over £3000. There were petitions from seamen and widows for a fairer allocation. The Admiralty supported them but Ogle yielded nothing. Despite repeated dunning he kept all the money, justifying its retention as a gift from the king. His recent ennoblement, he claimed covetously, was involving him in extra expenditure and necessitated his retaining every penny.[17]

With the examples of the merchant captain, Snelgrave, defrauding his loyal crew of their legitimate wages and of the naval captain, Ogle, refusing to share any part of his 'gift' with the officers and men of the *Swallow* whose bravery in battle had overcome the pirates it is not surprising that many common seamen preferred piracy to poverty. Chaloner Ogle's probable ancestor, Sir William Ogle of Michelmersh, Hampshire, a Royalist, defended Winchester Castle against Oliver Cromwell in 1645. Surrender was agreed on 6 October but delayed until 2 o'clock the following afternoon 'by reason the Governor and some of the Officers being unwilling to leave any wine behind them, had made themselves drunk – 700 men marched out and the Viscount Ogle as drunk as a beggar.'[18] The mercenary Chalnor Ogle was a less endearing character.

The pirates' story began at New Providence when they overpowered Woodes Rogers' sloops. Their first captain, Howel Davis, died violently at Principe. They rose to riches in the West Indies. Some fled to Scotland where they were hanged or to London where they skulked in poverty until the law found them. With Roberts other pirates plundered at a dozen ports, swaggered through the Caribbean, deserted, threatened, murdered, roistered and drank their ways to execution on the sunlit shores of Africa, their great captain killed in battle, their Company split in factions of greed, terror, envy and bitterness. They had risen and fallen in four short years. Not one of them died rich and at liberty.

Except perhaps Anne Bonny.

APPENDIX A

Pirates at Cape Coast Castle[1]

(1) Executed pirates. * = Bodies later hung in chains.
Valentine Ashplant*; Philip Bill; Charles Bunce; Robert Butson; James Clements; John Coleman*; Robert Crow; William Davies*; William Fernon*; Thomas Giles; Cuthbert Goss; Dan Harding; Richard Hardy*; Abraham Harper; Richard Harries; Robert Haws; Robert Hay; Israel Hynde*; Agge Jacobson*; John Jayson; Benjamin Jeffries; John Jessup from the *Diligence* captured in 1722; Marcus Johnson; Robert Johnson; Peter Lashly; William Magness*; William Mackintosh; William Main; Joe Mansfield; Michael Mare; Christopher Moody*; Joseph Moore; Joseph Nossiter; John Parker; William Petty; James Phillips*; William Phillips; John Philps*; Peter Scudamore*; David Simpson*; James Skyrme*; George Smith; John Stevenson; Thomas Sutton*; Peter de Vine; John Walden*; Edward Watts*; William Watts*; William Williams and William Williams, both from the *Sidbury* taken at Newfoundland in June, 1720; William Wood.

(2) A naval deserter hanged on the Weymouth[2]
Robert Armstrong.

(3) Pirates sentenced to death who successfully petitioned to become indentured servants of the Royal African Company.[3]
James Cromby; Henry Dennis; Samuel Fletcher; James

Greenham; John Griffin; Hugh Harris; Robert Hartley; John Horn; Thomas How; John Jessup from the *Princess of London*, 1719; John King; John Lane; Joshua Lee; David Littlejohn; John Mitchell; Thomas Owen; David Rice; Roger Scott; William Shurin; William Taylor.

(4) Pirates sent to the Marshalsea prison[4]

Altogether seventeen men were sent to England for trial. Of them the longest-serving was Henry Hunkins, forced from the *Success* sloop in the West Indies in June, 1720. Most unfortunate of the prisoners were Henry Graves, John Rimer and James Cosins, all of whom joined Roberts as late as January, 1722.

(5) Background details.[5]

Of these men the longest-serving pirates were those who had sailed with Howel Davis when he mutinied and took over Woodes Rogers' two sloops in 1718: Richard Hardy, Christopher Moody, William Magness and Thomas Sutton. Another, Thomas Jones, had returned to England and was imprisoned in the Marshalsea.

The average age of the pirates whose year of birth was recorded was 28. Only four of the 52 were over 40. The oldest of the condemned men, at 45 was Richard Harries, taken from the *Phoenix* in 1720. Not much younger was Peter de Vine, a Londoner of 42, and 'forced' volunteer from the *King Solomon*, a ship captured three months before de Vine's execution. He had 'enjoyed' exactly a month of piratical freedom from 5 January to 5 February, 1722. He was hanged on 9 April.

The youngest, aged 19, was Joseph Moore from the Wiltshire village of Mere twenty miles west of Stonehenge. He had enlisted from the *Mayflower* in February, 1721. He was executed two days after de Vine.

By far the majority, 42 per cent, were west country seamen from Cornwall, Devon and Somerset. The port of London provided a further 19 per cent and there were smaller numbers from northern England and Wales. Together they formed the greater part of a cosmopolitan crew whose remaining fourth came from places as far apart as Ireland, Scotland, the West Indies, Holland and Greece.

APPENDIX B

Captain Charles Johnson and the 'History'

The name of 'Charles Johnson', author of the A *General History of the Robberies and Murders of the most notorious Pyrates*, 1724, is almost certainly a pseudonym. His book was extremely popular. It had a second edition in its first year, a third in 1725 and a fourth with a second volume containing lives of additional pirates in 1726. By the present time there have been some seventy editions in four languages and the book was the inspiration for Stevenson's *Treasure Island* of 1883.[1] 'Johnson' was also credited as the author of *A General History . . . of Highwaymen*, 1734, but this was no more than a copy of Alexander Smith's book of 1714 with some lives of pirates appended. It gives no clue to the identity of the author.

Who he was is unknown. *The Dictionary of National Biography* lists a Captain Charles Johnson, fl. 1724–35, as the author but assumes that his was a nom-de-plume. Probably not by coincidence two men with that name were certainly connected with piracy. In 1682 Captain Charles Johnson, R.N., was employed to catch a notorious buccaneer, Jean Hamlin.[2] There was also an overweight, pedestrian playwright who wrote a play, *The Successful Pyrate*, about Henry Avery that was profitably performed at the Theatre Royal, Drury Lane, in 1712.[3] His verbal ability did not impress Alexander Pope.

'Johnson, who now to sense, now to nonsense leaning,
Means not, but blunders round a meaning'.

Alexander Pope, Dunciad.

It is feasible that whoever wrote the *History* deliberately
chose the pen-name of 'Charles Johnson', already doubly
associated with piracy, to conceal himsel under an appropriate
pseudonym, a practice often used by Daniel Defoe. In 1932
John Robert Moore actually proposed Defoe as the writer,
basing his arguments on stylistic and idiomatic correspondences
between the *General History* and Defoe's other works and on
the writer's liking for anonymity, Moore expanded this theory
in 1939.[4] Scholarly criticisms have been expressed about his
ideas by Furbank & Owens in their *The Canonisation of Daniel
Defoe*[5] although accepting 'that the largest part of his [Defoe's]
work was published anonymously and pseudonymously'.[6] Of
over two hundred works accepted by Furbank and Owens only
twelve have Defoe's name on them. In a polemical age of fierce,
sometimes physically violent, religious and political
controversies pen-names or anonymity were sensible and
usually successful precautions against prosecution or assault.[7]

Furbank and Owens argued incisively that many of Moore's
verbal and syntactical parallels between phrases in the *General
History* and in Defoe's known works such as *Robinson Crusoe*
were extremely weak and unconvincing. They also pointed to
several puzzling discrepancies between what was written in the
General History about pirates such as Gow and Low and
accounts given in other works attributed to Defoe like *An
Account of the Conduct and Proceedings of the Late John Gow*,
1725, claimed to be by Defoe by a forerunner of Moore's,
William Lee, and *The Four Years' Voyages of Captain George
Roberts*, 1726, assigned to Defoe by Moore although the book's
title stated it had been written by George Roberts himself.[8]

The story of Gow's life appeared in the *Account* of 1725 and
the short Chapter XVII in the *General History* repeated part of

it but included new material about John Smith, alias Gow, who persuaded his men to sail to the Orkneys so that he could be married there. There is no difficulty in accounting for the conflicting versions. Between 12 February and 5 June, 1725, no fewer than eight items were written about Gow in the *London Journal*. 'Johnson' could have merged that material into what had already been written in the *Account* by someone else.

The same explanation would hold good for Edward Low. In the *Voyages* the ruffianly Low of the *General History* is portrayed as a gentleman and genial host. This inconsistency in Low's character can be plausibly explained as the result of the *General History* and the *Account* being by different writers although in one instance it was ingeniously ascribed to a split personality. The pirate was 'a loving husband and father, and was usually kind to married men whom he captured. Otherwise he was feared as a ferocious beast of unequalled cruelty, who once killed 53 Spanish captives'.[9] The former suggestion is as plausible.

That Defoe, or anyone else, should have composed widely differing descriptions of Smith-Gow and Low, and both within a few months of each other, is improbable. But it does not invalidate Defoe as the author of the *General History*. The objections are valueless unless it can be demonstrated beyond doubt that Defoe was the author of the *Account* and the *Voyages* and therefore impossible as the author of the *General History*. Furbank and Owens poignantly exposed the fallacies in Moore's reasoning. What they did not do, probably could not, was offer conclusive proof that Defoe did not write the *General History*. Moore's arguments, not Defoe's identity as Charles Johnson, were their concern. A negative, moreover, can only be established by positive evidence supporting an alternative. It has been rightly observed that absence of evidence is not evidence of absence and Defoe must remain a possibility as the author who wrote under the name of Charles Johnson.

Several factors favour him. The style of *A General History of the Pyrates . . .* , is similar to others of his works. Its foible of suddenly changing tenses from the past into the present, its topics of maritime trade, 'shipbuilding, fisheries, storms, trials, executions and dying speeches' are characteristic of other works by Defoe.[10] His interest in piracy is proved by his two earlier novels about them, *The King of the Pirates*, 1719, and *The Life Adventures and Piracies of Captain Singleton*, 1720, both indubitably parts of his canon as were *Colonel Jacque*, 1723 and *A New Voyage Around the World*, 1724.

In 1719 he published *Robinson Crusoe*, about the marooned seaman, Alexander Selkirk. References to piracy were abundant. Turley pertinently remarked on that prevalence and the strange silence of commentators about it. 'The neglect of piracy in criticism of Defoe's canon is baffling because scholars have recently examined other traditionally popular literary genres such as crime literature to contextualise and offer new readings of Defoe's major texts and novels'.[11]

Crime fascinated him. Between 1722 and 1725 he wrote accounts of well-known criminals such as the burglar, petty highwayman and prison-breaker, Jack Sheppard. He was virtually the editor and writer of *Applebee's Weekly Journal* and in London he had access to newsheets such as the *Post Boy* and many others with their snippets of piracy provided by seamen returning from Africa and the Americas.

Another source of information was the naval surgeon John Atkins,[12] Registrar at the pirates' Cape Coast Castle trial. He returned to England in May, 1723, probably bringing a transcript of the trial with him. Even before then 'Charles Johnson' had access to details of the Court's proceedings. On 20 February, 1723, the *Daily Courant* printed 'An Account of the Tryal of All the Pyrates lately taken by Capt. Ogle', a work perhaps by Atkins himself and sent to London in a merchant ship returning from Africa between April and August, 1722 when the *Swallow* and *Weymouth* left Cape Coast Castle for the West Indies.

Such up-to-date material explains why 'Johnson' is trustworthy about the later history of Bartholomew Roberts.

Atkins would have learned about recent events from Roberts' crew. Only long-serving and probably uncommunicative hands such as Sutton and Ashplant, a man whom Atkins himself said would not talk to him, could have given him descriptions of episodes as early as 1719 and 1720. This accounts for Johnson's comparative unreliability about the beginning of Roberts' career for which only two men could have helped him. Most of Roberts' crew in the Marshalsea had joined the pirates too late to have anything but hearsay about Howel Davis or the forcing of Roberts or the raid at Bahia. 'Johnson' may, however, have spoken with Thomas Jones, a shipmate of Howel Davis on the piratical desertion from New Providence in 1718 and who would remember general, if vague, details of episodes so long ago. He died in 1724.

Three years earlier Walter Kennedy had been in the same prison. Although described as having a good memory he had only garbled recollections of Howel Davis and the mutiny in the *Buck*. He remembered vividly how he had survived the ambush on Principe where Davis was killed but confused Davis with Roberts when recalling the capture of the Portuguese treasure-ship at Bahia. Erratic reminiscences like these explain the inadequacies in the history of Roberts' early career.[13] Nevertheless, personal information such as that enabled Chapter IX of 'Captain Bartho. Roberts and his Crew' in the *General History* to be long and increasingly well-informed. For other notorious pirates such as Avery, Blackbeard and Anne Bonny the compiler would have been dependent on court proceedings and popular stories.

Against the arguments supporting Defoe as the writer of the *General History* is the fact that he may not have had the time. The *General History* was written fast explaining the occasionally clumsy prose. The book's first edition contained 250,000 words transcribed from trials and newspaper reports and then written at the longest between March and December, 1723, 800 words a day, to give the printer time to publish the book the following May. This is a problem. In spite of Defoe's reputation as 'the most prolific author in the English language' with a 'swashbuckling love of travel, adventure and piracy'[14] he was busy with a multitude of projects. In 1724 he published the novel *Roxana* and the first volume of *A Tour Through the Whole Island of Great Britain* and a *Narrative of Murder at Calais* and the *Life of John Sheppard* and the *Robberies, Escapes etc of John Sheppard*. To add the quarter of a million words of the *General History* would have been difficult even for him.

Although on page 477 of her magisterial *Daniel Defoe. His Life*, Baltimore, 1989, Paula Backscheider observed that between 1718 and 1721 'most of his serious attention [to criminals] went to pirates' she did not refer either to the *General History* . . . or to Johnson. The question was left unmentioned and unresolved.

In the absence of an alternative candidate Defoe remains a possible but unproven author of that splendid source-book about piracy. But should he really have been the chronicler then perhaps the *The General History of the* . . . *Pyrates* with its bullets, battles and bombardments might be sub-titled, *The 'cannonisation' of Daniel Defoe*.[15]

Notes

Abbreviations

Ad	Admiralty Papers, PRO.
AOWJ	*Appleby's Original Weekly Journal*, BC.
APC	Acts of the Privy Council, BMRR.
BC	The Burney Collection of 18th century news-sheets, BMRR.
BMRR	British Museum Reading Room.
CA	Court of Admiralty.
CO	Colonial Office Papers, PRO.
CSP (Col)	Calendar of State Papers, Colonial Series, BMRR.
DP	*Daily Post*, BC.
HCA	High Court of Admiralty Papers, PRO.
HCA 49	Cape Coast Castle trial, March 1722. Bracketed names refer to the testimony of individuals.
CA 1/54	London trial, July 1721, of Walter Kennedy.
JCTP	*Journal of the Commissioners for Trade and Plantation*, PRO.
LG	*London Gazette*, BC.
LJ	*London Journal*, BC.
OWJ	*Original Weekly Journal*, BC.
PB	*Post Boy*, BC.
PRO	Public Records Office.
RAC	Royal African Company.
SCHA	Criminal Records of the Scottish High Court of Admiralty, I. (1705–34), 316–400. Edinburgh trial, November, 1720. SCR.
SCR	Scottish Records Office.
T	Treasury Papers.
TRHS	*Transactions of the Royal Historical Society*.
WJ (BG)	*Weekly Journal or British Gazette*, BC.
WJ (SP)	*Weekly Journal or Saturday Post*, BC.

A General History . . . of the Most Notorious Pyrates . . . References to Charles Johnson's *General History* are from the 1972 edition edited by Manuel Schonhorn.

Black Barty

Introduction
1 The identity of Charles Johnson, author of *The General History . . .* is unknown. For a brief discussion of the problem see Appendix B.

Chapter One
1 Robinson Crusoe: Rogers, 121–31; Cooke, 36–7; Winston, 180–1, 183, 191. The Island: Souhami, 213–22. That *Robinson Crusoe* was based on Alexander Selkirk has been questioned. See: R. West, *Daniel Defoe. The Life and Strange, Surprising Adventures*, Carroll & Graf, New York, 2000, 237–8.
2 Woodes Rogers' expedition: CO 23/1. Sloops: Cordingly, 1995, 190–2.
3 Goats and ribbons: Anon., *Lives of the Most Notorious Criminals . . .*, London, 1735, ed. A.L. Hayward, London, 1927. 36 (Walter Kennedy).
4 Johnson, 142. Pirates surrendering: Dow & Edmonds, 345.
5 Vane: Johnson, 135–47, 616, 673; Carse, 164–5; Pringle, 186.
6 Rogers to Steele: CO 23/1. January 30, 1718/19; Little, 188, 189.
7 Mutiny of trading ships: SHCA, indictment 318–23 (evidence of Hews); 384–91 (Murray); HCA1/54, 122 (Kennedy).
8 Cape Franbarway: SHCA, indictment, 316–23.
9 Richard Jones; capture SHCA, 358 (Jones).
10 Vane's demotion and execution: Whipple, 126–7, 129.
11 Jones' escape: SCHA, 358 (Jones).
12 *Loyal Merchant:* HCA 1/54, 123 (Green).
13 Other merchant ships: HCA 1/54, 119 (Bennett); SHCA, 358–9 (Dowden). The Liverpool ship: SHCA, (indictment).
14 Royal African Company forts: Calder, 1981, 267.
15 Capture of Gambia fort: CO 31/15, 13ff; Anon (1806).
16 Olivier la Bouche: Johnson, 173; Mitchell, 124; Platt & Wright, 165–71.
17 Merchant vessel: CO 31/15, 13; SHCA 359–60 (Luntly).
18 Blackbeard: Johnson, 71–94 (treasure, 85); Sternbeck, 185–94; skull: Platt & Wright, 160. see also: Burg, 114–15.
19 Walking the plank: Pringle, 112, 1st century BC Cilician raiders are reputed to have tormented Roman captives in this way. see: Mitchell, 26.
20 Blackbeard's wife: Johnson, 76. Deadman's Chest: Stevenson, 5; Fuller & Leslie-Melville, 92–3; Verrill, 8–10; *Daily Telegraph*, 30 March, 1995.
21 *Queen Anne's Revenge:* BBC2 television broadcast, 2000, 'Blackbeard's Revenge' series, *Journeys to the Bottom of the Sea.*
22 Selkirk, 1711–18: R. Steele, *The Englishman* 26, December 3, 1713; Megroz, 142–59; Carse, 136 – Sophia 'Bunce'.
23 Jones as boatswain: SHCA 384–91 (Murray).

Notes

Chapter Two

1 *Mourroon* galley: CO 31/15, 479.

2 William Hall: SHCA 377–82 (Daw).

3 *Rising Sun*: Snelgrave considered 'Cocklyn and his crew to be a set of the basest and most cruel villains'. Christopher Moody: Johnson, 278. Johnson missed many details of Moody in the *Whitehall Evening Post* of 30 December, 1718 and 6 February, 1720, and in the *Weekly Journal or British Gazetteer* of 24 February, 1719. Such oversights suggest that the concept of a book about pirates had not yet occurred to him.

4 *Two Friends*: CO 31/15, 13.

5 'Crackers': Atkins, 40–2; Johnson, 1724, 226–7; Fuller & Leslie-Melville, 52.

6 Royal African Company: Ward (1948).

7 Royal African Company servants: Atkins, 90–4.

8 Cocklyn's flag: SHCA 377–82 (Daw).

9 Rackam: Whipple, 127–8, 129.

10 Anne Bonny and Mary Read: Sternbeck, 209–17; J. Wheelwright, 'Tars, tarts and swash-bucklers', 180, in: Stanley. For Bonny's life, see: Carlova; Johnson, 159–65, 623–6; for Read: Shay.

11 Anne Bonney: PRO CO 137/14/XC18757. Female pirates, Cordingly, 2001, 77–98; Turley, 96–101.

12 Ships taken at Sierra Leone: OWJ, July 25, 1719; CO 31/15, 13ff.

13 Attack on the fort: T 70/6.

14 Plunket and Cocklyn: Smith (1727). Smith said the argument was between Plunket and Roberts in 1720 but from the details he gives of Roberts having three ships and of the attack on the fort it seems that local gossip had mistaken the year and transferred the incident to the more notorious pirate. Smith added that a ship was sunk in a nearby creek. There is no reason to disbelieve him.

15 *Sarah*: CO 31/15, 13.

16 Thixton: SHCA 377–82 (Daw).

Chapter Three

1 The early parts of this chapter were taken mainly from: Snelgrave (1734). The conversations were reported verbatim.

2 Wages: Rediker, 121–5; Uring, xxviii. Naval pay: Rodgers, 124–37.

3 Bartholomew Roberts and a pirate's life: Johnson, 244. A verbatim report.

4 Cordingly, 1995, 193–4.

5 Captain Snelgrave, in his *New Account of Guinea*, gave a most plausible, detailed account of his tribulations and he ended his story with his return to London in August, 1719 when his employer gave him

some money to give to 'his poor sailors' who also had suffered but had stayed by him.

With this in mind it is ironical to read the *Weekly Journal or Saturday Post*, 7 November, 1719. 'Wapping, 28 October, 1719'.

On 8th November the — Galley, Captain —, commander, sailed out of the river for Holland. [It] arrived on the coast of Guinea 4 April and came to an anchor off the harbour of Sierleon; where they were the same night unfortunately surprised and taken by pirates. The captain was in the utmost confusion upon this occasion and it was with great difficulty his men preserved him from falling a sacrifice to the causeless fury of the pirates, they begging his life upon their knees. Eight of the ship's crew went with the Chief Mate at the head of them, immediately took on with the pirates and the greater part of the remainder dispersed themselves as the prospect of employment invited them. But the captain cast his eye on the third mate (who had then a tender made him of a profitable employ by another ship superior to his own) and entreated him in the most earnest moving manner that he would not forsake him in this his greatest extremity backing his pleas with mountains of promises of what he would do for him at his return to England. The captain's oratory prevailed with the young fellow's good nature and he determined to stay, and by his stay was chiefly, if not solely, instrumental in recovering upwards of a £1000 worth of the ship's cargo and in conjunction with the carpenter and gunner of securing the same to the owners, they not only taking care of it in the country to an infinite fatigue and hazard, but also continuing the same home to England, the captain all along issuing orders to them both written and oral, as employed by him and under his command.

The captain was well received by his owners and had the command of another ship immediately conferred upon him as placing, no doubt, the merit of his faithful men's service to his own account: but when they came to England and waited on the captain in expectation of their rewards, this promising gentlemanlike captain together with his fears had taken care to bid adieu to his Word of Honour and not only denied them any matter of favour but even the payment of their wages alleging they were lost together with the ship though no one who knows anything of the sea can be ignorant that there is a salvage of goods sufficient to answer the demands of men's wages. They are ever paid as a particular encouragement for their care and fidelity, and that not as a matter of favour but of right. I am unwilling to take up too much room on your paper and therefore only observe that those whose expense and much trouble, both which must be detrimental to persons in their present circumstances for they had neither insured at home or recovered anything from the pirates of their own though they lost their all, and that not a little, and cannot but think it hard to be thus severely dealt with and look upon it but small encouragement for men to forgo their own interest in favour of the owners',

Which shows that even 'honest' merchant captains were not above a little private piracy when the circumstances were right.

For Snelgrave and Sierra Leone, including the captains and the three coats, see also: Fuller & Leslie-Melville, 50–66.

6 Plunder: SHCA, 377–82 (Hews).
7 Cocklyn's quartermaster: Pringle, 258.
8 Release of the *Guinea Hen*: CO 31/15, 13.
9 Murder of the negroes: SHCA, 384–91 (Murray); *WJ or BG*, 10 October, 1719.
10 Small merchantman: CO 31/15, 262. The ship was the *Employ*.
11 Election of Taylor: SHCA, 382–4 (Cheape).
12 *Two Friends*: CO 31/15, 479.
13 Merchantman, the *Loyalty*: SHCA, 382–4 (Cheape); CO 31/15, 484.
14 Captains' quarrel: Johnson, 175, who quotes Davis' speech as though he had direct knowledge of it.
15 Separation of pirates: SHCA, 318–23, indictment.
16 La Bouche: Johnson, 117, 118, 671, note 3, retirement on Bourbon, now Reunion island. For another source with 'the buzzard' and Bel Ombre: Platt & Wright, 165–71, 184. Taylor: Johnson, 121, 127, 131, 134; in Cuba: Platt & Wright, 106–70. Cocklyn is said to have been hanged: Woodbury, 87; Dow & Edmonds, 345.
17 *Marquis del Campo*: SCHA, 318–23. Indictment.
18 Cape Coast Castle: Uring, 105–7.
19 Profits from slavery: Atkins, 41; Ransford, 130. Bill of Lading: Atkins, 160–6.
20 Anamabu: Atkins, 169–70; APC (Col. Ser), 24 August, 1721, ref. 17; WJ or BG, 10 October, 1719; HCA 1/54, 125 (Bradshaw); T 70/6; HCA 1/55 (Gittus), HCA 1/55, 51 (Lawrence). Price of slaves: Calder, 265–6; T70/6. Letters from Africa, 27 June, 1719. Received 29 September, 1719.
21 Date of the capture of Bartholomew Roberts. I have given June 6, 1719, from HCA 1/55, 5 (Stephenson); HCA 1/55, 51 (Lawrence).

Except for Richards, 20, every writer, including Johnson, 194, has put the date of Roberts leaving England for Africa as November, 1719, without realising that the Lisbon treasure fleet sailed from Bahia, Brazil, at that time. It would have been impossible for Roberts to have attacked if he had been forced to join the pirates at Anamabu, over two thousand miles away on the other side of the Atlantic, in the same month.

On 15 December, 1719, moreover, Kennedy in the *Royal Rover* captured the *Sea Nymph* near Barbados, having already fought at Principe and roistered in Cayen. The probability is that Roberts' ship, the *Princess of London*, left England with Snelgrave's *Bird* in November, 1718, as the *Weekly Journal or Saturday Post* reported a year later, arriving off the Guinea coast between March and April, 1719, and trading profitably for a while before its capture.

22 Stephenson and other sailors: HCA 1/55, 5 (Stephenson).

23 Roberts as third mate: Johnson, 194, wrote 'second' but this was impossible given the existence of Stephenson and the first mate. The error is typical of Johnson's inaccuracy about the early part of Roberts' career as is his mistake that the *Princess* 'left England, November, 1719, and arrived at Guiney about February following'. See also: Richards, 20, Note 4.

Roberts was certainly not the captain of the *Princess* as some books such as Cabal, 183–4, have claimed.

Chapter Four
1 Birthplace of Roberts: Johnson, 244; Richards, 19–20. Newydd Bach, between Letterston and Puncheston, grid reference SM 980 290.

2 Roberts born in 'Bridg(e)water' [sic]: *WJ or SP*, 15 October, 1720.

3 Seamen working without wages: *WJ or SP*, January 23, 1720.

4 England, Cocklyn & la Bouche: *WJ or BG*, 10 October, 1719; *Heroine*, HCA 1/55, 20 (Matthews).

5 Eastwell: SCHA, 5 (Stephenson); HCA 1/55 (Gittus).

6 Attempted escape in *Princess*: SCHA, 1 (Owen).

7 Steward forced from the *Marquis*: SCHA (Stewart).

8 Mary Read: Johnson, 155–6; Gosse, 204; Wheelwright, 187; Carlova, 161, 185–92; Cordingly, 2001, 91–3.

9 James Sail: SCHA (Sail).

10 Hanging of Captain Plumb: *Post Boy*, 4 July, *Morris*, APC, 24 August, 1721, Ref. 17 (Seinzac).

11 Plumb buying slaves: T70/6, 17 October, 1719.

12 Capture of French ship: HCA 1/55 (Lawrence).

13 Lust, wives and failure: Johnson, 192.

14 Ambush of the pirates: Johnson, 193; Hayward, 38 (Kennedy); *WJ or BG*, 29 July, 1721.

15 Attack on fort and town: Johnson, 195–6.

16 Dennis' speech: paraphrased from Johnson, 194–5; speeches by Sutton

and Roberts: ibid, 195. Sutton is called Simpson by Johnson, presumably the David Simpson later hanged at Cape Coast Castle. Simpson, however, was not captured until 10 January, 1720, in Tobago (CO 31/15, 1140). It is yet another of Johnson's errors in his account of Roberts' early career.

17 *Experiment*: HCA 1/54, 119 (Grant).
18 *Temperance*: CO 31/15. Barbados minutes, 518.

Chapter 5

1 Conditions at sea: Botting, 44; Pringle, 116, 239; Wheelwright, 165–7.
2 Roberts and the Lords: Johnson wrote that Roberts at first did consult with his leading men frequently, probably during his apprenticeship as captain. Later, confidence made him more autocratic.
3 Sallee Rover: AOWJ. 23 July, 1720.
4 Navigation: early Mediterranean seafarers used the astrolabe for reckoning latitude but because it had to be suspended for a reading it was unsuitable for the rougher seas of the oceans. The cross-staff replaced it and in turn this was superseded by the backstaff or quadrant.

   Longitude could not be determined properly until the invention of a precise sea-chronometer by Harrison in 1751. It took him a long time to receive the reward promised by the Admiralty: See: Sobel, D., *Longitude*, London, 1996.
5 Pierre le Grand: Exquemelin, 56–7; Fuller & Leslie-Melville, 75–6.
6 Name of the *Sagrada Familia*: WJ *or* SP, July 24, 1721.
7 The fight at Bahia: Johnson, 204–5; WJ *or* SP, 6 February, 1720; CSP (Col), 1719–20, no. 561.
8 Johnson, 288, said that Dennis Topping was killed, one of the six who had escaped in the *Buck*. Dennis Toppen, however, presumably the same man, was tried by the Scottish High Court of Admiralty in 1720. Mistakes like this constantly occur in Johnson.
9 The golden cross: Johnson, 205, Devil's Island: Richards, 31.
10 Rhode Island sloop: HCA 1/55, 51 (Lawrence). Cross given to the governor: Johnson, 205.
11 Anne Bonny, Mary Read and New Providence: Johnson, 624–5; Cordingly, 1995, 74–5.
12 Venereal disease and Blackbeard: Mitchell, 121; Pringle, 194; and Edward England: Pringle, 227–9, *Cassandra*, Botting, 59–63.
13 Desertion of Eastwell and others: as for Note 10.
14 Chase of brigantine: Johnson, 205–6; SCHA (Indictment; Owen).
15 Lack of food: Johnson, 206.
16 Desertion of Kennedy: Johnson, 206; HCA 1/54, 125 (Bradshaw); HCA

1/55, 51 (Lawrence). Desertion would be Roberts' natural interpretation of Kennedy's absence, and one that Johnson was told and accepted. There is another explanation, however, and this is given in Chapter 6. It is more likely because it accords with what is known of the pirates at this time.

Chapter 6

1. Many of the events in this chapter come from the Scottish High Court of Admiralty trial (SCHA) in 1720. A record of Kennedy's trial at the Old Bailey is held in the Public Record Office under HCA 1/54, 122. Additional data about Kennedy came from Hayward, 34–9.

2. Hamilton's letter: CSP (col), 1719–20, no. 561.

3. *Sea Nymph*: CO 31/15, 469; CO 31/14, 1.

4. South Sea Company: *New Cambridge Modern History, VII. The Old Regime, 1713–63*, London, 1957, 249–51.

5. Captain Knot: CSP (Col), 31 March, 1720, 18; *WJ or BG*, 30 July, 1720 AOWJ, 30 July, 1720 which says that three of the hanged pirates had sailed with Blackbeard.

6. *Eagle* snow: SCHA, (Indictment), (Murray), (Defence).

7. Kennedy on the *Eagle*: Johnson, 208.

8. *Royal Rover*. CSP (Col) 16 February and 28 March, 1720; WJ, 25 June, 1720; Holmes and Ottley, CSP (Col) 16 February and 28 March, 1720.

9. Captain Rose and the *Seaford*: CSP (Col) 16 February and 28 March, 1720; WJ, 25 June, 1720.

10. V. Cowles, *The Great Swindle. The Story of the South Sea Bubble*, London, 1960, 123.

11. Pirates in Scotland: Johnson, 208–9, gives the skeleton of the story but the details are given in SCHA where they are often confirmed by two or three separate pirates.

12. Extracts from the *Caledonian Mercury*, 8 and 29 November and 19 December, 1720, 9 January, 1721.

13. Hymen Saturly: SCHA, 396.

14. *The Last Speech and Dying Words of Richard Luntly, Carpenter Aboard the Eagle-snow*, Edinburgh, 1721.

15. Walter Kennedy. The movements and activities of Kennedy from Ireland to London: Johnson, 209–10.

16. Thomas Grant: LJ, 6 May, 1721. This suggests that Kennedy was arrested towards the end of April, 1721. If this is correct then improbably Bradshaw had been arrested before Kennedy. He may be the Jacob Bradshaw whose arrest on 19 March, 1721, was recorded at the Middlesex Guildhall.

17 Trial of Kennedy, see: HCA 1/54, 122; Hayward, 34–9. His bravado is mentioned in *WJ or BG*, 8 July, 1721. It also reported that Kennedy said that 'Roberts could have no peace of mind if only for murdering the French governor . . . who had executed one of his best men caught on shore'. This must refer to the governor of Martinique whose murder was first recorded in CSP (Col), Bermuda, 25 April, 1721. It probably was repeated in a lost news-sheet. Kennedy learned about it only by report. He could not have been present.

18 *Eastwell*: PB, 4 July, 1721.

19 Kennedy's committal papers still exist with the Keeper of the Records. There is a writ to John Cheeke, Marshal of the Court of Admiralty, for Walter Kennedy in Newgate for piracy and felonies at Justice Hall, Old Bailey, for 3 July, 1721. Also for Newgate: *LJ*, 29 July, 1721.

20 Execution of Kennedy: Hayward, 39, Silver oar: Dow & Edmonds, 367.

Chapter 7

1 Roberts' Articles: Johnson, 211–2.

2 Coinage: Thrower, 66; Verrill, 248–51; Winston, 12.

3 Lowther's Articles: Johnson, 307–8.

4 Lowther's suicide: Johnson, 217. The pirate died on Blanquilla island about a hundred miles north of the Venezuelan coast.

5 Phillips' Articles: Johnson, 342–3.

6 Sexuality at sea: Burg, 107–38; Turley, 16–17, 50–2, 75–8.

7 Pirates' boys: Burg. 126; Turley, 96–7.

8 Women at sea: Wheelwright, 176–93; Rodgers, 176–9; Cordingly, 2001.

9 Pirates' treatment of women: Burg, 115.

10 'Protectors' of women: Johnson, 212.

11 Burg, 118.

12 Marooning: Mitchell, 86; Pringle, 117; Thrower, 114.

13 Mary Read: Johnson, 158.

14 Buccaneers' compensations for injury: Exquemelin, 59.

15 *Philippa* sloop. CO 31/15, 1140.

16 Navigation Acts: Pringle, 126–7.

17 Naval List, 1717: Johnson, 39.

18 Member of Parliament on naval wages: *Hist. Parl.* XV, 839.

19 Press-ganging: Pares, 1937; Rediker, 32–3; Rodger, 164–82.

20 Naval convoys: CO 5/794.

21 *Benjamin*, CO 31/15, 1175.

22 *Joseph*: CO 31/15, 1140. Murder of Jelfes: Johnson, 358–9; HCA 1/85, Pt I, 22 June, 1725.

23 Montigny la Palisse. Conjectural. Roberts had two sloops a little later when fighting Rogers but only one when he took the *Joseph*. He either took another sloop and fitted it out himself or was joined by another pirate. The second is more probable. Montigny la Palisse was with him in a sloop at St. Christophers in June, 1720, and remained with him until April, 1721, with only occasional excursions on his own. It is likely that the two pirates met by coincidence off Barbados, were separated by Rogers, and rejoined a short while after Trepassy.

24 *Rose* and *Shark*: Ad 1/2649, 1/2650 (Whitney).

Chapter 8

1 Petition of the Barbadian merchants: CO 31/15, 1137.

2 Corrupt dealings of Governor Lowther: *Postmaster or The Loyal Mercury*, 28 October, 1720; *WJ or BG*, 29 October, 1720.

3 The attack of the *Summersett* on Roberts. The attack is well attested not only sketchily in Johnson, 215, but in WJ, 18 June, 1720 and 25 June, 1720, the same news-sheet in separate reports stating that both Rogers and Roberts won the fight! There was also a lengthy description in the *Boston News Letter*, 22 August, 1720.

The most important evidence, however, comes from the unpublished, personal statement of Rogers himself. CO 31/13, 1137ff. His journal covers the period 20 February to 3 March, 1720, and provides many otherwise forgotten details. The account is so detailed that it is accepted here. Greaves did behave as reported.

4 Preparations for a ship's defence: Ward, N, 1720.

5 Jettisoning heavy gear: Johnson, 215.

6 Marooned men on Dominica: HCA 1/49, Bundle 104 (Botson). Also Johnson, 215–16.

7 The stay at Carriacou: 216; HCA 1/55, 51 (Lawrence). It was probably at Carriacou, once known as Corvocoa, that Roberts decided to alter his methods. It was customary to attack lonely ships at sea. But Roberts had already taken the *Sagrada Familia* by unconventional means. His defeat by Rogers made him realise the dangers of having only one small sloop. From this time he preferred larger vessels and the invasion of harbours. The capture of individual ships was incidental to this strategy.

8 'Wine and women': D.C. Seitz, *Under the Black Flag*, London, 1925.

9 Martinician sloops: Johnson, 216.

10 Roberts' flag: Johnson, 234.

11 The raid on Ferryland: *WJ or BG*, 26 November, 1720. Newfoundland shipping: CSP (Col.) 3 October, 1720, 165–9, no. 251.

12 Tea and Bartholomew Roberts: Johnson, 211, 213. It does not follow that he was a dedicated teetotaller.

13 Shelvocke and the albatross: G. Shelvocke, *A Voyage Round the World, by Way of the Great South Sea*, London, 1726. Samuel Taylor Coleridge. 'The *Rime of the Ancient Mariner*', introd. R. Holmes, London, 1994, 8–9. Poolman, 45–7, 81–6.

14 The *Rose* and *Shark*: CSP (Col), 3 October, 1720 (Hamilton).

Chapter 9

1 Hurricane: *PB*, 13–16 August, 1720.

2 Newfoundland fishermen: Gosse, 1932, 206.

3 Blackstrap: Woodbury, 113.

4 Attack on Trepassy: *WJ or SP*, 1 October, 1720; *WJ or BG*, 26 November, 1720. There are also several letters from governors providing additional, corroborative material.

5 Copleston's brig: Johnson, 216.

6 Letter from Placentia: CO 194/6/83, 367.

7 The *Fortune*: Johnson, 217.

8 Return of Montigny la Palisse: This is conjectural. Roberts may merely have fitted out another sloop, even retained his old and injured *Good Fortune*. But as la Palisse was with him later in the West Indies it is possible that he did link with Roberts in Newfoundland.

9 Ships taken off Newfoundland: Johnson, 217; HCA 49, Bundle 104.

10 Anstis and Roberts: *WJ or SP*, 15 October, 1720.

11 The *Samuel*: *Boston News Letter*, 22 August, 1720.

12 Johnson, 217.

13 Harry Gillespie: The *Boston News Letter* of 22 August, 1720, receiving its information from Captain Cary calls the mate 'Gilespie'. Johnson, 222, 266–8, consistently calls him 'Glasby'. This was the name given at his trial but 'Gillespie', pronounced in a northern accent, easily misheard by a southern ear, is more probably correct. It was spelled that way in a report of the Cape Coast Castle trial in the *DP*, 21 June, 1722.

14 French man-of-war: *DP*, 26 November, 1720.

15 The two men-of-war: AOWJ, 1 October, 1720 and 28 January, 1721; JCTP, 1718–23 (2073), 190, 339.

16 Failure to attack: *LJ*, 1 April, 1721.

17 The Royal African Company: AOWL, 28 January, 1721; *WJ*, 20 January, 1722.

18 The *Swallow* and its companions: AOWJ, 23 July, 1720; *WJ or SP*, 6 August, 1720.

19 Insurance for the Company's employees: AOWJ, 28 January, 1721.

Chapter 10

1 Several events in this chapter are in an order different from Johnson.
   There are two reasons. Some written records disagree with Johnson. At
   other times there is a more logical sequence. As an example, Johnson
   puts the trial of Gillespie in Hispaniola. While it is known that Gillespie
   did desert there yet, according to his statement at Cape Coast Castle, he
   had previously tried to get away in Dominica. He added that Ashplant's
   intervention occurred during the first of his two trials by pirates.
   Dominica is more likely than Hispaniola. There is also an unconfirmed
   report that he had earlier tried to escape on Carriacou.

2 Roberts in the *Fortune*. The descriptions are mine but in keeping with
   Johnson's statements that Roberts liked tea, luxury and fine clothes.

3 Fensilon: *WJ*, 21 January, 1721.

4 Governors Lawes and Commodore Vernon: CO 140/16; *WJ*, 14 January,
   1721.

5 Dorothy Thomas: CO 137/14/ XC 18757; Wheelwright, 179.

6 Capture of Rackam: Johnson, 150; *WJ*, 14 January, 1721.

7 Jonathan Barnet: Carlova, 81–2.

8 Death Sentence: Cordingly, 2001, 96–7.

9 Anne Bonny and Mary Read: CO 137, Nos. 14, 73; Whipple, 137–51;
   Johnson, 150–2; Carlova, 253; Cordingly, 2001, 95–7.

10 Sanitary arrangements aboard the ship: Mitchell, 88; Course, 1969, 93.

11 Turtles and rumfustian: Woodbury, 108–10, 114.

12 Robert Dunn: CSP (Col), 3 October, 1720, no. 251.

13 St. Christophers: nearly all the evidence for the attack comes from CSP
   (Col), 3 October, 1720, 165–9. There is additional information in *WJ or
   BG*, December 3, 1720; CO 31/14; HCA 49, Bundle 104; LG January 28,
   1721; *AOWJ* 1 July, 1721. The letters are genuine.

14 Forcing the seamen: HCA 1/55, 53 (Weaver).

15 St. Barthélemy: HCA 1/55, 51 (Lawrence).

16 Tortola and St. Lucia: CSP (Col) 25–6 October, 1720; CO 31/14, 30
   January, 1721; *JCTP*, 19 May, 1721, encl. 501, iv.

17 Dominica CSP (Col) 28–30 October, 1720; CO 31–14, 31 March, 1721;
   JCTP 19 May, 1721, encl. 501, iv: Pringle, 241–2.

18 Armament: S. Richards, 59–60; Thrower, 102–4; CO 152/13, fol. 282.

19 Roberts' flag CO 31/14, 31 March, 1721.

20 Dominica's lake monster: Aspinall, 1939.

21 Desertion of Gillespie: Johnson, 222–3; HCA 49, Bundle 104 (Glasby
   and Harris).

22 *Swallow* and *Experiment*: *WJ or SP*, 10 September, 1720. *Weymouth*:
   Mégroz, 163. Frances Candis: ibid, 159–61. Sophia Bruce: ibid, 170–6.

Notes

Chapter 11

1 Captain Whitney and the *Rose*: CO 5/794.
2 *Thomas Emmanuel*: C) 152/14.
3 The Atlantic voyage: Johnson, 218–19. It is possible that Johnson confused this with the starvation voyage from Surinam. Yet Bennett said he was with the *Royal Fortune* from the end of October, 1720 until the middle of January, 1721. There is no reference anywhere to the activities of Roberts during that period. It is likely that the pirate had wished to return to Africa. He did so later. For those reasons Johnson's account has been accepted. Some details of starvation on other ships come from: P. O'Brien (ed), *A Book of Voyages*, 1947.
4 Drink and meat: Johnson, 220. Maroni river: Richards, 45.
5 St. Lucia, Simes and Bennett: CO 31/14. 31 January, 1721.
6 Porter and Tuckerman: Johnson, 221.
7 The flyboat at Basseterre: CO 31/14. 28 January, 1721; AD1/1649, 9.
8 Durrell and the *Seahorse*: Ad1/1649, 9; CO 31/14.
9 Stede Bonnet: Course, 1969, 97–8, 104–8.
10 Colonel James: HCA1/55, 4 (Rhett, Swale).
11 Dutch interloper, St Lucia: CSP (Col) 25 April, 1721. News from Barbados.
12 Roberts on Martinique: CSP (Col), 25 March, 1721; Johnson, 220.
13 Captain Whitney: CSP (Col), 20 February, 1721.
14 Hanging of the Governor of Martinique: CSP (Col) Bermuda, 25 April, 1721, 463, iii. Kennedy: HCA 1/54, 122. See also: *Notes*, Chapter 6, no. 17.
15 New Providence and Joseph Slinger: AOWJ, 29 July, 1721.
16 Rumours: LG, 29 July, 1721.
17 Departure of la Palisse. The date is conjectural. He had certainly left before April, 1721. Brazil Fleet: LG, July 29, 1721.
18 Whitney and Hamilton: CO 152/14, 23.
19 Rhode Island and Norton: Co 5/794; Ad1/1649/9. APC, Unbound Papers, 20 July, 1721; CSP (Col), nos. 501, iv, 721, 727 (1720–21 series); 1722–3, nos. 274, 300; 1724–5, no. 3.
20 Roberts' attitude towards his pirates: Johnson, 224.
21 Jones' assault on Roberts: Johnson, 224–5.
22 The French ship. Johnson places the episode earlier but Roberts did not have the vessel when he took Hingstone.
23 Desertion of Anstis: CSP (Col), 14 June, 1722.
24 Whitney: Ad1/2649; Ad1/2650.
25 Benjamin Jeffreys: HCA 49, Bundle 104 (Jeffrys).
26 The Royal African Company fleet: Atkins, 1; PB, 7 February, 1721; WJ or SP, 1 April, 1721; T70/7, 14 July, 1721.
27 Mishaps to the *Swallow* and the *Weymouth*; Atkins, 57.

Chapter 12

The main sources for this chapter come from: Dow & Edmonds; Jameson; and CSP (Col). Additional information came from the trial at Cape Coast Castle, HCA 49, Bundle 104, and also the testimony of Henry Treehill, HCA1/55, 65.

1 Career of Anstis: Johnson, 288–96.

2 *Two Sisters*: WJ or BG, 5 August, 1721.

3 H.M. *Hector* and deaths of crew: WJ, 13 January, 1722.

4 Anstis and rape: Johnson, 289, 678, note 1; Dow & Edmonds, 314.

5 Captain Marston: WJ or SP, 2 September, 1721.

6 Capture of *Hamilton* and ordeal of Ellwood: CSP (Col), 26 December, 1721, 507; HCA 1/55, 65 (Treehill).

7 Capture of John Phillips: Johnson, 341; Dow & Edmonds, 314.

8 *Don Carlos*: LG, 9 December, 1721.

9 *Morning Star*: DP, 13 January, 1722.

10 The Petition: CSP (Col), 14 June, 1722; CO 323/8, nos. 32, 32i; APC, Unopened Papers, 14 June, 1722; Johnson, 290.

11 Election of Finn: Johnson, 295, who calls the man Fenn, is very confused about this episode. Ellwood was quite clear that at the time of his capture Anstis was the captain. Seven weeks later Finn was, see: CSP (Col), June, 1722. This is corroborated by despatches from H.M. *Winchelsea* etc.

12 Captain Orm and H.M. *Winchelsea*: CO 239/1, no. 28; CSP (Col), 8 June, 1723.

13 Execution of Finn: CO 239/1, St. Christophers.

14 For the career of Phillips: Johnson, 341–51; Dow & Edmonds, 310–27.

15 Transportation and indentured servants: the facts are well-attested: Woodbury, 32–9; Ransford, 121–2. See also: Turbeville, 1933.

16 Trial of Phillips: Jameson, 1923.

17 Heads of Phillips and Burrill: Jeremiah Bumstead, *Diary*, 3 May, 1724, in: *New England Hist. Gen Reg. 15*, 201; Dow & Edmonds, 313.

Chapter 13

Much of the information in this chapter comes from Johnson, 225–38, who is far more reliable about this later period of Roberts' career than for earlier yeas. This is because the bulk of this information came from the testimony given by pirates at their trial at Cape Coast Castle, HCA 49/ Bundle 104.

Conversations are quoted verbatim from it. Altogether thirty episodes in this chapter come from that trial, twenty from Johnson corroborating them, six from news-sheets and none from the Calendar of State Papers. An edited transcript of the trial appeared in the *Daily Courant* of 20 February, 1723, and in *Mist's Journal*, 3 April, 1725. See also: Atkins, 1735, 191–4.

Notes

Other sources are specified below.

1 John Conny: Mégroz, 65–6; Uring, 100. The incident and others about the *Swallow* are described in detail by the ship's surgeon, John Atkins, in his account of the voyage and of the Cape Coast Castle trial: Atkins, 75–80. Atkins was the Registrar at the trial and returned to England in May, 1723, in the *Weymouth*. Johnson acknowledged his help, 'Mr Atkins, a Surgeon, an ingenious Man in his own Profession' who knew many details about Roberts 'and has been pleased generously to communicate them for the good of Others': Johnson, 7–8. Whether 'Johnson' met Atkins is not known.

2 Self-satisfied pirates: Johnson, 224.

3 Sierra Leone: Johnson, 228; 70/7, 10 July, 1721.

4 List of traders: Johnson, 227.

5 William Davis: Johnson, 280, Signor Joseph: Atkins, 54–6.

6 Diseases in West Africa: Richards, 68–9.

7 Yellow fever on the *Weymouth*: Atkins, 138–9; Mégroz, 166.

8 *Onslow*: Johnson, 228–9; *Robinson*: WJ, 6 January, 1722.

9 Elizabeth Trengrove: HCA 49/ Bundle 104; Richards, 67; Johnson, 266, 286.

10 Volunteering of soldiers to become pirates: Johnson, 228–9.

11 Revd Roger Price: Johnson, 229; T70/7, 1225, (Royal African Company Records).

12 Captain Gee: Johnson, 229.

13 *Joceline* brig: WJ *or* SP, 7 April, 1722. The captain is named Arthur Lowe in the report.

14 Calabar: Johnson, 229–30. Richards, 70, where it is mistaken for Ouidah.

15 Desertion of Jessup: HCA 49, Bundle 104 (Jessup); shipmate of Roberts: HCA 1/55, 5 (Stephenson).

16 Adventures of George Willson: HCA 49, Bundle 104 (Willson).

17 *Hannibal*; T70/7, 17 January, 1722. Ousley: Richards, 69.

18 *King Solomon*: Johnson, 231.

19 *Gertrouycht*: Johnson, 231–2.

20 Ouidah: Atkins, 110–32; Uring, 38; Johnson, 234. There called Whydah.

21 *Carlton*: T70/7. January 25 and 16 February, 1722. Farcical receipts: Johnson, 235. Sharks: Atkins, 45–6.

22 Conditions in slaveships: *National Geographic* 182 (3), 1992, 63–91; Ransford, 84–95. For seamen: Rediker, 45–50, 271–3.

23 Murder of the negroes in the *Porcupine*: WJ *or* SP, 30 June, 1722; Johnson, 235–6.

24 *Swallow* and despatches: T70/7, 18 September, 1721.

25 *Swallow*'s movements: Atkins, 191–2, 262; Johnson, 236, 238.

26   Death of Selkirk: Mégroz: 168; Souhami, 204–6.
27   Sophie: Mégroz, 159–61, 170–6; Souhami, 207–10.
28   Commander Powell: Richards, 7, footnote.

Chapter 14

1   *Swallow* and *Weymouth*: T70/7, 4 June, 1722; Ad 1/2242; Ad 51/954.
     Naval discipline and conditions at sea: Rodgers, 205–51.
2   Captain Bird: Johnson, 237.
3   Letters and despatches: Atkins, 186–8; Johnson, 237.
4   Mr Baldwin's letter: Johnson, 239. Baldwin was the R.A.C. agent at
     Ouidah: Johnson, 236. He would have known that contrary to Johnson's
     'seven leagues lower' Jacqueville was on the far side of Cape Coast
     Castle, not seven but one hundred and sixty leagues away.
5   Salmagundi: Woodbury, 112; Lane, 1978.
6   Walden's leg: HCA 29, Bundle 104 (Walden). Johnson, 241, confused
     the pirate with Skyrme who was uninjured. Walden had been taken from
     the *Blessing* of Lymington at Newfoundland in July, 1720. Skyrme came
     from the *Greyhound* of Bristol, captured in the West Indies in October,
     1720.
        Johnson, in his haste to finish his book, carelessly mistook Walden for
     Skyrme on page 241 but correctly identified him on pages 269–71 as the
     pirate who lost a leg and was 'rather solicitous about resting his Stump' at
     the trial.
7   Officer's conversation with Main. This is taken from Johnson, 241.
8   Roger Ball: Johnson, 241–2.
9   'Solomon Grundy': Course, 1969, 125; Richards, 87.
10   The sartorial splendour of Roberts: Johnson, 243.
11   Roberts' burial at sea: Johnson, 244.
12   The battle and a storm: Cordingly: 249.
13   Report of the battle and the showers: T70/7, 23 April, 1722. 'Letters
     from Africa'; *DP*, 21 June, 22 June, 6 July, and 10 July, 1722.
14   Captain Hill and the *Little Ranger*. Johnson, 245. Buried treasure.
     Roberts: Richards, 95. 'Easy come, easy go', Fuller & Leslie-Melville, 52.
     Kidd: Platt and Wright, 105–24; Carse, 179–80. Blackbeard: Platt &
     Wright, 151–64.
15   Scudamore and a mutiny: Johnson, 247, 272. Robert Louis Stevenson is
     said to have based his 'master surgeon' who amputated Long John Silver's
     leg on Scudamore whom he had read about in Johnson: Stevenson, 57.
16   Prisoners and jesting: Johnson, 246.

Notes

Facts about the trial at Cape Coast Castle come from the transcript in the Public Records Office, HCA 49, Bundle 104. It contains the individual depositions of prisoners. See also: HCA 1/99, 3; Ad L/S564.

Additional details in this chapter come from Johnson. Many of these extra observations are so detailed that it would have been difficult for anyone but the *Swallow*'s surgeon, John Atkins, to have known them. According to Johnson, 285–6, he acted as a chaplain or 'ordinary' and received the private confessions of condemned men before their execution. No one else except for a few soldiers would hear them.

'Johnson' may have met Atkins, who returned to England in 1723, well before the publication of the *History of the Most Notorious Pyrates . . .* in 1724, but more probably read the account in the trial in the *Daily Courant*, 20 February, 1723. It had already been given a short notice in the *Daily Post* of 21 June, 1722.

Curiously, Furbank and Owens (1988) in their excellent analysis of the possibility of Daniel Defoe being the author of the *History . . .* do no discuss Atkins or his transcript of the trial.

1 Pay of Registrar and Provost: Atkins, 194.
2 Fairness of the trial: Johnson, 248.
3 Indictment: Johnson, 253.
4 Testimony of the *King Solomon*: Johnson, 261.
5 Harry Gillespie: Johnson, 266–8; *DP*, 21 June, 1722.
6 George Willson: Johnson, 274–5.
7 Death of Willson: Johnson, 285.
8 Petition of Royal African Company indentured servants: Johnson, 283.
9 Execution of Armstrong: Johnson, 287.
10 Reprieve of Samuel Fletcher: Johnson, 286.
11 Atkins as a priest: Johnson, 285.
12 Elizabeth Trengrove: Johnson, 286.
13 Hanging in chains: Richards, 105–6. Charles Bunce: Johnson, 287.
14 R.L. Stevenson, *Treasure Island*, 160. Executions: M Rediker, *Between the Devil and the Deep Blue Sea. . .*, 1987, 283.
15 Departure of the *Swallow* and *Weymouth*: Atkins, 202. Hurricane at Port Royal: ibid, 237–42.
16 The *Ranger* at Rhode Island: CCL 11/42.
17 Chaloner Ogle and the prize money: Richards, 107–9; *The Compact Edition of the Dictionary of National Biography*, 2, 1975, 1532; Mist's Journal, 3 April, 1725.
   For Captain Snelgrave's dishonesty; see: Notes, Chapter 3, Note 5.
18 William Ogle: J Chambers, *St Mary's Church, Michelmersh*, 2002, 13.

Black Barty

Appendix A

1 Johnson, 281–2.
2 Johnson, 287.
3 Johnson, 282–5.
4 Johnson, 250–7, 281.
5 Richards, 111–15.

Appendix B

1 *Treasure Island*: Stevenson, 199, 210; Cordingly, 1995, 13–20. Numerous editions of *The General History. . . .* Gosse, 1927.
2 Jean Hamlin: Gosse, 1932, 165–6; Pringle, 85, 92; Verrill, 78–80.
3 Johnson the playwright, 1679–1748: *The Compact Edition of the Dictionary of National Biography*, I, 1975, 1086.
4 J.R. Moore, *Defoe in the Pillory and Other Studies*, Bloomington, Indiana, 1939.
5 Furbank & Owens, 1988, 100–17.
6 ibid, 1, 9–10. Defoe as Johnson: Pearson & Godden, 196–207.
7 Anonymity: Johnson, xxii–xxiii. Defoe attributions: Furbank & Owens, 1994.
8 Furbank & Owens, 1988, 103–5.
9 Low's split personality: Botting, 18. Low's ferocity: Johnson, 326–7; Low as a gentleman: Dow & Edmonds, 159–99.
10 Defoe's interests: Lloyd, 13; Backscheider, 476–92: Note 4, Ch. 5.
11 Turley, 1999, 74.
12 John Atkins, 1685–1757: *The Compact Edition of the Dictionary of National Biography*, I, 1975, 58.
13 Piratical recollections. Thomas Jones: Johnson, xxxiii, 224, 676, 677. Walter Kennedy: Hayward, 1927, 35, 37, 38; HCA 1/54, 122.
14 *The Cambridge Guide to Literature in English*, London, 1988, 266.
15 For more detailed arguments in favour of 'Johnson' being a pseudonym of Daniel Defoe, see: Lloyd, 12–16; Whipple, 277–8. But also see Note 5, above.

Public Records Office, London, References

Admiralty

Ad 1/1438A	Captain's letters to Admiralty, 1715–25.
Ad 1/1649/9	Captains' Letters.
Ad 1/2242	Captain Chaloner Ogle. Letters.
Ad 1/2282	Letters, 1717–26. Captain Pomeroy, *Shark*; Purvis, Dursley; Pearse, Phoenix.
Ad 1/2649	Captain Whitney, *Rose*, 1719–20.
Ad 1/2650	*ibid*, 1721–28.
Ad 51/954	Captain's Logs, *Swallow*.
Ad 51/801	Captain's Logs, *Rose*.
Ad 51/892	Captain's Logs, *Shark*.

Africa

CO 267/5	Sierra Leone. Secretary of State. 1694–1752.
T 70/6	Letters from Africa, 1714–19
T 70/7	Letters from Africa, 1720–32.
T 70/23	Committee of Goods. 1719–24.
T 70/26	Committee of Shipping. 1706–20.
T 70/53	Letters sent from Africa, 1720–28.
T 70/362	Sierra Leone. 1721–2.
T 70/384	Account Journals, Cape Coast Castle.
T 70/385	Cape Coast Castle. 1719.
T 70/386	Cape Coast Castle. 1720.
T 70/387	Cape Coast Castle. 1722–3.
T 70/921	Invoice Books. 1715–20.
T 70/973	Freight Books. 1716–20.

Trials

HCA 1/54	High Court of Admiralty. Oyer & Terminer, 1710–21.
HCA 1/55	High Court of Admiralty. Oyer & Terminer, 1721–25.

HCA 1/85	High Court of Admiralty. Parts I & II. Examinations, 1700–1830.
HCA 49	Trial at Cape Coast Castle, Africa, 1722. Bundle 104.

West Indies and America

CCL 11/42	Treasury Papers, Cape Coast Letters.
CO 5/4	America. Original Correspondence. 1711–39.
CO 5/12	America. Despatches. 1720–47.
CO 5/794	Massachusetts. Minutes.
CO 5/867W	New England. Original Correspondence. 1718–20.
CO 5/868X	New England. Original Correspondence. 1720–1820.
CO 5/868X	New England. Original Correspondence. 1720–3.
CO 7/1	Antigua. Secretary of State. 1702–1820.
CO 23/1	Bahamas. Board of Trade. 1717–25.
CO 23/12	Bahamas. Secretary of State. 1696–1731.
CO 23/13	Bahamas. Dispatches. 1718–27.
CO 24/1	Bahamas. Instructions, Commissions etc. 171–24.
CO 28/15	Barbados. Board of Trade. 1715–20.
CO 28/17	Barbados. Board of Trade. 1720–3.
CO 28/39	Barbados. Secretary of State. 1714–28.
CO 32/1	no. 18. Trial of Rackam and his crew.
CO 31/13–16	Barbados. Minutes. 1718–28.
CO 33/15	Barbados. Shipping Returns. 1708–26.
CO 37/10	Bermuda. Board of Trade. 1716–23.
CO 37/28	Bermuda. Secretary of State. 1706–27.
CO 137/13	Jamaica. Board of Trade. 1718–21.
CO 137/14	no. 9. Trial of Anne Bonny and Mary Read.
CO 137/14Q	Jamaica. Board of Trade. 1721–24.
CO 137/46	Jamaica. Secretary of State. 1702–28.
CO 140/16	Jamaica. Letters.
CO 142/14	Jamaica. Shipping Returns. 1709–22.
CO 152/13	Leeward Isles. Board of Trade, 1719–20.
CO 152/14	Leeward Isles. Board of Trade. 1721–24.
CO 152/39	Leeward Isles. Board of Trade. 1693–1720.
CO 152/40	Leeward Isles. Secretary of State. 1721–49.
CO 157/1	Leeward Isles. Shipping Returns. 1683–1787.
CO 166/1	Martinique. Secretary of State. 1693–1814.
CO 194/6M	Newfoundland. Board of Trade. 1715–20.
CO 194/7N	Newfoundland. Board of Trade. 1720–5.
CO 194/23	Newfoundland. Secretary of State. 1711–1805.
CO 217/3	Nova Scotia. Board of Trade. 1718–21. No. 1–47.

CO 217/31   Nova Scotia. Secretary of State. 1710–44.
CO 239/1   St. Christophers. Secretary of State. 1702–1812.
CO 243/1   St. Christophers. Shipping Returns. 1704–87.
CO 314/1   Virgin Isles. Secretary of State. 1711–91.

Bibliography

Acts of the Privy Council (Colonial Series) Unbound Papers, PRO.

Andrews, C. M. (1943). *The Colonial Period of American History*, Oxford U. P., Oxford.

Anon. (1735) *Lives of the Most Remarkable Criminals*, J. Osborn, London. (ed. Hayward, A.L., Routledge, London, 1927).

—— (1808). *The Dreadful Catastrophe of the Royal George at Spithead*, London.

Aspinall, A. (1939). *Pocket Guide to the West Indies*, Methuen, London.

Atkins, J. (1735). *A Voyage to Guinea, Brazil and the West Indies*, London.

Automobile Association. (1992). *Baedeker's Caribbean*, A. A., Basinstoke.

Backscheider, P. P. R. (1986). *Daniel Defoe: Ambition and Innovation*, Kentucky U. P., Lexington.

Baer, J. (2005). *Pirates of the British Isles*, Tempus, Brimscombe Port.

Botting, D. (1978). *The Pirates*, Time-Life, Amsterdam.

Burg, B. R. (1983). *Sodomy and the Perception of Evil: English Sea Robbers in the Seventeenth-Century Caribbean*, New York U. P., New York.

Carlova, J. (1964). *Mistress of the Seas*, Jarrolds, New York.

Carse, R. (1959). *The Age of Piracy*, Hale, London.

Cawthorne, N, (2003). *A History of Pirates. Blood and Thunder on the High Seas*, Arcturus, Leicester.

Chambers, R. (1861). *The Domestic Annals of Scotland*, III, London.

Clowes, L. (1948). *Sailing Ships, Their History and Development*, HMSO, London.

Compact Edition of the Dictionary of National Biography, I, II, (1975), Oxford.

Cordingly, D. (1995). *Under the Black Flag. The Romance and the Reality of Life Among the Pirates*, Abacus, London.

—— (1998). ed. *A General History of the Robberies and Murders of the most Notorious Pirates*, Captain Charles Johnson, 3rd ed., 1725. (Conway Maritime, London).

—— (2001). *Heroines and Harlots. Women at Sea in the Great Days of Sail*, Macmillan, London.

—— & Falconer, J. (1992). *Pirates in Fact and Fiction*, London.

Course, A. G. (1966). *Pirates of the Eastern Seas*, Muller, London.

—— (1969). *Pirates of the Western Seas*, Muller, London.

Bibliography

Criminal Records of the Scottish High Court of Admiralty, I, 1705–34, Edinburgh, 316–400 (4–22 November, 1720).

Defoe, D. see: Furbank & Owens; Johnson; Moore; Shinagel; West.

Dow, G. F. & Edmonds, J. H. (1923). *The Pirates of the New England Coast, 1630–1730*, Marine Research, Salem.

Esquemeling, A.O. (1684–5). *The Bucaniers of America, I, II*, 2nd ed., William Crooke, London.

Evans, H. (1949). *Men in the Tropics*, Hodge, London.

Feder, J. B. (1992). *Pirates*, Smithmark, New York.

Fuller, B. & Melville, R. (1935). *Pirate Harbours and their Secrets*, Stanley Paul, London.

Furbank, P. N. & Owens, W. R. (1988).*The Canonisation of Daniel Defoe*, Yale U.P., New Haven London.

Gosse, P. (1924). *The Pirates' Who's Who*, Dulau, London.

—— (1925, 1927). ed. *A General History of the Pirates, I, II*, 4th ed, T. Woodward, London. (Sainsbury, Stanhope Mews West).

—— (1926). *My Pirate Library*, Dulau, London.

—— 1927). *A Bibliography of the Works of Capt. Charles Johnson*, Dulau, London.

—— 1932). *A History of Piracy*, Longmans, London.

—— (1936). Foreword to *A Gallery of Rogues. Outlaws of Society in Fact and Fiction. Catalogue 630*, Maggs Bros, London.

Grant, N. (1976). *The Buccaneers*, Angus & Robertson, London.

Hayward, A. L. (1926). ed. *Charles Johnson. A General History of the Robberies and Murders of the Most Notorious Pirates*, Routledge, London.

—— see also: Anon, 1735; Smith, Captain Alexander.

Jameson, J. F. (1923). ed. *Privateering and Piracy in the Colonial Period. Illustrative Documents, 1670–1740*, Macmillan, New York.

Johnson, Captain Charles. (1724). *A General History of the Robberies and Murders of the Most Notorious Pirates, and also their Policies, Discipline and Government from their First Rise and Settlement in the Island of Providence in 1717, to the Present year, 1724. With the Remarkable Actions and Adventures of the two Female Pirates, Mary Read and Anne Bonny*, T. Weaver, London. see also: Cordingly, 1998; Gosse, 1925, 1927; Hayward, 1926; Lloyd, 1962.

Konstam, A. (2003). *The Pirate Ship, 1660–1730*, Osprey, Oxford.

Lane, K. E. (1999). *Blood and Silver. A History of Piracy in the Caribbean and Central America*, Signal Books, Oxford.

Lee, R. E. (1974). *Blackbeard the Pirate: a Reappraisal of his Life and Times*, Blair, Salem.

Leeuw, H. de. (1937). *Crossroads of the Buccaneers*, Philadelphia.

Little, B. (1960). *Crusoe's Captain. Being the Life of Woodes Rogers*, Seaman, Trader, Colonial Governor, Odhams, London.

Lloyd, C. (1962). ed. *Lives of the Most Notorious Pirates, by Captain Charles Johnson*, Folio, London.

Lucie-Smith, E. (1978). *Outcasts of the Sea*, Paddington, London.

Marley, D. F. (1995). *Pirates. Adventurers of the High Seas*, Arms & Armour, London.

Marx, R. F. (1967). *Pirate Port. The Story of the Sunken City of Port Royal*, World, Cleveland.

Mégroz, R.L. (1938). *The Real Robinson Crusoe*, Cresset, London.

Mitchell, D. (1976). *Pirates. An Illustrated History*, Thames & Hudson, London.

Mitchinson, A. (2004). *Alexander Selkirk. Survivor on a Desert Island*, Short, London.

Moore, J. R. (1939). *Defoe in the Pillory and Other Studies*, Indiana U. P., Bloomington.

—— (1940). 'Defoe, Selkirk and John Atkins', *Notes & Queries 1929*, 436–8.

—— (1958) *Daniel Defoe. Citizen of the Modern World*, Chicago.

National Maritime Museum, Greenwich. (1972) *Piracy & Privateering. Catalogue 4*, H.M.S.O., London.

Pares, R. (1937). 'Manning of the Navy in the West Indies', *Trans Royal Hist Soc.* 20, 31ff.

Pascall, J. (1978). *Pirates and Privateers*, Silver Burdett, London.

Pearson, M.P.& Godden, K. (2002). *In Search of the Red Slave. Shipwreck and Captivity in Madagascar*, Sutton, Thrupp.

Platt, C. & Wright, J. (1992). *Treasure Islands, The Fascinating World of Pirates, Buried Treasure and Fortune Hunters*, Fulcrum, London.

Poolman, K. (1999). *The Speedwell Voyage. A Tale of Piracy and Mutiny in the Eighteenth Century*, Naval Institute Press, Annapolis.

Pringle,. P. (1953). *Jolly Roger*, Museum Press, London.

Rankin, H. F. (1969). *The Golden Age of Piracy*, Holt, Rinehart & Winston, New York.

Ransford, O. (1971). *The Slave Trade. The Story of Transatlantic Slavery*, David & Charles, Newton Abbot.

Rediker, M. (1987). *Between the Devil and the Deep Blue Sea. Pirates and the Anglo-American World, 1700–1750*, Cambridge U. P, Cambridge.

Richards, S. (1966). *Black Bart*, Davies, Llandybie.

Roberts, G. (1726). *The Four Years' Voyages of Captain George Roberts, written by Himself*, London.

Rodger, N. A. M. (1986). *The Wooden World. An Anatomy of the Georgian Navy*, Fontana, London.

Rogers, Woodes. (1712). *A Cruising Voyage around the World*, A. Bell, London (Longmans Green, London, 1928).

Rogozinski, J. (2000). *Honour Among Thieves. Captain Kidd, Henry Every and the Story of Pirate Island*, Conway Maritime, London.

Bibliography

Rosenthal, E. (1957). *Cutlass and Yardarm, Timmins, Bailey & Swinfin*, Cape Town.

Senior, C. (1976). *A Nest of Pirates. English Piracy in its Heyday*, David & Charles, Newton Abbot.

Shay, F. (n.d.). *Mary Read: the Pirate Wench*, Hurst & Blackett, London.

Shinagel, M. (1975). ed. *Robinson Crusoe, 1719. An Authoritative Text, Background and Source*, Norton, New York.

Smith, Captain Alexander, (1714). *A Complete History of the Lives and Robberies of the Most Notorious Highwaymen, Footpads, Shoplifts and Cheats of both Sexes*, 5th ed, 1719, London. (ed. Hayward, A.L, Routledge, London, 1926).

Smith, W. (c.1727). *A New Account of some Parts of Guinea, and the Slave Trade*, London.

Souhani, D. (2001). *Selkirk's Island*, Weidenfeld & Nicolson, London.

Stanley, J. (1995). ed. *Bold in Her Breeches: Women Pirates across the Ages*, HarperCollins, London.

Sternbeck, A. (1930). *Filibusters and Buccaneers*, Ayer, London.

Stevenson, R. L. (1883). *Treasure Island*, ed. Letley, E. Oxford U.P. Oxford, 1985.

Thrower, R. (1980). *The Pirate Picture*, Phillimore, Chichester.

Turbeville, A. S. (1933). *Johnson's England, An Account of the Life and Manners of His Age, I, II*, Clarendon, Oxford.

Turley, H. (1999). *Rum, Sodomy and the Lash. Piracy, Sexuality and Masculine Identity*, New York U. P, New York & London.

Underhill, H. A. (1950). *Sailing Ships, Rigs and Rigging*, London.

Uring, N. (1726). *The Voyages and Travels of Captain Nathaniel Uring*, London.

Verrill, A. H. (1923). *In the Wake of the Buccaneers*, Parsons, London.

Visiak, E. H. (1910). *Buccaneer Ballads*, Elkin Mathews, London.

Ward, N. (1700). *A Trip to Jamaica*, London.

West, R. (2000). *Daniel Defoe. The Life and Strange, Surprising Adventures*, Carroll & Graf, New York.

Wheelwright, J. (1995).'Tars, tarts and swashbucklers', in: *Stanley*, 1995, 176–200.

Whipple, A. C. (1957). *Pirates. Rascals of the Spanish Main*, Gollancz, London.

Winston, A. (1970). *No Purchase, No Pay. Sir Henry Morgan, Captain William Kidd and Captain Woodes Rogers in the Great Age of Privateers and Pirates, 1665–1715*, (Eyre & Spottiswood, London).

Woodbury, G. (1952). *The Great Days of Piracy*, Norton, New York.

Zacks, R. (2003). *The Pirate Hunter. The True Story of Captain Kidd*, Review, London.

Index

Major entries in bold. Names of ships, titles of books etc, in italics.

Index

JUSTINIAN

John Moorhead

LONGMAN
London and New York

Longman Group UK Limited,
Longman House, Burnt Mill,
Harlow, Essex CM20 2JE, England
and Associated Companies throughout the world.

Published in the United States of America
by Longman Publishing, New York

First Published 1994

ISBN 0 582 06304 3 CSD
ISBN 0 582 06303 5 PPR

British Library Cataloguing-in-Publication Data

A catalogue record for this book is
available from the British Library

Library of Congress Cataloging-in-Publication Data

Moorhead, John, 1948–
Justinian / John Moorhead
        p.   cm. — (The Medieval world)
  Includes bibliographical references and index.
    ISBN 0–582–06304–3. — ISBN 0–582–06303–5 (pbk.)
      1. Justinian I, Emperor of the East, 483?-565.
  2. Emperors—Byzantine. Empire—Biography.   3. Byzantine
Empire—History—Justinian I, 527–565.   I. Title. II. Series.
              DF572.M66   1994
              949.5'013'092—dc20
    [B]   93–33762
                                                  CIP

Set by 14 in 11/12 pt Baskerville
Produced by Longman Singapore Publishers (Pte) Ltd
Printed in Singapore

CONTENTS

ACKNOWLEDGMENTS

I am grateful to the person who suggested that I write this book, and to David Bates, who not only accepted it for inclusion in the Medieval World series, but gave a most useful critique of the draft. While writing I have found myself footnoting with a light hand, which may disguise the degree of my indebtedness to the Australian Research Council for a grant which allowed me to work for a short while in a library with greater resources than those usually at my disposal.

But this is not to say that the resources available locally are negligible. This book has benefited from being written in a department headed by Geoffrey Bolton, and it has gained from the fresh enthusiasm and intelligence with which, year by year, Australian students approach the middle ages. It owes more than he can realise to Tom Poole, my collaborator in a course of which Justinian forms a part. This book is a small return for so much kindness and friendship.

John Moorhead

. . . . .
EDITOR'S PREFACE

The reign of Justinian is a period of central importance to our understanding of many aspects of the history of Europe, the Middle East and Asia. Its history is one of power exercised across a vast geographical range and against a background of a world into which new peoples and new interests were constantly intruding, and in which the often superficial unities and certainties which had existed under the Roman Empire were steadily giving place to local differences and political fragmentation. It must none the less have looked for a time as if Justinian was restoring the grandeur of the classical past, as his armies swept into Italy and North Africa, as Roman law was definitively codified and as magnificent buildings were constructed throughout his lands. The emperor's personality, and that of his remarkable wife Theodora, dominate the middle years of the sixth century. John Moorhead's most welcome addition to the Medieval World Series skilfully does justice to this immense panorama. He charts Justinian's complex doplomacy as he dealt *inter alia* with Persians to the east, Slavs to the north and Vandals and Lombards to the west, as he wrestled with the theological differences between the imperial Church and, on one hand, the Monophysites in Egypt, and, on the other, the emerging and distinctive opinions of the popes and the western Church, and as he grappled with court politics and apparently overbearing generals such as Belisarius.

As a scholar who has already written extensively on the fifth and sixth centuries, John Moorhead brings a wealth of knowledge and experience to this new assessment of Justinian and his reign. While the great histories of Procopius are inevitably central to the discussion, he also ranges over archaeological,

artistic and theological evidence, all of which is currently con-
tributing to a deeper understanding of this difficult period.
John Moorhead's Justinian is a restless and energetic man,
rather than a visionary. The early years of his reign are typified
by a determination to tackle the political, military and religious difficulties which the empire faced, and which he believed it to be his duty to confront. The 520s and 530s were a
time when numerous great initiatives were launched. If the
results were less decisive than the emperor might have hoped,
and even if fresh problems emerged while old ones proved
intractable, the agenda remains formidable and important.
John Moorhead's final assessment of Justinian is less than
eulogistic, but it is notably judicious. If the rhetoric which
accompanied many of the emperor's enterprises emphasized
the restoration of the past, the reign in fact turned out to be
in many respects notable for the increased intellectual and
political distance from its classical heritage. Although military
achievments were more apparent than real, it was only some
time after his death that the submerged antagonisms re-
emerged and defences crumbled. The life and achievements
of 'an extraordinary man' (the author's verdict) have been
authoritatively and stimulatingly assessed against their appropriate contemporary background.

David Bates

INTRODUCTION

The reign of the Byzantine emperor Justinian (527–565) was pivotal in late antiquity. From his headquarters in Constantinople he accomplished great deeds in the most diverse fields: major legal reforms were successfully carried out, vast numbers of architecturally distinguished buildings were erected, wars were launched and won against established powers in Africa and Italy, substantial innovations were made to the administration of the empire, and the position of the Christian religion and that of non-Christians in the empire were both changed considerably. There were other important events which the emperor did not initiate but to which he had to respond, such as the outbreak of a disastrous plague and depressing developments in foreign affairs. There can be no doubt that the activities of Justinian, which exhibit characteristics which can be readily labelled 'classical' side by side with others which seem 'medieval', marked an important stage in the move from the world of antiquity to that of the middle ages in the lands around the eastern half of the Mediterranean and beyond.

The historian of the period is fortunate, for it is extraordinarily well documented. Some of the wars for which Justinian was responsible are described in the work of one of the greatest of the Greek historians. Procopius was born in the Palestinian town of Caesarea, and became a legal adviser to the general Belisarius when he was based on the Persian front. Thereafter he accompanied him on expeditions to Africa and Italy, so when he began to write a history of Justinian's wars covering the period until 553 he was able to give an eyewitness account of much of the action until the time when, in the early 540s, he seems to have settled in Constantinople. Procopius was one

1

of those historians in the happy position of having found what he considered a major topic and being able to write a big book about it. The words with which his history opens, 'Procopius of Caesarea has written the history of the wars', constitute a direct borrowing of the words which Thucydides had used almost a thousand years earlier at the beginning of his history of the Peloponnesian war; when he went on to mention his wish that important events would not be 'obliterated' he was using a verb which Herodotus, writing before Thucydides, had employed early in his history of the Persian wars. But Procopius went beyond implicit assertions that he wished to be seen in the same company as the great historians of Athens in its golden age. Whereas Herodotus had set himself to recount 'great and marvellous deeds', Procopius was going to tell of 'immensely great deeds'; if Thucydides had told of a war 'great and noteworthy above all the wars which had gone before', Procopius' books were about 'the greatest and noteworthy deeds'. So it was that he felt able to boast, his eyes firmly fixed on his eminent predecessors, that the deeds carried out in the wars which formed the subject matter of his account were the most important and greatest in history. Here was an extremely positive way in which some of the achievements of Justinian could be evaluated.

His account of the wars was not, however, the only work which Procopius wrote. In his *Buildings*, apparently written between 553 and 555, he set himself to describe the buildings erected by Justinian in many parts of the empire. This book is extremely favourable to the emperor, whom it represents as instructing the most gifted architects how to overcome difficulties which had defeated them. But in another work which was written during the year 550, the notorious *Secret History* (Greek *Anecdota*), Procopius had already penned a portrait of Justinian and his wife Theodora which was bitterly hostile. His trenchant criticism of the royal pair, in some ways anticipated in the *Wars* but given far stronger expression here, and the scandalous manner in which this was conveyed, made the work dynamite. Procopius can have intended to publish it only after the death of Justinian, for although it was written fifteen years before this occurred Procopius expressed himself in a way which suggests that the emperor had already died, and its first reader known to us lived over four hundred years later. What seems to be a radical difference in tone between this and the

other works of Procopius led some scholars of earlier generations
to deny his authorship of the *Secret History*, but such a difference
may be more apparent than real, for modern work has made
it clear that his various works are more closely connected than
has often been thought.[1] As we shall see, the data provided by
Procopius in his various books are sometimes contradictory,
but it will be best to consider individual cases as they arise.

Other narrative sources complement the work of Procopius.
Agathias, a native of the town of Myrina in Asia, was a poet and
lawyer who practised in Constantinople. After the death of
Justinian he began working on a history of the wars the emperor undertook from the point at which Procopius had laid
down his pen, but he only reached 558. He was followed in
turn by Menander the guardsman, who, during the reign of
the emperor Maurice, wrote a work of which only fragments
incorporated in a text of the tenth century survive. A very
different kind of historical writing is the chronicle of John
Malalas, a rhetor from Antioch who moved to Constantinople
in the 530s. The last book of his chronicle, a comprehensive
work which begins with Adam, is devoted to the reign of
Justinian. Unlike Procopius and Agathias, John Malalas had no
pretensions to a fine style, but that his Greek was of a popular
kind far removed from that of the classical period does not
mean that he is a poor source of information. For the early part
of Justinian's reign Malalas was closely followed by the author
of the Paschal Chronicle, a text written in Constantinople early
in the seventh century which adds further information.

All these texts are in Greek, but two important chronicles in
Latin preserve data not known from other sources. Marcellinus
comes, an Illyrian who served Justinian in Constantinople
before he became emperor, wrote a chronicle extending to the
year 518, which was later extended by Marcellinus himself to
534 and then by another author to 548, while the chronicle by
Victor of Tunnunna, an African bishop who suffered from
Justinian's church policy, goes as far as 563. Easterners to write
on church matters included Evagrius, a layman living in Antioch whose Ecclesiastical History continued a genre two centuries old by the time of Justinian, and John of Ephesos, who
also wrote a fascinating book on the lives of eastern holy men.

1. Averil Cameron *Procopius and the Sixth Century* London 1985 is out-
    standingly the best work on the subject.

Interesting traditions are also preserved in some texts from later periods; among these the most important is a work by Theophanes, a monk who wrote in Constantinople early in the ninth century and had access to material now lost.

We have, then, an extraordinary richness of narrative evidence. But, as is so often the case, the sources have a great potential to mislead. That different works by Procopius provide contradictory data is obviously awkward. More subtly, that some of Justinian's wars are recounted at great length by a major historian has often caused modern scholars to assign them an importance in his reign greater than that which they really had.[2] Further, certain kinds of bias may be built into our sources. While some of the texts emanate from Asia, one notices immediately how much of our information is provided by authors writing in Constantinople. Egypt, in particular, is poorly represented in these sources, which overwhelmingly speak with a metropolitan accent. In terms of the ability of these texts to document the deeds of Justinian this may be all to the good, for the emperor rarely stirred beyond the walls of his capital. Yet oddly enough, those who wrote them were not natives of Constantinople. One can only be struck by how much of our knowledge of the reign of Justinian is provided by authors of provincial backgrounds who had come to the capital, done well for themselves, and were then understandably prepared to look with kindly eyes on the regime from which they had profited. Further, Justinian was not averse to orchestrating a positive image of his reign. Procopius's *Buildings*, which, if not commissioned by him (cf. 1.3.1), may well have been undertaken in an attempt to win his favour, goes out of its way to interpret his activities positively; a scholarly civil servant, John the Lydian, represents Justinian as having suggested to him that he write the history of his war against the Persians (*Powers* 3.28); and the chronicle of John Malalas may contain propagandistic material put into circulation by the government.[3] Hence the plethora of sources is a mixed blessing. In the sixth century, as much as in other times, the

---

2. For example, over a third of the space devoted to Justinian in the second volume of J.B. Bury *History of the Later Roman Empire* 2 London 1923 is taken up with narratives of the reconquest of Africa and Italy.
3. As argued by Roger Scott 'Malalas, *The Secret History* and Justinian's propaganda' *Dumbarton Oaks Papers* 39 1985 pp. 99–109.

intelligent exercise of patronage by a powerful figure could easily lead to that person's disappearing from the sight of later generations behind a veil of benevolent primary sources. These texts are supplemented by the voluminous non-narrative sources for the period. Justinian presided over a great enterprise of codifying Roman law, so that the shape given the law by the commissioners he appointed to revise it is perfectly known. But at least as important for the historian are the novels, or new laws, which he issued piecemeal in response to matters as they arose. These provide exceptional insight into the social life of the empire, and the way in which they are framed allows us to see how the government sought to present itself to the people, although here again it is the official line which is heard. The affairs of the church generated a large bulk of material, among which that concerned with an ecumenical council held at Constantinople in 553 is particularly extensive. It must be said that much of this is of purely doctrinal interest, but some of it has the merit of originating in circles hostile to Justinian, and so allows critical voices to be heard. The *Collectio avellana*, a collection of correspondence between the papacy and various dignitaries which was preserved in Rome, contains a large volume of material bearing on ecclesiastical relations between East and West in the time of Justinian.

The activities of this emperor and the times in which he lived are therefore illuminated by written sources of a prodigality for which historians of the century which was to follow would be grateful. Beyond this we have the rare luxury of a small number of texts which Justinian himself may be presumed to have written. Apart from a hymn in Greek of which he may have been the author[4] and some theological works, as we shall see it is highly likely that some letters in Latin written to pope Hormisdas in his name which are preserved in the *Collectio avellana*, together with a few laws, also in Latin, which were issued in his name, were the work of the emperor himself rather than the officials who customarily wrote such documents on behalf of the emperor. So it is that we have a degree of unmediated access to Justinian which provides direct evidence for his concerns and the furnishings of his mind.

Apart from these texts, we have a good number of other

---

4.   V. Grumel 'L'Auteur et la date de composition du tropaire 'O Μονογενὴς' *Echos d'Orient* 22 1923: 398–418.

sources of information for Justinian's reign. Many of the buildings for which he was responsible, such as the great cathedral of Hagia Sophia which was erected in Constantinople during the 530s, can still be seen, as can the beautiful mosaics with their pictures of Justinian and Theodora which were installed in the church of S Vitale at Ravenna late in the following decade. Increasingly, the work of archeologists is uncovering the remains of buildings, streets and indeed whole towns of the sixth century, to the extent that it is now impossible for historians to avoid considering evidence of this kind, however difficult it may be to integrate it into the narrative treatments which written sources most naturally generate. Evidence provided by archaeology is making us better informed as to the changing conditions of rural and urban life, and so allowing broad social and economic contexts to be understood far more clearly than they have been in the past. It seems safe to predict that future excavations will further modify our interpretations of the period.

But the discovery of new evidence is not the only way in which our understanding of the past develops. Each generation of historians approaches the same sources looking for different things. The feminist movement, for example, has led us to address quite new questions to bodies of evidence which have long been available, and historical understanding is being revised in the light of the answers which have emerged. And beyond this, there is always the task of assessing our evidence and arranging the various bits and pieces into the patterns which seem to do justice to them best. In working through the sources for the reign of Justinian I have been struck by the possibility of disentangling various events which historians have often lumped together. In the discussion of Justinian provided by a standard introduction to Byzantine history we can read that it was the 'sacred mission of the emperor to free Roman lands from the yoke of barbarian invaders and Arian heretics, and to restore the ancient frontiers of a single Roman and orthodox Christian empire. And it was towards this end that the whole of Justinian's policy was directed'.[5] But we may take leave to doubt this generalization. Careful analysis of the constituent parts of his reign may seem

5. George Ostrogorsky *History of the Byzantine State* trans. Joan Hussey Oxford 1968 69. See further below ch. 3 n. 1.

a grey business, but it suggests that actions which have been interpreted in the light of overarching ideological purposes need not be and probably should not be taken in this way.

It may be worth going into some detail at this point. As we shall see, historians have sometimes thought that Justinian concluded a peace treaty with Persia in 532 so that he would be free to make war on the Vandals in Africa and subsequently the Ostrogoths in Italy. But the adoption of this framework may involve the kind of improper privileging of the role of the western wars in our understanding of Justinian's reign to which, it was suggested above, the great work of Procopius may predispose us, so that other developments are wrongly seen in the light of what is taken to be the central event. If we accept that the peace of 532 was desirable to Persia for its own domestic reasons and to Justinian because his troops had been faring poorly, that the African and Italian wars were launched in the context of circumstances which had recently developed in those lands, and that the happy outcome of the first war, that against the Vandals, was something hoped for rather than expected, the case for seeing the capture of Ravenna in 540 as the motive for which peace with Persia was concluded in 532 looks decidedly weak. To be sure, there are some passages in Justinian's laws which could be used to support an interpretation of the wars as a single operation undertaken to restore the boundaries to their old limits, but they were written at the high point of what then seemed surprisingly effortless success, and it would be risky to use them as evidence for policy when the wars were begun, or indeed were further advanced; still more to conclude that peace with Persia had been concluded towards this end.

Another possible context for Justinian's decision to launch the wars is biographical. Justinian was born in the small Latin-speaking area which remained in the empire by the late fifth century, and so, it could be argued, he would have been more keen than most emperors to regain the Roman territories in the West which had been lost during that century. But this consideration, which would have applied equally to the emperor who preceded him, a man who nevertheless betrayed no sign of thinking in such terms, would entail the survival in a man who had come to Constantinople decades earlier of casts of mind and attitudes brought from the provinces, the very things which life in the cosmopolitan capital tended to neutralize. There can be no doubt that in some ways Justinian did remain out of place in the great city: his gauche Latin, the narrow strain of his piety and, most of all, his loyal adherence over the decades to advisers and associates of unimpressive backgrounds who had themselves come from the depths of the provinces is enough to suggest this. Nevertheless, the depth of learning Justinian achieved in the theological literature of the Greek-speaking East indicates his success in transcending his western background. His roots in the West were not enough to make him launch wars there. Neither is there any need to locate his legal reforms against the background of the wars, on the grounds that both betray a concern for Roman universalism,[6] for the great reform of the laws can be seen as looking back to its partial anticipations in the preceding century more naturally than forward to the wars in the West which were undertaken shortly afterwards.

Perhaps, then, it will prove difficult to organize our understanding of Justinian's reign around a few central themes. Perhaps it was characterized more than has sometimes been thought by policy being made on the run, and it will emerge as more disordered than one had thought it to be. Be this as it may, the reign of Justinian provides far more than the spectacle of a busy emperor coping on an *ad hoc* basis with the spectacular challenges which late antiquity threw before him. His initiatives, many of them launched in an extraordinary burst of activity shortly after he came to the throne, were frequently bold, original, and successful, so that he had a greater impact on the history of the world than any other head of state of the period. He largely redrew the political map of the Mediterranean region, but his other achievements were longer lasting. Of no other figure in late antiquity could it be said that his legacy triumphantly survives in legal texts, theological definitions and stones. Justinian confronts the historian with a massive achievement.

Yet it brought trouble in its wake. Paradoxically, among the most intractable of the various problems which came to occupy Justinian's attention as the decades passed were those

6. As does John Meyendorff, affirming that 'Roman universalism . . . led Justinian to military conquest of the Western provinces lost to the barbarians' (*Imperial Unity and Christian Divisions* Crestwood NY 1989 p. 207) and that his legal work 'reflected his dream of a universal and Christian Roman order' (ibid. p. 248).

of his own creation. As it turned out the wars in the West were ultimately successful in military terms, but they took far longer and required far more resources than would have seemed likely in the first flush of success. Not all of those who lived in the conquered territories were pleased at the manner and results of Justinian's victories, and it may be that his successes were responsible for turning western opinion against him. Another unlooked for response to his early victories was that of the shah of Persia, who retaliated by launching attacks on imperial territory in the East which had to be dealt with. The wars also meant that the military resources of the empire were being spread dangerously thinly at a time when the Balkans were coming under increasing pressure. The flexible Justinian tried to cope with this problem in a number of ways, but one of his solutions, which involved buying the friendship of some unsavoury and greedy allies, was itself to produce further difficulties.

The outcome of his ecclesiastical endeavours was similar to that of the western wars. They may seem to have reached a triumphant climax at the council of Constantinople (553), which is still accepted as an Ecumenical Council by the Orthodox and Roman churches. Yet, seen in the light of the purpose for which it was called, the council was a disaster. Not only did it fail to achieve its purpose of reconciling the warring parties within the church, but by turning members of the majority against each other it sowed disunion where none had existed before. In short, Justinian was the victim of his own successes. And so it was that the energies which early in his reign had been responsible for dramatic initiatives were increasingly devoted to mounting holding operations.

Such an interpretation of Justinian may seem to fall short of the heroic. Yet the man remains as fascinating as ever. If his ambitious plans were important, he was at least as remarkable for his energies, and these continued in play throughout the period of his rule, the second longest of any Byzantine emperor prior to the long reigns of the tenth century. But they only make sense in the context of late antiquity, to which we shall now turn.

Chapter 1

EARLY YEARS

. . .

THE LATE ROMAN EMPIRE

In the time of the Roman empire the lands around the Mediterranean were knit together more closely than at any other period in human history. Spreading outwards from a peninsula in the centre of the sea, the arms of Rome had conquered a wide swathe of territory throughout which the imposition of the one government, the practice of Roman law, the use of a unified system of coinage and, ultimately, the existence of one state religion progressively tended to lessen regional distinctions. The empire constituted a vast, largely self-sufficient common market within which areas could specialize in the production of such items as grain, wine, oil, pottery and papyrus; every summer what Julius Caesar nonchalantly referred to as 'our sea' was filled with cargo ships. Its cohesiveness was displayed in the remarkable uniformity of its towns, from Britain to Syria, which a fine network of roads brought close together.

But as the centuries passed the political expression of this unity evaporated. Late in the third century the emperor Diocletian divided the empire into eastern and western parts, each with its own emperor, and in 324 his successor, Constantine, ordered the beginning of work on a 'new Rome' named after himself, not far from where Diocletian had based himself in the East. Constantinople, inaugurated in 330, was built on the site of Byzantium, a former colony Greeks had founded nearly a thousand years earlier. The site was a good one, for it controlled the straits which linked the Mediterranean and

Black seas and was the point where the continents of Europe and Asia approached each other more closely than anywhere else in the empire. It was also at the easternmost end of the Via Egnatia, an important road which ran almost due westwards to the coast of the Adriatic Sea, across which Italy was a short trip away, while on the other side of the Bosphorus was the terminus of the main highway leading towards Persia. So it was that Constantinople enjoyed excellent communications by both sea and land.

The work of Diocletian and Constantine marked a change in the political centre of gravity in an empire of which Rome had earlier been the undisputed centre. Subsequent dramatic events were to speed up this process. In the late fourth century a group of people called Visigoths crossed the Danube, and in 401 they invaded Italy. Before long the other key northern frontier, that of the Rhine, was seriously breached, and the effective reach of the western government was increasingly restricted until 476, when a barbarian strongman deposed the last Roman emperor in the West. Within the lifespans of a few generations all the provinces to the west of Croatia had been politically detached from those parts of the empire in the East.

The remaining portion of the empire was, at first site, a heterogeneous agglomeration of territories. In Europe, its western frontier ran northwards from the Adriatic coast to the Danube. On the other side of this border lay territories ruled from Italy, where the Ostrogoths were to establish a strong kingdom under their king Theoderic at the end of the fifth century. The border proceeded along the Danube to the Black Sea. The land to the north of the river remained the home of barbarians, as it had for centuries, but the hold of the empire on the Balkans had been weak for much of the fifth century, and the movement westwards of groups such as the Goths opened the way for other Germanic groups, as well as peoples of Hunnic and Slavic ethnicity, to move into the region. So it was that the government was unable to exercise effective power over much of the territory south of the Danube which was nominally part of the empire. The eastern border began at the south-eastern corner of the Black Sea, from which it proceeded in a southerly direction to the Euphrates. Here the empire's neighbour was Persia, a long-established and powerful state quite capable of looking its rival in the eye. From the Euphrates the border continued with a more westerly orientation across a desert populated by bedouin Arabs to Aqaba, whence it followed the Sinai peninsula and the west coast of the Red Sea. Much of the wealthy Nile valley was part of the empire, as was a strip of coastal territory to the west of Alexandria. Imperial territory came to an end at a point almost due south of its most westerly section in Europe.

A conventional way of periodizing history encourages us to see the sundering of the empire in the fifth century as constituting a dramatic break in the history of Europe. But care is called for, as it can certainly be argued that over most of the territories which came under the power of people the Romans called barbarians, although they did not call themselves this, the basic structures of society continued largely unchanged. To be sure, the rolling back of the imperial frontiers was impressive, but for generations power in the West had been passing from the state to such organs as the army, the land-owning aristocracy, and the church, and over most of the lost territory these happily outlived a political apparatus which had been of steadily diminishing importance. Indeed, many Romans were pleased to accommodate themselves to the changed political realities, while many barbarians imitated the Romans as closely as they could. Oddly enough, the perception that the empire had ended in the West in 476 is first given explicit utterance in the chronicle of Marcellinus comes, who wrote in Constantinople in *c.* 518/519, and there is good reason to see this perception as an eastern rather than a western one.[1] However mild the response of many westerners to the redrawing of the map which occurred in the fifth century, the government of the east could hardly have looked on the process with equanimity.

Political life was not the only way in which the eastern and western parts of the old empire were moving apart. The export of the distinctive pottery which Africa had been shipping overseas in large quantities for centuries declined; the leading churches in each area, those of Rome in the West and Constantinople in the East, found themselves out of communion after 482; and government in Constantinople was increasingly conducted in the Greek language rather than the

1. B. Croke 'AD 476: The manufacture of a turning point' *Chiron* 13 1983: 81–119.

Latin which continued to be used in the West. But the survival of the empire in the East was never in question. Its major political problem in the fifth century was a comparatively benign variant of the process which had brought imperial government in the West to an end. Whereas Italy had come during the fifth century to be controlled by barbarian generals who governed through puppet emperors and finally decided that the office of emperor was redundant, the East suffered from generals of provincial origin who felt themselves called to greater things. Such a man was Zeno, who made his way from his native soil in Isauria, an area in southern Asia Minor, to Constantinople. He was given a military command, married Ariadne, the daughter of the emperor Leo, and, on the death of his father-in-law, became emperor himself (474–491). Zeno's had been a stunning rise, at the end of which he had neither the name nor the wife with which he had begun. But his career was found worthy of imitation.

Indeed, his own reign was troubled by a series of attempts by generals to depose him. One of these was mounted by the brother-in-law of his predecessor Leo, but more serious were the challenges which came from his fellow Isaurians. When he died there was no obvious successor, and Ariadne's eye fell on an elderly administrator with strong but suspect religious interests, Anastasius, who was crowned emperor and then married the woman to whom he owed the throne. His reign (491–518) was not devoid of incident.[2] Zeno's brother had hoped to succeed the dead emperor, but Anastasius banished him to Egypt, where he later died of starvation, and within a few years a series of military actions had overcome the problems caused by the Isaurians. Another general, Vitalian, who seems to have had a barbarian father, led the troops under his command against Constantinople itself in 513, in 514, and again in 515, but was repulsed. There were also problems emanating from the church, repercussions of a widespread failure to accept the teaching of the council of Chalcedon (451), which led Anastasius to depose the patriarchs of Constantinople and Antioch in 511 and 512 respectively. But under Anastasius the empire enjoyed more peace than it had been used to. The emperor put his leisure to good use by introducing a new system of taxation and applied his

2. C. Capizzi *L'imperatore Anastasio I (491–518)* Rome 1969.

administrative skill to bring about savings in the operations of government. He died in 518 leaving 320 000 pounds of gold in the treasury and a number of relatives who could hardly be blamed for being interested in exploiting his good reputation.

The death of the emperor was followed by one of the unexpected transfers of power so characteristic of the period. Anastasius had not groomed a successor. He had three nephews, Hypatius, Pompeius, and Probus, and a story was later told that on one occasion the old emperor, wondering which of them would succeed him, gave them lunch and then told them to take a nap in a room with three couches. Imperial insignia had been hidden under the pillow of one of the couches, and Anastasius waited to see which nephew would choose that couch. But none did. He then prayed that God would reveal who was to follow him on the throne, and one night was told that the first person to be announced to him the following morning would be his successor. Not surprisingly, this was the leader of the imperial bodyguard.[3] It is an interesting story, implying as it does that Anastasius' nephews, apparently the sons of his sister Caesaria,[4] had some claim to the throne, and as we shall see they were to remain an important element in succeeding reigns. But the tale also provides a context for the unexpected accession of Justin.

. . .

THE NEW EMPEROR AND HIS NEPHEW

Following the death of Anastasius on 9 July 518 the senators were not able to agree on a successor. The most likely candidate, Hypatius, was serving as commander-in-chief in the East, and out of the city. Amantius, a powerful eunuch, bribed Justin, the leader of the bodyguard, to obtain its support for a claimant whom he hoped to control. But Justin spent the money winning support for himself, and on the next day he became emperor.[5] The new ruler could charitably be

3. Anonymous Valesianus 74–76, of which there is an inaccurate translation by J.C. Rolfe, in vol. 3 of his Loeb edition of Ammianus Marcellinus (London 1952).
4. Alan Cameron 'The house of Anastasius' *Greek Roman and Byzantine Studies* 17 1978: 259–76.
5. On Justin see A.A. Vasiliev *Justin the First* Cambridge Mass. 1950.

described as a rough diamond. He had been born at the town of Bederiana near Niš, in an area where Latin rather than Greek was spoken, and, rather like Zeno, had made his way to Constantinople to follow a military career. He was said to have been illiterate, and his wife, apparently a barbarian, was thought to have been a slave and the concubine of another man before she caught Justin's eye and he bought her. On the elevation of her husband she changed her name from Lupicina, a name unfortunately similar to a slang word for prostitute, to Euphemia. The accession of such a man as Justin was unexpected, and contemporaries expressed surprise that members of the family of Anastasius had been elbowed aside (Procopius *Wars* 1.11.1). Given the tensions which had surrounded successions during recent decades, it was unlikely that members of the supplanted family would simply go away.

Justin began his reign with vigour. Letters were sent to pope Hormisdas announcing a change in ecclesiastical policy, and in the following year the schism which had separated the churches of Rome and Constantinople since 482 was healed, on the terms of the former. Zeno and Anastasius were condemned, an extraordinary concession by the man who succeeded them as emperor. Justin also moved rapidly to deal with potential enemies. Among them was Amantius, who became involved in disturbances in the cathedral of Hagia Sophia; within a few months he and the man he had hoped to install as emperor had been put to death. People whose careers had languished under Anastasius found themselves gaining preferment. The patrician Apion, a member of a famous Egyptian family, who had been sent into exile and ordained a priest in 510, was recalled and appointed praetorian prefect. Eminent soldiers who had been exiled by Anastasius were also recalled: one was appointed commander-in-chief of the forces of the East, and another enjoyed a consulate in 525.

But Justin did not come to power alone. Like every emperor, he was surrounded by a group of men who, naturally enough, found themselves competing for influence. Among them was Anastasius' old enemy Vitalian. Ambitious generals of his kind had long been a problem in the Roman empire, and they had been particularly prominent in the politics of the preceding century. No-one would have thought that their hour was passed.[6] Indeed, the rank to which Justin appointed Vitalian in 518, magister militum praesentalis, was that which Zeno had held immediately prior to becoming emperor in 474. Vitalian was to the fore in a group which met legates sent to Constantinople by pope Hormisdas in 519, and in 520 he held the office of consul. But in July of that year he was brutally murdered in the palace. Another important military figure was Germanus, a nephew of Justin, but he was a loyal officer whose office, that of commander-in-chief in Thrace, kept him removed from the palace and its intrigues.

In the royal city, power was in the hands of disparate people. There could be no doubting that the empress wielded significant influence, although we shall later see that this may have been less than some people thought, and other members of the emperor's family could be important in varying degrees. The eunuchs of the bedchamber, who controlled access to the emperor and empress, were in a position where they could wield power. Having become important in administration during the fourth century, they were notorious for their corrupt engagement in politics. Another well-positioned group was the imperial bodyguard, whose members were able to play a prominent political role; Justin was the first of three of its commanders who became emperors in the sixth century. The complex administration of the empire was in the hands of powerful officials. Chief among these was the praetorian prefect, who discharged a very mixed bag of responsibilities. He could almost be regarded as a deputy emperor, and one important holder of the office in the sixth century was accused of harboring imperial ambitions. There were also the quaestor, who had responsibility for legal affairs, the master of the offices, and various financial officials. The responsibilities attached to some of these positions were ill-defined, and so there was frequently rivalry between different parts of the administration. The chief positions were in the gift of the emperor, and they were traditionally enjoyed for short tenures, doubtless a device to prevent those who held them from gaining too much power. The upper reaches of the bureaucracy in the time of Justinian had changed little since major reforms in the fourth century, but one body in public life was

6. For the general context, see W.E. Kaegi *Byzantine Military Unrest 471–843. An Interpretation* Amsterdam 1981.

far older. The senate, which traced its origins to early Rome, continued to meet in Constantinople. It was less distinguished in membership than that of Rome, and the functions it discharged, most of them advisory or of local import, were not onerous, but it was a place where traditionalist sentiments found a home.

So it was that, while the empire was effectively an autocracy, there were various positions which ambitious people could use to further interests which did not necessarily coincide with those of the emperor. Relatives, generals, eunuchs, bodyguards, administrators and senators all had places in the power structure which could easily be exploited. Among these the military men were the most dangerous, for successful generals such as Vitalian always had the potential to cause trouble. But it quickly became clear that the key figure in the group around Justin was the person everyone blamed for the murder of Vitalian. The emperor's nephew was the figure to watch.

Justinian, the son of Justin's sister and her husband Sabbatius, came from the same region as his uncle, having been born at the village of Tauresium, near Scupi, in about 482.[7] Nothing is known of his early life, but he followed his uncle to Constantinople where he occupied himself in making a name for himself; indeed, he had been mentioned as a possible emperor in 518. Early in Justin's reign he wrote many letters to the pope concerning the ending of the schism in which he can be seen letting the pope know that he played a special part in ecclesiastical affairs. He also built a church dedicated to SS Peter and Paul, for which he sought relics of the martyr S Laurence from Rome, and at some stage he mastered a good deal of the voluminous Greek theological literature of the period. He was also interested in foreign affairs, and cultivated Hilderic, a member of the royal house of the Vandals, before he became king of their African domain in 523. But most importantly, he took care to establish himself in Constantinople. As its name implies, the office of magister militum praesentalis in which he succeeded Vitalian in 520 allowed him to be present at the palace, and in 521 he held a consulship, which gave him an opportunity to make blatant

7. According to Zonaras (*Epitome* 14.5.40, ed. M. Pinder 1897), he was 42 when he became emperor in 527.

attempts to win favour with both the people and the senators. The consular games at which he presided were spectacular, featuring 20 lions, 30 leopards and other wild beasts; in all, he spent 4000 pounds of gold. He sought the favour of members of the senate by giving them ivory diptychs bearing at the top his full name, Fl. Petrus Sabbatius Justinianus, and in central medallions a dedication: 'I, the consul, offer to my fathers these gifts, of little value but with deep respect'.[8]

No less than his uncle, Justinian was a provincial. He had been born in a part of the empire where Latin was the dominant language, and his laws contain several references to it as his native tongue, but letters he wrote to pope Hormisdas in Latin were composed in a clumsy and awkward fashion which contrasts to the smooth style in which the letters sent in Justin's name were composed by the chancery.[9] He must have cut a decidedly rustic figure in the capital. There was nothing sophisticated about his deep religious convictions. It was said that during Lent he lived on water and wild herbs pickled in salt and vinegar; a text of the tenth century states that he was once cured of a disease of the kidneys by drinking the water of a spring outside Constantinople. Perhaps there is little to wonder at here, for the Byzantine empire, while famous for its conservatism, was frequently ruled by people who had come up the hard way, with consequent tension between the boorish ways of the sovereign and the smart ways of the capital. As far as we can tell, Justinian was a modest man. According to John the Lydian, who knew him quite well, when he was emperor he could, in his humility, just tolerate being addressed as 'master', a word John glossed as 'good father' (*Powers* 1.6). In his *Buildings* Procopius described him in a phrase from Homer as being 'as gentle as a father' (1.1.15), and likeable characteristics emerge even in the bitterly hostile *Secret History*, for he could be described as approachable and kindly (13.1), an easy going man (15.11) who seemed good-natured (15.17). But in his early years in the royal city Justinian must have been feeling his way.

8. The diptychs are the only evidence for him bearing the names other than the last. There is a good representation in K. Weitzmann ed. *The Age of Spirituality* New York 1979 p. 51.
9. A.M. Honoré 'Some Constitutions composed by Justinian' *Journal of Roman Studies* 65 1975: 107–23.

. . .

AN UNUSUAL WIFE

Justinian also equipped himself with a wife some years younger than he with an unusual past.[10] According to a famous story told by Procopius in his *Secret History* (9.1–32, 47–51), Theodora had an unsavoury background, her father having been a keeper of bears in the employ of the Green faction of the circus at Constantinople and her mother a professional dancer and actress. Following the death of her husband and the failure of the Greens to support her young family, Theodora's mother put her three daughters on the stage, and as Theodora, the second of the three sisters, grew she naturally turned towards a career as a prostitute. In time she became notorious throughout the city for her novel practices, lack of modesty, and gargantuan sexual appetite. Among her clients was one Hekobolos, who took her with him when he was appointed governor of Libya Pentapolis. But following a lovers' quarrel Theodora made her way back to Constantinople by way of Alexandria, earning a living by her accustomed means. When she was back in the royal city Justinian fell under her spell, and they began to live together. Justin's wife Euphemia, whose own background was scarcely distinguished, refused to hear of the couple getting married, and in any case the law prevented a senator from marrying a woman of Theodora's background. Only after the death of Euphemia did Justinian prevail upon Justin to issue a law which made their marriage possible.

It is an extraordinary tale which loses nothing by the degree of explicitness with which it is told, and the narrative has formed the basis of countless retellings by male historians with varying degrees of enjoyment and innuendo. None has carried the exercise off with greater style than Gibbon, who resorted to quoting passages of the Greek text of Procopius in footnotes, alleging that 'her murmurs, her pleasures, and her arts must be veiled in the obscurity of a learned language'.[11] Nudging and winking, of course, is precisely the

10. For what follows there is the study of H.-G. Beck *Kaiserin Theodora und Prokop* Munich 1986. Also of interest is the gallant study of Ch. Diehl *Théodora, impératrice de Byzance* Paris 1904.
11. Edward Gibbon *The History of the Decline and Fall of the Roman Empire* ed. J.B. Bury 4 London 1898 p. 213.

response Procopius sought from his readers, but the extent to which his story is true is not immediately clear. The description of Theodora's sexual excesses is obviously designed to titillate, but this does not mean we have to write off all he says. We know from elsewhere that Theodora was a prostitute early in her life, and she is known to have had children before she married Justinian. While Hekobolos is known from no other source, an Egyptian text of the late seventh century states that Theodora met the patriarch Timothy of Alexandria. His tenure of office (517–535) fits comfortably with the period during which Procopius says she was in Alexandria, and her coming under his influence could account for the adherence to Monophysite Christianity she was later to display.

Procopius' narrative is also born out by a law enacted by Justin which, having been addressed to an official who was in office in 521/522 but had been replaced by 524, can be dated to this period.[12] Roman law prohibited a member of the aristocracy from marrying an actress. Further, not only was the condition of having been an actress life-long, but the children of an actor or actress could not marry people of senatorial rank. For that matter, neither could former slaves, such as Justin's wife Euphemia. But Euphemia probably married Justin before the latter acquired senatorial rank, and she may well have been not merely manumitted but made legally freeborn. Such a legal fiction would have nicely anticipated the law Justin enacted in the interests of Justinian and Theodora, which proclaims that an actress who desisted from her dishonourable profession could be 'so to speak handed back to her pristine, native condition'. She could therefore contract a marriage with whomever she chose. It can be seen that this would have neatly solved the difficulties of the couple, and when the law went on to declare the children subsequently born into such a marriage to be legitimate it betrays dynastic preoccupations.

We may take it, then, that there is a fair amount of truth in the story Procopius tells. But why did he deck it out with such inflammatory material? Perhaps because attacking the past of

---

12. Codex 5.4.23, well discussed by David Daube, 'The marriage of Justinian and Theodora. Legal and theological reflections' *Catholic University of America Law Review* 16 1966/7: 380–99, whom I follow. No source other than Procopius states that Euphemia was dead by then, but she certainly died before Justin, so a death before the time of the marriage is quite plausible.

a woman who had died just a few years earlier offered him a way of expressing the disgust he had obviously come to feel for the government by the time he was writing in 550. As we shall see, there were those who were unhappy as Justinian's reign developed, and the contents of the *Secret History* reflect the state of mind of the author as much as what had really happened some decades earlier. There is no need to take the *Secret History* as a true guide to the subjects it discusses. Indeed, it is possible to respect Justinian's choice of wife. In a period when marriages were often contracted with an eye to the advantages a partner could bring, he chose a woman who could offer no possible benefit beyond what could be gained from an intelligent and resourceful spouse. She was also faithful; not even in Procopius' hostile account does a whisper of scandal touch her after she married Justinian.

That Justin was prepared to enact a special law in the interest of Justinian and his future wife is a pointer to the position his nephew occupied. Justinian was certainly ambitious: as early as 521 he had written to the pope of 'our state', implying that the empire was his to do with as he pleased, and it was widely believed that he was the power behind the throne. In the vivid image of Procopius, Justin was a donkey with flapping long ears, obedient to the one who pulled the reins (*Secret History* 8.3), and in later years the reign of Justinian was sometimes calculated as having included that of Justin.[13] But we may doubt whether Justinian enjoyed such power as people later thought he held. When he became emperor he immediately launched a number of major initiatives, and if he had been in a position to have gone ahead with these matters during the reign of Justin he surely would have done so, particularly given that he was well into his forties when his uncle died. As late as 526, when pope John visited Constantinople, he crowned Justin, but not Justinian. At some stage, however, Justin adopted his nephew, and on 1 April 527, as his end drew near, he made Justinian co-emperor.[14] Coins were

13. Procopius *Wars* 3.9.5.; *Secret History* 6.19, 18.45; *Buildings* 1.3.3 (ed. and trans. H.B. Dewing, London 1914–1940). If we accept that the *Secret History* was written in 550, Procopius reckons Justinian as having governed from 518: 18.33, 23.1, 24.29.

14. This was three days before Easter Day (Procopius *Secret History* 9.53; Zacharias rhetor *Historia ecclesiastica* 9.1 trans. E.W. Brooks *Corpus Scriptorum Christianorum Orientalium* 42 (*Scriptores Syri* 6)). I cannot explain this odd choice.

quickly minted showing the two emperors seated side by side. So it was that when Justin died from complications arising from an old wound in a foot on 1 August the succession caused no difficulties.

. . .

THE NEW BROOM

Justinian approached government with the enthusiasm of a reforming head of state who had been waiting for years to enter office, and his early years as emperor were marked by a series of bold initiatives. But before turning to these it will be worth our while to examine how he dealt with a major piece of unfinished business.

The most important neighbour of the Roman empire was Persia. Relations between the two states were always difficult, and they had recently grown worse, for shah Kavad, who had ruled since 488, was increasingly concerned with the succession to his throne. He had a number of sons, but it was the third, Khusrau (Greek Chosroes), whom he wished to succeed him. With this end in view he approached Justin in about 525 asking the emperor to adopt Khusrau. Justin and Justinian were prepared to accept the unusual proposal, but they were dissuaded by the quaestor Proculus, a man of conservative convictions who believed that if Khusrau were to be adopted he would be in a position to lay claim to the Roman empire when the childless Justin died. The only fitting way for Justin to adopt Khusrau, he argued, would be by making him his 'son–in–arms'. There was recent precedent for this procedure, for not long after he became emperor Justin had adopted as his son in arms the man who seemed likely to take over the Gothic kingdom in Italy when the great king Theoderic died. But Kavad was not prepared to see his son treated in the same way as a Goth, and war followed.

The leaders of the Roman forces were a mixture of old and new faces. Hypatius, a nephew of the emperor Anastasius, was the commander-in-chief of the East, an office he had held on and off since late in his uncle's reign. His immediate subordinates, however, were from far more humble backgrounds. The commander in Armenia was Sittas, the bearer of an unusual name which may be Thracian or Gothic, and a man who had come to Justinian's attention while serving in his bodyguard. The duke of Mesopotamia was another officer from

Justinian's bodyguard, Belisarius, who had come to Constantinople from his birth-place in what is now western Bulgaria. In 529, however, Hypatius was relieved of his post, the last military command he would ever enjoy, and replaced by Belisarius. The staff of this young general included Procopius, a scholarly man from Caesarea whose observations when campaigning against the Persians, Vandals and Ostrogoths were to form the basis of a major work of history.

Unfortunately, the early stages of Procopius' work are heavily biased in favour of Belisarius, but reading between the lines of his narrative it is clear that in the opening years of Justinian's reign the Roman forces were finding it difficult to hold their own against the Persians. A major victory was won in June 530, when they put a large invading force to rout near the stronghold of Daras, and we know of one and possibly two equestrian statues of Justinian erected to commemorate it. But in the following year Belisarius, following a defeat at Callinicum by the Euphrates River, was summoned back to Constantinople. It has sometimes been thought that he was recalled because Justinian proposed to send him to make war on the Vandals in Africa, but the only evidence for this interpretation is two passages in Procopius which were almost certainly concocted to conceal the unpleasant reality that the general had been recalled because of his incompetence.[15] The outlook was not encouraging, but in September Kavad died and Khusrau, whose grip on the throne was not strong, sought peace. After a good deal of haggling a treaty was duly agreed to in 532.

The terms of the peace may seem to have favoured Persia. While each side was to return the territory it had won during the war, the Roman duke of Mesopotamia was henceforth to

---

15. Robert Browning *Justinian and Theodora* rev. edn London 1987 p. 77; John Julius Norwich *Byzantium the Early Centuries* London 1988 p. 206. It is true that Procopius asserts that Belisarius was recalled so he could lead the expedition to Africa (*Wars* 1.21.2, 3.9.25). But at this stage of his narrative Procopius was happy to distort the facts in favour of Belisarius, and here he simply attempts to conceal the unpleasant reality that his hero was relieved of his command and recalled after the incompetence and cowardice he displayed at the battle of Callinicum (John Malalas 464, 466; Zacharias rhetor *Historia ecclesiastica* 9.6); in another passage of the *Wars* (2.21.34) he uses a very similar form of words to hide a similar unpleasant reality (see further below p. 98).

reside at Constantina rather than the forward site of Daras which had been fortified at great cost by Anastasius, and the Romans were to pay 11 000 pounds of gold. Some historians have argued that Justinian's agreeing to pay such a high price indicates that he wished to free himself to make war elsewhere.[16] But it is hard to accept this. It is not surprising that Justinian agreed to make some payment. The Persians argued that by manning defences in the Caucasian Passes they were serving Roman as well as their own interests, so that it was reasonable for the Romans to contribute to their upkeep. Whatever degree of plausibility attached to this argument, it is hard to escape the conclusion that the Persian government looked on the empire as a useful source of revenue, for Persian attacks on imperial territory were often no more than plundering expeditions. But while 11 000 pounds of gold may have represented desirable income to Persia, Justinian may have thought that it was well spent. In 521, after all, he had been prepared to spend 4000 pounds on the celebration of his consulship. In 468 Zeno had spent over ten times this sum on a futile expedition against the Vandals in Africa, and in 545, when Justinian negotiated a peace with Persia which was to last for just five years, he paid 5000 pounds. By these standards the peace of 532 offered remarkably good value, for it was to be permanent. Justinian himself, according to the text of a law, seriously believed that the peace would last for ever.[17] As it turned out this expectation was woefully optimistic, for Khusrau was to open hostilities again in 540. But this occurred after a radical shift in the balance of power between the states which Justinian can hardly be held to blame for not anticipating.

The early years of Justinian's reign were also characterized by intense diplomatic activity on a number of fronts, which it will be as well to consider later. But external affairs were not

16. A.H.M. Jones *The Later Roman Empire 284–602* Oxford 1964 p. 273, and apparently E. Stein *Histoire du bas-empire* 2 Paris 1949 p. 295. Yet Khusrau seems to have had the greater need for peace, and the only source to make a connection between the peace with Persia and the onset of the Vandal war in the following year is Procopius, in the two passages cited in the preceding note.

17. This is the only way of interpreting a phrase in a law of 534, which states that through Christ Justinian had 'ratified with the Persians a peace for all time to come (in aeternum)': Codex 1.27.2pr.

the only concern of the new emperor. Another aspect of the activity of this period were the moves he took against people who were not orthodox Christians.

Correct belief in matters of religion was of the greatest importance to Justinian, a religious enthusiast who had transformed himself into a competent theologian. Unfortunately he was a man of settled opinions, able to issue a law which contained the passing observation 'we hate heretics' (novel 45pr.), and he never wavered from firm convictions. One important group of Christians whom Justinian considered deviates, the Monophysites, were spared his attentions, for reasons we shall consider later. But for other groups, the coming to power of Justinian marked the onset of persecution. Shortly after he had become co-emperor with Justin in April 527 a persecution of Manicheans, adherents of a dualist form of belief originating in Persia, was set under way. Some of them were put to death. This policy was carried out in accordance with a law passed some decades earlier, but at the beginning of his reign Justinian extended the applicability of the penalty so that it also applied to people who had been baptized but secretly engaged in pagan practices. Sometimes Justinian used to debate with Manicheans, and those who proved stubborn were burned. Doubtless the Persian origin of their belief made them particularly undesirable, but they were not the only group to suffer persecution.

Action was also taken against the Samaritans, people who claimed to follow the original teachings of the first five books of the Bible and who had a history of rebellious behaviour. In a law published between 527 and 529 Justinian ordered the destruction of their synagogues, and took away their right to bequeath property to people of non-orthodox belief. Many Samaritans in Palestine pretended to embrace Christianity, but in the summer of 529 others revolted, crowning one Julian as their ruler. The time was well chosen, for during that year an Arab ruler who was allied to Persia, al-Mundhir, invaded Syria and penetrated as far as Antioch. Julian found himself leading a movement which attracted considerable popular support. He based himself at Nabulus, not far from Mt Gerizim, the holy place of the Samaritans, where he presided over the chariot races, just as the emperor did in Constantinople. Lack of co-ordination between the Roman civil and military authorities worked in favour of the rebels, but when an army was sent against Julian he was defeated. His head and the diadem he had worn were sent to Justinian. The Samaritans did not find such treatment to their liking, and during the following year it was discovered that a group of them was planning to betray Palestine to Persia, a move which was quashed. Similar measures were enacted against the Montanists, a group in Phrygia which had broken away from the church as early as the second century. In despair they shut themselves in their churches, which they then set alight.

Much milder was Justinian's policy towards the Jews. By the early sixth century they were subject to a variety of legal disabilities, and a body of clerical opinion was not well disposed to them. It was the practice of a Monophysite holy man, Sergius, to gnash his teeth and assert that those who had crucified Christ did not deserve to live. With a band of followers he destroyed a synagogue near Amida, and built a church dedicated to the Theotokos[18] where it had stood. Needless to say, attempts to erect a new synagogue were successfully thwarted. Justinian's early flurry of legislation against non-Christian groups left the Jews largely untouched. But changes were made in their position, for the worse: for example, whereas previously Jews had been allowed to keep Christian slaves provided they respected their religion, henceforth no Jew was to have a Christian as a slave.

As time passed, however, more measures were taken against them. In 535 Justinian ordered that the synagogues of Africa were to be turned into churches, together with what were described as the 'caves' of pagans and heretics; it is not surprising that in the following year, when one of Justinian's armies was seeking to take Naples from the Ostrogoths, the Jews of the town were to the fore in urging resistance to the Roman army.[19] He is reported to have ordered that the Passover was never to be celebrated ahead of Easter, and he certainly intervened in the conduct of synagogue worship. In 553 a curious law was published which provided that a

18. Literally 'God-bearer', the term by which Byzantines most commonly referred to the Virgin Mary. Its technical meaning is discussed below, p. 121.
19. An odd story told in Procopius *Buildings* 6.2.21–23 may represent the application of the African policy. There is no indication that the far larger Jewish communities of Italy suffered in such a way following the Gothic war.

translation of the Jewish Bible rather than the original Hebrew text could be read in synagogues; the Septuagint was recommended as the best translation into Greek, in preference to that which Aquila, a convert of the second century, had produced. He also forbad the use of the Mishnah and ordered that Jews who denied the resurrection, the last judgment or the creation of angels were to be expelled from their communities. It is hard to imagine the Jewish community welcoming such interference in their affairs.

The early years of Justinian's reign were also important for a development in the high culture of the empire. By the sixth century non-Christians in the west could be looked down on as 'pagans', a disparaging word which seems to have meant 'country folk',[20] but in the east they were called 'Hellenes', implying that they were familiar with the sophisticated thought of Greece. To be sure, there were still non-Christians living in parts of the countryside, and in 542 Justinian sent John of Ephesos to Asia Minor to preach against them. He began his work in the hills near Tralles in Lydia, and as the decades passed he enjoyed remarkable success, being said to have baptized 70 000 or 80 000 pagans. Earlier, Justinian had ordered that all pagans were to present themselves for instruction in the Christian faith and, thereafter, baptism; the property of any who failed to comply was to be confiscated, and they were to be exiled. Such people were also forbidden to teach or receive any income from the state. Indeed, we are told of a decree posted in every city of the empire which gave pagans a period of three months to accept orthodox belief; those who failed to do so were to be exiled (John Malalas 449). However, such a decree is not to be found among the laws collected in Justinian's great Codex, and may never have been issued. There was some concern in church circles about the sincerity of pagans who presented themselves for baptism and of schismatics who came forward to take communion. Persecution was directed against some distinguished persons, such as Thomas the quaestor, one of the legal experts working on a new Code of law, who was arrested in 529, and Phocas, a patrician who was to commit suicide later in a subsequent period of persecution.

20. It is possible, however, that the word may have been used in another sense, with the meaning 'civilians'.

Such activities on the part of the state formed the background to a development with important consequences in intellectual history. In the fifth century Athens had become the home of a group of keen Neoplatonic philosophers. In about 430 a young philosopher, Proclus, had arrived there, and for the ensuing five decades he advocated in his teaching and writing a Neoplatonism which was both explicitly non-Christian and intellectually attractive, even to Christians; among those who drew on him was an important Christian author of a slightly later period who is generally known as pseudo-Dionysios. One of the pupils of Proclus, Agapius, lectured in Constantinople, where his lectures were attended by John, a Lydian who had come to Constantinople at the age of twenty-one seeking a career, while another, Ammonius, returned to his hometown, Alexandria, to publish distinguished work on a variety of topics and teach a galaxy of brilliant students. Ammonius was a pagan, but was able to come to some agreement with the patriarch of Alexandria. His students were of diverse persuasions. One of them, John Philoponos, was a Monophysite Christian who attacked the teaching of Proclus that the world was eternal, but he was himself criticized by another of Ammonius' students, the pagan Simplicius, who made his way to Athens, where a third student of Ammonius, the Syrian Damascius, was head of the Neoplatonist school. Early in the sixth century Athens was home to some distinguished scholars, some of whose works survive, the products of minds and intellectual traditions of real distinction.

Byzantine intellectual culture in late antiquity was subject to currents which flowed in different directions. A fire which broke out in Constantinople in 475 is said to have destroyed 120 000 books, among them an illustrated roll of Homer written on the intestines of snakes in letters of gold, 120 feet long.[21] But the contemporaries of the thinkers we have been considering included people with very different interests, such as Romanos Melodos, the most famous writer of hymns in the history of Byzantium. He was a Syrian who had found his way to Constantinople during the reign of Anastasius, yet another of the important figures of the time to have come to

21. P. Lemerle *Byzantine Humanism* trans. Helen Lindsay and Ann Moffatt Canberra 1986 p. 71.

the capital from a distant province. There he wrote hymns which unashamedly relish the paradoxes inherent in the Christian doctrines of the incarnation and resurrection. For the great writers of classical Greece he felt nothing but contempt:

> Why do the Greeks snort and chatter?
> Why do they make a show of Aratus, the thrice-accursed?
> Why are they led into error by Plato?
> Why do they love Demosthenes, the weak?
> Why do they not see that Homer is a flitting dream?
> Why do they keep talking about Pythagoras who is justly to be muzzled?[22]

The hymns of Romanos were popular in their time and have never ceased being copied, sung and imitated. So it was that by the early sixth century the philosophers were aware of swimming against the tide. Some time after the accession of Khusrau to the throne of Persia in December 531 a group of seven of them, depressed at the status Christianity had gained in the empire, made their way to his domain, in the hope of finding there a land ruled by the kind of philosopher king of whom Plato had written.[23] They included Damascius and Simplicius of Cilicia, a pupil of both Ammonius and Damascius, although not all of their party need have been from Athens. But the philosophers were hard to please. They were soon disillusioned with Persia, and when Khusrau and Justinian concluded their peace treaty in 532 its provisions included a clause allowing them to return home and continue the practice of their old beliefs.

22. Romanos Melodos hymn 33.17, trans. Marjorie Carpenter *Kontakia of Romanos, Byzantine Melodist* 1 *On the Person of Christ* Columbia Missouri 1970 p. 367. Romanos is best approached by way of H. Hunger 'Romanos Melodos, Dichter, Prediger, Rhetor – und sein Publikum' *Jahrbuch der Österreichischen Byzantinistik* 34 1984: 15–42.
23. Note the important study of Alan Cameron, 'The last days of the Academy at Athens' *Proceedings of the Cambridge Philological Society* 195 1969: 7–29. The assertion of John Malalas (451) that in 530 a law forbad the teaching of philosophy at Athens and prohibited the Athenians from gambling, apparently because gamblers had been detected in Constantinople uttering appalling blasphemies, has no more weight than the suggestions of archeologists that statues and busts found in a well in Athens were placed there in response to anti-pagan measures in 529.

This they did. We know an epigram composed by Damascius in 538 at Emesa. But there is good reason to believe that Simplicius and some if not all of the scholars made their way to Harran, a town near the Persian frontier in northern Mesopotamia.[24] Its inhabitants were staunch devotees of the old religion: in 363 the emperor Julian had offered sacrifice there while on his way to fight the Persians, and the last pagan temple in the town was only destroyed late in the eleventh century. The temple, however, was not the only centre of pagan activity in Harran. There is also evidence that the town, for centuries after the coming of the Arabs, remained home to a Neoplatonic school, and it may well have been there that the scholars returning from Persia after the peace of 532 settled. It is certainly true that paganism in the eastern parts of the empire was a long time dying. In about 579 a leading citizen of Edessa, a town some 40 kilometres from Harran which was famed for the strength of its Christianity, was found guilty of being a pagan and condemned to torture, being thrown to the beasts and crucifixion. Not for the last time, one wonders at the gap between Justinian's ambitions and his achievement.

This aside, there can be no mistaking the energy displayed by Justinian in the opening years of his reign. Like many other reforming heads of state, he lost no time in surrounding himself with assistants who were themselves new to office. In 530, as we have seen, the commander-in-chief in the East, Belisarius, and the magister militum praesentalis, Sittas, were both former officers in Justinian's bodyguard. Belisarius had married an older woman of a questionable past who was close to Theodora, while Sittas had shown more ambition in marrying Komito, Theodora's elder sister. Following the dismissal of Thomas the quaestor in 529, this important civil office was filled by Tribonian, a lawyer from an obscure background in Pamphylia. Waiting in the wings were John, a man from the Cappodocian town of Caesarea whose career in the bureaucracy was moving ahead rapidly thanks to the patronage of Justinian, Narses, an Armenian eunuch of the sacred bedchamber, and Solomon, another eastern eunuch who was serving in the household of Belisarius. One is confronted with

24. See the fascinating study of M. Tardieu '«Sābiens» coraniques et «Sābiens» de Hārran' *Journal asiatique* 274 1986: 1–44.

a group of talented people of humble backgrounds whose careers were starting to take off early in the reign of Justinian. The new emperor would owe much to them, but they, dependent on his patronage, would owe more to him. Inevitably, before long many of them were to be the subjects of hostility and gossip.

But if their servants had risen from obscurity, how much more could this be said of the emperor from the backwoods and his disreputable spouse? Tongues were ready to wag; early in his reign reports reached Justinian that Probus, a nephew of Anastasius, had been slandering him, but he decided not to pursue the matter. He and his wife set about the business of government with all the spendthrift vulgarity of the nouveau riche. Justinian's first consulship had been expensive, but when he held his second in 528 it was thought that the largesse distributed was on a scale unmatched by any earlier emperor on becoming consul. When Theodora set out in the summer of the following year for the town of Pythion in Bythinia, to enjoy the hot springs which were popular with the inhabitants of Constantinople, she travelled in style, to a town which was to do well from the beneficence of the emperor: a palace, public baths, and an aqueduct were all built there during the reign of Justinian, while improvements were made to a church and an infirmary. Theodora was accompanied thither by a mixed entourage of patricians, eunuchs of the bedchamber and other staff, to the number of 4000. Among those in her party was the count of the sacred largesse, the chief minister of finance, whose presence must have been useful, for Theodora made many gifts to churches, poorhouses and monasteries. Doubtless such generosity had a purpose, but her unashamed display must have grated on members of the prestigious and wealthy families which had been in Constantinople for generations. They can only have wondered at the direction the government was taking under Justinian, his remarkable wife, and those who were beginning to prosper under their patronage.

Chapter 2

THE MAJESTY OF THE EMPEROR

. . .

REFORM OF THE LAWS

One of the supreme achievements of Roman civilization was law. At its best this provided an efficient administration of justice within a framework of highly developed intellectual principles. The endeavours of the Romans in this field have won the admiration of many others, and even now it is hard not to be moved by the words of Ulpian, an author of the early third century: 'Justice is a fixed and everlasting desire to give to each person what is properly just ... These are the precepts of the law: to live honourably, not to harm another, to render to each person what is rightly theirs'.

Yet all was not well with Roman law in late antiquity. For centuries emperors had been enthusiastically issuing new constitutions. A particularly dangerous practice was the issuing of rescripts, in which specific questions were answered in terms which did not necessarily agree with the general principles of the law but which nevertheless themselves had the force of law. Further, laws were not systematically published, and to make matters worse the imperial archives did not always keep copies of new legislation, so that lawyers and judges found it difficult to determine what the law was on specific points. Another problem was the jungle of opinions on points of law offered by the learned jurisconsults of the second and third centuries, which were sometimes contradictory and often hard of access. Towards the end of the third century two collections of laws were published, and attempts were made in the following years to update them. But as time

passed their usefulness diminished, and the practical administration of justice remained difficult. In 426 the western
emperor Valentinian III had attempted to deal with these
problems by ordering that the opinions of just five commentators could be cited before the courts; the opinions of some
earlier writers cited by them could also be taken cognisance
of, on condition that the passages containing these opinions
were confirmed by a comparison of manuscripts. When the
opinions of the commentators differed, the opinion of the
majority was to be accepted; if the numbers were equally
divided, the authority of the group which included Papinian,
a jurist of the second century, was to be accepted.

Theodosius II, an eastern emperor, took a more important
step. In 427 and again in 434 he set up commissions to prepare
a new collection of the laws issued since 312. The outcome was
the Theodosian Code, which was issued in 438. We still have
the minutes of the meeting of the senate in Rome which was
held when the code was issued. As was their wont on such
occasions, the senators broke into acclamations, many of which
reveal concern at the way the law was operating. Among other
things, the senators wanted many copies of the Code to be
made for the state offices, copies to be kept under seal, copies
to be written out in full to prevent interpolations, and the
promulgation of no new laws in response to petitions. These
anxieties are extraordinary testimony to the inability of the
state to make its laws known, the danger of illicit emendations
being made, and the threat posed by ad hoc legislation. Some
of these problems arose from inefficiencies which were doubtless beyond the power of any pre-modern administration to
deal with. But others were of such a kind as to pose a challenge
to a vigorous emperor. Such an emperor was Justinian.

On 13 February 528, comfortably within his first year as
emperor, he appointed a commission to produce a new code
of imperial law.[1] It comprised ten experts chaired by one John,

1. Very important work in this area has been done by Tony Honoré, in
   particular in his *Tribonian* London 1978, which makes important points
   about Justinian as well as its subject. In some respects, however, such
   as his conclusions as to the precise divisions into committees and the
   timetables to which they worked, his findings are controversial: W.
   Waldstein 'Tribonianus' *Zeitschrift der Savigny-Stiftung für Rechtsgeschich-
   te* Romanistische Abteilung 98 1980: 232–55, and D.J. Osler 'The
   composition of Justinian's Digest' ibid. 102 1985: 129–84.

who had formerly held the office of quaestor, or chief legal officer of the empire, and was to take in hand the contents of the three collections made in the preceding centuries as well as the various supplementary new laws, technically termed 'novels,' issued since the Theodosian Code was promulgated. The mass of material was to be systematized and simplified. The commission carried out its task with great efficiency, and the Codex Justinianus was published on 7 April 529.

One success led to another. On 15 December 530 a commission of 16 was set to work on a more demanding task, that of codifying the works of the Roman jurists. It was said that the state of the laws, which went back to the time of Romulus, was so disordered that it was beyond human power to take its measure. Some said that the job could not be done, or that it would take ten years, and Justinian's practice of keeping a close eye on the activities of the commissioners need not have been conducive to its efficiency. But the team discharged its responsibilities amazingly well. At its head was a highly skilled lawyer, Tribonian, who had already served on the commission which had prepared the Code. The commission claimed to have worked through 2000 books, a 'book' being notionally the length of a papyrus roll, and to have read three million lines. The outcome of its labours, the Digest or 'Pandects' as they were called in Greek, was published on 16 December 533. A remarkable feat of compression, it amounted to 50 books and 150 000 lines. Justinian hoped that the work would be definitive: no commentaries were to be made on it, although it would be permissible to make indexes and supply headings, while literal translations into Greek were also acceptable. Some of the steps which were taken may seem extreme: thus, the numbers of the sections of the Digest were to be written out in full, rather than expressed as numerals. But they express a desire to prevent corruption of the text and, hence, for the efficient exercise of the will of the emperor.

Meanwhile, a committee consisting of Tribonian and the leading academic lawyers of Constantinople and Beirut had also been preparing a short textbook for the use of students. A preface, addressed to 'young men desirous of the laws', encouraged its readers to work hard and relish the prospect of holding posts in the government at the end of their study. Towards its beginning stood the words from Ulpian quoted at the beginning of this chapter. This work, which is heavily indebted to Gaius, a lawyer of the second century, was published as the Institutes on 21 November 533. Finally, a revised version of the Codex Justinianus which took into account developments since 529 was prepared, and it was published on 16 November 534.

The energy with which these works were produced and their degree of success are both astonishing. They constituted the final, definitive form of Roman law. But Justinian's legislative achievement did not end with them. In 535 he began to issue novels which supplemented or replaced earlier legislation, of which a large number were compiled after he died. Unlike the Digest, Code and Institutes, which were cast in Latin, the traditional language of Roman law, the great bulk of the novels were issued in Greek. Over half the novels promulgated during Justinian's reign were issued in the 530s, and some of them dealt with important issues.

Among the needs which Justinian felt was that of overhauling the administration of the provinces to make it more efficient and less corrupt, and a series of novels dealt with piecemeal reform to this end. One novel, citing the biblical teaching 'the love of money is the root of all evils', and acknowledging the advice received from Theodora, stated that provincial governors and other high officials were to take an oath that they had not made any payments for being appointed to office. The sale of offices was an old and intractable problem, but the issue was important, for it was feared that governors who paid for office would be led into exploiting the provincials, and they could easily find themselves owing favours. But Justinian, like many other rulers, found it impossible to control his officials. When the inhabitants of a village in Egypt sent a petition complaining about the behaviour of a tax collector there was little he could do. Other legislation changed the administrative set-up of a number of provinces, in particular by amalgamating civil and military power. Here Justinian was striking out in a more radical direction. For centuries the separation of civil and military authority had been a fixed policy, but as the initial success of the Samaritan revolt of 529 indicated it was not necessarily a good one, and by bringing together the two areas of competence Justinian was anticipating later developments in Byzantine history. Officials in the provinces were given increased authority to hear appeals, so as to keep litigants away from the capital.

Marriage and sexual matters were other areas occupying Justinian's attention. A law of 534 dealt with the problem of prostitution. Constantinople, the law complained, was full of brothels, staffed by women who had been enticed from the country, some of them were mere girls, less than ten years old. The keeping of brothels in the city was henceforth forbidden. Perhaps we are to see here the influence of Theodora, whose shady background led her to take an interest in the plight of women trapped in prostitution. She was certainly involved in the transformation of a palace on the Asian shore of the Bosphorus into a convent which housed former prostitutes, although not all the women placed there seem to have been happy with their new way of life, and was known to have bought girls out of prostitution. In 536 a long law on marriage was published; among its provisions lurked the implication that marriages could be dissolved. The status of concubines was another matter to receive attention, and here a liberal policy prevailed, the inheritance rights of a man's faithful partner and their children being improved.

When it came to male homosexuals, however, there was no mercy. As early as 528 some bishops accused of homosexual practices were summoned to Constantinople. One of them was tortured and exiled, while another was castrated and paraded through the city. Justinian ordered that, henceforth, those guilty of this offence were to be castrated. The Institutes had legislated against homosexual behaviour (4.18.4), and in 535 a novel was published which drew a grim lesson from Scripture: the just wrath of God punished not only those who committed deeds against nature but also the cities in which they lived, so that famine, earthquakes and disease could be expected as a result of their activities (novel 77.1). They were to be put to death. The penalty applied only to male homosexuals, lesbians escaping the attention of the law. It may be significant that another novel dealing with male homosexuals was published in 559 (novel 141), the year after an outbreak of the plague in Constantinople.

'We are lovers of chastity, but we know that there is nothing more powerful than sexual madness.' (novel 74.4pr.) The expression is borrowed from Plato (*Laws* 839B) but the sentiment is Christian, and it is clear that Justinian's legislation represents a compromise between a desire to impose proper standards of Christian behaviour and the knowledge that people could not be expected to act as he would have wished. Divorce was a particularly difficult area, because the exacting standards taught by the church conflicted with both pre-Christian legislation and the wishes of many citizens of the empire. In 528 Justinian had provided a new reason for divorce, the failure of the husband to consummate a marriage within two years (Codex 5.17.10) But a law of 542 reduced the grounds for divorce and explicitly denied divorce by mutual consent (novel 117.8) In some respects the law improved the position of women, who could now divorce husbands who were unfaithful, made false accusations of adultery, or were held captive, but women who sought to divorce their husbands on grounds other than those specified were to be handed over to the local bishop and sent to a convent (117.13), and from 548 men seeking to act in this way were committed to monasteries (novel 127). But in 566 Justinian's successor, Justin II, was to admit defeat. Although Justinian had prohibited divorce by mutual consent, his successor was aware of many cases where peoples' lives were being made a misery by domestic battles and combats, and restored this ground for divorce (novel 140).

Doubtless ultimate fine-tuning of the laws was impossible. In the early 530s Justinian must have looked on his legal endeavours as having been overwhelmingly successful. The immense effort which went into them and the measure of success which attended them naturally encouraged a certain arrogance. At one point in the Institutes Justinian is represented as striving to surpass Augustus (2.23.12), but this is nothing compared to a passage in the constitution describing how work on the Digest came to be undertaken. It asserted that before Justinian's reign no-one had hoped for such an achievement, the pathway of the laws, which came down from the founding of Rome and the time of Romulus, being so hard to follow that it went on for ever (constitution *Deo auctore*). But who could blame Justinian, amid the achievements of the first years of his reign, for feeling buoyant? Pieces of legislation issued in 535–537 introducing reforms in provincial administration contain important prefaces, almost certainly written by the quaestor Tribonian, which contrive to suggest classical antecedents, frequently spurious, for the reforms being imposed. It may well be that they, too, reflect continuing optimism.[2] But this is to anticipate matters which will concern us later.

Justinian's legislation suggests a persistent interest in the situation of women, and as we have suggested with reference to the issue of prostitution, it may not be fanciful to see the influence of Theodora here. This raises the general question of the position of the empress during Justinian's reign, and it will be worth our while to broach it now.

. . .

THE POWER OF THE EMPRESS

In his *Secret History*, Procopius painted an alarming picture of Justinian having been under the thumb of his wife, a situation he suggested may have been brought about by sorcery (22.28, 32). No-one would take his statements at face value, but as with his lurid account of Theodora's early days it may be that some truth lay behind the exaggerations. John the Lydian described her as 'co-reigning' with Justinian (*Powers* 3.69), while Zonaras, an author of the twelfth century, believed that her power had been greater than that of her husband (*Epitome* 14.6.1, 5f). One of Justinian's laws mentions his having taken counsel with 'the most pious spouse whom God has given us' (novel 8.1, issued in 535) and provided the wording of an oath by which holders of office were to swear good service 'to our most holy lords Justinian and Theodora, the wife of his majesty' (ibid., *ad fin.*) Inscriptions were erected 'in the most happy times of our lords Justinian and Theodora', and the estates of the empress, which had their own administration, gave her economic independence. During the last desperate years of their kingdom in the 530s the sovereigns of the Ostrogoths found it worth their while to address five letters to her. From one of these we learn that Theodora had told king Theodahad that any matters which were to be placed before Justinian should be brought to her prior notice.[3] Given this, it would

2. See the important study of Michael Maas 'Roman history and Christian ideology in Justinian's reform legislation' *Dumbarton Oaks Papers* 40 1986 pp. 17–31, where the rhetoric of the prefaces is seen as a bid for support from various elements.

3. Cassiodorus *Variae* 10.20.2 (ed. Th. Mommsen, *Monumenta Germaniae Historica Auctores Antiquissimi* 12; trans. S.J.B. Barnish, Liverpool 1992); the other letters addressed to Theodora are 10.10 (from Amalasuintha), 10.21 (from Theodahad's wife Gudeliva), 10.23 (from Theodahad) and 10.42 (from Gudeliva).

not have been surprising had Theodora played a role in the framing of legislation.

Some years before her death Theodora had displayed power in moving against one of her husband's chief officials, John the Cappadocian. She brought it about that John's daughter was befriended by Antonina, the wife of Belisarius, who led her on to say that John would co-operate with Belisarius in a coup against Justinian. John fell into the trap. In 541 Antonina arranged for him to pledge himself to move against the emperor while friends of Theodora were secretly listening. John fled to a church and later took holy orders, being assigned to a church near Cyzicus. Justinian retained a friendly interest in his former minister, and saw to it that a large part of the property which had been confiscated from him was returned. But imperial favour was not enough to shield him from his enemies. Before long John, now accused of murdering the bishop of Cyzicus, was beaten with rods and exiled to Egypt, and his house was given to Belisarius. In 545 Theodora sought to revive the charge that John had been responsible for the murder of the bishop, but to no avail. Only after Theodora had died did Justinian recall him to Constantinople.[4]

Yet one wonders. Theodora's name did not appear on coins. Her power cannot be compared to that exercised during the preceding century at the court of Theodosius II by his sister Pulcheria, who was quite capable of fostering developments in the cult of the Theotokos to her advantage, and to a lesser extent by his wife Eudocia.[5] Indeed, it may be that the accusations of intrigue which her enemies levelled against Theodora, such as an implausible claim that fear lest the attractive Gothic queen Amalasuintha become a rival for her husband's affections caused her to see to the murder of the woman, are themselves indicative of a lack of genuine power.[6]

4. The basic source for the fall of John is Procopius *Wars* 1.15.13–44 (ed. and trans. H.B. Dewing, London 1914–1940), but Theodora's involvement is also clear from John the Lydian *Powers* 3.69 (ed. and trans. A.C. Bandy *On Powers* Philadelphia 1983).

5. K.G. Holum *Theodosian Empresses: Women and Power in Late Antiquity* Berkeley Calif. 1982.

6. Procopius *Secret History* 16.1–6 (ed. and trans. H.B. Dewing, London 1914–1940). The charge is implausible because Justinian never displayed 'fickleness' of the kind Theodora is said to have feared.

Mosaics which were installed in the church of S Vitale at Ravenna not long before Theodora died (see below pp. 112–15) are interesting in this connection. They show Justinian in the company of clergy, an archbishop among them, of secular men whose dress marks them out as the holders of high office, and of his bodyguard. Theodora, on the other hand, is shown with two men and a following of seven ladies in waiting, but the latter were not considered important, for the mosaicists only bothered to take pains with the faces of the two of them nearest the empress. Justinian spent his life surrounded by men of power, whereas Theodora did not. The resources available to her were not to be despised, but they were much more limited than those Justinian could mobilize, and in a sense 'illegitimate', for they were not those through which power was formally exercised. In other words, they were of precisely the kind liable to be given exaggerated importance by people who distrusted her, and perhaps would have been made uneasy by any woman with an appearance of strength. Theodora certainly had character and possessed enough power to help the advancement of her friends and orchestrate the fall of some of her enemies, but it was limited. As we shall see she was not able to secure the victory of the theological cause to which she was strongly committed.

· · ·

RIOTS IN THE CAPITAL

By the time of Justinian Constantinople was home to some hundreds of thousands of people. The massive walls built by Theodosius II early in the fifth century enclosed fourteen hectares, but the site was not fully built up, and the inhabitants of Constantinople, like those of cities in the modern world with a high density of population, lived largely out of doors. The broad main street of the city, the Mese, was flanked by shops, in accordance with a trend in late antiquity for the agora or forum of earlier times to be replaced by colonnaded streets as the centre of retail activity, a development which pointed the way towards the souk familiar in middle eastern countries today. One has the feeling of the city's people living cheerful lives, largely in public. Early in Justinian's reign they were able to see a wonderful dog which had, among other abilities, the power of detecting pregnant women, brothel keepers, adulterers, misers, and the magnanimous (John

Malalas 453). Many must have found the animal's prowess disconcerting, yet throngs formed around it and its master. The amenities of the city were certainly such as to cater for people who lived in public. The citizens had at their disposal a number of heated bath-houses, decorated with impressive statues. But the most important place where the people of the city congregated was the Hippodrome, capable of seating perhaps 100 000 spectators at the chariot races. Built in imitation of the Circus Maximus in Rome on a site immediately flanking the palace, no less than the bath-houses it represented continuity with a classical, urban past. The size of the crowds made it the place where public feelings could be expressed most directly. Intellectuals were accustomed to gather by the bookshops near the Basileios Stoa, where they engaged in acrimonious controversy on theological issues. Outdoor processions organized by the church were another way in which communal feeling was expressed, as were the services conducted within stately basilicas, for congregations worshipped while standing. Whereas for the last few centuries Christians of the western traditions have worshipped in pews, which encourage a sense of isolated individuals being spectators or auditors of a service, Byzantine congregations worshipped as a group on their feet. The liturgy was marked by solemn processions, and the generous size of late antique chalices, which sometimes have a capacity of one litre, indicates that large numbers came forward to share in the sacrament of the Eucharist. Religious devotion, which was to become an increasingly private matter in succeeding centuries, was given public and communal expression in sixth-century Constantinople.

Not all the inhabitants of the city were gainfully employed. There were many beggars, and on one occasion the state acted to have people of sound physique not earning a proper living put to work on public works, at the bakeries, in the gardens or elsewhere; those who resisted were to be expelled. Among those who made their way to Constantinople were country people unable to support themselves from the land, perhaps because of the efficient way in which taxes were being collected under Justinian, or because of damage caused by passing armies. The population of the city also included prostitutes, girls who had been lured by promises of shoes and clothing to the capital where they worked for a modest income,[7] ambitious clergy who had come to further their careers or causes, and doubtless large numbers of transient sailors; it was believed that speakers of each of the 72 languages thought to be spoken in the world lived in the city. But it would be wrong to think of Constantinople as being similar to a cosmopolitan city of the present day. In the ancient world cities were places of consumption rather than production, funerary inscriptions of the period indicating that the labour force was devoted to providing services rather than producing goods.[8] This was certainly true of Constantinople, and the large fleet which conveyed grain there from Egypt each year can have had little cargo to carry on the return journey. The large numbers of Christian clergy during this period (see below p. 52) is testimony to the spectacular success of one 'service industry' which did not create wealth. More than the inhabitants of modern cities, those of Constantinople had time on their hands. This circumstance may help account for the volatile nature of life in the great city.

In 507 disturbances had broken out when the emperor Anastasius refused to release prisoners. Stones were thrown at him while he sat at the Hippodrome in the kathisma, the imperial box which was entered directly from the palace, and fires were lit which consumed much of the centre of the city. A new prefect of the city was appointed, but he had his hands full when, five years later, rioting broke out over the addition of a few words to the liturgy. The citizens congregated at the Forum of Constantine, threw down the images and statues of Anastasius and cried out for the husband of Juliana Anicia, Areobindus, to be made emperor, but when they came to his home they found that Areobindus had prudently fled. Anastasius resorted to a desperate expedient. He went to the Hippodrome and took his seat in the kathisma without wearing the diadem which proclaimed his office. There he beseeched the people to refrain from rioting, and they, moved

---

7. Their rate of three folleis per customer (Procopius *Secret History* 17.5) may be compared with the incomes of other workers given by A.H.M. Jones The *Later Roman Empire 284–602* Oxford 1964 pp. 448, 858.

8. While it would be wrong to think that the situation in Constantinople would have been the same as that in a small town, there is food for thought in the discussion of inscriptions at Korykos in Cilicia provided by E. Patlagean *Pauvreté économique et pauvreté social à Byzance* The Hague 1977 pp. 158–69.

by the address of an emperor over eighty years old, asked him to put on the diadem. Other cities around the Mediterranean were not immune from such disturbances. The early years of the sixth century saw rioting in Alexandria, which was famous for its civil disorders, Rome, where people fought in the streets over who should be pope, Ravenna and Antioch. Interestingly the troubles in the latter two cities were linked with anti-Jewish feeling, although it seems unlikely that this was the basic point at issue; rather, Jews seem to have been made scapegoats for problems, hard for modern historians to understand, which were confronting cities at the time. Urban disturbances were certainly a concern for Justinian, several of whose novels seek to guard against the inhabitants of various cities fighting each other.

Civil disturbances were often the work of members of the two great factions of the Hippodrome, the Greens and the less numerous Blues. Originally their function had been to supply items needed for entertainment, and so they employed people such as Theodora's father to look after animals, but as time passed they had increasingly become supporters' clubs. There was bitter rivalry between the factions, which enjoyed some political power. This arose from their function of orchestrating applause at the Hippodrome, where the massed crowds and anonymity of the individuals allowed discontents to become manifest, often in the presence of the emperor. They had powerful backers, for Justinian himself had been a supporter of the Blue faction in his young days, as was Theodora following the bad treatment of her mother by the Greens. But essentially the Greens and Blues were a rowdy lot, who frequently took to vandalism and the lighting of fires after a day at the races. There is no need to see the factions as having represented any particular social, economic or religious interests, nor to see them operating as primitive political parties, although the behaviour of the large crowds which assembled at the Hippodrome could easily assume political significance. They were similar to the fans of soccer teams today, and the descriptions we have of their flamboyant hair-cuts and clothes, which they were thought to have borrowed from barbarians, and their habit of carrying weapons, together with references to the fear their wild behaviour inspired among those who considered themselves respectable citizens, suggest the kinds of things we would associate with a youth culture of the twentieth century.

The games held at the Hippodrome on the Ides of January 532 were the occasion for the beginning of the most severe rioting ever experienced in Constantinople.[9] Having failed to obtain the release of some prisoners, the Blues and Greens joined forces. Adopting as their slogan a word familiar in both the races and imperial acclamations, 'Nika' (Victory), they made their way from the Hippodrome to the praetorium of the city prefect, where they seized the prisoners and set fire to the building. Fires spread in the city, the beginnings of a series of conflagrations which, within a few days, were to destroy various buildings in its central part, including the cathedral of Hagia Sophia, the senate house, the Chalke Gate of the palace and the city's most famous bath-house. On 14 January the rioters demanded the dismissal of some of Justinian's key officials. One of them was Eudaimon, the prefect of the city who was the official responsible for the quiet of Constantinople, but the other two were figures of much greater substance.

Not long before a man named John had been appointed praetorian prefect. He had been born at Caesarea in Cappadocia, and his small-town background may account for the animosity he aroused among the scholar bureaucrats who, even then, were a feature of Byzantine life. John created a big impression on his contemporaries, who took delight in professing horror at the sensuality of his life-style. He redesigned the living quarters in the praetorium and caused scandal by having a smart bath installed outdoors; stories were told about the debaucheries in which he indulged, as well as the ambiguity of his religious position. He was an agent in the move away from Latin towards Greek in the administration of the empire. A major switch in this direction had occurred in about 440 when the office of praetorian prefect was held by an Egyptian, Cyrus, some of whose poetry in Greek survives; a century later, conservatives could look back on his tenure of

---

9. For what follows, our most detailed sources are Procopius *Wars* 1.24, John Malalas 473–76 (*The Chronicle of John Malalas* ed. L. Dindorf, Bonn 1831; trans. E. Jeffreys, M. Jeffreys and Roger Scott Melbourne 1986), and *Chronicon paschale* (ed. L. Dindorf, Bonn 1832; trans. M. Whitby and M. Whitby Liverpool 1989) pp. 114–27.

the office as marking the beginning of a long decline which was still under way when John cut back the use of Latin in the eastern prefecture.[10]

But the chief reason for John being disliked was quite different. The reign of the emperor Anastasius was remembered as a time of prosperity, and he had died leaving the treasury full. But when Justinian and Theodora came to power it seemed as if the big spenders had taken over and were determined to fritter away the state's wealth. Doubtless some items of heavy expenditure were justified: if Theodora's trip to Pythion had been an exercise in conspicuous consumption and Justinian's consular expenses set new records, the outlay involved in the perpetual peace with Persia, for example, could only have been seen as money well spent. But the government needed money, and John proved himself highly skilled at raising funds. The animosity revealed in our two sources most hostile to him, Procopius and John the Lydian, can be seen as reflecting not merely the contempt of traditionalist scholars, but the financial losses which John's activities on behalf of Justinian may have inflicted on the members of at least one social class.[11]

The third victim of the factions was Tribonian, a Pamphylian who had been much involved in Justinian's legal work. He is named sixth in the list of the commissioners appointed to draw up the Codex in 528, but his work must have been exemplary, for in 529 he was appointed to the office of quaestor, Justinian's first appointee to this key office which gave its holder great access to the emperor, and in the following year was given charge of work on the Digest. Unlike John, Tribonian was a genuine intellectual. As we have seen, the Institutes and Digest were in Latin, the traditional language of Roman law, and John the Cappadocian's partiality for Greek may be a sign of divergence between the two men who may well have been rivals for the ear of the emperor. But in 532 they fell together. In his desperate situation Justinian found the services of John and Tribonian as dispensable as

10. Their cause, however, was a lost one. After the dismissal of John from the office of praetorian prefect in 532 the new appointee, the learned Phocas, was not familiar with Latin.
11. Their data are helpfully summarized in J.R. Martindale *The Prosopography of the Later Roman Empire* 3A Cambridge 1992 pp. 627–35.

those of Eudaimon. But the removal from office of unpopular officials was not enough to bring peace to the city. By now people were thinking of the replacement of Justinian as emperor, and their thoughts naturally turned to the family of the well-regarded Anastasius. A crowd went to the house of his nephew Probus, who had been accused of slandering Justinian just a few years earlier, thinking to proclaim him emperor. Not finding him at home, they burned his house down.

Sunday 18 January was to be one of the most eventful days in the history of the city. Early in the morning Justinian appeared in his box in the Hippodrome carrying the Gospels, on which he swore to the assembled crowd that he would not take reprisals. The gesture recalled that of Anastasius in 512. But Justinian received a mixed reception from the people. While some chanted 'May you be victorious!' others cried 'You lie, donkey!' On returning to the palace Justinian told the senators who were there to go to their own homes. They seem to have included the two other nephews of Anastasius, Hypatius and Pompeius, although they may have been asked to leave the preceding evening. A crowd assembled outside the house of Hypatius and took him to the forum of Constantine, where he was proclaimed emperor. Thereafter he was conducted to the Hippodrome, whether or not of his own free will. But when he sat on the kathisma, the seat from which emperor presided at the games, he could only be seen as acting as an emperor, and an African text explicitly refers to him as having assumed the position of tyrant, the wielder of illegitimate power.[12]

Justinian, closeted in the palace with his closest advisers, discussed what could possibly be done. The situation was desperate: the government had largely lost control of the capital city, and a nephew of a recent popular emperor had come out in open rebellion. According to a passage in Procopius, a rousing speech by Theodora was responsible for stiffening the resolve of the meeting. Arguing against leaving the city, she expressed the hope that she would never be separated from her purple robe and live to see the day when petitioners did not address her as mistress. While it would be possible to take flight across the water, she agreed with the old saying that

---

12. Victor of Tunnunna *Chron. s.a.* 530 (ed. Th. Mommsen, *Monumenta Germaniae Historica Auctores Autiquissimi* 11).

'Royalty is a fine burial shroud' (*Wars* 1.24.32–7). It is an excellent story, but unfortunately there are good reasons for not trusting Procopius' account, which cannot be corroborated from any other source. In addition to the general circumstance that no ancient or medieval historian expected accounts of speeches to be taken literally, and the particular one that Procopius was almost certainly not present at the meeting, aspects of the reported speech seem to reflect the author's uneasiness at the power of the empress and the nature of the government, for the concluding quotation is false. The old saying which Theodora is said to have quoted actually runs 'Tyranny is a fine burial shroud'.[13] Rather than attributing the quotation to Theodora, we may find it more plausible to believe that, by altering the first word, Procopius is signalling to alert readers to his unhappiness with Theodora, and perhaps the government of Justinian. We cannot tell, but Justinian decided to resist, and loyal army units were brought into play.

It was not long since Belisarius had returned from the Persian frontier with a large retinue, while Mundus, a barbarian general in Roman service, also happened to be in Constantinople. Justinian ordered Belisarius to enter the Hippodrome through one of the gateways and approach Hypatius through the crowd, a tactic which made heavy civilian casualties inevitable. After Narses, the commander of the eunuch bodyguard, distributed bribes in an attempt to divide the people, Belisarius, Mundus and Narses himself led their troops into the Hippodrome through different entrances and attacked the unarmed populace. A massacre ensued. Contemporaries placed the number of deaths in the tens of thousands. Hypatius and Pompeius were taken captive, and their professions of innocence were not persuasive. One source claims that Justinian was inclined to be merciful to them and that it was the harsher counsels of Theodora that prevailed; be this as it may, they were put to death on the following day, 19 January, and their bodies cast into the sea. Their property, and that of those senators who had supported them, was confiscated. The patricians who had been with them, people whose identity we unfortunately do not know, fled.

13. J. Evans 'The "Nika" rebellion and the empress Theodora' *Byzantion* 54 1984: 380–2.

Civil unrest on such a scale took contemporaries by surprise, and in seeking to account for it they fell back on a standard explanation: in the punning words of John Malalas (473), it was caused by the activity of demons while Eudaimon was prefect. Writers paraded their disdain for the 'barbarous and merciless mob' involved in the riots in the most overt manner.[14] But their evaluations certainly reflect a tendency, one also found in writings about civil disturbances at other periods, to disparage those involved in crowds, and in any case disturbances over the issue of prisoners were only the beginning of troubles which escalated in two stages.

Firstly, demands were made for the sacking of officials. The wish to see the end of Eudaimon is easy to understand, for as prefect of the city he was responsible for prisoners and so the issue which sparked the riots. The man who replaced him in this office, Tryphon, was the brother of a man who had held it for four previous tenures; doubtless Justinian, no less than Anastasius when faced with a similar situation in 507, felt the need for a steady hand at the wheel. But John the Cappadocian and Tribonian were the two officials most closely associated with the reforms Justinian seemed to be introducing willy-nilly. They were replaced respectively by Phocas, who had been suspected a few years previously of being a pagan, and Basilides, a former colleague of Tribonian on the commission which worked on the Codex in 528/529. They were figures of no particular distinction, neither of whom enjoyed office for long: by the end of the year John had returned to the prefecture, and Tribonian, who did not give up his work on the Digest, had returned to the quaestorship by 535. Demands for the replacement of John and Tribonian expressed discontent with the policies of Justinian.

From this it was only a short step to direct attack on the emperor, and once this reached a certain level it was inevitable that a potential successor would emerge. No-one could have been surprised that it was one of the nephews of Anastasius. It is impossible to tell now whether genuine feeling on the part of the people of Constantinople induced Hypatius to make his fatal grab for power, or whether senatorial money

14. The quote is from John the Lydian *Powers* 3.70; compare Procopius' 'people of the common herd, the whole rabble' (*Buildings* 1.1.20 ed. and trans. H.B. Dewing, London 1914–1940).

was behind the apparently spontaneous behaviour of the crowd. One of our sources explicitly attributes the riots to the nephews of Anastasius, acting in concert with the many nobles who had sworn to support them and the seditious throng of the people.[15] Whichever it was, Justinian was in a wretched position after the riots. Between him and disaster there had stood just a small group of soldiers, and many of the senators, the very people whose support he had carefully sought by distributing modestly worded diptychs on the occasion of his first consulship, may have been plotting to overthrow him. More than the behaviour of the rioters, that of Hypatius, who had been so trusted that he was still in the palace late in the disturbances, must have hurt. The Nika riots mark a major turning-point in the reign of Justinian.

One member of the senatorial class was of particular importance. Juliana Anicia was of unmatched parentage. Her father, Olybrius, had been a man whose illustrious antecedents reached far back into Roman history and who had briefly been emperor in the West in 472, while her mother, Placidia, had herself been the daughter of the western emperor Valentinian III (425–455). Valentinian's wife Eudoxia had herself been the daughter of the eastern emperor Theodosius II (402–450) and his wife Eudocia, so an inscription could accurately summarize a complex family tree in describing Juliana as inheriting royal blood to the fourth generation. A letter sent to her by pope Hormisdas in 519 drew attention to her imperial blood.[16] Her own husband, Areobindus, was inevitably of less distinguished ancestry, although according to a story current in Rome at the beginning of the sixth century his great grandfather Aspar had been offered the throne by the senate, and it was Areobindus whom discontented elements in Constantinople had sought to make emperor during the riots against Anastasius in 512. But the family was loyal to Anastasius. Indeed, Olybrius, no less than Anastasius' nephews, may have been seen as a potential successor when the old emperor died in 518, but his path to the throne was blocked by the quick action of Justin. In comparison to

15. Marcellinus comes *Chron. s.a.* 532 (ed. Th. Mommsen, *Monumenta Germaniae Historica Auctores Antiquissimi* 11).
16. *Collectio avellana* 179.1 (ed. O. Guenther *Corpus scriptorum ecclesiasticorum Latinorum* 35).

Juliana and her family, Justinian and his wife could only look shabby.

Some of the activities of this remarkable person are known to us. She was well regarded for charitable activities, it being said that when she died she had filled Constantinople with her good works, corresponded with the pope on church affairs, and was responsible for the building or rebuilding of several churches. Among these was a church in honour of the Theotokos at Honoratai, across the Bosphorus from Constantinople, where the citizens seem to have expressed their gratitude by commissioning for her a splendid copy of a Herbal written by a scholar of the first century CE, Dioscorides. The book can still be seen in the National Library in Vienna. The illustrations in the Herbal exploit to the full the wonderful opportunity such texts provided to depict plants, although some would say that the series of illustrated Arabic texts of Dioscorides produced from the tenth century onwards are more pleasing to the eye. The manuscript contains 498 miniatures, and a frontispiece shows a portrait of Juliana herself, sitting between figures representing magnanimity and prudence. She was also responsible for a church dedicated to S Euphemia, where an inscription recorded that her mother Placidia and grandmother Eudoxia had also been involved in work on the church.[17]

But Juliana's most famous work was a church dedicated to the martyr Polyeuktos, erected on a site where her great-grandmother Eudocia had already built a church dedicated to that little-known saint. Thanks to recent work we know far more about this church than would have seemed possible a few decades ago, for its site was uncovered in 1960 when work was under way on the building of a new city hall in what is now Istanbul.[18] Erected within the period 524–527, it was a large church, perhaps the largest in the city at the time of its construction, almost a square with sides of 51.90 and 51.45 metres. The thickness of the foundations of some of the walls make it very likely that it had a dome. As far as can be deduced from fragmentary remains, the apse was decorated with

17. The dedication to this martyr may be significant, for it was in the church dedicated to her that the council of Chalcedon met in 451.
18. There is a convenient summary in Martin Harrison *A Temple for Byzantium* London 1989.

mosaics depicting figures against a gold background, and there were other mosaics, pieces of carved architectural sculpture, and busts of Christ, the Virgin and Apostles, which must have made the interior of the church dazzling. Its decorations included a remarkable inscription of 41 lines of hexameter verse, in letters eleven centimetres high, parts of which could almost be taken as a challenge to the reigning emperor: 'Who has not heard of Juliana? ... Every land, every city cries out that she made her parents more famous by better works. The inhabitants of the whole earth celebrate in song your ever-memorable toils ... For you alone, I believe, have constructed temples beyond counting throughout the whole earth'.[19] The inscription ended by expressing the wish that the saints to whom Juliana had given presents or in whose honour she had built churches would give their protection to her, her son, and his daughters, and that the glory of the family would last for as long as the sun drove his chariot across the sky.

We have no way of telling what Justinian may have thought of this church, but the family background, intellectual sophistication and private wealth of such a person as Juliana must have grated on an emperor with such lowly origins as his. Moreover, the concluding words of the inscription, which can only have been installed a few years before the Nika riots, contained an uncomfortable reminder that there was at least one great family in the city capable of paying for a massive church, and Olybrius, the son referred to but not named in the inscription, had married Irene, a niece of the popular emperor Anastasius. Indeed, Olybrius, no less than Hypatius and Pompeius, may have been seen as a potential successor when the old emperor died in 518, but any ambitions he had would have been blocked by the prompt action of Justin. Hostility Justinian may have felt towards such people before the Nika riots must have been strengthened by the attempted usurpation of Hypatius. The wife of Pompeius, Anastasia, counted Juliana Anicia among her friends; when the holy man S Sabas had visited the royal city in 511–512 they visited him frequently. But after the events of 532 Hypatius and Pompeius were executed, while Olybrius was sent into exile, from which he was recalled in the following year. In other words, the Nika riots could be seen as having developed from being a

19. *Greek Anthology* 1.10.14–32 (ed. W.R. Paton, London 1931).

manifestation of popular discontent to a vehicle for the frustrations of an old ruling class which had lost power. Such an interpretation need not have been correct, but it was easy to make, and Justinian was not slow in striking against those who now seemed clearly revealed as his enemies.

. . .

JUSTINIAN THE BUILDER

The devastation of large parts of the monumental centre of Constantinople provided Justinian with a golden opportunity to make his mark on the city. Just as the great fire which devastated Rome in AD 64 had allowed Nero to make his mark on the capital by rebuilding it, so now the way lay open to Justinian in Constantinople. There was still plenty of money in the treasury, and Justinian set to work with a will.

Among the buildings destroyed in the fires was the cathedral church of Hagia Sophia, or Holy Wisdom, a term which designated one of the attributes of Christ (cf. I Cor 1:24). The cathedral dominated the religious life of Constantinople, for it was not only located in the heart of the city but played a role unchallenged by the martyrs' shrines which competed with the cathedral for supremacy in cities such as Rome. Hence the size of its staff, which is known to us from a law of 535 announcing that no further appointments of clergy were to be made until the staff had fallen to 60 priests, 100 male deacons, 40 female deacons, 90 subdeacons, 110 readers, 25 singers, and 100 doorkeepers. Admittedly, these people had to serve the needs of three smaller churches as well as the cathedral, but even so it was hardly a modest establishment. The first cathedral on the site had been dedicated in 360 but had been severely damaged by fire in tumults associated with S John Chrysostom in 404, and it was the restored building, dedicated in 415, that was destroyed in the Nika fires of January 532. Justinian set matters in hand with the decisiveness he so often demonstrated. Two highly competent men, Anthemius of Tralles and Isidore of Miletus, were placed in charge of operations. The former, a member of a well-known family of intellectuals and the author of books on technical subjects, was a man whose talents allowed him to play a practical joke on an enemy: he harnessed steam power which made the apartment in which his victim lived shake so that the man thought an earthquake had occurred and made a fool of himself. But Anthemius was known for his ability to 'apply geometrical speculation to material objects' (Agathias 5.6.3, trans. Frendo), while Isidore was the author of a commentary on a work by Hero of Alexandria on vaulting. Yet again, Justinian availed himself of talent from the provinces. With their grasp of theory, Anthemius and Isidore were not the men to design an ordinary building.

Work on the new cathedral began on 23 February. According to a source written a few centuries later, two teams of 5000 workers were employed, and it must have quickly become clear to passers-by that work on a huge building was under way. But it would also have been obvious that the church being erected was of an unusual design. Large churches had traditionally been built in the form of a basilica, a rectangular Roman public building which usually had side aisles, and often a semi-circular apse at the east end. While the design had been developed for secular buildings, it was found very suitable for the purpose of Christian liturgy, so that the cathedral which had been destroyed in the fires, like the major early churches in Rome and elsewhere, had been built along these lines.

Early in the sixth century, however, people were experimenting with other designs. The church of SS Sergius and Bacchus built in Constantinople early in Justinian's reign is octagonal, with a central dome. A similar design was followed at the church of S Vitale in Ravenna, a town in which earlier churches had been designed according to the basilican pattern. We are told work on S Vitale was begun by bishop Ecclesius (521–532), and a mosaic in the apse implies that he was responsible for its construction. Nevertheless the building contains monograms of bishop Victor (537/8–544/5), which suggests that the actual building was carried out during his episcopate, although as we shall see mosaics were installed there a few years after he died. The church of S Polyeuktos which Juliana Anicia had built a few years earlier was nearly square in shape, its sides just under 52 metres long, and seems to have had a dome. The new cathedral of Hagia Sophia can be located against the background of these experiments. It was of ample proportions, being 79 metres in length and 72 metres in width, and hence approaching a square in shape. Four enormous piers supported four arches, of which those on the east and west alarmed people by rising 'above empty air', and these supported the mighty dome, 31 metres in diameter, its top 55.6 metres above the ground. The task of raising a dome of this size over what was virtually a square was immensely difficult; indeed, the dome was to collapse in May 558, while further collapses occurred in 989 and 1346. Hence Justinian's decision to entrust the work to a pair of theoreticians rather than to practising architects. Amazed contemporaries thought the church like no other in the world; its golden dome seemed to be suspended from Heaven.[20]

In the late tenth or early eleventh century a new mosaic was installed over an opening into the narthex of the cathedral. It shows an enthroned Virgin holding her Son; to their right is a representation of Justinian presenting them with a replica of Hagia Sophia, while to their left is Constantine offering a replica of the city of Constantinople. Each emperor, then, offers the work for which he was responsible. The image of the church offered by Justinian is extremely distorted: the dome is too large and steep, and the windows at its base too big. But oddly enough the oversized dome and clean lines of the inaccurate representation coincide with what modern people often have in mind when they think of Hagia Sophia; visitors approaching it have been disappointed at the ungainly exterior. But Hagia Sophia was not designed to be seen from the outside.

For contemporaries, the important part of the cathedral was the interior. They particularly admired the quality of light within it. The forty windows at the base of the dome would pick up the rays of the sun from whatever angle they were coming, while a mass of lamps provided light by night. The decor was such as to enhance the light: the ceiling was covered with gold, while surfaces were covered with marble or mosaics, the latter probably non-figurative. The sanctuary was embellished with 40 000 pounds of silver, indicative of a generosity far in excess of that Constantine had displayed when adorning the basilicas of Rome after his conversion, while a large silk hung showing Christ flanked by SS Peter and Paul; it

20. Like no other in the world: Marcellinus comes *Chron. s.a.* 537.5 (singulariter in mundo). Golden dome suspended from heaven: Procopius *Buildings* 1.1.46 (cf. Homer *Il.* 8.19). In a powerfully written passage Procopius writes of the church as soaring, looking down, glorying, dominating and exulting (*Buildings* 1.1.27f; small wonder that the sentence immediately following refers to its pride!).

shimmered, according to a classicizing poet, with gold, with the rays of rosy-armed dawn.[21] Procopius commented that all the details of the interior produced an extraordinary 'harmony' (συμφωνία, literally 'concord of sound', *Buildings* 1.1.47; he also writes of the harmony of the exterior proportions, 1.1.29). Despite this, he observed that people in the church always found their eyes moving on to other parts (*Buildings* 1.1.39). This has been the experience of many modern visitors to Hagia Sophia, who find it hard to keep their eyes from wandering, and one of the reasons why no photograph of the interior is satisfying, for there is a sense of incompleteness about any part of the whole. Procopius described the sensation produced by the church on the minds of those who entered it to pray: their minds were raised up to God and soared aloft (*Buildings* 1.1.61). But the chief purpose of the building was to provide a setting for the celebration of the Eucharist, in which the emperor would naturally take a prominent part.[22] It is said that a group of Russians who attended a celebration of the liturgy, almost certainly in Hagia Sophia, towards the end of the tenth century, felt that they did not know whether they were in heaven or on earth. Such was the impact of Hagia Sophia.

Given that the cathedral was named for an attribute of Christ, it was fitting that its dedication occurred in the season of Christmas. On 27 December 537 a procession left the church of the martyr S Anastasia, known for its odd practice of having passages of the Bible read in Gothic on feast days, a testimony to generosity it had received at the hands of a barbarian general. Amid throngs of people, Justinian and the patriarch Menas made their way to the new cathedral for a solemn service of dedication. The time which the erection of the new cathedral had taken, no less than the time needed for the completion of the great legal works, indicates the extraordinary speed with which Justinian could complete major

21. Paul the silentiary *Descriptio Sanctae Sophiae* (*Patrologia Graeca* 86) 1.769.
22. Just what part he would play is not clear. The intriguing arguments of Thomas F. Mathews *The Early Churches of Constantinople: Architecture and Liturgy* University Park Penn. 1971, in particular the suggestion that the imperial throne would have been in the central bay of the southern ، aisle, have not found favour with R.J. Mainstone *Hagia Sophia* New York 1988 pp. 223–6.

rank beside the Hippodrome as a place of imperial ceremony, he is alleged to have cried out 'Solomon, I have been victorious over you!'

Various other churches were erected by Justinian in the royal city. By 520 he had built SS Peter and Paul, and the church of SS Sergius and Bacchus mentioned above was erected early in his reign. Just over 100 metres north of Hagia Sophia lay the church of Hagia Eirene, Holy Peace, which was also rebuilt after the fires of 532. The large church of the Holy Apostles had emerged unscathed from the Nika riots, but Justinian rebuilt it in the shape of a cross with a dome over the middle. Theodora was said to have laid its foundation stone, and while work was proceeding three coffins, believed to contain the bodies of SS Andrew, Luke and Timothy, were uncovered. The church was dedicated in June 550. A church of similar design was built in Ephesos in honour of S John the Theologian. In Constantinople and its suburbs alone, according to the data provided by Procopius, Justinian built or rebuilt 33 churches. Authors of the time were generous in their attributions, and it would certainly be wrong to credit Justinian with major work on all of these churches, but it is hard to escape the impression of immense activity amid which the new cathedral was only a part.

These, however, were not the only works for which Justinian was responsible in and around his capital. One of the problems the government faced was providing water for the inhabitants of the capital city, which had grown so quickly. The need for drinking water was especially acute during the dry Mediterranean summers, but the lack of storage facilities was also a military handicap, for it meant that the city was vulnerable to enemy attacks on the aqueduct which supplied it. Early in his reign Justinian, following the examples of earlier emperors, saw to the construction of large underground reservoirs which collected the overspill of the aqueduct. The results can be seen by tourists to this day. He also saw to the completion of a public bath which Anastasius had begun.

The efficient deployment of the fleet which carried the grain sent from Egypt to Constantinople was another practical matter to occupy the state's attention. Each August ships bearing what was optimistically known as the 'happy shipment' set out from Alexandria, but sometimes they found it difficult to enter the Hellespont. The waters flowing into the

Mediterranean from rivers are not enough to compensate for the loss caused by evaporation, and hence at the Dardenelles and the Strait of Gibraltar currents flow in, from the Black Sea and Atlantic Ocean respectively. If the wind was adverse the ships could not make progress against the hostile current. Sometimes they had to lie at anchor and let their cargo rot, yet if the early ships could make good speed to Constantinople they were able to make a second or even a third trip from Egypt before the onset of winter ended the sailing season. The ancient city of Troy had been built close to where the ships sometimes had to bide their time, and from there the island of Tenedos lay not far out to sea. This was the place, according to Vergil's account of the fall of Troy, to which the Greeks retired having left the Trojan Horse outside the walls of the doomed city, and it was there that Justinian saw to the building of an enormous granary. If the winds were contrary, the ships could unload their cargo there and go back to Egypt, leaving other ships to carry it the rest of the way to Constantinople when the winds changed.

Justinian was also an active builder in the most diverse parts of the empire. Following a request from the holy man S Sabas he saw to the completion of the Nea (new) Church in honour of the Theotokos in Jerusalem. Partial excavations conducted in the Jewish quarter of the Old City during recent years have revealed that its northern lateral apse was five metres wide, which suggests that the whole was of vast proportions. In Ephesos, as we have seen, a large church shaped like a cross was built in honour of S John the Evangelist, who was believed to have settled in the town, while in the remote African town of Ceuta, not far from the Strait of Gibraltar, a church was erected in honour of the Theotokos.

Perhaps the most interesting of Justinian's undertakings was in another remote setting. Between the Gulf of Suez and the Gulf of Aqaba lies the desolate Sinai peninsula, towards the south of which stands Mt Sinai, or Gebel Musa, 'Mt Moses', as it is called today. It was there, Byzantines believed, that Moses had two dramatic encounters with God. In the first he saw God in the form of a burning bush and heard him name himself by the mysterious and resonant words 'I am the one who is'. Later, according to the Bible, Moses received the Law there amid thunder and lightning. For centuries the spot had been the site of a Christian cult, and it was there that Justinian built a famous church. A surviving inscription on a roof beam, 'For the memory and repose of our late empress Theodora', allows it to be dated to the period of Justinian's reign after 548. It was part of a monastic complex attached to a fort in a remote area, and owed its importance to the religious significance of the site. The dedication of the church to the Theotokos was appropriate, for the Byzantines saw the burning bush as foreshadowing her uncorrupted virginity. A beautiful mosaic in the apse of the church which seems to date from the time of Justinian takes up these biblical themes. It depicts another theophany on a holy mountain, the Transfiguration of Christ. On his right stands Elijah and on his left Moses, while Peter, James and John are below. Around the central scene are portrayals of various noteworthy people from the Bible, with king David holding pride of place in the centre foreground. Clad in a purple chlamys and wearing pearl ear-hangings, he is oddly reminiscent of a portrait of Justinian at S Vitale in Ravenna.

Justinian's patronage here and in many other places was lavish, and such as to impose financial burdens on the state. It made a joke of the claim expressed in the inscription in Hagios Polyeuktos that Juliana Anicia alone had built countless churches throughout the world. Nevertheless, the central work in Justinian's building of churches was Hagia Sophia, and, as we have seen, a later tradition states that when he entered the cathedral for the first time he exclaimed 'Solomon, I have been victorious over you!' It is hard to disentangle the thoughts behind this statement, which may answer to similarities between the First Temple built by Solomon in Jerusalem and Hagia Sophia,[23] but, assuming that it may be genuine, there is almost certainly more to it than meets the eye. Solomon has played a large part in the imagination of later builders. A few years after the death of Justinian a new cathedral at Nantes in Gaul was described as having surpassed the Temple of Solomon, and at the end of the seventh century the caliph 'Abd al-Malik erected the most beautiful building in Jerusalem, the Dome of the Rock, on the site of the Temple, thereby appropriating to the world of Islam some of the significance of the site. The twelve lions in the Court of Lions

23. See the evidence presented by Georg Scheja 'Hagia Sophia und Templum Salomonis' *Istanbuler Mitteilungen* 12 1962: 44–58.

which was built within the Alhambra at Granada in the fourteenth century stand in some relation to the twelve carved lions which stood by Solomon's Throne (I Kings 10:20, II Chron 9:19), and inscriptions in the Sistine Chapel erected in renaissance Rome compared this edifice with Solomon's Temple. It was therefore entirely reasonable for contemporaries to compare Justinian's achievement to that of Solomon, as did Romanos Melodos in one of his kontakia and Corippus in his panegyric on Justin II. It may also be possible that Justinian's boast of being victorious deliberately echoed the name given to the uprising which had allowed him to build the cathedral, 'Victory' (Nika).[24]

But there may have been more to Justinian's claim than this. Recent work suggests, on the basis of units of measurement and the form of its decoration, that the large church recently built in Constantinople by Juliana Anicia was itself designed in imitation of Solomon's Temple, and an inscription placed in that church boasted of Juliana's having gone beyond the wisdom of Solomon.[25] It would therefore be plausible to see in Justinian's claim of victory over Solomon an indirect claim to have surpassed the work of Juliana. Be this as it may, Juliana stood at the end of a line of private patrons, if indeed she saw herself as a private person. Procopius claims that during Justinian's reign the building and repair of churches throughout the empire could only be undertaken with state funds (*Buildings* 1.8.5). This charge was not true, and Procopius cannot have expected his readers to take it seriously, but it points to a feeling that the building of churches by private individuals could be done away with. In any case, Juliana was the last private patron responsible for the erection of a large

24. On Justinian and Solomon, Romanos Melodos hymn 54.21 (Romanos Melodos trans. Marjorie Carpenter *Kontakia of Romanos, Byzantine Melodist* 1 *On the Person of Christ* Columbia Missouri 1970); the footnotes to the French translation accompanying the edition of J. Grosdidier de Matons *Hymnes* (vol. 5, Paris 1981) bring out the difficulties Romanos found in sustaining a comparison favourable to the emperor. Note as well Romanos' playing with the word 'victory' at 54.16.7, 54.18.8, and Corippus *In Laudem Justini Augusti minoris* 4.283 (ed. and trans. Averil Cameron, London 1976).
25. Harrison, *Temple*, *Greek Anthology* 1.10.48. Solomon, of course, was famed for his wisdom, and it was Wisdom (Sophia) to which Justinian's church was dedicated.

church in Constantinople until the last centuries of the Byzantine empire.

. . .

NEW DIRECTIONS

There can be no doubt that the reign of Justinian marked a turning away from the elite. At the end of August 537 a law was issued which stated that the name of the emperor and the year of his reign were to be placed at the beginning of legal documents; only then could dates be supplied in accordance with the methods which had traditionally been used (novel 47). It must be said that the old methods were far from satisfactory. Dating in accordance with the name of the year's consul or consuls involved ambiguity when similarly named consuls held office in different years, as had happened in the West in 501 and 502, and was shortly to become less practical when the office of consul was restricted to the emperor and held intermittently, which meant that most years would have to be given dates according to the number of years which had passed since a particular consulate. Another system involved dating with respect to the position of a year in the indictional cycle of fifteen years, but this meant that after a while it was hard to tell in which cycle a document had been issued. It is odd that the Romans, a practical people in many ways, used such cumbersome methods of dating, and Justinian's reform was obviously sensible. But pride stood behind it as well. The preface to the law announcing the new system, which mentioned Aeneas, Romulus, Numa, Caesar and Augustus, left no doubt as to the company in which Justinian expected to be viewed. The reform was not limited to documents, for in the twelfth year of Justinian's reign, that is the twelve months beginning in April 538, copper coins dated according to Justinian's regnal year were being minted in Constantinople and elsewhere.[26]

One of the main functions of the office of consul was giving one's name to the year, so the reform in dating could be seen as having weakened the standing of that office. Some scholars have held that the consulship was on its last legs by the time of Justinian and that its suppression was timely. In 537 a law

26. M. Hendy *Studies in the Byzantine Monetary Economy c. 300–1450* Cambridge 1985 pp. 539f.

had made the distribution of consular largesse optional, which could be held to suggest that potential consuls were coming to find the office financially onerous. But the last surviving consular diptych, issued by Justin in 540, depicts slaves energetically performing the gesture of *sparsio*, the scattering of largesse, and people were still coming forward to hold an office which, even under Justinian, could still be described in traditional terms as the mother of the freedom of the Romans. Indeed, there is ample evidence from a slightly earlier period for the office having been keenly sought. The status which came, prior to the reform of 537, from giving one's name to the year, and the popularity to be won from distributing money drawn from one's own wealth so generously that, in the image of a contemporary, it had the appearance of snowflakes,[27] made the office desirable. Of the fifteen years from the accession of Justinian until 541, when the last private holder of the office enjoyed his tenure, there were consuls during eleven, including each of the last four years. This record is more impressive than it may seem, since it had been standard but not invariable practice for one eastern and one western consul to hold office each year; the war in Italy, however, caused a gap in western appointees after 534. Following the consulship of Belisarius in 535 there was no consul for two years; then the office was successively held by John the Cappadocian; by Apion, a member of a prominent Egyptian landowning family; by Justin, a great-nephew of Justinian; and finally by Basilius, a member of a distinguished Roman family which had held many consulships.

John the Cappadocian hardly shone in such company, and his consulship is a reminder that if there were losers in the empire which was emerging under Justinian, there were also winners. As we have seen, John and Tribonian were reinstated not long after their removal from office during the Nika riots. They went on to enjoy their posts for remarkably long tenures: John was praetorian prefect from 531 until 541, with the exception of a period in 532, while Tribonian, having been quaestor from 529 until 532, was to hold the office again from 535 until 542. No comparable tenure for either office is recorded for the fifth or early sixth centuries, and had John and Tribonian not been removed from office by Theodora

27. John the Lydian *Powers* 2.8.

61

and, apparently, the plague respectively, they presumably would have continued to hold them indefinitely. As it turned out, their abruptly terminated tenures pale into insignificance beside the heroic career of Peter the Patrician, who was master of the offices for a totally unparalleled period, 539 until 565. At the time of the Nika riots no-one could have foretold the loyalty Justinian would display to those who served him well, but it became clear that Justinian was not only prepared to raise up the talented but would continue to back them.

Perhaps, then, we should see the suppression of the consulate not as a prudent piece of statecraft but as a stage in Justinian's turning away from the senatorial aristocracy, and hence as the culmination of a policy which had been followed steadily for a decade after the Nika riots. In the middle of the century, when an author came to describe the senate house which Justinian had rebuilt after the Nika riots, he commented that it was the place where the senate came together once a year to celebrate a festival.[28] This does not suggest a body of any importance in the affairs of the empire. But after the role senators played in the riots it was hardly likely to have been.

28. Procopius *Buildings* 1.10.7; cf. the description of the senate at *Secret History* 14.8.

1. (*opposite*) A.H.M. Jones *The Later Roman Empire 284–602* Oxford 1964 p. 270. Compare F. Martroye *L'Occident à l'époque byzantine Goths et Vandales* Paris 1904 p. 216; John Julius Norwich *Byzantium the Early Centuries* London 1988 p. 205. It may be worth noting the comment of Tony Honoré that Justinian's historical imagination reached back no more than a century (A.M. Honoré 'Some Constitutions composed by Justinian' *Journal of Roman Studies* 65 1975: 107–23).

Chapter 3

WARS IN THE WEST

When the first edition of Justinian's Codex was published in 529 the decree which confirmed it opened with the observation that the safety of the state chiefly proceeded from arms and laws. From these, Justinian felt, the state derived its strength. Such a juxtaposition of **military** and legal activities is common in texts of the period. It occurs in the decree which announced the beginning of work on the Digest in 530, and in the preface to the decree which confirmed that work in 533. Justinian would have agreed with a sentiment Cassiodorus put in the mouth of Theoderic the Ostrogoth: 'It is our purpose to set the provinces the help of God has made subject to us in order by the laws, just as we defend them with arms' (*Variae* 4.12.1). Justinian's endeavors to reform the laws had seen remarkable success, and it was not surprising he turned his attention to war.

The account of the wars provided by Procopius, an eye-witness of many of the scenes he describes, is voluminous. It is also enthusiastic, reflecting the tremendous optimism felt in at least some quarters during the early years of Justinian's reign. The evaluation of the importance of the wars fought in this period which it offers is extremely positive, and in this Procopius has often been followed by modern scholars. But some have gone further, and argued that the wars Justinian launched in Africa and Italy were central aspects of an ideology. Hence, it has been suggested that a 'planned reconquest of the West' was evidence of 'a mission to restore the ancient glories of the empire', and one of the guiding principles of his reign.[1] But as we shall see, the only evidence which can be cited in support of such assertions comes from texts written after the unexpected early success against the Vandals. Here, as elsewhere, some of the main themes of Justinian's reign developed as the years passed.

. . .

WAR IN AFRICA

Among the barbarian states which emerged in the West during the fifth century, the kingdom established by the Vandals following their crossing from Spain into Africa in 429 was in a most important area. Not only had Africa traditionally been a major exporter of grain and olive oil within the Roman empire, but a trade in pottery which had developed from the end of the second century had ensured its prosperity in the generally depressed economy of the later Roman West. Towards the end of the fourth century a Roman author, with some exaggeration, represented the capital of Africa, Carthage, as the third city of the empire. But Africa was not merely wealthy. The intellectual powerhouse of early western Christianity, it produced an unending stream of combative theologians. Taken over in the years following 429 more or less *en bloc* by a barbarian people who quickly developed an unnerving naval capacity, to which a devastating assault upon Rome in 455 bore witness, Africa retained an important role in Mediterranean affairs. The plunder taken from Rome in 455 included Eudocia, the daughter of the emperor Valentinian III; she subsequently married Geiseric's son Huneric. Such was the reputation of the Vandals that when a Gothic chieftain came to an agreement with the emperor in the early 470s he specified that he would fight against any of the enemies of the empire except them!

But Vandal Africa was notorious for another reason. One of the major early Christian heresies was Arianism, a form of belief which asserted that the Son was not of the same substance as God the Father, not having existed from eternity but having been created by the Father in time. This belief was condemned by the Council of Nicaea in 325, and the wording of many passages in the so-called Nicene Creed, sung to this day in Christian churches, was designed to exclude Arian understandings. By the sixth century Arianism had become extinct among the Romans, but by then many of the barbarians who had gained power in the West had come to accept its teachings. It is hard to establish how committed its initial barbarian adherents, and other barbarians later converted through them, were to its theology, and it may be that the appeal of Arianism to them lay simply in its being a form of Christianity distinct from that of the Romans, who by this time were overwhelmingly Catholics.

Needless to say, Catholics living in a state ruled by Arians need not have found life unpleasant; Ostrogothic Italy, for example, is attractive for the religious tolerance which its Arian government practised. But this was not the experience of Africa under the Vandals. A savage persecution, which owed something to the wish of the Vandal state to gain control over the assets of the church and its members, took place. On the other hand, the polemical traditions of African Christianity ensured a lively response to the hostile activity of the new rulers. Already under the reign of Geiseric (428–477) there were outbreaks of persecution, but conditions markedly worsened under his successor Huneric (477–484), who ordered that all the Catholics of his kingdom were to become Arians. Some obeyed, but the hold of Catholicism was too strong to be broken.

During times of persecution, the Catholics of Africa took comfort from remembering that they were adherents of a faith which had spread throughout the known world. Surely, they felt, they could expect sympathy from their co-religionists. A veritable diaspora of African clergy and dispossessed members of the landowning class scattered around the Mediterranean, visible evidence of the malignity of the Vandals, while stories of their atrocities circulated widely. The story of the townspeople of Tipasa who could still speak after a Vandal official cut their tongues out was well known, and was recorded in five Byzantine sources. Indeed, a dramatic account of the persecution written in the 480s by Victor of Vita may well have been read in Constantinople. Given that people were coming to see the emperor as the protector of orthodox Christians, wherever they might be, it is possible to see persecution by the Vandals as playing into the hands of their potential enemies in Constantinople.

The imperial government had continued to keep an eye on the affairs of Africa, despite its having concluded a treaty recognizing the Vandal control of its wealthiest parts in 440. In 468 an expedition was sent from Constantinople at great expense against the Vandals, but it came to nothing. Attempts which were made to ameliorate the condition of the Catholics of Africa were similarly to no avail. Nevertheless, as time passed relations between the Vandals and Constantinople became less cool. King Thrasamund (496–523) was described as a 'friend' of the emperor Anastasius, while his successor Hilderic (523–530) had visited Justinian in Constantinople; one wonders whether he called on his cousin Juliana Anicia in the city. On coming to power Hilderic was quick to recall the exiled bishops and open the Catholic churches. But he was not universally popular among the Vandals, and after a military defeat in 530 he was deposed and replaced as king by his cousin Gelimer. From his imprisonment Hilderic appealed to Justinian for help, and in 533 his ally struck.

As it happened, Justinian found himself in a good position to make war on Gelimer, having concluded his perpetual peace with Persia in 532.[2] But when Justinian broached the plan with his advisers their response was not positive. Procopius represents John the Cappadocian as having given a strong speech advising against making war, but states that a vision from a bishop which conveyed a promise of divine aid encouraged Justinian to persevere (*Wars* 3.10.1–21). At the very least there is a degree of artifice in Procopius' account, which may have been constructed so as to give the emperor sole credit for the launching of a war the successful outcome of which was known to the author. But we may accept that the decision to invade Africa was Justinian's, and the story of a vision receives some indirect confirmation from an African source which states that he had a vision of Laetus, a bishop who had been committed to the flames under Huneric. As so often, Justinian leaped where others feared to tread.

A fleet was prepared, and at about the summer solstice in 533, after prayers had been offered by Epiphanius, the patriarch of Constantinople, it set sail. On board was a youth who had recently been baptized and become the adopted son of Belisarius and his wife, Antonina; later it was believed that Antonina and the young man had a long-running affair. Belisarius had under him a force of 10 000 infantry, 5000 cavalry, and a following of barbarian troops. Great authority was invested in the commander of the expedition, for Jus-

2. The language John uses when mentioning this (*Powers* 3.28, ed. A.C. Bandy *On Powers* Philadelphia 1983 p. 176.24f) is reminiscent of Procopius *Wars* 1.1.1 (ed. and trans. H.B. Dewing, London 1914–1940), itself reminiscent of Thucydides (above p. 2).

tinian gave Belisarius a document granting him the power of the emperor (Procopius *Wars* 3.11.20). Our source uses the noun βασιλεύς, which can mean 'king' as well as 'emperor', but in the context in which it occurs here it clearly means that at this stage in their relationship Justinian was prepared to grant Belisarius authority to act in his stead while on a major campaign far from home.

Good progress was made. A problem arose when the biscuits provided for the soldiers went bad, a consequence of what Procopius represents as an ill-advised cost-cutting strategy on the part of the praetorian prefect, John the Cappadocian, who had arranged for the dough to be baked over the fires of a public bath-house. Having crossed the Aegean Sea and rounded the Peloponnesos the fleet took on water at Zakinthos before crossing the Adriatic. The army now proceeded with a feeling of trepidation; a story was told of how Geiseric had once enslaved 500 of the leading men of Zakinthos, and then chopped them into pieces which he threw into the Adriatic. But there was no opposition as the fleet made its way to Sicily where, thanks to an agreement which had been concluded with the Gothic government of Italy, it landed near Mt Etna. Here Belisarius received some reassuring news: Gelimer, unaware of the approaching force, had sent the bulk of his army to put down a rebellion in Sardinia which had been encouraged by Justinian, and was himself some distance inland from Carthage. So the order was given to sail to Africa. Proceeding by way of Malta, the invading force made land at Caput Vada, the modern Ras Kaboudia in Tunisia.

Now a decision had to be taken. There were two possible ways by which the invaders could approach Carthage, the capital: the army could continue to sail or it could disembark and march overland. It was decided to disembark, and the army commenced its march, following the coast northwards as the fleet accompanied it offshore. The soldiers encountered only friendship from the native Africans. Gelimer, on learning of his imminent danger, ordered the execution of Hilderic, whom he had kept in prison, and prepared to resist. When the vanguard of the invading army reached Decimum, about 15 kilometres from Carthage, it defeated a Vandal detachment; the ferocious appearance of a small invading force of Massagetes was alone enough to drive away another group of Vandal warriors; and finally the main Vandal force under Gelimer was routed. The Africans noted that the day on which this occurred, 14 September, was the day of the festival of the martyr Cyprian, a former bishop of Carthage. The city lay open to the invaders, and on the next day Belisarius led his army in. Entering the palace he sat down on Gelimer's throne and ate for his lunch food which had already been prepared for the Vandal king. Procopius' description of the scene is curious, and of a kind to suggest doubt as to Belisarius' precise status, for he observes that 'palace' is the word used by the Romans for where the emperor lives, and that the place where Belisarius had his lunch, the 'delphix', took its name from imperial ceremonial at Rome (*Wars* 3.21.2–4). The soldiers, for their part, exercised what seemed amazing restraint and bought their lunch in the forum.

Meanwhile, Gelimer had fled westwards with his forces and recalled the troops which he had earlier sent to Sardinia. So it was that in mid-December the two armies encountered each other at Tricamarum, not far from Carthage. Before long the Vandals were put to flight, falling back as far as the camp where the women and children were taking shelter, but when Belisarius advanced towards it with his forces Gelimer leaped on his horse and rode away. Having eluded his pursuers he took refuge amid the Moors on a mountain in Numidia, where he displayed a taste for the melodramatic. He asked the officer Belisarius had appointed to guard the mountain for a lyre, a loaf of bread and a sponge: the lyre so that he could accompany himself singing an ode he had composed on his misfortune, the loaf because he had not been able to eat bread on the mountain, and the sponge because of a swelling in an eye which he had not been able to wash. After some months in his lofty refuge he gave himself up, and was taken to Carthage a captive. Belisarius had already gained control of Sardinia, Corsica, the Balearic Islands, and Septem (the modern Ceuta), a fortress near the Strait of Gibraltar, but had not been able to persuade the Goths to relinquish a fortified site in Sicily which the Vandals had held.

Belisarius' achievement in overthrowing the mighty state of the Vandals within a few months was stunning; Procopius was not sure whether deeds of that kind had ever occurred before (*Wars* 4.7.20). The early part of his first book dealing with the Vandal war depicts many of the preceding Roman emperors as a collection of remarkable incompetents, of whom even the best had failed to resolve the situation in Africa, but now the tables had been turned. News of the defeat of the Vandals was received with joy in Constantinople. The preface to the Institutes, published in November 533, exultantly refers to the return of Africa and countless other provinces to Roman power and the rule of Justinian, while a constitution published in the following year concerning the government of Africa, one of the few items of legislation published in the name of Justinian which seems to have been written by the emperor himself rather than the chancery, began: 'The mind cannot conceive nor the tongue express what thanks and praise we should show forth to our Lord and God Jesus Christ'. It goes on to give full voice to the optimism of the period: 'Africa, which was taken captive a hundred and five years ago by the Vandals, those enemies of souls and bodies, has regained its freedom through us'. After listing some of the excesses of the Vandals, Justinian continues: 'By what work or deeds can I thank God who has seen fit to avenge the wrongs of his church and pluck the people of mighty provinces from the yoke of servitude through me, the least of his servants?'[3] The mood in Constantinople was buoyant, and at some time during the mid-530s a medallion was issued showing on its reverse the emperor on horseback, nimbed and holding a spear, following a winged Victory.

But Justinian had to depend on informants for news from the theatre of war. Whereas his Persian counterpart Khusrau led armies into the field, it was decades since a Roman emperor had commanded his troops, and only the grossest flattery could lead to Justinian being described as a general.[4] Justinian's ignorance of developments far from home created a situation which the unscrupulous sought to exploit more than once. Before long it was whispered that Belisarius was

---

3. Codex 1.27.1. Apart from the claim that the Vandals turned churches into stables, the list of Vandal atrocities could have been written by someone with access to the *History of the Vandal Persecution* written by Victor of Vita (trans. John Moorhead, Liverpool 1992); cf. R. Bonini 'Caduta e riconquista dell' impero romano d'occidente nelle fonti legislative giustinianee' *Felix Ravenna* 111f 1976: 293–318 at 304. Stables were not mentioned by Victor, but such activities were known to Procopius: *Wars* 3.8.20, 23. On the authorship of Codex 1.27, Honoré 'Some Constitutions'.

4. As was the case in *Greek Anthology* (ed. W.R. Paton, London 1931) 1.97.4, 1.98.2.

planning to set up an independent government in Africa. When he was given the choice of returning to Constantinople with Gelimer and the leading Vandals, or staying in Africa and sending captives, the general wisely chose the former, and on his return to Constantinople Belisarius took part in ceremonial acts which made his subordination to Justinian explicit. He made his way from his own house to the Hippodrome on foot, and there advanced to the throne on which Justinian was sitting. He and Gelimer, the latter stripped of his purple garment, fell to the ground before it. No less than the defeated king, Belisarius, as he performed the rite of proskynesis, made it clear that he was a suppliant of the emperor. A Persian ambassador was looking on.

One hundred years of Vandal rule had come to a sudden end, and there was a need to reintegrate Africa into the empire. In April 534 Justinian issued detailed legislation concerning its administration. A praetorian prefect was appointed to head the civil administration. There were to be 396 officials working under the prefect and another 350 working under his subordinates; with a thoroughness typical of much of Justinian's legislation, the salary payable to each was itemized. The post was a new one. In earlier days Africa had fallen under the oversight of the praetorian prefect of Italy and Africa, based in Italy, but this ceased to be so when the Vandals took Africa. Now, however, Justinian created an African prefecture, distinct from the prefecture of Italy, an office which the Goths had maintained in Ravenna. Its first holder was an experienced administrator who had already held prefectures in Illyricum and the East. The chief holders of power in Byzantine Africa were therefore a Greek-speaking general and a Greek-speaking bureaucrat.

But all was not to be plain sailing. Despite their reputation for ferocity, the Vandals had not been able to defend their territory from enemies in the interior of Africa, and their last decades had been marked by defeats at the hands of the Moors, also known as Berbers, indigenous transhumant people who lived in a symbiotic but inevitably awkward relationship with the settled farmers and townspeople. Indeed, the absence of Gelimer when Belisarius landed seems to have been due to his fighting the Moors. They saw in the collapse of the Vandals a chance to make further gains. Solomon, a eunuch from Mesopotamia, was given the task of dealing with the unanticipated threat they posed. He took resolute action against them in the field and set under way a campaign to erect defensive works; some of the massive fortifications erected in Africa during the reign of Justinian can still be seen.[5] But progress was held up by a major revolt of the army which broke out in 536. Some of the troops had married Vandal women and stood to lose by the confiscation of the lands the Vandals had taken over. Justinian dealt with the problem by recalling the general and replacing him with a relative, Germanus. The efforts of the new general met with success, and in 539 Solomon was sent back to Africa.

The two postings of Solomon to Africa, however, had an unusual feature, for in 534 and again in 539 he combined the functions of praetorian prefect and of the commander-in-chief, magister militum. This flew in the face of standard practice in the later Roman empire, where the civil and military arms of the state had functioned independently of each other for centuries. It is easy to see how the special circumstances of Africa could be thought to have called for an amalgamation of the offices. Nevertheless, the unusual concentration of powers enjoyed by Solomon proved to be a straw in the wind.

The general who emerged with most credit from the war against the Vandals, however, was a man whose career had hitherto not been impressive. Belisarius, appointed consul for 535 in succession to Justinian himself, used some of the spoils won from the Vandals as largesse. But it was an even greater success for his master. The throne from which Justinian received the proskynesis of a powerful and hostile king and of a general who had been accused of plotting against him was the very one which Hypatius had occupied in state during the Nika riots, scarcely two years previously. Belisarius had brought to Constantinople the enormous treasure of the Vandals, enriched by the plunder Geiseric had taken from Rome in 455. Among these items were some of the treasures of the Jews which Titus had removed from where king Solomon had placed them in Jerusalem; these Justinian sent to

---

5. E.M. Ruprechtsberger 'Byzantinische Befestigungen in Algerien und Tunisien' *Antike Welt* 20 1989: 3–21 is a beautifully illustrated discussion. See in general D. Pringle *The Defences of Byzantine Africa from Justinian to the Arab Conquest* Oxford 1981.

churches in that city. Gelimer was given estates in Galatia, an inland area of Asia Minor where he could do no harm, and Justinian began to contemplate the future. Astonishingly fortunate in his African gamble, he looked further afield.

The widening of his ambitions can be seen in the titles which were applied to him in official documents. In November 533 a law was issued with a new intitulature, in which Justinian was described as 'Alammanicus, Gothicus, Francicus, Germanicus, Anticus, Alanicus, Vandalicus, Africanus'.[6] The title 'Anticus' relates to successes against barbarian enemies in Thrace in the period 530–533, while the following three all refer to Belisarius' success against the Vandals and their Alan comrades, which was conventionally attributed to the emperor. The first four words, on the other hand, represent a revival of traditional terms. Yet they had a contemporary resonance, for the Alammani, Goths, Franks and 'Germans', a general term which included Franks, had made themselves at home on formerly Roman territory no less than the Antai, Alans and Vandals. A law issued in the spring of 535 is evidence for Justinian looking further afield, for it expresses the hope that, Africa having been regained and the Vandals reduced to slavery, Justinian would be able to undertake many still greater projects, with the help of God (novel 8.10.2). From Africa, the obvious direction to move was northwards. And so it was that, in the words of a contemporary chronicler: 'After Carthage and Libya with its king Gelimer had been made subject, the emperor gave thought to Rome and Italy'.[7]

. . .

WAR IN ITALY

At its closest the African coastline is 150 kilometres from Sicily, and at some stage Justinian conceived the plan of launching a follow-up expedition against Italy. As Africa had been, Italy was under the control of a barbarian government, that of the Ostrogoths, but their government was utterly unlike that of the Vandals. Whereas the Vandals had invaded part of the empire as its enemies, the Ostrogoths under king Theoderic

6.   See on this G. Rösch ΟΝΟΜΑ ΒΑΣΙΛΕΙΑΣ Vienna 1978 pp. 101–3.
7.   Marcellinus comes *Chron. s.a.* 535.1 (ed. Th. Mommsen, *Monumenta Germaniae Historica Auctores Antiquissimi* 11).

had been sent to Italy in 488 by the emperor Zeno to overthrow the rule of Odovacer, holder of power since he deposed the last Roman emperor in the West in 476; whereas the Vandals had simply helped themselves to the possessions of the inhabitants of Africa, the Ostrogoths were supported in accordance with a traditional Roman mechanism which may well not have involved the transfer of property;[8] whereas the Vandals were notorious for religious persecution, the Ostrogoths, no less Arians, respected the Catholic church. Much of the credit for their benign ways belongs to king Theoderic, who held power in Italy from the defeat of Odovacer in 493 until his death in 526, and who was remembered for good by both Goths and Romans. It was clear that any rationale provided for war against the Ostrogoths would have to be different from that supplied for war against the Vandals.

Such a rationale was forthcoming. If an invasion of Africa could be justified by the appalling conduct of the Vandals towards local people, the Goths were vulnerable because of their constitutional position. It was agreed by all that Theoderic had led them to Italy in accordance with a commission from Zeno to overthrow Odovacer's 'tyranny', a word which had the sense of 'illegitimate government'. But the status of the government Theoderic established on the ruins of that of Odovacer, which preserved Roman ways but was to all intents and purposes independent of Constantinople, was vague. Was it the case that Italy under the Goths enjoyed 'libertas', that freedom which especially pertained to Romans, or did it not? In a letter to Justinian nominally written on behalf of the senate of Rome, but which reflected the thinking of the Gothic government, Cassiodorus could assert in 535 that, if Africa had deserved to regain its freedom, it would be cruel for Italy to lose what it had always been seen to possess (*Variae* 11.13.5). Yet, scarcely ten years previously, an allegation that he had sought 'Roman freedom' was one of the charges the enemies of the philosopher Boethius made against him before Theoderic. Not persecution, then, but an alleged lack of freedom, with the broader implication of illegitimacy, was the weakness in the Ostrogothic state which Byzantine propaganda sought to exploit.

The issue was academic for most of the reign of the great

---

8.   Walter Goffart *Barbarians and Romans* Princeton NJ 1980.

Theoderic. Towards its end various senators had been accused of corresponding with the empire in a way disloyal to the Gothic government, and suspicions of treason brought about the execution of Boethius. But there is no need to believe that any correspondence which took place was disloyal, nor that the senators were in any way set up by Constantinople.[9] Nevertheless, the years after 526 were not easy for the Ostrogothic state. Theoderic's son-in-law Eutharic, whom he had hoped would succeed him and who had been accepted by Justin as his son-in-arms, predeceased him, and the succession passed to a boy, Athalaric, a grandson of the great king. Effective power, however, was wielded by the boy's mother, Amalasuintha. A letter was sent to the emperor Justin in the name of the new king seeking peace and friendship which, by using the phrase 'let hatreds be put away together with those who have been buried' (Cassiodorus *Variae* 8.1.2), tactfully suggested that the tensions which had disfigured the last years of Theoderic's reign be put away.

Coming to power in 527, Justinian had to deal with a state in Italy which was still formidable. Trouble between Gothic and Roman soldiers had broken out more than once during the reign of Theoderic, and the Goths continued to cause difficulties after his death. A letter written in 533 rejoiced that, contrary to what 'the ruler of the East' wanted, Amalasuintha had made the Danube Roman; indeed, given that the emperor kept sending embassies to Italy, it was clearly the case that 'her unique power has caused the awesome loftiness of the East to bend down, so that it elevates the Italian lords' (Cassiodorus *Variae* 11.1.11). Such words could not have been to Justinian's taste, but they could not disguise the shaky nature of Amalasuintha's power. Tensions among the Goths which had remained latent during the powerful rule of Theoderic now came into the open, finding expression in controversy over how Athalaric was to be educated. At one time Amalasuintha found her position so threatened that she arranged with Justinian to live as an exile in Constantinople, an arrangement which would have given the emperor the ability to have intervened forcefully in Italian affairs. But the

---

9. Henry Chadwick *Boethius the Consolations of Music, Logic, Theology and Philosophy* Oxford 1981 pp. 66–8 seems to me to place too dark an interpretation on Byzantine policy.

resourceful regent succeeded in arranging to have three of her enemies murdered and decided to remain in Italy.

Amalasuintha, however, was not the only relation of Theoderic on the stage. The accession of Athalaric in 526 had entailed the exclusion of another potential successor, Theoderic's nephew Theodahad, a wealthy landowner who owned great estates in Tuscany. Annoyed at the treatment he received from Amalasuintha, he made contact with bishops Justinian had sent with the overt purpose of discussing theology with the pope, and asked them to tell the emperor he was prepared to hand over Tuscany to him, in exchange for a large sum of money, the rank of senator and freedom to live in Constantinople. Meanwhile Amalasuintha, concerned at the deteriorating health of her son and plots which were being mounted against her, was herself entering into further negotiations with Justinian, and she agreed with a senator who was accompanying the bishops that she would place all Italy in the hands of the emperor. Justinian, having received these proposals from the ruler of Italy and her chief enemy, was in a strong position.

For some time, he had being showing ominous signs of wanting to intervene in Italian affairs. In 530 he had promulgated a law on ecclesiastical affairs which would apply to Rome as well as Constantinople and the rest of the Christian world, and a passage in the introduction to the Digest (533) which orders that copies of his legal works were to be transmitted to students in 'the royal cities' as well as Beirut implies that he expected his legislative work to be observed in Italy as well as the territories under his direct control (constitution *omnem* 7).[10] After Gelimer's assumption of power in Africa in 530, Justinian sent a message to Italy warning Athalaric's government not to recognize the usurper, and apparently the Goths did as he wished. In 534 a law was issued addressed to the senate of Constantinople and of Rome (Codex 6.51), while in the following year another was promulgated concerning the possessions of the Roman church (novel 9), and Justinian wrote to Theodahad on behalf of a monastery which was paying too much tax and a Gothic woman who had in some

10. But the constitution goes on to forbid students in 'this most splendid city' (Constantinople) and Beirut, but not those in Rome, to play tricks on their teachers (9f). Perhaps Justinian felt that the students of Rome were better behaved.

way been made to suffer for converting to Catholicism. It would be interesting to know how Justinian came to know of these matters, but the Gothic government can hardly have been pleased to have the emperor intervene in such trivial things. The apparent failure of the Gothic government to publish the name of the eastern consul for 534, Justinian himself, may be a sign of increasing tension between Ravenna and Constantinople.

On 2 October 534 Athalaric died, whereupon his mother, now queen, attempted to strengthen her position by associating Theodahad with her on the throne. The move was not wise. Letters were sent by both Amalasuintha and Theodahad to Justinian explaining the turn of events and asking for his friendship, and before long Amalasuintha wrote a letter to Theodora assuring her of her love and asking for news. Before long, however, Theodahad imprisoned the queen on an island in Lake Bolsena. The murky situation was one which Roman diplomacy could turn to its own ends, especially when one of the ambassadors Theodahad sent to Justinian to explain his actions failed to conceal his bad behaviour. This was the patrician Liberius, who had been in the service of the Goths for four decades, and that he chose not to return to Italy can be taken as a straw in the wind. Shortly afterwards, probably at the end of April 535, Amalasuintha was murdered on Theodahad's orders. People believed she had been strangled in a bath-house. It was not a good time to murder a woman who had been the friend of Justinian, and the situation was taken advantage of by the emperor's ambassador, a young intellectual from Mesopotamia named Peter who, like so many of those found working for Justinian in the early years of his reign, would grow old in his service. Peter threatened Theodahad with a war admitting of no truce.

Justinian was extraordinarily optimistic, and expressed hopes beyond those he had entertained at the time of the Vandal war. The disintegration of the Gothic government had occurred at precisely the time when, thanks to the outcome of the Vandal war, he was free to exploit it. In 535 he launched a two-pronged attack against the Goths. While Mundus, the commander-in-chief in Illyricum, led a force to Dalmatia, where he was soon to be killed in battle, Belisarius sailed to Sicily with 7000 regular, allied barbarian and Isaurian troops, and small detachments of Huns and Moors. In other words, he had at his disposal something like half the troops he had commanded in Africa. But fortune smiled on him. Having landed at Catania he proceeded to occupy the towns of the island, encountering resistance only at Palermo. On the last day of the year, which was also the last day of his consulate, he marched into Siracusa and distributed largesse.

Theodahad's responses were futile. He continued to negotiate with Justinian's ambassador Peter, at one point intimating that he was prepared to resign his office.[11] A Gothic force was sent to Rome, to the disquiet of the senate, and a series of letters written in the names of the king and his wife were sent to Justinian and Theodora, seeking peace and concord. Somewhat later, pope Agapetus was dispatched to Constantinople to plead the cause of the Goths. Relations between the Roman church and Justinian were at that moment cool, for an imperial pronouncement that the bishop of the new city of Justiniana Prima was to enjoy the rank of metropolitan and archbishop had elicited from the pope a guarded response in November 535. But the pope had his own agenda. Two emissaries of the patriarch of Antioch, a doctor and an architect, had recently arrived in Rome with news of the growing power of the Monophysite heretics, and following his arrival in Constantinople in late February or March 536 Agapetus busied himself in church affairs but achieved nothing to the benefit of the Goths.

Following the capture of Sicily the mood in Constantinople was more buoyant than ever. During the spring of 536 Justinian issued a law expressing the hope that God would allow him to reconquer the lands formerly held by the Romans which had been lost by indolence; God had allowed Justinian to come into the possession of all Africa and Sicily, and to have good hope that he would allow him to take back other lands as far as the two shores of the Ocean which the old Romans had held; trusting in the help of God, the emperor was hastening to change things for the better.[12] At about the same

11. Negotiations which preceded this offer are discussed by E.K. Chrysos 'Die Amaler-Herrschaft in Italien und das Imperium Romanum: Der Vertragsentwurf des Jahres 535' *Byzantion* 55 1981: 430–74.
12. Novel 30.11.2; compare on indolence John the Lydian *Powers* 218.2,7, 108.2,22. Neglectfulness is a characteristic of the Romans which emerges from the scornful introductory pages of Procopius *Wars* 3, where their leaders are portrayed as buffoons whose follies are effortlessly exploited by the barbarians.

time Belisarius crossed to the mainland of Italy and marched northwards. He met with no resistance until he reached Naples, where there was a Gothic garrison. Here the inhabitants asked him not to proceed with an attack on their town, but Belisarius is represented by Procopius as having recommended that they choose freedom rather than slavery. Of course there is no reason to suppose that Belisarius said precisely these things, but at the very least it is interesting that when Procopius wrote these words the justification for the war could be so expressed. His advice was not followed, and only after a siege of about three weeks was the town taken by storm. It was the first victory of this kind in the war, and the troops behaved wildly. They were said to have killed thousands while sacking the city, with priests and consecrated religious among their victims. The Massagetes, the mere sight of whom had earlier been enough to terrify Vandals, were to the fore.[13]

Theodahad remained impassive in the face of these losses. One of the prime functions of a barbarian king was that of providing leadership in war, and the Goths were quick to turn against a monarch who showed himself so incompetent. Meeting at a site near Terracina, roughly midway between Rome and Naples, the Gothic warriors who were in that part of Italy elected as their new king Vitigis, a man of military experience who was the first Ostrogothic sovereign in Italy not to have been a member of the Amal family. Theodahad, who had been in Rome, left the city for Ravenna, but was overtaken on the road and murdered in December 536. Vitigis sent ambassadors to Constantinople to plead for peace. They took with them letters written by Cassiodorus addressed to Justinian and the master of the offices, affirming that the murder of Theodahad was a good deed.[14] But it was far too late for such

13. The account of the sacking in the *Liber Pontificalis* (trans. R. Davis, *The Book of Pontiffs (Liber pontificalis)*. Liverpool 1989 p. 54) paints a grimmer picture than Procopius (*Wars* 5.10.26–37), but the sources are not contradictory. Note too the laconic words of Marcellinus comes: 'Neapolim vastat' (*Chron. s.a.* 536.3).

14. Cassiodorus *Variae* 10.32f (ed. Th. Mommsen, *Monumenta Germaniae Historica Auctores Autiquissimi* 12; trans. S.J.B. Barnish, Liverpool 1992). A phrase towards the end of the second letter, in which Cassiodorus urges that hatred should be buried with the death of a sinner (10.33.3) is remarkably similar to a phrase the same author had used a decade earlier writing to Justin on the death of Theoderic: 'hatreds should be closed up with tombs' (*Variae* 8.1.2).

measures, and the new king was soon to follow in the footsteps of his predecessor and take the road to Ravenna.

Vitigis can be criticized for his retreat, which effectively abandoned much of Italy to the invaders, but it may have been dictated by fear of the Franks. During the reign of Clovis (*c.* 481–511) this people, advancing from the northwest, had made rapid progress into Gaul. Having rejected the attempts of Theoderic to make peace between himself and the Visigoths, Clovis had gone on to defeat them at the battle of Vouillé in 507. The Franks had a tradition of alliance with Constantinople, and after the battle of Vouillé the emperor Anastasius showed his pleasure by conferring on Clovis an honorary consulship.[15] Following the death of Theoderic the Franks had shown themselves interested in making gains which threatened the Ostrogoths, and they would clearly be in a position to influence the outcome of a major war fought in Italy. Hence the Roman invaders and the Gothic defenders both sought the support, or at least the benevolent neutrality, of the Franks. At the beginning of the war they had promised Belisarius that they would fight as his allies, but in 536 Theodahad, in return for a promise of help, had agreed to give them a part of Gaul which the Ostrogoths had gained under Theoderic and a large sum of gold. On coming to power Vitigis carried out the Gothic side of the bargain, and received an agreement from the Franks to send non-Frankish troops to assist him. Nevertheless, caution was called for whenever the Franks were involved, and the move to Ravenna may have been an attempt to cover his rear.

But it played into the hand of Belisarius. The central parts of Italy were left dangerously exposed, and the inhabitants of Rome were emboldened to invite the invaders to occupy their city. On 9 December 536, as its Gothic garrison left northwards through the Flaminian Gate, the army of Belisarius entered the city from the south through the Asinarian Gate. It was a happy day, the significance of which Procopius emphasized by the solemnity of its dating: Rome became subject to Romans again after an interval of sixty years, on the ninth day of

15. Gregory of Tours *Historiarum libri X* ed. W. Arnolt, B. Krusch, W. Levison (*Monumenta Germaniae Historica Scriptores Rerum Meroringicarum* 1/1), trans. as *History of the Franks* (O. M. Dalton, Oxford 1927; L. Thorpe, Harmondsworth 1974), 2.38.

the month called by the Romans 'December', in the eleventh year of Justinian's reign.[16] When news of the loss of Rome came to Vitigis he prepared a host which his enemies believed numbered 150 000 and advanced on the city. Making no attempt to take various towns which the invaders had captured, he arrived at Rome towards the end of February. But the city, surrounded by walls which were for the most part in sound condition, would have defied an army more competent at siege warfare than that of the Goths. They could only surround about half of it, and Vitigis, despite some successes, was unable to gain a decisive edge. Nevertheless, there were only 5000 troops available to defend the city, so neither side was able to bring about a speedy victory. In the spring of 537 Belisarius wrote to Justinian explaining that the imperial army was heavily outnumbered and asking for reinforcements. The emperor replied that more men were on their way.

One of the problems the defenders faced was the provisioning of the city. While the Goths were not able to block all its entrances, they were able to restrict the entry of food. Similarly, they were able to cut the aqueducts, and while there were springs in Rome these could not supply sufficient water for its inhabitants. It became clear that the city contained not enough soldiers but too many civilians, and Belisarius ordered that those in the city who were not involved in the fighting were to go to Naples. One night a group tried to force open the doors of the temple of Janus, near the forum. Traditionally, the gates had been opened in time of war, perhaps to suggest the departure of the god from his temple to aid the Romans, and recourse to such a frankly pagan practice suggests the desperation of some of the inhabitants of the city.[17]

16. *Wars* 5.14.14, evidence of a perception characterized above as being eastern rather than western (p. 12). Note however that there is some uncertainty about the reference to December, which has been supplied from a parallel passage in Evagrius (*Historia Ecclesiastica* 4.19) (*The Ecclesiastical History of Evagrius*, ed. J. Bidez and L. Parmenties, London 1898; trans. E. Walford, London 1851).

17. Needless to say the practice had long fallen into abeyance. There are references to the doors being closed in Ammianus Marcellinus 16.10.1 ed. and trans. J.C. Rolfe, London 1950–2 (on the visit of Constantius to Rome in 357) and Claudian *de cons Stil II* 2.287 ed. and trans. M. Platnauer, London 1922 (with reference to the early fifth century), but these are purely metaphorical.

In a time of such low morale, accusations of treachery were rife.

One such accusation was particularly important. Pope Agapetus had died while still in Constantinople, and after news of this reached Rome a successor, Silverius, was elected, early in June 536. The new pope was the son of an earlier pontiff, pope Hormisdas, but he was imposed on the church by Theodahad, as a result of bribes it was believed. Despite his owing his elevation to the Gothic sovereign, he was chief among the Romans who urged Belisarius to come to Rome late in 536. Nevertheless, a few months later he was accused of treasonable negotiations with the Goths and brought before Belisarius. But the accusation of treachery was merely a pretext which allowed a more sinister operation to be effected. While in Constantinople, pope Agapetus had obtained the deposition of the patriarch of that city. This was not a universally popular action, and a Roman cleric of senatorial family who happened to be in Constantinople when Agapetus died, the deacon Vigilius, let it be known to Theodora that if he were to become pope he would reinstate the patriarch. Stories circulated that he told the empress that he was prepared not only to reinstate him but also to do away with the council of Chalcedon; a promise of 700 pounds of gold may have helped him reach this position. When it became clear that Silverius had no intention of rescinding what his predecessor had done, Vigilius was sent to Rome by Theodora with an order that he was to be made pope.

When Silverius was brought before Belisarius and his wife Antonina in the palace the general was occupying on the Pincian Hill, he must have realized that his days as pope were over. Accused of treason on the basis of a forged letter, he was stripped of his papal vestments, led away, and sent in exile to Patara, a town on the southern coast of what is now Turkey. Here he found himself the recipient of the good offices of the local bishop, who travelled on his behalf to Justinian. The emperor was moved by the bishop's argument that, while there were many kings in the world, there was only one pope, and ordered that Silverius be returned to Rome and that the correspondence on the basis of which he had been accused of treason be examined. But when Silverius returned to the city Belisarius, who had in the meantime imposed Vigilius on the papal throne, delivered him into the hands of his successor.

Vigilius took no chances. Silverius was sent to Palmaria, a small island in the Tyrrhenian Sea some forty kilometres off the Italian coast, and was dead before the end of the year. There were reports of miracles occurring at his tomb.

The events were a first indication of what reintegration into the empire would mean for the papacy. The elevation of Vigilius showed that a posting in Constantinople could be an important item in the curriculum vitae of an ambitious member of the Roman clergy. More importantly, the influence Constantinople could have on the Roman church was clear for all to see. Whereas the Gothic kings had sometimes exerted an influence on the election of a pope, they had never sought to depose one. Emperors did not behave in such a gentlemanly fashion: of the 52 patriarchs of Constantinople who held office from the reign of Justinian until that of Alexios Comnenos (1081–1118), 19 or 20 were deposed or forced into temporary retirement,[18] and the fall of Silverius showed that popes were similarly at risk while Rome was part of the empire. For those with eyes to see, it was an event of ill omen for the freedom of Italy.

Meanwhile, the siege continued. While it was certainly eventful, 69 encounters being mentioned as having taken place (Procopius *Wars* 6.2.37), neither side was happy at the way it progressed. The Goths took care that no supplies entered the city, the inhabitants of which began to put pressure on Belisarius to risk all on a decisive battle; in reply, he affirmed that a mighty army was on its way to bring help. Disease became a problem in the city. But the Goths as well were suffering from hunger and disease, and as Roman reinforcements began to arrive they despaired of success. They sent three men to treat for peace, and a truce was concluded so that Gothic envoys could be sent to Constantinople to discuss terms of peace.

Roman advances in other parts of Italy hastened the ending of the siege. While it had been dragging on, Belisarius' lieutenants had captured various towns, among them Rimini, a town on the Adriatic coast perilously near Ravenna, the Gothic capital. The Roman general, John, was the nephew of Justinian's old rival Vitalian, and it was soon clear that he was

18. H.G. Beck 'Konstantinopel Zur Socialgeschichte einer früh-mittelalterlichen Haupstad' *Byzantinische Zeitschrift* 58 1965: 11–45 at 27 n. 52.

no less ambitious than his uncle. He made contact with Matasuentha, the granddaughter of Theoderic. Vitigis had married her, but she was an unhappy wife, who was pleased to discuss the betrayal of Ravenna and a possible marriage with John. Alarmed by this course of events and despairing of taking Rome, the Goths, who had received no news from the envoys sent to Justinian, abandoned their siege in mid-March 537. It had lasted one year and nine days.

The proper course of action for the invaders after their success was not clear, and ironically the capacity of the Romans to plan effectively was hampered by the arrival of another general. Narses came accompanied by 5000 troops, but he was a friend of Justinian and Theodora, a circumstance which weakened the authority of Belisarius. Following his advice Belisarius marched on Rimini, which the Goths had besieged. The town was relieved, but the advent of a new general who was reluctant to take orders from Belisarius in a situation already marked by animosities between the Roman commanders was awkward, so that the remaining period of the war was marked by disputes over both strategy and tactics.

Meanwhile, another Roman force had been sent to Liguria. Having sailed to Genoa and defeated a Gothic army at Pavia it was able to enter the great city of Milan unopposed. But the success was shortlived, for a Gothic force supported by 10 000 Burgundians sent by Theudebert the Frank captured it. Their task had been made easier by a falling out between Belisarius and Narses. The Goths are said to have razed the city to the ground in the early months of 539, killing 300 000 males and making slaves of the women. Among the victims was the praetorian prefect Reparatus, the brother of pope Vigilius, who had been appointed to the office after his predecessor Fidelis had been killed by Goths. The body of Reparatus was cut into small pieces and thrown to the dogs.[19]

Effectively, Italy had been divided into two zones. The invaders had occupied much of it, but the Gothic government continued to function in Ravenna. In 537–538 it took steps to

19. These details are known from Procopius *Wars* 6.21.39f. There may be distortion here, but as with this author's description of the taking of Naples in 536 his account seems likely to be basically accurate; cf Marcellinus comes *Chron. s.a.* 539 (Gothi . . . omnes Romanos interficiunt) and Marius of Aventicum *Chron. s.a.* 538.

buy supplies in Istria, the peninsula in the north of the Adriatic which was far from the invaders. Justinian could not allow the progress of the war to be hampered by disputes between his generals, and in the spring of 539 Narses, who had accused Belisarius before a meeting of the commanders of acting contrary to the interests of the state, was recalled. Vitigis, meanwhile, took an enterprising step. In the belief that the best hope for the Goths lay in distracting Justinian's attention, he arranged for two Roman clergy to convey a message to Khusrau in Persia. His ambassadors represented Justinian as planning to take hold of all the earth; if he overcame the Goths, the Persians would be next, so it would be to the advantage of both Goths and Persians if Khusrau were to act against him (Procopius *Wars* 2.2.1–11, 6.22.17–20). Distracting an enemy by creating a diversion was an excellent idea, and recent history had seen various examples of interaction between eastern and western affairs. In the early years of the century Theoderic had made trouble for Anastasius when he was occupied with Khavad, and later it was rumoured that he and Vitalian planned to co-operate against the emperor. Similarly, a rebellion launched by the general Basiliscus against Zeno in 475–76 and that of Odovacer in Italy in 476 need not have been unco-ordinated. As it happened, in 540 the Great King was looking for reasons to make war on the emperor. Hence Justinian, on learning of the ploy of Vitigis, decided to make peace.

But before word of his intention reached Italy the military situation had changed. Belisarius invested Osimo, a strongly fortified town south of Ancona, and Vitigis, despite appeals from the besieged force, made no attempt to relieve it. The Goths finally surrendered and joined Belisarius' army, which made its way towards Ravenna and invested the city. Here a hard task awaited them, for the Gothic capital was difficult to take by siege, Theoderic himself having spent several years before its walls before the surrender of Odovacer in 493. While Vitigis was contemplating his options envoys from the Franks arrived proposing that, in return for an alliance, they and the Goths would share the rule of Italy. But a force of Franks led by king Theudebert had recently conducted a raid in Italy, and its behaviour towards the Goths had been abominable; at Pavia, Gothic women and children had been sacrificed. The Franks were scarcely desirable allies. Then envoys from Belisarius appeared before the king arguing that it would be more in the interest of the Goths to throw in their lot with the emperor's forces, and this the king decided to do. Discussions had begun between the Goths and the Roman forces when ambassadors arrived from Constantinople, with news that Justinian was prepared to partition Italy: Vitigis and the Goths were to be allowed to hold that part north of the Po, while the remainder was to go to the emperor. Likewise, the treasure of the Goths was to be divided in two.

The Goths were prepared to accept these terms, and the war would have been ended on this basis had it not been for the refusal of Belisarius to give his consent. According to Procopius this was because he felt that he could win an outright victory over Vitigis (*Wars* 6.29.4), but some of the Romans felt he was plotting against the interests of the emperor and so protracting the war. It was then that some of the Goths hit upon a novel idea. They proposed to proclaim Belisarius emperor of the West, and privately asked him to assume this office.[20] It had lapsed in 476 when a barbarian chief deposed its last holder, Romulus Augustulus; now another group of barbarians was proposing to revive it and give it to Justinian's general. Belisarius would thereby have joined the long list of military men who had become Roman emperors. In his history of the wars, Belisarius' friend Procopius represents him as only pretending to be receptive to the overture of the Goths (6.29.20), but he may have found their proposal appealing. As we have seen, accusations had been made after the defeat of Gelimer that he was planning to establish his own monarchy in Africa. Further, accusations of

20. Procopius uses the noun βασιλεύς to describe the office which the Goths asked Belisarius to assume. It is the word he customarily uses for 'emperor', but it can also mean 'king' (see for example *Wars* 5.11.5, where it is applied to Vitigis). Hence the office of 'basileus of the Italians and Goths' which Procopius suggests the Goths dangled before Belisarius (*Wars* 6.29.26) could have been the imperial office, or it could have been nothing more than barbarian royalty. But a term Procopius uses elsewhere in this passage, 'emperor of the West' (*Wars* 6.29.18), seems technical. I am therefore uneasy with the translation offered by H. B. Dewing at *Wars* 6.30.28, which suggests a distinction between 'emperor' and 'king' not present in the Greek. See for further discussion of the point E. Stein *Histoire du bas-empire* 2 Paris 1949 p. 367 with n. 1, and H. Wolfram *History of the Goths* trans. T. J. Dunlap Berkeley Calif. 1988 p. 349 and n. 670.

disloyalty had recently been made against Belisarius, who had come to enjoy vast powers in Italy during the war. He seems to have been able to appoint praetorian prefects without reference to Justinian, and while he had been in the Pincian Palace in Rome people approached him through curtains. To be sure, he had taken oaths of loyalty to the emperor, but these need not have stood in the way of ambition.

Whatever Belisarius really intended, the Goths were led to believe that he had accepted their proposal, and they offered no resistance as he marched into Ravenna in May 540. Gothic leaders in other centres submitted to him, with the exception of Ildibad, the commander in Verona. But inevitably, word of the agreement Belisarius had purportedly made with the Goths reached Justinian, who immediately ordered his general to return. His feelings must have been mixed, for Belisarius had succeeded in obtaining better terms than those which he had been prepared to accept himself. There may have been other reasons for the decision to summon Belisarius back to the east, for relations with Persia had been deteriorating and in March 540 Khusrau launched a major invasion of Roman territory. Justinian may have felt the need for the services of Belisarius, who had emerged as his star general, in this theatre. In any case, accompanied by Vitigis, his wife Matasuentha, other important Goths, and the Gothic treasure, Belisarius made his way to the royal city. But the contrast with his return in 534 was apparent. Then, he had been given a choice of remaining in Africa or not, and had been ceremonially greeted. In 540 he was recalled and held in suspicion.

But this aside, the wars of the 530s had fulfilled Justinian's steadily escalating hopes. It would be possible to make too much of these successes: the territory conquered amounted to somewhat less than half that of the old Empire in the West, and the combined budgets of the praetorian prefects of Italy and Africa and Illyricum were barely a quarter that of the prefecture of the East.[21] Nevertheless, Africa was the wealthiest region in the West, while Italy enjoyed immense prestige

21. M. Hendy *Studies in the Byzantine Monetary Economy c. 300–1450* Cambridge 1985 p. 171.

because of the significance of Rome from both classical and Christian perspectives.[22] God, it must have seemed, had smiled on the ventures of his servant.

The clearest indication of what the victories meant to Justinian comes from the description of a mosaic he had installed in the ceiling of the Chalke ('Bronze') Gate, as the vestibule through which people entered the palace from the Mese was called. Originally erected by Anastasius, it had been rebuilt by Justinian after the Nika riot. The vestibule must have been impressive: some idea of what Anastasius' structure looked like can probably be gained indirectly from the depiction of Theoderic's palace in S Apollinare Nuovo in Ravenna, which is itself oddly similar to the facade of the sanctuary of the Great Mosque at Damascus which was constructed in the Umayyad period. In any case, we know from a carefully worded description that the mosaic Justinian placed in the ceiling depicted the taking of towns in Africa and Italy, and the victories he achieved through Belisarius, who was shown giving the emperor booty, kings and kingdoms. In the middle stood Justinian and Theodora, before whom the kings of the Vandals and Goths were brought as captives, while members of the senate stood around them, all keeping festival. The mosaic showed them exulting and smiling, as they gave the emperor honours equal to God (Procopius *Buildings* 1.10.16–19). Being depicted as receiving honours equal to God suggests in Justinian a vanity unusual even among Byzantine emperors. But everyone knew that the victories had really been due to Belisarius, whose conduct at the end of the Italian campaign can only have worsened suspicions already present in Justinian's mind. A curious passage in Procopius may be a pointer to Justinian's concerns. Late in 539 some Armenians were encouraging Khushrau the Persian to make war on Justinian, and one of the points they made was that he had nothing to fear from Belisarius, for the emperor was never going to see his general again. Indeed, the Armenians alleged, Belisarius was paying no attention to Justinian but remaining in the direction of the setting sun, having power in Italy (*Wars* 2.3.52). It is hard to know how to evaluate this passage, but it

22. So it is that John the Lydian refers to 'sacred Rome' (*Powers* 10.18, 168.9, 218.16), and that eastern authors generally thought of Rome as the capital of contemporary Italy.

is one of a number in our sources which reveal elevated perceptions of the kind of power Belisarius had come to enjoy. A strange passage in a work written in Constantinople about a decade after Belisarius entered Ravenna states that 'Justinian the emperor, victorious and triumphant, and the consul Belisarius, shall be called Vandalicus, Africanus and Geticus'.[23] The bestowal of such titles was customary for emperors (cf. above p. 72), but not their subjects. At some stage, whether in the 530s or 540s, Belisarius made offerings to the Roman church. They were lavish, and the most significant was a jewelled gold cross of 100 pounds which, a contemporary source tells us, had an inscription about his victories.[24] Yet the description of the mosaic at the Chalke Gate describes them as Justinian's victories, merely achieved through Belisarius. As we shall see, a story was later told that, while Justinian lay ill with the plague in 542, Belisarius and some other generals fighting the Persians agreed that if another Justinian were to become emperor they would not put up with it (Procopius *Secret History* 4.2). Some of this evidence is anecdotal, and some of it from after 540. We have no direct evidence that Belisarius was tempted to disloyalty at the end of the Italian campaign, but jealousy could always be reckoned within the circles around an emperor, where courtiers could be relied on to fan the flames of suspicion. Roman history was full of examples of successful generals who had gone on to better things, and while Belisarius had won the victories for which he had been sent to the West, Justinian cannot have seen the manner in which the Goths were successfully defeated as an unmixed blessing.

23. Jordanes *Getica* 315 (ed. Th. Mommsen, *Monumenta Germaniae Historica Auctores Antiquissimi* 5; trans. C.C. Mierow, Princeton NJ 1915).
24. Davis *Book of Pontiffs* p. 56.

Chapter 4

YEARS OF FRUSTRATION

. . .

THE PROBLEM OF PERSIA

Late in the sixth century some elephants which had been
captured from the Persians were accustomed to walk in single
file through the streets of Constantinople. Whenever they
passed a church the leading elephant turned to the east,
bowed down and made the sign of the cross with its trunk;
those following each did the same in turn.[1] The pious behaviour of the animals can be compared to a statue which
Justinian erected in the Augusteum, an open space to the
south of Hagia Sophia and the west of the senate house, two
works he had built after the Nika riots. Here, atop a lofty
column, was a huge statue of Justinian on horseback, perhaps
three or four times larger than life. Looking towards the east,
the figure of the emperor held in his left hand a globe,
representing the world, surmounted by a cross, the symbol of
Christian victory, while his right hand was extended eastward
in a gesture which contemporaries recognised as a command
to the barbarians in that direction to remain seated at home.
(Procopius *Buildings* 1.2.1–12)

Despite the wars in the West, Justinian's priorities remained
still largely eastern. They were clearly revealed in the midst of
cut-backs which were made to the *cursus publicus*, the costly
state post which was maintained for the use of officials travelling on official business and the transport of materials for

1. John of Ephesos *Historia ecclesiastica* trans. E.W. Brooks, *Corpus Scriptorum Christianoram Orientalium* (Scriptores Syri 3rd ser. 3) 2. 48.

military or other state purposes. In some areas it was abolished and elsewhere it was restricted, to the loss of the rural producers who had sold produce to the stations where horses and oxen were kept and accommodation provided. But on the road leading to Persia the service was retained intact. Indeed, at Nicaea the quarters of the couriers were improved by the restoration of a bath. Persia was still seen as the major threat to the empire.

The power of Persia had been an intermittent problem for the peoples of the eastern Mediterranean for centuries. Based as they were on the vast uplands between Mesopotamia and the Indus River, the Persians could look in various directions, but when their capital was in the west a policy oriented towards the Mediterranean was always likely. This had been the case just over a thousand years prior to the time of Justinian, when Darius and Xerxes attacked Greece. During the Hellenistic period Persian power had diminished, but in AD 226 a new dynasty, the Sasanians, came to power. The diplomatic protocol of the time described the shahs of Persia as the brothers of the emperors, but their relations with Constantinople were only one of their concerns. After the calamitous Arab invasion of the seventh century it made sense for the last Sasanian monarch to appeal for aid to the Chinese, with whom the Persians had extensive trade relations; in the eighth century, members of the royal family were still living at the cosmopolitan Tang capital. But the title Persian rulers used in correspondence, 'King of kings of Iran and non-Iran', whatever its precise meaning, could be interpreted by other powers in an alarming way. In 363 the emperor Julian the Apostate invaded Persia in a campaign which may have been designed to recall the days of Alexander the Great, but after he died of wounds sustained on the campaign hostile encounters between the states tended to take the form of raids rather than invasions.

As is so often the case with ancient peoples adjacent to the classical world, the bulk of our documentary evidence about the Persians comes from works written by their enemies. Indeed, the very word 'Persia' is Greek, for the inhabitants of this state referred to it as Iran. Procopius, like Herodotus before him, described Persian affairs in some detail, but theirs are obviously the works of outsiders. Procopius' continuator Agathias based his discussion of Persian matters on material excerpted on his behalf from the Persian royal annals (4.30), and his account has interesting similarities with traditions preserved in later eastern sources; despite this, the impression he gives of the Persians is negative. While the Sasanians were Zoroastrians, adherents of a religion preached in the distant past which had developed a cult of fire worship and a class of powerful clergy, the Magi, they ruled over a state which included flourishing minorities of Jews, who produced the Babylonian Talmud, and Christians, whose school at Nisibis became important from the late fifth century. It is clear from the magnificent silverware preserved in the Hermitage at St Petersburg that Sasanian society was one of wealth and sophistication, and Justinian seems to have been well-matched in Khusrau (Greek 'Chosroes'), his great contemporary.

Under Khusrau's father Kavad (488–531), Persia had become stronger, and his own reign (531–579) was to prove the high-water mark of Sasanian power. He was given the nick-name 'Anushirwan', 'of immortal soul'. It seems that Khusrau was more inclined to look towards the empire than other Sasanians. A reform of the tax system he instituted was apparently modelled on that of the empire, and he was reputed to be a scholar of Greek philosophy; it was to his court that the seven philosophers fled early in Justinian's reign. But it was also believed that a king of India had sent him a game of chess, and perhaps Khusrau was interested in all the neighbouring civilizations. In any case, he was a rival worthy of Justinian. The massive brick vault of a palace he built at his capital on the Euphrates, Ctesiphon, still stands, some thirty metres in span and a little more in height. A new town built by Khusrau near Ctesiphon was given a name which mocked the chief city of Syria: it was Veh Antiok Khusrau, 'Better than Antioch has Khusrau [built this]'.[2] Eight hundred years later the Arab author Ibn Khaldun was to quote Khusrau as an authority on good government.

The frontier between Persian and Roman territory was part of the long eastern border of the empire, which extended southwards from the eastern shore of the Black Sea. To the eastern side of the northernmost section of the frontier were the Armenians. Further south, in the region between the

---

2.   R.N. Frye 'The political history of Iran under the Sasanians' in E. Yarshater ed. *The Cambridge History of Iran* 3 *The Seleucid, Parthian and Sasanian Periods* Cambridge 1983 pp. 116–80 at 155.

Tigris and Euphrates known as Mesopotamia, the frontier separated Roman and Persian territory. The defence of this border was a great concern to the empire, which was reflected in the way Procopius organized his material in the *Buildings*: after a first book devoted to works carried out in Constantinople, he passed immediately to describing the fortifications built on the Persian frontier. South of the Euphrates the border proceeded in a more westerly direction towards the Gulf of Aqaba. The border in this third section, running as it did through country which was largely desert, was not well defined. The territory on its eastern side was controlled by Arabs, people then coming to be known as 'Saracens', an obscure word, possibly of Arabic origin, which means 'easterners'. Plenty could go wrong along a long border such as this, and as it happened by 540 there was trouble right along it.

The Armenians were restless. It has been the misfortune of the Armenian people at various stages of their long history to have had to accommodate themselves to more powerful neighbours, often transient by Armenian standards, and in the time of Justinian the Roman and Persian states were such neighbours. At the beginning of the fourth century Christianity had been adopted as the religion of Armenia. Ultimately this decision tended to pull it into the Byzantine sphere of influence, but this consequence cannot have been foreseen, for at the time it was taken Christians were still being persecuted in the Roman empire, and the path of the Armenian church was to be one of sturdy independence. Important manifestations of this were the invention of the Armenian alphabet in *c.* 400 and the subsequent growth of a vernacular literature, and the failure of the Armenians to accept the teachings of the council of Chalcedon (451).

Late in the fourth century the Romans and Persians had partitioned Armenia. Initially the portion of Armenia which fell to Rome remained under the control of hereditary Armenian satraps, but their ill-advised support of an unsuccessful claimant to the throne in the 480s and Justinian's reforms of the 530s had cost them their power. One of the consequences of Justinian's administrative reforms was that in 536 the satrapies were finally abolished in all the region under Byzantine control. Justinian must have viewed this as nothing more than the tidying up of a local administrative anomaly, but the development was not well received by the Armenians, and the changing of the name of Martyropolis, the city on which the Byzantine administration was based, to Justinianopolis can have done nothing to smooth irritated feelings. Before long they were in revolt. In 538–539 Justinian despatched against them Sittas, a rising general who had married Theodora's sister Komito, but the Armenians succeeded in killing him. Following this bold stroke they desperately needed support, and sent ambassadors to Khusrau. A report of their speech suggests that they painted an alarming picture of Justinian: the entire earth, they maintained, could not hold a man with his ambitions for conquest, they claimed, and following his victories in the West he was already plotting against Persia. Now, the Armenians declared, while the bulk of his armed forces was still in the West, was the time for Khusrau to strike (Procopius *Wars* 2.3.32–53).

Trouble also loomed in the desert to the south of Mesopotamia, the home of the Arabs. In the early days of the empire Rome had dealt with the threat they posed by supporting client kingdoms. This method was later replaced by a system of fortifications manned by frontier troops, the *limitanei*, but from the early fifth century no new forts were built, and by the mid-sixth century at least some of them had been abandoned. At Umm el-Jimel in north Jordan, for example, a large fort built in the third century was given over in the fifth century to domestic and possibly commercial uses. On the other hand, we know that one fort, Hallabat, was restored in 529, so generalization seems difficult. But there is no doubt that a move away from forts occurred, and it is possible to interpret this development in a sinister light. Centuries later Muslim authors told how the Prophet Muhammad, although still a boy, had been recognized by Bahira, a monk or hermit of Bostra (the modern Bosra), the capital of the Roman province of Arabia, when he passed through the town as a member of an Arab caravan.[3] Perhaps, it might be thought, the move away from forts opened the way to a rise in Arab

3. Historians are not certain what weight to place on Arab trade of the period: compare Patricia Crone *Meccan Trade and the Rise of Islam* Oxford 1987 and I. Shahid *Byzantium and the Semitic Orient Before the Rise of Islam* London 1988. Concerning the legendary encounter between Muhammad and Bahira, see A. Abel 'Bahira' in *The Encyclopaedia of Islam* 2nd edn 1 1960 pp. 922f.

influence which had as its climax the extraordinary expansion of Arab power in the years after the death of the Prophet. But the region enjoyed prosperity in Justinian's time: in Umm el-Jimel the construction of domestic houses came to a climax in the sixth century and most if not all of its fourteen churches were built between the late fifth and early seventh centuries.[4] The abandonment of forts can be seen not as a policy of retrenchment but as part of a change in military strategy which saw the Romans reverting to their earlier policy of cultivating some of the Arabs.[5]

So it was that Justinian's eye fell on a Monophysite Christian, Harith, the ruler of the Ghassanid Arabs. His father had already had dealings with the Romans, and it seemed that he would be a worthy representative of Roman interests. In about 528 he was given the title Phylarch, and made his headquarters at the caravan town of Sergiopolis, the modern Rusafah, 25 kilometres south of the Euphrates. Harith found his position advantageous, for after the Samaritan revolt in 529 there came into his possession 20 000 Samaritan children whom he was able to sell in the markets of Persia and India. But Persia was also interested in strengthening its ties with the Arabs and opposed to Harith was a long-standing ally of Persia, al-Mundhir, the ruler of the Lakhamids of al-Hira, an experienced commander based at al-Hira with several raids into Roman territory to his credit. A staunch pagan, on one occasion he was reputed to have sacrificed 400 Christian virgins to his deities.

Both the great powers, then, sought to use the Arabs. Nevertheless, they remained a constant irritant. In 536 a body of them estimated to number 15 000 responded to dry weather by crossing into Roman territory south of the Euphrates, where the local duke had to deal with them. A few years later Harith and al-Mundhir fell out over the control of

4. Bert de Vries 'Urbanization in the Basalt region of north Jordan in late antiquity: the case of Umm el-Jimel' in A. Hadidi ed. *Studies in the History and Archaeology of Jordan* 2 Amman/London 1985 pp. 249–56. Note as well the comment of M. Piccirillo that in the period from the fifth to the seventh centuries Jordanian territory reached its maximum development of sedentary life and urbanization (ibid. vol. 3 p. 165).
5. S. Thomas Parker *Romans and Saracens: A History of the Arabian Frontier* Winona Lake In. 1986. But see below p. 163 for the erection of a military complex in Syria late in Justinian's reign.

a stretch of impoverished country to the south of Palmyra (the modern Tadmur), named Strata. Justinian sent two officials to enquire into the dispute, but they gave different advice, one recommending that the Romans not give way and the other that they not press the issue and so supply Khusrau with a pretext for the war he seemed to want to wage.

Developments concerning the Armenians and the Arabs therefore gave Khusrau reason to think of ending the peace. They occurred against the background of the desperate appeal of the Ostrogothic king Vitigis that he attack the Romans. A speech Procopius represents the ambassadors of Vitigis making before Khusrau described Justinian as wanting to lay his hands on the whole earth (*Wars* 2.2.6), a charge similar to that which the Armenian legates are said to have made, and Justinian's remarkable successes during the 530s may have made such an assertion plausible. When hostilities broke out the Romans naturally attributed Khusrau's aggression to his being filled with malice and fury after Justinian's successes in the West, and it may well be that Khusrau thought that the balance of power between Persia and Rome had changed for the worse since the perpetual peace had been agreed to in 532.

So it was that Khusrau struck boldly during the early spring of 540. With a large force he advanced along the lightly populated southern side of the Euphrates. Crossing into Roman territory, Khusrau captured the town of Sura, which he proceeded to destroy, and advanced further, seeking sums of money from various towns. Justinian, on hearing of the threat, had sent his cousin, Germanus, to Antioch, with three hundred men, but he achieved little. He and the patriarch Ephrem had already seen fit to leave the city when Khusrau reached it in June and demanded a thousand pounds of gold. When payment was not forthcoming Khusrau stormed the walls. Its defenders, regular soldiers supplemented by members of the factions of the Hippodrome, were no match for the Persian troops, who were quickly able to scale the walls. Many of the inhabitants of the city were massacred, and Khusrau, who suffered from no love of Christianity, helped himself to the wealth of the cathedral. Those of the inhabitants who did not flee were enslaved, and the city fired. Oddly enough, the cathedral was to be spared.

The loss was devastating for Justinian. Antioch had been

founded by one of the generals of Alexander the Great late in the fourth century BC, and had grown to become the capital of Syria and the third city of the empire. Located on the Orontes River some thirty kilometres upstream from the coast, it was a true Mediterranean city, and its capture in 540 was the first occasion since the third century on which Persians had taken it. Its sack in 540 came after a number of other misfortunes: Antioch had suffered from a great fire in 525 and earthquakes in 526 and in 528, after the second of which it had been renamed Theopolis, 'City of God'. Following the disaster of 540, Justinian rebuilt the city. The enterprise is described at length by Procopius (*Buildings* 2.10.2–25), but in terms which suggest that the new city was a scaled-down version of the old.

But this lay in the future. After his capture of the city Khusrau demanded 5000 pounds of gold. Justinian's representatives on the spot accepted the terms, but had to send to Constantinople for confirmation. Meanwhile, Khusrau made his way to Seleucia and bathed in the waters of the Mediterranean, a rare pleasure for a Persian shah, before going to Apamea, where he took the treasure of the town and attended the races at the Hippodrome, whence he proceeded homewards through Mesopotamia. For as long as he was in Roman territory he helped himself to plunder along the way. The last town he attacked, Daras, was near the border, and important to the Romans. One of the set-pieces in Procopius' *Buildings* (2.1.4–3.26) is the long passage on the fortifications at Daras, which is placed at the beginning of the book devoted to Mesopotamia. The emperor Anastasius had begun to fortify the site, but Procopius describes major activities undertaken by Justinian, which included strengthening the walls and towers and the construction of cisterns to save water. Modern scholars have found it difficult to establish the respective contributions of these two emperors,[6] but Justinian was furious when he heard of Khusrau's futile attempt to take the town. He treated it as a hostile act which abrogated the agreement which his representatives had concluded with Khusrau.

6. See the differing assessments of Brian Croke and James Crow 'Procopius and Dara' *Journal of Roman Studies* 73 1983: 143–59, and M. Whitby 'Procopius' description of Dara' in P. Freeman and D. Kennedy eds *The Defence of the Roman and Byzantine East* Oxford 1986 737–83.

Inconclusive hostilities were to last for several years. In the spring of 541 Belisarius, fresh from the war in Italy, was sent to the Persian frontier, commanding a force which included Gothic troops he had brought to Constantinople in the preceding year. Khusrau, however, had turned his attention to the east of the Black Sea, where a people called the Lazi lived. The territory they occupied was of some strategic importance, for it blocked passes which otherwise would have been open to potential invaders from the steppes to the north of the Caucasus. Justinian, who seems to have had the knack of effortlessly antagonizing the small neighbours of the empire, had annoyed the Lazi by sending military forces to Lazica and establishing a major fortification at the town of Petra on the coast of the Black Sea. So it was that the Lazi followed the example of the Armenians and sought an alliance with Khusrau. Pleased with the prospect of access to the Black Sea, he accepted their appeal, and in 541 led an army to Lazica. The town of Petra was captured and Khusrau helped himself to its wealth. An expedition which Belisarius led into Persian territory while this was going on accomplished little, but when Khusrau heard of his activities he left Lazica, bringing to an end a campaigning season which had worked in his favour. In 542 Khusrau again led an army into Roman territory, but this time Belisarius was able to turn his expedition aside. Shortly afterwards, however, the general was recalled to Constantinople. This puzzling incident is mentioned by Procopius in two of his works, where very different interpretations are placed on it. In his history of Justinian's wars Procopius asserts that Belisarius was recalled to Constantinople by the emperor so that he could be sent to Italy again (Procopius *Wars* 2.21.34). But in his *Secret History*, a work allegedly written to correct the untruths of his earlier writing, Procopius states that a report reached the army fighting the Persians that Justinian had died from the plague, whereupon Belisarius and other generals engaged in some loose talk to the effect that they would not tolerate another emperor like Justinian. This came to the attention of Theodora, who summoned the generals to the royal city. One of them, Buzes, disappeared into a dungeon, from which he was to emerge two years later in poor condition, while Belisarius was relieved of his command (*Secret History* 4.1–16). Unfortunately, the latter version is likely to be correct, for Belisarius was only sent to Italy in

97

544, inexplicably late if he had been recalled for this purpose in 542; further, the words Procopius uses to describe his recall in the former version are formulaic, being suspiciously similar to those he used when he described the recall of Belisarius from the Persian front under a cloud a decade earlier (*Wars* 1.21.2).[7] We may take it, then, that whatever words Belisarius uttered to his military cronies in 542 came to form another item in Justinian's steadily lengthening dossier of grounds for mistrusting him.

By 543 Romans and Persians were each suffering from the plague, and little came of attacks launched by both sides. In particular, an immense Roman force marched into Armenia, but it was defeated. In 544 Khusrau led an army against the town of Edessa. The city withstood a siege with vigour, and Khusrau departed after receiving 500 pounds of gold. But the shah's appetite for war was diminishing, and in 545 the two powers came to an agreement that there would be peace for five years. Justinian paid Khusrau 5000 pounds of gold. He sought the return of Lazica, but Khusrau would not relinquish his gain. Each party could take some satisfaction from this result. Khusrau received a payment which would have been in line with expectations if he had continued to launch raids into Roman territory, and had made a useful gain in Lazica, while Justinian, who was by now confronted with a deteriorating situation in both Italy and Africa, became free to turn his attention elsewhere. But the terms of the peace were scarcely glorious, and in retrospect the inconclusive war could be seen as marking a turning of the tide after the successes of the 530s. When Procopius wrote his *Secret History* in 550, he claimed that after Belisarius failed to stand up to the empress Theodora in a personal matter just prior to Khusrau's attack of 542, the power of God opposed him in everything he did (3.30). The judgment was made with the aid of hindsight, and concerned Belisarius rather than Justinian, but it is clear that Justinian was going to find it difficult to sustain the momentum of the extraordinary accomplishments of the early years into the 540s.

7. The chronicle of Marcellinus comes also indicates that Belisarius was recalled in disgrace: *sub anno* 545.3 (*Chron.* ed. Th. Mommsen, *Monumenta Germaniae Historica Auctores Antiquissimi* 11). See further above, p. 23.

. . .

THE PLAGUE

In the spring of 542 many people in Constantinople found themselves suffering from a strange disease.[8] They began to experience fevers, and then bubonic swellings appeared on their groins, armpits or other parts of their bodies. Before long some sunk into comas, while others became delirious, their wild behaviour making life difficult for those who were looking after them. Large pustules broke out on some, who soon died; others died when they vomited blood. Effective treatment of the disease proved beyond the skill of the doctors. It spread mysteriously, but apparently not by contact with those afflicted by it.

The disease which terrified the inhabitants of the empire was a variant of the bubonic plague. Spreading from Egypt, where it had struck in 541, it passed across the empire, reaching Constantinople in 542 and Italy in 543, before proceeding further into western Europe. Its impact was grim. In one Egyptian town a boy of ten was the only survivor, while some communities in Syria were wiped out. The plague was exceptionally savage in Constantinople. According to a contemporary estimate, there were 16 000 victims in the city on one day, and when the number of fatalities came to 230 000 people stopped counting. The city became filled with corpses, so Justinian ordered one of his officials, Theodore the referendarius, to hire labourers who would dig a number of great ditches on the far side of the Golden Horn, each large enough, we are told, to hold 70 000 bodies. The corpses were flung into them and then trampled underfoot to allow as many as possible to be squeezed in. Other bodies were piled in towers which had been erected for military purposes. This lack of respect for the dead was a sad state of affairs in a society which placed great importance on burial arrangements, and was widely noted. Many turned to the practice of religion in their despair. At the town of Sykeon in Galatia a boy of about twelve fell victim to the plague. His family took him to a shrine

8. For what follows, see Pauline Allen 'The "Justinianic" plague' *Byzantion* 49 1979: 5–20, and the richly documented study of Karl-Heinz Leven, 'Die «Justinianische» Peste' *Jahrbuch des Instituts für Geschichte der Medizin der Robert Bosch Stiftung* 6 1987: 137–61.

where he was healed; later he became a famous holy man. A monk in Palestine who was asked to pray that God turn his wrath aside explained that things would have been worse had it not been for the prayers of three good people. The impact of the plague on the morale of the empire is impossible to measure, but it may have been devastating.

We lack precise evidence which would allow us to determine the incidence of mortality. The plague stimulated writers to flights of rhetoric which, depending on the author, could take the form of an imitation of Thucydides' description of the plague in Athens or quotations from Jeremiah or Ezechiel. One contemporary felt that half the population died. As it happens there is good reason to doubt this,[9] but there are signs that the impact of the plague was severe. In 543 legislation was enacted dealing with the rights of the heirs of people who had died without having made a will, and in the following year problems arising from litigation after deaths were dealt with. Earlier law had not dealt in a satisfactory way with the system of inheritance to be followed when someone died intestate, but that Justinian legislated on the topic when he did is a sign of the contemporary urgency of the question. Moralists claimed that those who had inherited large sums, greedy for yet more, were taking wealthy widows rather than virgins for their wives.

As we have seen, among those who suffered from the plague was Justinian himself, who developed a swelling in his groin. It did not prove fatal, but for as long as he was ill there was a change in the balance of power in favour of Theodora. Of more lasting importance were the social consequences of the plague, which was to break out again in Constantinople in 558. According to one report, after the plague struck the launderers put up their prices, and legislation of 544 complained that traders, craftspeople, farmers and sailors had doubled or tripled the prices of their goods or labour, a development which was attributed to avarice. Legislation attempting to fix maximum wages was introduced in England in 1349 and 1351, shortly after the arrival of the Black Death, and we may conclude that in sixth-century Byzantium, as in fourteenth-century England, a high incidence of mortality had caused a

9.   E. Stein *Histoire du bas-empire* 2 Paris 1949 p. 765 n. 1.

scarcity of labour. It may not be accidental that there was a shortage of wine in Constantinople in 543.

One other consequence of the plague deserves mention. While the army of the empire in the West had become progressively barbarized during the last decades of its life in the fifth century, the forces which Belisarius led to Africa and Italy were substantially indigenous to the empire. This was no longer the case with armies after the plague struck. Not only were reinforcements grudgingly sent to theatres of war, but the new troops were more likely to be barbarians than had been the case earlier.[10] Such circumstances go a long way towards explaining the curiously inconsequential nature of Justinian's military enterprises against the Persians, as well as in Italy, Africa and the Balkans, in the 540s.

. . .

DISTRACTIONS IN THE WEST

It was against this unpropitious background that the position of the Goths in Italy underwent a major resurgence. This development, quite unanticipated after the apparently definitive victory won by Belisarius in 540, would have been unwelcome at the best of times, and it occurred when Justinian's capacity to respond had been weakened. Resources had been transferred to the eastern frontier to deal with the sudden threat posed by the inroads made by Khusrau, with the result that the generals who had helped Belisarius defeat Vitigis were as likely to turn up on the Persian frontier as in Italy during the following decade. Moreover, the impact of the plague made it harder to dispatch armies where they were needed. As time passed Justinian was made uncomfortably aware that the cause of the Goths was by no means defunct, and that coping with them effectively required resources on a scale beyond those Belisarius had needed to defeat Vitigis.

When Belisarius entered Ravenna in May 540 it must have looked as if the Gothic war had been brought to a triumphant conclusion. But this was far from the case, for unlike the Vandals the Goths had not been decisively defeated in the field. Some of them, stung by Belisarius' refusal to become emperor, chose a new king, Ildibad, a nephew of Theudis who,

10. John L. Teall 'The barbarians in Justinian's armies' *Speculum* 40 1965: 294–322.

although an Ostrogoth, was then king of the Visigoths. Before accepting the office Ildibad sent Belisarius an embassy which repeated the offer the Goths had already made, but Belisarius again turned it down. When the loyal general left Ravenna shortly afterwards with Vitigis and other prominent Ostrogoths as his captives, as well as a good part of the Gothic treasure, the way was open for Ildibad, with no Roman commander-in-chief to oppose him, to set about restoring the fortunes of the Goths. This he did in no uncertain way.

The Goths quickly made advances. Before long all of Italy north of the Po was under Ildibad's control, while the failure of the Byzantine administration to pay its troops effectively meant that the opposing forces were low in morale and full of potential defectors. The administration of the Goths had been efficient, but when Justinian placed the financial affairs of Italy in the hands of a notorious penny-pincher the tax-payers found themselves far worse off. Ildibad was murdered in 541, as was his successor, but this opened the way for the accession of one of the greatest Gothic kings, Totila, later in the same year.[11] For the first time, Justinian was faced by an enemy in the west of undoubted competence. In 542 Totila marched south of the Po to win a great victory at Faenza. Quickly moving into the south of Italy he took Benevento, Cumae and Naples. It was an amazingly quick reversal of the situation of 540, and it occurred at the same time as Justinian's illness. A sensible response to the deteriorating situation would have been the posting of Belisarius back to Italy, where he had not only been successful but was respected. But the strategy would have depended on the good faith of Belisarius, and as we have seen, much power passed into the hands of Theodora, who had no love for the empire's star general, during the illness of her husband. Hence, following his recall from the Persian front, Belisarius languished in Constantinople. Only in 544 was he appointed to Italy again, arriving in Ravenna towards the end of the year. Desperately short of troops, he was powerless to stop the Gothic advances, and an appeal he made to Justinian in 545 for reinforcements fell on deaf ears. Nevertheless, his attempt to gain additional support had one

11. I give the name of the new king in the form provided by the majority of written sources. On coins, however, his name appears as Baduila or Baduela, and forms like this occur in some written texts.

unexpected result. His ambitious emissary John, the nephew of Vitalian, was the man who had earlier been interested in marrying Theoderic's grand-daughter Matasuentha. Now he took advantage of his presence in the royal city to contract a marriage to Justina, the daughter of Justinian's cousin Germanus.

In December 545 Totila besieged Rome. Cut off from military aid and food supplies, and under the control of a corrupt general, the city was in poor heart. In the absence of pope Vigilius, the people looked for leadership to a deacon, Pelagius, who happened to be a friend of Justinian. The cleric made his way out of the city to negotiate with Totila, but nothing came of their talk. Belisarius was unable to relieve the city, and in December 546 the Goths entered it. Totila summoned the senate and reproached its members for disloyalty to the cause of the Goths, but at the insistence of Pelagius did them no harm. He sent Pelagius and another ambassador to treat with Justinian, but the emperor refused to deal with them, and told them to speak with Belisarius, a significant sign of confidence in his general's loyalty. But as it happened Belisarius was able to turn the tables on Totila. The Gothic king had decided to tear down the walls of Rome, set fire to its buildings and, people believed, turn the city into a sheepwalk. Hearing of this, Belisarius wrote to his enemy, pointing out the beauty of the city and the damage that would be done to his reputation if he destroyed it. Astonishingly, Totila evacuated the city, taking the senators with him and sending its other inhabitants into Campania, and left it empty. For forty days, a contemporary noted, Rome lay desolate, inhabited by neither humans nor animals. After this Belisarius had the pleasure of entering it, rebuilding its walls, repopulating it, and sending its keys to Justinian. To his shame, Totila was unable to recapture the city he had so foolishly abandoned.

The tide had apparently turned in favour of the invaders. But they were still desperately short of resources, and in 548 Belisarius' wife Antonina made her way from Italy to the capital to seek help. She hoped to use ties of friendship to prevail upon Theodora, but when she arrived in Constantinople it was to learn that the empress had died, on 28 June. Feeling that her mission could not now succeed, Antonina asked that Belisarius be recalled. This was done, and he left Italy later in the same year.

But Belisarius was not the only person to make the journey from Italy to Constantinople in these years. As we shall see, from January 547 pope Vigilius was in Constantinople, and he was soon joined by aristocrats who had fled from Rome after Totila's capture of the city at the end of 546. They included Cethegus, a patrician and the most senior of the Roman consuls, who persistently urged Justinian to step up the war effort. We know from ecclesiastical documents that Cethegus was in Constantinople in 550 and 553, so presumably he remained there until the end of the war, after which he lived in Sicily. Another Italian to find his way to Constantinople during the war was Theoderic's old official Cassiodorus. Doubtless such people found congenial company in the royal city. Justinian himself and members of his family were good at Latin, the master of the offices was Peter the patrician, an intimidating intellectual who had spent some years in Italy as a prisoner of the Ostrogoths, and Constantinople was also home to authors such as John the Lydian, who was capable of writing a text in Greek which contained allusions to Homer and Vergil in equal numbers. To be sure, there were those with narrower horizons; the chronicler John Malalas, for example, seems to have been all at sea when it came to Vergil. But the strength of the Latin-speaking element in Constantinople was notably enhanced by the arrival of refugees in the middle of the century, and Justinian found himself under increasing pressure to deal with a war which showed no sign of ending. But he had other concerns. In 547–548 a wily Persian ambassador, Isdigousnas Zich, spent ten months in Constantinople. Justinian treated the ambassador with the utmost respect, giving him money and presents valued at a thousand pounds of gold. That he was so generous to such an inconsequential purpose and at such a time indicates that Justinian remained vitally concerned with his eastern neighbour.

Developments in Africa were also worrying.[12] In 543 the Moors rose in revolt, and in the following year Solomon, the

12. Averil Cameron 'Byzantine Africa – the literary evidence' in J.H. Humphrey ed. *Excavations at Carthage 1978 conducted by the University of Michigan* 7 Ann Arbor 1982: 29–62, offers an excellent discussion of its topic; see too P.-A. Février 'Approches récentes de l'Afrique byzantine' *Revue de l'Occident Musulman et de la Mediterranée* 35 1981: 25–53, and Y. Moderan 'Corippe et l'occupation byzantine de l'Afrique: pour une nouvelle lecture de la Johannide' *Antiquités africaines* 22 1986: 195–212.

Syrian general to whom Justinian had entrusted the highest military and civilian offices in Africa simultaneously, was killed. Justinian appointed the dead man's nephew, Sergius, to the offices his uncle had held, but it was a poor choice, for Sergius quickly made himself unpopular with both the army and the civilians of Africa, while the Moors held him in utter contempt. In 545 the emperor thought to retrieve the situation by sending another official, Areobindus, to share the command with Sergius. The new man was closely connected with Justinian, having married Praeiecta, the daughter of the emperor's sister, but quickly showed himself incompetent. He was unable to deal with the Moors, who found themselves able to sack the capital, Carthage, and in 546 a rebellious officer slew him after a banquet. If this was not enough, at about this time a Visigothic force crossed the Strait of Gibraltar and attacked Septem. The invaders were overcome, a circumstance which a Spanish source attributes to their having been attacked after they had laid aside their weapons in honour of the Lord's Day, but the incident was a reminder that aggression could flow from Spain into Africa as easily as from Africa into Spain. Justinian took matters in hand later in the year by appointing a new commander. John Troglita was an experienced general with a good record against the Moors, and he set about restoring the situation. He was able to win a major victory in 548, after which Africa knew peace.

In Italy, meanwhile, things went from bad to worse following the departure of Belisarius. Totila made some handy gains, and in 549 he besieged Rome, which fell in the following January, having been betrayed by imperial troops. This time he made it clear that he was there to stay, and when he went on to preside over races in the Circus Maximus he was clearly asserting that he was the legitimate sovereign of the city. Indeed, the inhabitants of the city felt that Totila lived among them like a father with his children. In the same year he responded to a failure by Justinian to discuss peace by plundering Sicily. Justinian sent Liberius to Sicily, but the general's advanced age prompted second thoughts and he was replaced by an Armenian, Artabanes who, as we shall see, had recently been involved in a conspiracy against the emperor. But more serious measures were needed, and in 550 Justinian finally took decisive action.

In that year he appointed his cousin Germanus to lead a

large expedition. It was a sensible decision, for Germanus had a good deal of military experience and had received a higher education in Latin as well as Greek. His appointment also reflected a change in the balance of power at court. The murder of Areobindus in Africa had made a widow of his wife Praeiecta. The emperor's niece was a desirable match, and she agreed to marry Artabanes, an ambitious Armenian general serving in Africa. Artabanes made his way to the capital in 546 where he was well received by Justinian. However, he had neglected to tell Praeiecta that he was already married, and after his estranged wife appealed to Theodora for assistance he was forced to resume living with her. Praeiecta went on to take another husband. This was John, the grandson of Anastasius' nephew Hypatius who had been put to death after being acclaimed emperor during the Nika riots of 532. It is a striking sign of the continued prestige of the house of Anastasius that Justinian was prepared to accept this marriage, which must have set the members of the palace recalculating the probabilities of the succession after the death of Justinian, whose marriage had been childless.

But this was not the end of Artabanes. When Theodora died in 548 he dismissed his wife, and began paying attention to the treacherous suggestions of Arsaces, another disaffected member of the old Armenian royal house, that they strike against Justinian. The story of the conspiracy is known only from one source (Procopius *Wars* 7.31f) which may well be inaccurate. Those involved were playing a risky game for high stakes and must have sought to cover their tracks, while the historian could scarcely have allowed himself the luxury of supporting them. But it seems that the conspirators tried to inveigle Justin, the elder son of Germanus, into joining a plot against Justinian which would see his replacement as emperor by Germanus. However, the young man told his father what was afoot. Germanus then arranged to meet an associate of the plotters while a trustworthy person eavesdropped, and overheard a plan to kill Justinian, Belisarius and the commander of the bodyguard together. The matter was finally brought to the attention of Justinian, who ordered that torture was to be applied to the conspirators to force them to confess. Artabanes was dismissed from his posts and held at the palace, while Germanus and his son were acquitted.

So ended the first-known conspiracy against Justinian; it was not to be the last. Perhaps we can interpret it as a stage in the development of hostility towards the emperor. In any case, it is a reminder that the career of Germanus had not flourished while Theodora was alive. The empress had never shown enthusiasm for Justinian's relatives, preferring to forward the careers of those who would be under obligation to herself, and her demise may have freed Justinian to appoint Germanus. He prepared himself for the expedition to Italy by taking an enterprising step. Among the members of the Gothic royal family taken to Constantinople by Belisarius in 540 was Matasuentha, Theoderic's granddaughter, whom Vitigis had married on becoming king. Vitigis had died, as had Germanus' first wife, and so he was able to take Matasuentha in marriage, believing that if the grand-daughter of the respected Theoderic accompanied him to Italy the Goths would no longer fight on behalf of Totila. One would like to think that love played some part in what was obviously a prudential marriage.[13] Germanus set to work organizing a large force, but before he was able to advance on Italy he fell ill and died. By that time Matasuentha was pregnant, carrying a child in whose veins would run blood of both Roman and Gothic royal families. He would be named Germanus, after his father.

The death of Germanus was a blow, but it made no difference to Justinian's determination to finish the Italian war. The Armenian Narses, who had already had a record of loyal service, was appointed to take over the expedition, and enormous financial resources, such as would allow him to raise a huge army, make up arrears in the pay of the soldiers already in Italy, and seek to win the loyalty of troops who had defected to Totila, were placed at his disposal. He was not, however, given a title, so our sources describe him in vague terms such as 'commander-in-chief' and 'general'. Rather than sailing, Narses chose to march overland, at the head of a huge force which included 5500 unruly Lombards. Among the Romans was Artabanes, who had been restored to favour. In the spring of 552 he left Salona, entering Ravenna in June at the head of

13. As we have seen, in 538 there had been talk of a marriage between Matasuentha and John, the nephew of Vitalian; in 545 John married Germanus' daughter Justina. The marriage of Germanus and Matasuentha a few years later gives one the feeling of how limited the number of really desirable spouses was.

an army of some 30 000. It was beyond the power of the Gothic army, weakened by years of fighting, to resist such a force. In 551 Totila, in a display of bravado, had ravaged the coasts of Greece, but such acts could do nothing to change the situation. Narses moved quickly. Late in June or early in July the armies met at Busta Gallorum, a site in the Apennines. Hitherto the war had mainly been fought by siege and skirmish, but now, when the opposing armies were drawn up for a decisive battle, it was clear that the Goths were hopelessly outnumbered. They fought with valour and their king displayed heroism, but were overwhelmed by their opponents. We are told that 6000 Gothic troops were killed. Totila died of a wound sustained in the battle, and the war was effectively over.

There was still mopping-up to be done, but before seeing to this Narses dismissed his Lombard allies, whose wild behaviour could not be controlled. Rome was occupied, and at the end of October a Gothic army was defeated at Mons Lactarius, a site in the south of Italy. Narses allowed the survivors to return to their own lands and become subjects of the emperor.[14] Some hostile Goths were still ensconced in strong points, and the Franks took advantage of the demise of the Gothic state to launch a major expedition which had to be dealt with. Justinian only received the keys of Verona and Brescia from Narses in November 562, but we may take the battle of Busta Gallorum as marking the end of substantial Gothic resistance. In this fashion the Gothic period of Italian history came to a definitive end. The extensive properties of the Arian religious establishment of Ravenna passed to the Catholic church, and the Arian churches of the town were turned over to the Catholic cult and rededicated, to saints of largely eastern and anti-Arian orientation. It is a small detail, but the rededications left no doubt as to the direction Italy's new rulers saw it as taking.

One more expedition rounded off the western wars. In 551 a member of a noble Visigothic family, Athanagild, sought to

14. Agathias 1.1.1 (*Histories* ed. R. Keydell, Berlin 1968; trans. Joseph D. Freudo, Berlin/New York 1975), whose testimony is to be preferred to the claim of Procopius that the surviving Goths were allowed to leave Italy forthwith (*Wars* 8.35.33–6 ed. and trans. H.B. Dewing, London 1914–1940). Many Goths continued to live in Italy, as can be deduced from the correspondence of pope Gregory the Great (590–604), which refers to many bearers of Gothic names.

enlist the aid of Justinian in a revolt against the king, and in the summer of the following year the emperor despatched a force under the command of the patrician Liberius to Spain. This man had begun his career in his native Italy under king Odovacer, and given that Odovacer had died in 493 his appointment to a command as late as 552 is surprising. Indeed, he had been recalled from an expedition to Italy not long before on the grounds that he was ἐσχατογέρων ('in extreme old age', Procopius *Wars* 7.39.7). The expedition made useful gains in Spain, but in 555 Athanagild became king and asked the imperial forces to withdraw. This they refused to do, and Justinian was left holding a slice of coastal territory which included Cartagena and Malaga, but did not extend far inland.[15] A mint was established which continued to issue coins until the reign of Heraclius in the seventh century. Hence the Spanish expedition, unlike those directed against Africa and Italy, failed to topple the barbarian state into whose territory it had been directed. But this may not have been the aim of Liberius' mission. As we have seen, the Visigoths offered a threat to Africa, and Justinian may have been merely erecting a defensive barrier along the Spanish coast nearest to Africa. In any case, the Spanish expedition was the final touch to an impressive re-drawing of the political map of the Mediterranean, at the end of which, a poet observed, a traveller could go as far as the sandy shore of Spain where the Pillars of Hercules lay and still be in imperial territory.[16]

. . .

THE WEST AFTER THE WARS

Yet the fruits of success were bitter for the West. The Italians who had been sitting out the latter stages of the war in Constantinople set off for home. Pope Vigilius left in 555, although he died before arriving in Rome. Cethegus retired, to estates in Sicily rather than Rome, while Cassiodorus founded a monastery in Bruttium. His foundation, Vivarium, boasted a fine library, and in some ways the community Cassiodorus established there marked the fruition of a plan to found a centre for Christian higher studies in Rome which

15. E.A. Thomson *The Goths in Spain* Oxford 1969 pp. 320–3.
16. Agathias, in *Greek Anthology* 4.3.83ff (ed. W.R. Paton, London 1931).

he had talked over with pope Agapetus in happier times. In those days he had planned to imitate the kind of school which had formerly existed in Alexandria and which in his own time flourished in Nisibis.[17] But no-one would have thought of founding such an institution in Rome after the war. Many of its most distinguished inhabitants had been killed, and the countryside which produced the wealth necessary to sustain the activities which had flourished there under the Goths had been devastated.

How could the Italians not have felt unhappy? Thanks to the long war Justinian had launched, their land was in a terrible state. Cities had lost their populations, and the rural economy had been devastated, with the landowning aristocracy, which had flourished under the Goths, being left to contemplate the ruin of its estates. Pope Pelagius I (555–561) wrote to Gaul and Africa seeking financial help. Moreover, the restoration of Italy to the empire had not been accompanied by a restoration to the position it had enjoyed prior to 476. No emperor ruled from Ravenna, still less from Rome. Important posts of the empire in the West which had been maintained under the Ostrogoths, such as the master of the offices and quaestor, simply lapsed. Those which were not dependent on the presence of the sovereign continued to be filled, but often not by Italians. While the first two praetorian prefects appointed by Belisarius were natives respectively of Milan and Rome, later appointees were career men sent from Constantinople. One of them, Athanasius, was successively praetorian prefect of Italy and praetorian prefect of Africa, and indeed the administration of Africa, no less than that of Italy, came to resemble that of a branch office in which the upper echelons were filled by Greek speakers reporting to headquarters by the Bosphorus. Until he was recalled in 568, supreme power in Italy was in the hands of Narses, an Armenian who is not known to have held a formal title and is described in dark terms by Italian sources. The contrast with the administration of Egypt, which, as we shall see, was for practical purposes in the hands of wealthy indigenous landowners, could not be more clear. Increasingly, Italians occupying positions of leadership were to be found among the bishops, but even this was not necessarily an area of local autonomy,

17. Cassiodorus *Institutiones* 1 praef. 1 (ed. R.A.B. Mynors, Oxford 1937).

for as we shall see, key members of the episcopate were often appointed by Justinian.

The clearest sign of the state of Italy after the war comes from the Pragmatic Sanction Justinian issued to regulate its life in August 554. The conclusion of the Vandal war was followed by the enactment in 534 of precise and detailed legislation concerning the governance of the newly won territories in Africa, but nothing on a similar scale followed the Gothic war, and the Pragmatic Sanction has a feeling of the *ad hoc* about it.[18] While it deals with important issues such as the ownership of land, there is no attempt to recast the government, such as had happened after the victory over the Vandals in Africa; the status of Narses, for example, is not touched on. There were no celebrations when the drawn-out war against the Goths was finally brought to a conclusion. Indeed, far from pulling Italy out of the barbarian West, the wars of Justinian were to implicate it there more deeply: the lingering presence of the Franks, something unthinkable in the Ostrogothic period, was ominous, but of more importance was the presence of so many barbarian soldiers in the army led by Narses. Among them were Lombards, who were to return *en masse* not long after the defeat of the Goths, and it was to prove impossible to dislodge them.

The impact of the war on the intellectual life of Italy was also grim. Cassiodorus' first surviving work was a collection of letters written on behalf of the Ostrogothic sovereigns, some of them bursting with delightfully recondite pieces of information; his last was a book on how to spell. Contrary to what might have been anticipated, the war failed to integrate the conquered lands into the thought-world of the wider empire: in the library Cassiodorus established in his monastery at Vivarium the books in Greek were relegated to an eighth bookcase, and oddly enough the Byzantine conquest of Italy seems to have been followed by a decline in Greek scholarship in Italy. As we shall see, by the middle of the sixth century the centre of Latin literary culture was Constantinople, and it is possible that the hostile western response to a major theological initiative undertaken by Justinian during the 540s and

18. The study of G.G. Archi, 'Pragmatica Sanctio pro petitione Vigili' *Festschrift für Franz Wieacker* Göttingen 1978: 11–36, is a good example of the light historians of law can cast on non-legal issues.

early 550s can be interpreted as betraying uneasiness as to the situation of the West.

It may well be, then, that after the war the inhabitants of the conquered territories looked with less favour on the empire than they had before they were a part of it. In the same way, it has been plausibly suggested that the inhabitants of the East became increasingly aware of the differences between themselves and westerners in the years of war.[19] Paradoxically, then, far from healing the split between the eastern empire and its lost western territories, the wars of Justinian may have tended to drive them apart.

But if we wish to get the feel of at least some of the aspirations of the ruling class in Italy towards the end of the Gothic war, we can do no better than consider the famous mosaics in the church of S Vitale at Ravenna, where two exquisite works depicting processions were executed in the sanctuary in about 547.[20] One, flanking on the right the figure of Christ which is depicted in another mosaic in the apse of the church, has two deacons at its head, the first carrying a thurible and the second a gospel book. They are followed by a bishop identified by an inscription as Maximianus, a lay person who cannot be securely identified, and Justinian. Thereafter come two court officials and finally a group of soldiers, apparently bodyguards. The figures are located in a space devoid of characteristics which would define it, but various details, such as the movement of the left hand and foot of the figure furthest to the right, who seems in the act of moving outside the scene, show that they are to be understood as moving towards the right. Facing this mosaic is another on the women's side of the church which shows two court officials leading Theodora, who is followed by a group of splendidly

19. Maria Cesa 'La Politica di Giustiniano verso l'occidente nel giudizio di Procopio' *Athenaeum* 59 1981: 389–409.
20. Of the large amount of writing on this subject I have found most helpful G. Rodenwaldt 'Bemerkungen zu den Kaisermosaiken San Vitale' *Jahrbuch des Deutschen Archäologischen Instituts* 59f 1944f: 88–110, and F. W. Deichmann *Ravenna, Haupstadt des Spätantiken Abendlandes* Wiesbaden 1958–76, vol. 1 pp. 220–56, vol. 2/2 pp. 47–230, which is noteworthy for its illustrations as well as its detailed commentary. Otto G. Von Simson *Sacred Fortress* Chicago 1948 is interesting, but the interpretation seems to me fanciful, as does that of E. Manara 'Di un ipotesi per l'individuazione dei personaggi nei pannelli del S. Vitale a Ravenna e per la loro interpretazione' *Felix Ravenna* 125f 1983: 13–37.

attired women; there are no explicitly religious figures in this procession. Here the figures are clearly moving towards the left, and seem to be about to enter a building, outside which there is a small fountain, through a curtained entrance. In accordance with convention, the main figures in the mosaics, although shown moving in such a way as would make only the profiles of their faces visible to beholders, are shown looking directly out at the beholder; in each case the figures are moving in the direction of the altar of the church.

The identity of the most important person in each mosaic may seem clear. In the former, Justinian occupies a central position. He wears a distinctive purple chlamys with a rich tablion, fastened over his right shoulder by an extraordinarily rich brooch, from which hang jewels.[21] On his head is a diadem, on his feet low shoes. Around his head is a nimbus, and he appears to be the only figure in the mosaic not partly obscured by a neighbour. For her part, Theodora, while not occupying a central position, is distinguished by being the tallest person in the scene, although she is known to have been a person short in stature, is wearing a purple robe over a white dress with a golden fringe, has a nimbus, and stands beneath a canopy.

But there is an alternative way of interpreting the scene of which Justinian is a part which it will be worth our while examining. If the group of soldiers at the end is taken away from the scene, and it is clear from the low competence of the mosaicist responsible for their faces that they were regarded as the least important people in the composition, Justinian and Maximianus can be seen as jointly the most important. It is true that the unidentified lay person between them occupies the central place, but he is a figure of no importance, whose body disappears below his chest: there is no sign of him in the space between the clothing of Justinian and that of Maximianus, while he has no feet. Not only do the emperor and the bishop become central in the composition of the mosaic, but each can be seen as having two lesser individuals, respectively

21. Interesting in this connection is a passage from Corippus describing the clothing of Justin II prior to his coronation: it included a clasp from which hung jewels gained by victory in the Gothic war and which Ravenna had conveyed, as well as some which Belisarius had carried away from the Vandal court (*In Laudem Justini Augusti minoris* 2.123–5 ed. and trans. Averil Cameron, London 1976).

secular officials and junior clergy, between himself and the margin of the composition. Indeed, each seems to stand at the head of a line of people: to the left of Justinian the left side of the body of each figure is blocked by the figure to the right, while to the right of Maximianus the reverse is true. Emperor and bishop both wear brightly coloured and distinctive clothing, Justinian a chlamys and Maximianus a pallium, and they make almost identical gestures with their arms. Further, while Justinian's left arm obtrudes in front of the bishop, the latter's cloak comes dangerously near to blocking the lowest part of the imperial chlamys, and Maximianus, with his two deacons, stands further into the foreground than do the others in the scene. Finally, Maximianus is the only figure whose name the mosaic supplies. There are, then, reasons for seeing emperor and bishop as being equally weighted, or indeed for Maximianus as being seen as marginally the more important.

The solemnity of the scenes, and the overt ecclesiastical nature of one of them, suggests that they have some religious significance. Each depicts a procession in which an imperial personage carries a vessel, a round dish with a raised rim in the case of Justinian and a capacious chalice in the case of Theodora. In other words, they are carrying the vessels used to hold the bread and wine used in the sacrament of the Eucharist. Scholars have debated as to whether they are to be seen as participating in one of the processions of the Orthodox liturgy, and it is certainly interesting that the first clear reference to something like the Great Entrance of the Orthodox liturgy occurs in a document of just this time. But this is not the only context in which such processions could be seen. Some decades earlier the emperor Justin had presented S Peter's in Rome with a paten and chalice, each made of gold, and it is possible that the mosaics are meant to suggest the presentation of similar gifts to the church of S Vitale in a procession of a kind which would have occurred had the imperial couple ever visited Italy. The theme of the offering of gifts is taken up in a design embroidered on the bottom of Theodora's cloak, which shows the three Magi carrying the gifts they were to present to the infant Jesus, a eucharistic theme to be found in other mosaics in the church, which depict Abel, Melchizedek and Abraham, three figures from the book of Genesis whose offerings were pleasing to God.

Nevertheless, it would be going too far to argue that the mosaics were designed to convey any ideological message devised by the emperor. There is no reason to see in them an imperially sponsored statement of victory in the Gothic war, which was still to be won when the mosaics were installed, still less any covert reference to the Arianism of the Goths. Of course their content, particularly in the mosaic including Justinian, is Christian, even down to the monogram made up of the superimposed Greek letters XP (chi and rho), which occurs on the shield held in front of the members of the bodyguard, these being the first two letters in the word 'Christ'. But this does not mean that the soldiers were meant to represent an orthodox army fighting heretical Arians: they have much more the look of the imperial bodyguard. Any statement the mosaic was intended to convey may have been episcopally rather than imperially inspired. Bishop Maximianus had recently been in Constantinople, having been consecrated there by pope Vigilius in October 546, and he may have brought back from the royal city the idea for the mosaics, and perhaps rough plans for the imperial portraits. Nevertheless, the importance given the bishop in one of the mosaics could be held to suggest that episcopal rather than imperial inspiration lay behind them. Maximianus, who came from Pola, a coastal town in the south of Istria, was not a native of Ravenna, and, like so many of those who held power in post-conquest Italy, he owed his appointment to the favour of Justinian. It is possible that the assertion of his own position governed the composition of the mosaic as much as a desire to make a statement about the emperor and his consort. If this is so, the work answers to the needs of the imperially imposed hierarchy which found itself in power after the armies of Justinian had allegedly restored freedom to Italy. But this raises issues which it will be better to consider in the context of ecclesiastical affairs.

Chapter 5

THE CHURCH

. . .

THE CHRISTIAN EMPIRE

No century has seen greater change in the role played by the Christian church in society than the fourth. In 303 the last of the great persecutions began, but the tide turned decisively during the reign of the first Christian emperor, Constantine (306–337), and by the end of the century the pagan temples were closed and sacrifices prohibited. The progress of the Christian religion from being the victim of state-sponsored persecution to definitive triumph had occurred comfortably within the span of two generations. It is true that pockets of paganism displayed disquieting resilience and that Judaism remained a tolerated faith, but the status of Christianity as the religion of the state had become overwhelmingly secure long before the reign of Justinian.

This, however, was not the end of its development. As time passed the Christian religion continued to become more central to the life of the empire, the cities of which steadily took on a more ecclesiastical character. Constantine is known to have built only two or three churches in Constantinople, and a document of 425 indicates the presence in the city of fourteen churches, although it certainly errs on the low side. But Justinian is reported to have built or rebuilt thirty-three churches in the city and its suburbs. At Philippi two large basilicas were built in around 500, an octagonal church followed shortly afterwards, while by 540 a larger church had been erected. The chronology of the building of churches in

Syria is particularly interesting.[1] At Gerasa, the modern Jerash, the urban site continued to be dominated by pagan temples, but despite a general economic decline it came to be well catered for by churches, largely built out of the stones of the temples. By the time of the Arab conquest in about 636 the town was served by eleven places of Christian worship. The cathedral had been erected in the fourth century and two further churches in the second half of the fifth century, but the great boom occurred in the sixth century when seven churches, among them those containing the most impressive mosaics in the town, were erected, while the last church was built early in the seventh century. At Rihab, some 25 kilometres to the east, the boom in building came later: inscriptions indicate that the churches on the site were built during the period 533–635.

The rise in the number of churches was not an unmixed blessing, however, for people were more prepared to gain prestige by erecting buildings than to pay for their staffing and upkeep. The Great Church in Constantinople found it difficult to pay its large staff (see above p. 52). By the time of Justinian its 40 deaconesses, women who had to be no less than 40 years old and married only once, may have been anomalous, but neither can the male members of its enormous clerical establishment have been overworked. They constituted a drain on the resources of the Great Church, and the burden of large numbers of clergy may have been common; early in the sixth century the church of Antioch was so heavily in debt that the patriarch was reluctant to carry out further ordinations. But despite their expenses, the churches enjoyed substantial assets. The Great Church controlled 1100 workshops or small businesses, and the wealth of the society was increasingly finding its way towards religious institutions; an early piece of Justinian's legislation deals with the problem caused by the many people who left wills simply naming Jesus Christ as heir (Codex 1.2.25). Doubtless not all the citizens of the empire were this pious. In 546 a law threatened actors who dressed up as monks, nuns or ascetics with bodily punishment and exile (novel 123.44). But there can be no mistaking the

1. For Gerasa, C.H. Kraeling ed. *Gerasa City of the Decapolis* New Haven Conn. 1938 remains the standard treatment; for Rihab, I follow M. Piccirillo *Chiesi e mosaici della Giordania settentrionale* Jerusalem 1981.

importance of religion in the empire, and its continuing growth.

One pointer to this was the rising power bishops enjoyed in their cities. To an extent this was a consequence of the episcopate's expanding its functions to fill the vacuum created by the atrophy of town councils in late antiquity. But in the sixth century we find bishops discharging an extraordinary variety of functions. In the 530s the loyalty of the bishop of Rome was of concern to both sides in the Gothic war, and in the 540s it was taken for granted that bishops could treat with invading Persians on behalf of their towns. The Pragmatic Sanction that Justinian issued in 554 gave local bishops as well as leading secular persons the power to nominate provincial governors in Italy, and gave the pope and the senate authority to regulate the weights and measures used by the tradespeople of Rome. Justinian's legislation authorizes bishops not only to carry out such pastoral tasks as visiting prisoners on Wednesdays or Fridays (Codex 1.4.22) and helping actresses who sought to leave the stage (Codex 5.4.29), but to report officials who were lax in enforcing the laws against heretics to him (Codex 1.5.18.12), and bishops were among those enjoined to keep an eye on the administration of local affairs (Codex 1.4.26). It is not surprising that stories were told in Egypt that Justinian tried to induce a patriarch of Alexandria to support his theological line with the promise that he would be governor as well as patriarch, and when the Arabs invaded Egypt in 640 they found that the one man, Cyrus, was both patriarch and governor.

But the Christian religion was far more than a cult performed in impressive buildings and a source of administrative talent. Since the time of Constantine emperors had believed that its correct practice would assure the good-will of God towards the state. The belief was given forceful expression in the Henotikon which Zeno issued in 482: as long as Christ approved and accepted the praise and service rendered by the empire, the power of its enemies would be swept away, and peace with its blessings, favourable temperature, abundant produce, and all beneficial things would be forthcoming. As did many people in late antiquity and the middle ages, Justinian placed great faith in the prayers of monks. If they prayed for the state with pure hands and naked souls, he was sure that the army would enjoy peace, the cities would enjoy tranquillity, the earth would produce its fruits, and there would be plenty of seafood as well (novel 133.5).

For the Byzantines, then, Christianity was a religion harnessed to the purposes of the state. Justinian felt that the two greatest gifts for which the kindness of God were responsible were the priesthood and the imperial power, and that if both carried out their functions properly there would be harmony (novel 6pr.; the word συμφωνία is that which Procopius used to describe the relationship between the component parts of Hagia Sophia). In some respects, his doctrine of the priesthood was a high one. He accepted that the pope was the first of all bishops, followed by the 'most holy archbishop of Constantinople, the new Rome' (novel 131.2). But, to express the relationship in terms which may not have occurred to people in the sixth century, the harmony he sought involved a high level of state interference in church affairs. Justinian felt it was within his competence to forbid the clergy to play board games, or to legislate concerning the election of abbots and abbesses. Personal qualities and the support of other members of the monastery or convent were to be sought rather than seniority, and the local bishop had to approve. He also issued a law stating that monks were to sleep in dormitories. These principles were obviously sensible, and had much in common with those enunciated at almost the same time by S Benedict in Italy, so much so that some scholars have unwisely suggested that one legislator influenced the other. But whereas Benedict was a monk writing a personal document of no official status, the issues he dealt with were the subject of legislation by the state in the empire.

Justinian's concern for the maintenance of correct doctrine and proper standards was therefore partly a matter of state. But he was concerned with more than this. He was a devout and sincere believer, who thought that intervention of two saints had once saved him from a serious illness, and that on another occasion he had been healed from an ailment, which rigorous fasting had worsened, by the application of the relics of forty martyrs. While the legal code issued by Theodosius II in 438 concluded with a statement of belief, the code of Justinian opened with one, and as we have seen the steps he took against pagans and Jews at the beginning of his reign represented a hardening of official policy. Further, he insisted that the canons of the ecumenical councils of the church were

119

to be considered as laws of the empire, so that this part of the law of the church was incorporated into the law of the state. He wrote various works expressing his convictions, the first emperor to do so since Julian the apostate, and it is possible that he was the author of a hymn, 'O only-begotten Word and Son', which is sung to this day.[2] There can be no mistaking his conviction.

. . .

THE SEARCH FOR SOUND DOCTRINE

Virtually since its foundation, the adherents of the Christian religion had been engrossed in controversies over doctrine. Many of these arose out of attempts to express the teachings of their faith in accordance with philosophical understandings which had arisen among the Greeks. In principle this was an excellent idea, and over the centuries Christian thinkers have found it useful to appropriate Greek terminology and concepts, such as those of 'substance' and 'nature', to help elucidate their concerns. But in practice the operation turned out to be awkward. It was difficult to make Greek concepts fit the data of the Bible, by and large the product of a very different thought-world. To make matters worse, Christian thinkers were prepared to defend their ideas and attack those of others with a doggedness not often found among pagan intellectuals. And as the church became more important in society, the temptation to use divergent theological understandings in struggles for power became stronger. From the time of the emperor Constantine the holding of correct doctrine became a concern of the state, as the government became concerned with matters of doctrine to a degree rarely found among Christian states of the West. And so the stage was set for the controversies which followed.

The focal point for disagreement was the status of Jesus of Nazareth. Almost everyone agreed that he was both God and a human being. Yet surely these two categories were mutually exclusive. Early in the fifth century Nestorios, a theologian from Antioch who became patriarch of Constantinople (428–431), tried to deal with the question by positing a Christ in whom the divine and human elements were quite separate.

2. V. Grumel 'L'Auteur et la date de composition du tropaire 'O Μονογενὴς' *Echos d'Orient* 22 1923: 398–418.

For this reason he held that it was improper to refer to the Virgin Mary as one who had given birth to God; rather, she had merely given birth to a man, Christ's divine characteristics having come from the Father. It seemed to most people that this way of looking at things created too wide a gulf between the divine and human aspects of Jesus, and the teaching of Nestorios was condemned by the Council of Ephesos (431), which taught that Mary was truly 'Theotokos', a word which is often translated 'Mother of God' but should more accurately be rendered 'God-bearer'. In using it the council was not, in the first place, making a statement about Mary; rather, by asserting that she gave birth to Jesus as God as well as Jesus as a human being, it was expressing the closeness of the relation between the divine and human components of the individual, Jesus.

Some, however, thought that the council had not gone far enough. A school arose which taught that the divine and human aspects of Jesus were bound together so closely as to constitute a unity. Among those thinking in this way was Eutyches, a monk of Constantinople, but the most important exponent of the view was Cyril, patriarch of Alexandria (412–444). But if this were granted, surely it could be said that Christ had only one nature. So there developed the understanding later called 'Monophysite', or 'one nature,' which it is convenient to refer to by this title from its beginning. Not all were persuaded by this teaching. Its opponents included pope Leo I (440–461), and after some abortive preliminaries a council met in 451 at Chalcedon, just across the Bosphorus from Constantinople, to consider the issue. It expressed its condemnation of the Monophysite position in precise terminology which owed something to Greek philosophy and something to an eastern Christian fondness for expressing understandings in negative terms: Christ was to be acknowledged as one person in two natures 'without confusion, without change, without division, without separation'.

But neither the council of Ephesos nor that of Chalcedon was universally accepted. The opponents of the former, a group generally referred to as Nestorians, tended to live in territories under Persian power, and hence their opposition was of little concern to the empire. The Monophysites were a very different kettle of fish. Their theologians in the period after Chalcedon were superior to those who supported the council, and they were able to argue, against the Chalcedonian formulation of 'in two natures', that Christ could be more accurately described as 'of two natures', which would allow them to predicate 'one nature of the incarnate word'. It is tempting to see such disputes as nothing more than frivolous games of intellectual football, but Justinian took them very seriously. While a concern with church affairs was common among emperors, Anastasius having been spoken of as a potential bishop of Antioch, the dogged persistence with which Justinian devoted himself to church affairs is remarkable. Adherence to the council of Chalcedon was strongest in the West, and it may be that Justinian's western origin was connected with his commitment to its teaching. But he found himself opposed by most of the inhabitants of Egypt, and many of those of Syria, who were of the Monophysite persuasion. Moreover, the ecclesiastical politics of Egypt and Syria were notorious for the vigour with which they were conducted.

. . .

EGYPT

Egyptians had a history of taking their theology remarkably seriously. In 415 a crowd of monks had murdered Hypatia, a well-known pagan intellectual, although their implements were probably tiles rather than the oyster shells which they have sometimes been thought to have used.[3] Supporters of the council of Chalcedon believed that in 507 unclean spirits had taken possession of the people of Alexandria and all Egypt, so that they began to bark like dogs and ate their hands and arms. In 457 the bishop of Alexandria was lynched in his cathedral while celebrating the eucharist on Maundy Thursday, and neither of his successors was able to impose himself on the patriarchal throne. More relaxed views prevailed in Syria, but even here successive patriarchs of Antioch were murdered, deposed and banished. Some scholars have seen the enthusiastic acceptance of Monophysitism in Egypt and Syria as an expression of national identity *vis-à-vis* Constantinople. There is no need to accept this hypothesis, but there

3. As by Gibbon, in a memorable passage (*The History of the Decline and Fall of the Roman Empire* ed. J.B. Bury 5 London 1898 p. 110).

can be no doubt that Egypt, in particular, was a region to be treated with care.

Indeed, Egypt was an exasperating land. Its capital, the mighty city of Alexandria, had been founded by Alexander the Great in 331 BC on a site ideally located for trade, for it stood at the junction of routes linking the Mediterranean, the Indian Ocean and large parts of Africa. Roughly midway between Sri Lanka, then a key trading centre, and Britain, it was home to such people as the merchant Kosmas Indicopleustes, who sailed down the Red Sea and claimed to have gone as far as Sri Lanka. It was certainly better located for trade than Constantinople, which Alexandrians could look down on as a young upstart. Their city was famous for its imposing buildings, while the great lighthouse on the island of Pharos was one of the wonders of the world. A large and alert Jewish community lived there, it being in Alexandria that the Septuagint, the standard translation of the Old Testament into Greek, had been prepared, while the city produced an unfailing stream of Christian heresies. But Egypt owed its importance in the time of Justinian to another reason. The inhabitants of Constantinople, a large city in the midst of fairly poor agricultural land, depended on imported grain. Bread was then the basic food of the Mediterranean region to a far greater extent than today, and the average person probably ate several pounds of it each day. So it was that the harvests which were so bountiful along the Nile valley supplied the want of the royal city. Every year the 'happy shipment' of grain saw perhaps a tenth of the Egyptian crop conveyed to the docks of Constantinople, in sufficient quantity, it has been estimated, to have fed 600 000 people.[4]

By and large, the government was prepared to let Egypt go its own way as long as the grain shipments and taxes were forthcoming. No emperor since Diocletian had set foot there, and in the remarkably short section devoted to Egypt in his *Buildings*, Procopius only gives Justinian credit for one work; significantly, it was to do with the storage of grain (6.1.1–5). As far as we can tell from the surviving fragmentary evidence, the administration was almost entirely conducted by native Egyptian landowners at all levels except for the topmost office, that of praefectus augustalis. Power was in the hands of

4.   A.H.M. Jones *The Later Roman Empire 284–602* Oxford 1964 p. 698.

wealthy, self-regarding landowners such as the egregiously named Fl. Marianus Michaelius Gabrielius Sergius Bacchus Narses Conon Anastasius Domninus Theodorus Callinicus. Another Egyptian, Fl. Ioannes Theodorus Menas Chnoubammon Horion Hephaestus, went to Constantinople where it was believed that he was a descendent of Hephaestus, the first king of Egypt. The confident names betray no sign of the breakdown of the traditional system of Roman names which was then occurring in Italy, where increasingly people were being known by just one name. The native-born heads of the Egyptian church, the patriarchs of Alexandria, were feared for their ambition, and referred to as pharaohs by others. While the adoption of Christianity had given Egypt a religion held in common with the rest of the empire, the concomitant rise of the Coptic language meant that for the Egyptians, as for the Armenians and Goths, Christianity came to encourage a specifically local form of written culture. But what sane emperor would wish to intervene in the ecclesiastical affairs of Egypt? Precedents were not encouraging: in the fourth century emperors had deposed and banished the intransigent patriarch Athanasius, the great opponent of the teaching of Arius, five times, but he had the last laugh. Surely it was best to have as little as possible to do with Egypt.

Justinian found himself in a difficult position. There were good reasons for generosity towards the Monophysites, particularly those of Egypt. Yet any move towards weakening the formulations of the council of Chalcedon would have been contrary to his personal inclinations and, conceivably, would bring the wrath of God on the empire. Further, such a move would be strongly opposed. From the time of pope Leo the Great the papacy had been unswervingly committed to the defence of the Chalcedonian position, and the entire western church was of one mind, even if it was not an educated mind. The success of the wars in the West made western opinion less easy for Justinian to ignore. There were also influential circles in Constantinople committed to the council of Chalcedon, among which the family of Juliana Anicia was prominent. Yet the family of the former emperor Anastasius, which retained a degree of influence throughout the reign of Justinian, was of the contrary persuasion, as was the empress. It was small wonder that Justinian's policy, while firm in its principles, tended to wobble in its execution. The imposition of a formula which sought to mediate between different theological understandings, the appointment of apparently pliable figures to high office in the church, the kidnapping and browbeating of a pope and the calling of an ecumenical council were among the expedients Justinian adopted. Ultimately, all were in vain.

. . .

THE SEARCH FOR COMPROMISE

In 482 Zeno, advised by the patriarch Acacius, issued his Henotikon which attempted to solve the matter by observing that there is in Christ one person. But the pope reacted in a hostile fashion, and the Acacian schism between the churches of Rome and Constantinople began. Not for the last time, an imperial manoeuvre aimed at reconciliation was a cause of division. The following emperor, Anastasius, was a Monophysite sympathizer, and a tide began to flow which led to the most competent theologian among the Monophysites, Severus, becoming patriarch of Antioch in 512. But the coming to power in 518 of Justin, a staunch adherent of the council of Chalcedon, was a triumph for that side. In the following year communion with the church of Rome was re-established, and the emperors Zeno and Anastasius anathematized. Before long Monophysite bishops were being deposed. Some found their way to Egypt, where no attempt was made to move against them. Among them was Severus, who found it impossible to hold his ground in Antioch.

Nevertheless, the new government's actions were not entirely to papal liking. In September 518 Justinian wrote an imperious letter to pope Hormisdas informing him that he was anticipating the pope's arrival in Constantinople without any delay, an ominous straw in the wind, but Hormisdas stayed in Rome. The patriarch of Constantinople used language in his dealings with the pope which was calculated to enhance the standing of his see, and he seems to have been the first occupant of it to have adopted the title 'ecumenical patriarch', the use of which was to create problems in relations between the sees of Rome and Constantinople towards the end of the century. Further, contrary to papal hopes, the government did not go out of its way to antagonize Monophysite opinion, refusing to depose all the bishops to whom Rome objected.

To make matters worse, Justinian became aware of a formula which he hoped would reconcile the adherents of the council of Chalcedon with the Monophysites: 'one of the Trinity suffered in the flesh'. This doctrine, technically termed Theopaschitism (from the Greek for 'God suffered'), may seem tendentious, but arguably it is inherent in the Nicene creed, given its teaching that 'Jesus Christ ... very God of very God ... became man and was crucified'. Justinian took these words at face value: the one who was 'very God' was the one who was crucified, for when the creed spoke of his becoming man it did not mean that he stopped being one thing and was turned into something else, but rather that he remained God when he assumed humanity. But not all were convinced. When Justinian put pressure on pope Hormisdas to accept the formula, the pope equivocated for as long as he could before coming down against it. Not for the last time, however, Justinian decided to proceed regardless of what Hormisdas or anyone else thought.

In 532 he arranged for conversations to be held in the royal city between Chalcedonian and Monophysite theologians. Their dialogue had no lasting result, and was chiefly noteworthy for the latter group producing a work which they said had been written by Dionysios the Areopagite, an Athenian converted by S Paul. This is a very early reference to the writings of the unknown Neoplatonist scholars now referred to as the pseudo-Dionysios. Its authenticity was shrewdly queried by the chairperson of the discussions, bishop Hypatius of Ephesos, who was certainly correct to see it as spurious. But Justinian was sufficiently encouraged by the meeting to issue an edict in the following year addressed to the inhabitants of thirteen cities and towns. None of them was in Egypt, however; it is clear that Justinian's strategy was to bring the supporters of Chalcedonian to a position from which reconciliation with the Monophysites would be possible. While the edict reaffirmed adherence to the council of Chalcedon and condemned the teachings of Nestorios and Eutyches, it made no mention of the nature or natures of Christ, and could therefore be said to have tiptoed around the central issue which divided Chalcedonians and Monophysites. A team was sent to Rome, led by bishop Hypatius. The pope, John II, had recently assumed office in difficult circumstances, and he was not the man to make difficulties. The generous gifts which Justinian prudently sent may have made the imperial argument seem more compelling. In any case, John retreated from the ground Hormisdas had occupied, and accepted a form of words remarkably close to a Theopaschite position. A fulsome exchange of correspondence took place between emperor and pope, which Justinian placed towards the beginning of the Codex, promulgated in November 534. His plans were maturing well.

In June 535 a new patriarch of Constantinople, Anthemius, was appointed. A famous ascetic, who was said never to have eaten bread or drunk wine, he had been one of the Chalcedonian theologians in the discussions of 532, but before long he revealed himself as a Monophysite. A few months earlier the patriarch of Alexandria had died, and his replacement, Theodosius, was a friend of Severus. People thought that the hand of Theodora could be detected behind both appointments. She certainly gave help when Theodosius found it difficult to secure his position: 6000 troops commanded by Narses were despatched to Alexandria. Oddly enough this may have weakened the position of Theodosius, who could now be seen as an imperial lackey. But when the veteran Severus turned up in Constantinople it must have seemed that the triumph of an imperially sponsored moderate line was at hand.

Against this background pope Agapetus, who had succeeded John in May 535, arrived in Constantinople in late February or early March 536. As we have seen, he had been sent to conduct an embassy on behalf of the Ostrogoth Theodahad, but he had his own agenda, and was determined to strike at recent developments. The pope declined to enter into communion with the patriarch, and before long not only Justinian but also Theodora, usually an ally of Monophysite clergy, had turned against him.[5] Anthemius was deposed and Agapetus had the satisfaction of consecrating his successor, Menas. Having achieved nothing on Theodahad's behalf, Agapetus was in no hurry to return home, and died in Constantinople in April. Not all mourned him. The pope's sojourn in the royal city had given no joy to the Monophysites. They later recalled that his entrance had been accompanied

5.   W. Ensslin, 'Papst Agapet I und Kaiser Justinian I.' *Historisches Jahrbuch* 77 1958: 459–66 at 462 n. 30. But I know of no study which brings out the complexities of the mission of Agapetus.

by an earthquake and a dimming of the sun and moon, while his death was attributed to a curse from a Monophysite holy man: the pope's tongue grew so long that it hung down over his breast, and after suffering for several days he died. Such stories bear the hallmarks of emanating from a persecuted community, and they were easily told, for these events marked the beginning of a decline in the fortunes of the Monophysites.

Later in the year a council was held which excommunicated and banished Severus and Anthemius, and ordered that books written by the former were to be burned. He retreated to the Egyptian desert where he died a few years later; a story was told that as he lay dying his doctors tried to persuade him to take a bath, but the holy man replied that since promising Christ that he would become a monk he had never looked on his body, and when he was finally prevailed upon to bathe it was with his clothes on. Anthimius, on the other hand, was able to remain in the royal city, merely retiring to a palace belonging to Theodora. Theodosius, the patriarch of Alexandria who had owed his elevation the preceding year to Justinian, was summoned to Constantinople, where he was lodged in the palace of Hormisdas and deprived of his see. His replacement, the monk Paul, was the first supporter of the council of Chalcedon to be patriarch of Alexandria for over 50 years, and had a hard road in front of him. It was thought prudent to have him consecrated in Constantinople before he set out for his see, which he was not to occupy for long. In 539 Rhodon, the augustal prefect, and he were accused of being responsible for the murder of the deacon who controlled the finances of the diocese. Justinian sent the patrician Liberius to step into Rhodon's shoes and investigate the matter at first hand. Rhodon was sent to Constantinople and beheaded, while Paul, after proceedings in which Pelagius, a Roman deacon, had been involved, was deposed and replaced by Zoilus. Meanwhile, Ephrem, an adherent of the council of Chalcedon was appointed patriarch of Antioch. So it was that in territories where many or most of the people were Monophysites there came into being a 'Melchite' church. The name, which comes from the same root as that of the biblical character Melchizedek, means 'royal', and it was applied to church officials who followed the emperor's line, but it is semitic. The people who used it were Monophysites who came to see the emperor's church as different from their own.

There can be no mistaking the attitude Monophysites came to adopt towards Justinian:

> This very pit of the abyss was opened again in the days of the emperor Justinian. Again that soul-destroying madness, again the torrents of lawlessness flowed in their ravines to shake the house of the faithful.[6]

But Christian groups have frequently flourished in the midst of persecution. As early as 529/530 the Monophysite bishop John of Tella, a town in east Syria, had begun to ordain to the diaconate and priesthood men from distant regions who came to him with testimonials. This was only the beginning. In 541 Justinian's Arab ally Harith the Ghassanid asked Theodora to supply him with Monophysite bishops. As Theodosius, latterly patriarch of Alexandria, was living in the royal city, it was an easy matter for him to consecrate two bishops. One of these, Theodore, was to be based at Bostra, and the other, James, was notionally bishop of Edessa. Before long James equipped himself with two assistant bishops, so that it was possible for him to consecrate additional bishops in a canonically regular fashion. He travelled incognito, and came to be called Bar 'Addai, 'the rag', from the old clothes he wore to escape detection. The underground activities of this energetic figure resulted in what contemporaries believed was the ordination of 100 000 men to the priesthood and the formation of a Monophysite hierarchy outside Egypt. The success of his strategy is evident from the survival to this day of the 'Jacobite' church which takes its name from him. But considered from the point of view of the unity of Christians, his work was disruptive. Hitherto there had been in each town one bishop, whether a supporter or an opponent of the council of Chalcedon; hereafter, in many towns there would be two bishops, one Melchite and the other Jacobite. Instead of one church within which there were two rival points of view, James created a situation in which there would be two churches.

Meanwhile, Justinian was still considering how to bring

---

6. Trans. K.H. Kuhn, 'A panegyric on Apollo archimandrite of the monastery of Isaac, by Stephen bishop of Heracleopeolis Magna', in *Corpus Scriptorum Christianorum Orientalium* 395 (=*Scriptores Coptici* 40f), 10f. For the 'pit of the abyss' cf. Rev 9:1.

about unity between the adherents and opponents of the council of Chalcedon, and took advice from bishop Theodore Ascidas of Caesarea. He was a controversial figure, for he was an enthusiastic supporter of the doctrines of Origen, a theologian of the third century many of whose ideas were generally held to be unorthodox.[7] Having taken counsel, in 543 or 544 Justinian published an edict which anathematized the person and works of bishop Theodore of Mopsuestia, some of the writings of bishop Theodoret of Cyrrhus, and a letter of bishop Ibas of Edessa. The edict has not survived, but the three anathemas it presumably contained were termed the Three Chapters.[8] However, this term quickly changed its meaning, and came to be understood as referring not to the propositions of the lost edict but to the person and bodies of work which it anathematized. The three condemned theologians were writers of the fifth century who were held to be of Nestorianizing tendency, and so their condemnation could be taken as a conciliatory gesture towards Monophysite opinion. As with his Theopaschite manoeuvre, Justinian was trying to find common ground. But Theodore had died in communion with the church, while Theodoret and Ibas, although their teachings had come under criticism, were accepted by the council of Chalcedon, so a move against them could be construed as an indirect attack on Chalcedon. Justinian was playing with fire.

⁃ The issuing of the edict was a high-handed act. As so often, Justinian was going his own way; it does not seem to have crossed his mind to seek the opinion of a church council, the pope, or the patriarch of Constantinople. Nevertheless, he made it clear that he expected the leaders of the church to condemn the Three Chapters. The patriarchs of Alexandria, Antioch and Jerusalem were prevailed upon to sign the document which Justinian placed before them, but Menas of Constantinople was only prepared to sign subject to the agreement of the Roman church. As it turned out this was not forthcoming. But Justinian was in no mood to tolerate papal opposition

7. An anti-Origenistic tendency in Justinian's policy which was evident in the 540s and 550s may have arisen from a conviction that Origenism was connected more with the important questions of Christology, or it may have represented an attempt by Theodore to cover his tracks.
8. É. Amman 'Trois chapitres (affaire des)' *Dictionairre de théologie catholique* 15 1950: 1868–1924, remains a full guide to the ensuing controversy.

to his plans, especially when it emanated from Vigilius, who owed his position to intrigues in Constantinople. On 22 November 545, not long before Totila laid siege to Rome, the pope was arrested while celebrating the feast of the martyr S Cecilia in the church dedicated to her in Trastevere. It is one of the churches in Rome closest to the Tiber, and Vigilius was easily bundled onto a ship. After spending a long time in Sicily, he arrived in Constantinople in January 547. Initially Vigilius maintained a high line, refusing to enter into communion with Menas, who had accepted the condemnations made by Justinian. But the circumstances of his elevation to the papal throne and his failure to carry out any promises he may have made to Theodora made him vulnerable to pressure, and Justinian was in no mood to compromise. In the preceding year another persecution of pagans had broken out, and the respected Phocas, whom Justinian had appointed praetorian prefect in succession to John the Cappadocian in 532, committed suicide; Justinian ordered that he was to be buried like an ass. The pope's resistance weakened. In June he resumed communion with Menas, and after taking the advice of various bishops he issued his *Iudicatum* in April 548. Addressed to Menas, it condemned the works which had not found favour with Justinian.

But two developments occurred which complicated matters. Justinian and Vigilius had reckoned without western opinion. Clerics from the West resident in Constantinople made their opposition felt, and a council of the bishops of Dacia declared Benenatus, the archbishop of Justiniana Prima, deposed. More important, however, was the response of the African church. Since its earliest days this had been a church of superabundant energies, and the Africans, who had been effectively insulated from involvement in the affairs of the universal church during the century of Vandal power, quickly began to make up for lost time. Ferrandus, a deacon of Carthage, bombarded contacts in Rome, southern Italy and Constantinople with letters arguing for a strict Chalcedonian position; among his correspondents was the Roman deacon Pelagius, later to become pope. Bishop Facundus of Hermiane wrote an enormous *Defence of the Three Chapters* addressed to Justinian which concluded by inviting him to acknowledge that he was wrong, a move not calculated to win the favour of the emperor. In 550 the African bishops met in synod and excommunicated the bishop of Rome, writing to the emperor to explain their hostility to his policy.

Justinian was quick to respond. While Benenatus continued to enjoy his office, the emperor's African opponents were summoned to Constantinople. The bishop of Carthage was exiled and replaced by a more pliable man who had hitherto been his apocrisarius in the royal city, a sequence of events closely paralleling the fall of pope Silverius, but the new appointee found it difficult to gain acceptance. Other bishops who resisted the emperor were sent into exile. Zoilus, the patriarch of Alexandria who had been installed in place of Paul, was removed from his post and replaced by a man thought to be reliable.

But Justinian had not only to confront the unexpected level of resistance to his plan. The situation was further complicated by the death of Theodora in June 548. This occurred not long after the inhabitants of Constantinople had been alarmed by a severe storm of thunder and lightning, and there may have been those who saw a connection. An African author, Victor of Tunnunna, is our only source to give a reason for her death, and he expressed himself starkly: 'The empress Theodora, an enemy of the council of Chalcedon, finished her life in a way which constituted a portent, stricken by disease throughout her body'.[9] The Latin word 'cancer', here translated 'disease', can mean cancer, but has a range of other meanings, and Victor did not necessarily mean that Theodora died of the disease now called cancer. But theologically committed authors of the period delighted in attributing gruesome deaths to those of other persuasions, which they were always ready to see as punishment, and there is no doubt that the death of Theodora was welcome to Victor, who was content to describe Monophysites as 'the faction of the empress Theodora'. She had been unpopular with the adherents of Chalcedon, such as S Sabas, an influential supporter of the council of Chalcedon in Palestine, who had refused her request to pray that she would bear Justinian a child. He contented himself with praying for the welfare of the state.

Monophysite authors, on the other hand, referred to Theodora as 'the believing queen', and clerics of their persuasion

9. Victor of Tunnunna *Chron. s.a.* 549.2 (ed. Th. Mommsen, *Monumenta Germaniae Historica Auctores Antiquissimi* 11).

who turned up in Constantinople could count on being made welcome by her. Some of them were men of wild eccentricity, such as Mare the solitary, who, on being presented by her with a hundredweight of gold, threw the bag away as if it were full of light apples. Antics of this kind endeared ascetics to their patrons, and Mare was given the use of a villa outside the city, where so many important people visited him that robbers concluded he was receiving gold. At the end of his life, when he was informed by God that he would shortly die from the plague, Mare was able to use his contacts in the palace to have his tomb built in advance. Theodora was estimated to have sheltered 500 Monophysite clerics in a palace where holy men continually gave themselves up to vigils, fasts and prayers. After his fall in 536 the patriarch Anthemius had been hidden by Theodora in her palace, and it was believed that Justinian only became aware of this after his wife died. She also supported Monophysite clergy elsewhere: on the island of Chios, for example, she built a refuge for monks where banished bishops could live, while it was estimated that she maintained some 300 clerics at a fortress in Thrace. Theophanes, writing early in the ninth century, believed that she had been responsible for the reconciliation between Vigilius and Menas in June 548, and a wide variety of Monophysite texts credit her with having exerted a wholesome influence over Justinian.[10] When Justinian determined to see to the conversion of the Nubians to Christianity, she was credited with bringing it about that, contrary to his plan, a team of Monophysite missionaries was first in the field.

It is hard to know how to interpret this. Perhaps Theodora brazenly defied her husband by pursuing policies contradictory to his. On the other hand, it is possible that the wily Justinian was making use of his wife to keep doors open to the Monophysites, and that the couple merely pretended to disagree (cf. Procopius *Secret History* 10.14f). In any case, the vigour of the western response to his policies, together with the death of Theodora, weakened the Monophysite cause in

10. See for example A. Campagnano 'Monaci egiziani fra V e VI secolo' *Vetera Christianorum* 15 1978: 223–46; *History of the Patriarchs of the Coptic Church of Alexandria* 2 ed. and trans. B. Evetts *Patrologia Orientalis* 1/4, 460; John of Ephesus *Lives of the Eastern Saints* ed. and trans. E.W. Brooks *Patrologia Orientalis* 17/1, 18/4, 19/2, *passim*.

a game which Justinian found himself playing for increasingly high stakes. But it was not in his nature to admit defeat. If his attempt to use the pope to bring about concord between warring theological positions had failed, there remained the possibility of placing the matter before an ecumenical council, as earlier emperors had done with important issues.

. . .

AN ECUMENICAL COUNCIL AND ITS AFTERMATH

Justinian prepared the ground by issuing, in July 551, a carefully argued edict containing thirteen anathemas.[11] Vigilius, who had not been consulted, fled from the palace where he had been staying to S Peter's church at the Hormisdas palace, from which, in the following month, he excommunicated Menas again. Justinian sent troops to arrest the pope, but he grabbed the altar and could not be removed from the church. The next day he was visited by a high-powered delegation comprised entirely of Latin speakers. Its members were Belisarius, to whose actions Vigilius may have felt he owed his accession to the papal throne, Cethegus, the prominent senator who had fled to the royal city a few years earlier, Peter the patrician, a diplomat with Italian experience, and Justin, the emperor's nephew. They took an oath that Vigilius would be unharmed if he returned to his old quarters, whereupon he made his way back. But he was still marginal to the life of the city. When the church of S Eirene across the Golden Horn was dedicated in September, it was the patriarch of Alexandria who sat with Menas in the imperial carriage. Vigilius remained unhappy, and on the night before Christmas Eve in 551 he fled across the Bosphorus to the church of S Euphemia. The choice of refuge was significant, for it was the church where the council of Chalcedon had met just a one hundred years earlier. On 28 January 552 Belisarius again waited on the pope with a group sent by Justinian, but it was some months before Vigilius returned to Constantinople.

Other developments worked in Justinian's favour. In August 552 Menas, the patriarch of Constantinople, died; before he was buried his successor had been enthroned. Eutychius, the son of one of Belisarius' officers, was a monk who was in

11. The edict is one of the documents translated by Kenneth P. Wesche *The Person of Christ the Christology of Emperor Justinian* Crestwood NY 1991.

Constantinople representing the sick bishop of Amesia, and the emperor was sure he would not let him down. Further, the success of Narses in Italy meant that there was less need for Justinian to be wary of offending Italian opinion.

So it was that Justinian summoned a great council, which is regarded to this day as the fifth of the ecumenical councils of the church, the second among them to have been held in Constantinople. It held its first meeting on 5 May 553. The biographer of Eutychius represented the council as a new Pentecost, bishops having come to Constantinople, which he described as the new Jerusalem, from every nation, but of the 145 bishops who attended very few were from the West.[12] Vigilius declined invitations to join them, preferring to sulk nearby. Justinian refrained from attending the meetings of the council, despite the precedents set by earlier emperors, but a letter which was read at its first session made his wishes clear, and its meetings took place in the complex of Hagia Sophia, disquietingly close to the palace. On 14 May Vigilius produced a document which made some concessions to Justinian's demands, but it was not enough, and late in the month Justinian played his trump card. The quaestor Constantine told the council that Justinian had evidence that the pope had agreed to condemn the Three Chapters, including one document in his own handwriting and another which bore his signature. Vigilius now payed the penalty for his earlier temporizing. Justinian proposed to the council that the name of the pope be struck from the diptychs, the lists of the names of hierarchs in the communion of the church proclaimed during the eucharist, and this was agreed to. There was little left for the bishops to do. At its last session on 2 June the council affirmed the council of Chalcedon, but it also accepted the validity of the formula of Cyril of Alexandria, 'one nature incarnate of God the Word', an ambiguous phrase which could certainly be understood in a Monophysite sense. The Three Chapters and teachings of Origen and his followers were condemned in accordance with Justinian's wishes.

The pope had been humiliated. Still in Constantinople, in December he wrote to Eutychius saying that he had changed

---

12. E. Chrysos *Die Bischofslisten des V. Ökumenischen Konzils (553)* Bonn 1966. On the council as a new Pentecost, *Vita Eutychii* 4.27 (*Patrologia Graeca* 86:2305), with reference to Acts 2:5.

his mind: after all, if S Augustine had written a book of Retractions, he was in good company in renouncing an erroneous opinion! He explained that he had come to see that the Three Chapters should be condemned. It may be that news of the successes of Narses in Italy had encouraged Vigilius to trim his sails. But Justinian wanted more than this, and in February 554 the pope issued another document explicitly accepting the decrees of the council. It was a disingenuous piece, claiming, for example, that the letter of Ibas read at the council of Chalcedon was not authentic, but it was enough to gain him freedom. In the following year Vigilius left for Rome, but had only reached Sicily when he died. His body was taken to Rome, where it was buried not in S Peter's but outside the walls of the city.

His successor, Pelagius, was a man of varied experience. He had negotiated with Totila in Rome but was well known in Constantinople, having previously acted as Justinian's agent in dealing with a scandal in the church of Alexandria, and he played a complex role in the dealings of popes with Justinian and Theodora. He had initially been a supporter of the Three Chapters and taken a firmer stand than Vigilius, but the possibility of further preferment proved stronger than his principles, and Pelagius soon became an enthusiastic supporter of Justinian's line. His docility was rewarded.

Pelagius, however, was by no means the only cleric of the time to owe promotion to Justinian. The middle of the sixth century saw imperial involvement in appointments to important sees on a scale for which church history offered no precedent. On one occasion pope Vigilius had celebrated the liturgy in Hagia Sophia with the patriarchs of Constantinople, Alexandria and Antioch. The mood around the altar must have been one of tension, but it may have occurred to the minds of some of the participants how much their careers owed to the patronage of Justinian. Vigilius had been appointed pope while Silverius was alive, just as Apollinaris had become patriarch of Alexandria while Zoilus lived, an irregularity which even evoked a protest from the usually complaisant Vigilius, who doubtless forgot how he had come to be pope. In such company the accession of Eutychius of Constantinople, whom Justinian had appointed to his see while the body of his predecessor lay in the cathedral, had been dignified. The occupants of other important sees similarly owed their preferment to Justinian: Primosus of Carthage had been appointed after the sacking of Reparatus, Vitalis of Milan had been appointed to his see after the death of the previous occupant in 552, and Maximianus of Ravenna had been appointed while in the royal city.

Justinian's policy of interference did not, however, prove to be an effective one. When Pelagius arrived in Rome as the nominee of the emperor only two bishops could be found who were prepared to consecrate him, and it was believed among the people that he had been a party to the death of Vigilius. In 556 he issued a profession of faith addressed to the whole Christian people, which marked a wholesale retreat from the position Justinian had taken: by its acceptance of four ecumenical councils it tacitly denied the ecumenical status of the council of Constantinople, by affirming the orthodoxy of Ibas and Theodoret it contradicted their condemnation by the council, and by accepting the letters of popes as far as Agapetus it passed over Vigilius in silence. Pelagius was prepared to abandon the line taken by his imperial patron, but this was not enough to win him the support of the West. In northern Italy the bishops of Milan and Aquileia withdrew from communion with the see of Rome, and refused to be placated. Pelagius, who had picked up some of Justinian's ways, hoped the recalcitrant pair could be arrested and shipped to Constantinople, but Narses refused to co-operate. The schism over the Three Chapters which began in the pontificate of Pelagius was to last until the end of the seventh century.

One of the Italians who was in Constantinople for the greater part if not the whole of pope Vigilius' stay there was Cassiodorus. As we have seen, in the 530s he had hoped to found a centre for Christian studies in Rome after the pattern of an institution in Nisibis, a city of the Syrians. It is true that Cassiodorus states that instruction there was given to Jews (Hebreis), but this may be a conventional expression for 'Nestorians'.[13] One of the most boring theological texts ever

13. G. Fiaccadori 'Cassiodorus and the school of Nisibis' *Dumbarton Oaks Papers* 39 1985: 135–7 argues for a school of Nestorians. It has occurred to me to wonder whether Cassiodorus only came to know of the school at Nisibis while he was in Constantinople, for the words 'sicut . . . exponi' of *Institutiones* 1 praef. 1 (cited above, ch. 4 n. 17, 3.8–10: ed. R.A.B. Mynors, Oxford 1937) do not necessarily reflect knowledge he had during the 530s. If he only came to know of the school while in the royal city, perhaps he owed his information to Junillus.

written is the short *Institutes* composed by an African, Junillus, whom Justinian appointed to the office of quaestor in succession to Tribonian in 541/542. At the beginning of the work, which he addressed to the African bishop Primasius at a time when the latter was in Constantinople, Junillus explains that he had benefitted from the teaching of a certain Paul, a Persian who had been educated in the school of the Syrians at Nisibis, a place where the divine law was transmitted by teachers who taught in public, just as the worldly subjects of grammar and rhetoric were transmitted in areas with which he was himself familiar. But Paul was himself a tributary to another scriptural scholar, Theodore of Mopsuestia, one of Justinian's *bêtes noires*.

Presumably Cassiodorus was familiar with the circles in which Justinian's theological antagonist Junillus moved. An exposition of the Psalms on which he was working during the time Vigilius was in Constantinople contains frequent references to the two natures of Christ. Cassiodorus once breaks into a citation of the council of Chalcedon, and on another occasion refers to the two natures in Chalcedonian language as having been 'unmixed, unchanged, undivided and not separated'. The sentiments are unexceptionable, but suggest a degree of dogmatic concern not always found in works of scriptural commentary. Cassiodorus also refers to two books on the two natures of Christ 'which the venerable bishop Facundus, who destroys heretics with penetrating acuteness, recently wrote to the *princeps* Justinian', and goes on to cite a definition of a heretic provided by 'one of the fathers', who seems to have been Justinian's enemy Primasius.[14] In his *Institutiones* Cassiodorus recommended the work of Primasius on the Apocalypse and his work *Quid faciat hereticum*; elsewhere he recommended among introductory works on the Bible that by Junillus. A final pointer to Cassiodorus' attitude to Justinian's activities is his having an Ecclesiastical History prepared on the basis of translations from three Greek authors, one of whom was Theodoret of Cyrrhus. Cassiodorus, then, may be seen as having taken a decidedly cool attitude to Justinian's theological activities. He consistently wrote in favour of the council of Chalcedon, which some felt had been

---

14. *Expositio in psalmam* 138.548–52, 560–4 (=*Corpus Christianorum Series Latina* 98:1255).

endangered by the council of 553, and Justinian's theological opponents.

Nor did Justinian carry the day in Africa. It is from an African source that we learn that immediately after the council of 553 an earthquake rocked Constantinople. In the early 560s the archdeacon Liberatus of Carthage wrote his *Breviarium* to provide the background to the entire controversy, starting with the forerunners to Nestorios. In his preface he lists among his sources an Ecclesiastical History recently translated out of Greek into Latin, which must be the Historia Tripartita for which Cassiodorus had been responsible, and the work is unsympathetic to Justinian. Another hostile African, the chronicler Victor of Tunnunna, finished writing his Chronicle in 565/566, and it contains no sign of any softening towards the emperor.

In Spain as well the line taken by Justinian was not popular. Writing in the early seventh century, Isidore of Seville could assert that there had been four 'venerable synods' held by the church, implicitly denying the claims of the council of 553 to ecumenicity, that the list of Roman legislators concludes with Theodosius, implicitly denying the importance of Justinian's work in this field, and that the sending of the Byzantine expedition to Spain in 552 was at the behest of an illegitimate power. In his work on famous men, Isidore is complimentary about some of the African opponents of Justinian, and an anonymous Spanish author of the seventh century made the drift of the original explicit by inserting additional material critical of the emperor.[15]

So it is that in the three areas of the West which were the subjects of invasion by Justinian there is good reason for believing that the emperor came to be regarded in a bad light. Indeed, the only major see in these territories which supported Justinian's theological line was Ravenna. As we have seen its bishop, Maximianus, was an imperial appointee, and other kinds of evidence suggest that his see was the recipient of a good deal of imperial largesse: the grant of a forest in Istria, the bestowing of the title 'archbishop' on its incumbent, and the expansion of his power over other churches all point

15. This work must be consulted in the edition of C.C. Merino, *El 'De viris illustris' de Isidoro de Sevilla Estudio y edicion critica* Salamanca 1964 (=*Theses et studia philologica salmanticensia* XII).

in this direction.[16] Even in Gaul there was rumbling discontent which tactful measures on the part of pope Pelagius were not able to overcome. Bishop Nicetius of Trier wrote a blunt letter to Justinian informing him that all Italy, the whole of Africa, Spain and Gaul together grieved over him and anathematized him, and asked the rhetorical question 'Oh sweet Justinian of ours, who had deceived you?'[17] It is hard to imagine the emperor losing any sleep over this letter from a backwoods bishop outside the empire. But Nicetius' estimate of the extent of western opposition to Justinian's religious policies, which is only a little exaggerated, encourages one to speculate why the opposition developed on the scale it did. It is hard to credit the condemnation of three scholars almost unknown in the West with having excited passions of this depth, and one wonders whether we have here another symptom of a deep unease in the West at the outcome of the wars Justinian had launched there.

If this was not enough, the council of 553 had totally failed in its purpose of reconciling the opponents of the council of Chalcedon with its supporters. Its decrees seem to have left Monophysite opinion unmoved, and the progress towards reconciliation which was under way early in the 530s was stone dead. Only in the ecumenical climate of the late twentieth century have Orthodox and Monophysite theologians agreed to put behind them the problems caused by the definition of the council of Chalcedon. Further, Justinian's years of effort not only failed to bring about reconciliation between Chalcedonians and Monophysites, but occasioned a division among the former which was not quickly overcome. His efforts not only failed, but backfired. Just as the East and West came to feel further apart thanks to Justinian's wars, so did his ecclesiastical policies contribute to a distancing between the Christian groups he sought to bring together.

16. See the important study by T.S. Brown, 'The Church of Ravenna and the imperial administration in the seventh century' *English Historical Review* 94 1979: 1–28. The rise of the bishops of Ravenna and Justiniana Prima, and generous treatment which the bishop of Carthage received from Justinian, suggest a policy of granting churches a status linked with the importance of their respective towns within the political framework of the empire. Such a principle would have been disastrous for the see of Rome.

17. *Monumenta Germaniae Historica Epistolae* 3:118f. (*Epistolae Austrasicae*, ed. W. Gundlach).

. . .

MISSIONARY ENTERPRISE

But it would be a mistake to conclude that Justinian's involvement in church affairs was a total failure. In one area, Justinian's policy concerning the church worked very well, for it was in his reign and that of his uncle Justin that a great flowering of Byzantine missionary activity occurred.[18]

We have already seen how Justinian had sponsored the preaching activities of John of Ephesos in Asia Minor. But he was more interested in the conversion of people outside the empire. One group to be converted were the Abasgi, who lived on the eastern coast of the Black Sea. Justinian built them a church dedicated to the Theotokos and sent clergy, and put pressure on them to cease making eunuchs of attractive boys.[19] Early in his reign he was sponsor to Grepes, the king of the Heruls, at his baptism. In about 542 missionaries were sent to Nubia, the land to the south of Egypt. Christian influences had been at work there for some time, and in about 535 a general, acting on orders from Justinian, destroyed the pagan shrines. Before long, plans to convert the Nubians were under way, but as we have seen, Justinian and Theodora were thought to have sent rival teams of evangelists, respectively orthodox and Monophysite. Contemporaries believed the success of the latter was due to the skulduggery of the empress, who threatened the duke of the Thebaid with the loss of his head if her missionaries were not the first to arrive. It is hard to know how seriously to take this story, but the conversion of the Nubians proceeded.

It would be naive, however, to think of the expansion of Christianity under imperial auspices as nothing more than a stage in the history of the triumphal march of Christianity across medieval history. The diffusion of Christianity is one of the most significant things to have occurred in the middle ages, and the missionary can stand with the knight and the merchant as an agent in the spread of western European and

18. See in general I. Engelhardt *Mission und Politik in Byzanz Ein Beitrag zur Strukturanalyse byzantinischer Mission zur Zeit Justins und Justinians* Munich 1974, comprehensive if rather schematic.
19. The Abasgi had sold the eunuchs to the Romans. In 558 Justinian issued a novel (no. 142) seeking to suppress the making of eunuchs within the empire, a practice which may have become more common following the conversion of the Abasgi.

Byzantine influence in this period. But the different relationships between ecclesiastical and secular power which obtained in the medieval west and east led to their diffusing Christianity by different means. In the west the missionaries who found their way to such lands as England and Germany usually did so under papal, or at any rate ecclesiastical, auspices. But in the east the process of conversion tended to occur under the aegis of the state, and so could easily be harnessed for the political purposes of the empire.

A good example of this is the conversion of a Hunnish ruler, Grod (John Malalas 431f). In 528 he came to Constantinople, was baptized, with Justinian himself being his sponsor, and returned home laden with gifts. His base was the Crimean city of Bosporus, where he was expected to act in support of Roman interests. But he proved too enthusiastic a Christian. He ordered that the idols of silver and electrum were to be melted down, whereupon the pagans killed him and the garrison which guarded the city. Justinian mounted an expedition against the murderers of his ally, part of which proceeded by sea and part by land, making the difficult march around the Black Sea coast. The Huns fled, and Bosporus remained under Roman power.

The coming of Christianity to another people, the Tzani, is also interesting from this point of view. Procopius explains that, as a result of the activities of the general Sittas, Theodora's brother-in-law, they changed their way of living so as to be more gentle, signed up for service with the Roman forces, and abandoned their own way of thinking for the more pious one of the Christians (*Wars* 1.15.25). Elsewhere he provides details of the package of which Christianity was a part: roads were improved to make the Tzani more open to external influences, and fortresses manned by Romans were built in their territory (*Buildings* 3.6.9–13). So it was that they came to prefer toilless servitude to dangerous liberty.[20] Justinian was using methods remarkably similar to those by which western influence is transmitted to third world countries today. Before long the Armenians were complaining to Khusrau that Justinian had made slaves of the hitherto independent Tzani, having set a Roman ruler over their king (*Wars* 2.3.39), and indeed the preface to Justinian's first novel, issued in 535, refers to the Tzani as for the first time being able to be considered among the subjects of the Romans.

It is therefore possible to see the expansion of Christianity as part of a process we would now term imperialism.[21] Justinian is an early example of a tradition which was to remain potent for much of the history of the Byzantine empire and beyond, and the empire was later to derive great benefit from the application of this aspect of his religious policy. But another point deserves emphasis. One cannot help but notice that the bulk of these activities occurred within a few years of Justinian's coming to power. Indeed, they occurred at about the time he concluded his alliance with Harith, the Ghassanid Arab, and, as we shall see, at about the time when he sent an ambassador to distant Axum. This, of course, constitutes further evidence, of an indirect kind, for interpreting his overtly evangelistic activities in a somewhat sinister light, as having been in part politically motivated. It also gives us yet more reason for judging the opening years of his reign to have been a time of powerful initiatives in the most diverse fields. Time would tell whether Justinian would prove capable of keeping so many balls in the air at once.

20. (*opposite*) *Buildings* 3.6.6 (ed. and trans. H.B. Dewing, London 1914–1940), with which compare Milton:

nations grown corrupt
And by their vices brought to servitude
Then to love Bondage more then Liberty
(*Samson Agonistes* 268–70), and

Preferring
Hard liberty before the easie yoke
Of servile pomp (*Paradise Lost* 2.255–7).

21. Compare the words John of Nikiu attributes to a group of Lazi who came before Justinian: 'We wish thee to make us Christians like thyself, and we shall then be subjects of the Roman empire' (*Chronicle*, trans. R.H. Charles, London 1916, 90.37).

Chapter 6

THE NORTH

The boom which has occurred in the study of Byzantine history over the last few decades has made historians far more prepared to give due weight to the role of the empire in late antiquity and the early middle ages. Yet this new emphasis has meant an eastward shift in a perspective of which the centre of gravity still remains firmly centred on the Mediterranean. Of course there are good grounds for adopting such a perspective, which was that of contemporaries. It is well caught in a large mosaic map which was installed on a pavement at Mabada in Jordan, probably in the second half of the sixth century. The part of the map which survives includes a fascinating depiction of some of the buildings of Jerusalem, Justinian's Nea Church among them, although in its original form the work must have covered a block of territory extending approximately from Thebes in Egypt to Damascus, if not beyond. But the difference in direction between the coastlines of Palestine and Egypt is largely smoothed out, which suggests that the point of observation for each coast is the Mediterranean.[1] Similarly, when a writer in Gaul drew up a list of twenty noble cities of the Roman world late in the fourth century, half of them lay on the Mediterranean coast, while the remainder were all close to a sea or on major rivers.[2] In the ancient world political, commercial and ecclesiastical power was concentrated on coastal cities, which prospered

1.   O.A.W. Dilke *Greek and Roman Maps* Ithaca NY 1985 pp. 151f (not accurate in all respects).
2.   Ausonius *Ordo urbium nobilium* (ed. and trans. H.G.E. White, London 1919).

144

thanks to the wealth and human talent transferred to them from their hinterlands. Roman and Byzantine political history is full of men, such as Zeno, Justin and Justinian, who came from a province to find their fortune in the capital, and for every one who succeeded there must have been hundreds who failed. So it was that when the inhabitants of the empire thought about its geographical extent it was natural for them to envisage it as a great expanse of land lying around the Mediterranean.[3] And Justinian's wars in the West, rarely fought far from the coast, strengthened the Mediterranean axis of the empire.

Yet inland areas persisted in forcing themselves onto the attention of the state. Although Justinian's legislation immediately after the stunningly quick victory over the Vandals bespeaks a confidence that all of Africa had been successfully reintegrated into the empire, as it turned out the Vandal war was merely the prelude to a much longer period of fighting against the Moors who were based in the interior, just as the Gothic war was followed by trouble from the Franks and, far more seriously, the Lombards. What was true of the conquered western areas was also true of the empire's north. Just a few hundred kilometres to the northwest of Constantinople lay the Danube frontier, a river which the army found it difficult to police effectively. Any invading force which crossed it could seek to plunder the Balkans, the hilly landscape of which made it ideal for raiding expeditions, while for the more ambitious, the coastal cities of Thessaloniki and Constantinople itself were glittering temptations. While Constantinople was excellently located with respect to the sea, commanding as it did the passage between the Black Sea and the Sea of Marmara, beyond which lay the Mediterranean, it was a different story when it came to the land; any force which crossed the Danube and headed towards the east would inevitably end up before its walls.

.   .   .

PROBLEMS IN THE BALKANS

In the disturbed conditions of late antiquity the Balkans had

---

3.   Procopius *Wars* 3.1 (ed. and trans. H.B. Dewing, London 1914–1940), a fascinating attempt to conceptualize Roman territory.

become a major concern for the government.[4] What textbooks call the fall of the Roman empire is generally described in a narrative which begins in 376, when large numbers of Goths entered the empire not in the West, where they were to end up, but across the Danube. Just two years later they won a victory at Adrianople (Erdine), killing the emperor Valens in the process. In the winter of 394–395 further instability was caused by a crossing of the Danube by Huns, a pastoral people from central Asia who were being led by changes in the ecological situation to abandon their homeland. Romans and barbarians all looked on this people with dread, and their arrival was enough to cause the Gothic leader Alaric to lead his people towards Constantinople, from which he was deflected by the promise of land in Macedonia. Here the Goths were to be based until they moved into Italy in 401, by which time another group of Goths had briefly occupied Constantinople in 400. In 408 another group of Huns crossed the Danube, and before long the Romans were paying them an annual subsidy to desist from further attacks. But a later ruler of the Huns, the famous Attila, was able to increase the payments. In 441 Niš (the classical Naissus) had been destroyed; a diplomat who passed by in 449 reported that the city was uninhabited, and a hundred years later its wall was still in ruins.

Before long Attila tired of his remarkably successful extortion racket. He turned his attention to the West, only to die in 453. His sons were unable to maintain his power, and in 469 the head of one of them was taken to Constantinople to be publicly displayed. But the demise of the Huns opened the way to the rise of Germanic peoples whom they had kept under their thumb. For decades Goths ravaged areas of the Balkans and dabbled in the politics of the empire; some of them attacked Constantinople itself in 471, 481 and 487, and it may have been simply to rid himself of the threat they posed that in 488 Zeno commissioned Theoderic the Ostrogoth to invade Italy. But troubles continued. Relations between Theoderic's kingdom, which extended across the Adriatic to

4. For the Goths, P.J. Heather *Goths and Romans 332–489* Oxford 1991 is a sound guide; for the Huns, O.J. Maenchen-Helfen *The World of the Huns* (ed. M. Knight) Berkeley 1974 is a work of amazing erudition, if somewhat eccentric.

include Dalmatia, and the empire were uneasy, and on more than one occasion tensions escalated into open warfare. Another general, Vitalian, who seems to have been of Gothic ancestry, attacked Constantinople from the European side three times towards the end of the reign of Anastasius, even though he fought for the empire.

But despite the traumas they caused, the presence of the Huns and Goths in the Balkans was transient, and their impact minor. Urban life continued, even if it was sometimes poured into new channels. The inhabitants of Nicopolis-ad-Istrum in the northern foothills of the Stara Planina, for example, migrated 18 kilometres to the better protected site of Veliko Turnovo, where an active building programme was sustained in the fifth and sixth centuries. It was not the Huns and the Goths but the various groups of people who followed on their heels who were destined to have an important impact. Ominously, in 493 a force which seems to have been comprised of Bulgars crossed the Danube. The ethnic origin of this people is not clear, but like the Huns they seem to have been a steppe folk from central Asia; only centuries later were they to be Slavicized. Their raids met with some success, and it was probably to protect Constantinople against them that Anastasius built, or at any rate strengthened, what contemporaries called the Long Wall.

These were not the first walls to protect the city. Constantine and his son Constantius had equipped it with a set of walls, and early in the fifth century Theodosius II responded to the rapid expansion of the city by erecting new walls, six kilometres long, which almost doubled the enclosed area. Eleven metres high and amazingly solid, they were not successfully breached until 1204, and are the best-preserved Roman walls to be seen anywhere today. The Long Wall, however, answered to a different defensive need. Some 65 kilometres west of the city, it ran from the Black Sea to the Sea of Marmara, and so protected not only the city but its environs as well. It may have run for 45 kilometres, and we know from surviving portions that it was 3.3 metres thick and up to five metres high. But it could offer no protection to areas more distant from Constantinople. In 499 Bulgars defeated a Roman army sent against them in Thrace, 4000 imperial soldiers dying in the encounter, and three years later another force of Bulgars met with no resistance in Thrace. In 517 enemies penetrated as far south as the pass of Thermopylai in Greece, although these may not have been Bulgars but members of another group of raiders which troubled the empire.

Worse troubles lay ahead. Before long other peoples, called Sklavinoi and Antai, came on the scene. In the sixth century it was held that they had the same origin, and they could be described as being somewhat reddish in appearance, in contrast to the fair-haired Goths. Debates have raged about the ethnic identity of these peoples, but it is widely believed now that they can be seen as southern and eastern Slavs respectively. The origin of the Slavs is itself a controversial topic, but in very general terms it seems clear that while the Germanic peoples were moving towards the west in late antiquity, Slavs were following in their footsteps, the Sklavinoi coming to settle in large numbers on the northern bank of the Danube and the Antai basing themselves in the modern Ukraine. The Sklavinoi in particular posed a long-term threat, for they were not so much warriors as farmers, steadily working their way across the map; as the experience of parts of the sub-Roman West was to prove, these were the barbarians who made the greatest impact.

The outlook in the early sixth century was therefore confused, but it was not entirely depressing. During the reign of Justinian's uncle Justin a large army of Antai which crossed the Danube was defeated by the emperor's nephew Germanus, and that a Roman army could march from Constantinople to the Crimea, as happened following the murder of Justinian's ally Grod, suggests that the position of the empire in the eastern Balkans was healthy. Meanwhile, the baptism of Grepes, the king of the Heruls, in Constantinople in 528 and the grant to his people of land in the area of Singidunum (Belgrade), presumably in imperial territory, would have strengthened its position in the west, while the difficulties the Ostrogoths found themselves in following the death of Theoderic in 526 were a source of satisfaction. There were also some useful military successes early in Justinian's reign which, in time-honoured fashion, were often the work of barbarian generals whom the empire used to deal with other barbarians. Justinian responded to a savage raid by the Bulgars by appointing a Gepid, Mundus, commander-in-chief in Illyricum, while in 530 or 531 Chilbudius, a Slav, was appointed to keep Huns, Antai and Sklavinoi from crossing the Danube. He discharged his office well, taking warfare into the territories of his opponents. The empire was adept at putting northerners to good use: when Vitalian attacked Constantinople in 513 his force included Huns and Bulgars, and in the 530s an Utigur fought in Belisarius' host in Africa, while some Sklavinoi from the region of the Danube were part of the first Roman army sent against the Ostrogoths. Progress was also made further to the west, where Sirmium, which had been a part of the Ostrogothic kingdom of Italy, was occupied at the beginning of the Gothic war. As in so many other areas, there seemed grounds for optimism during the early part of Justinian's reign. Indeed, a document of 533 accords the emperor the title 'Anticus', implying military success over the Antai.

More importantly, work began on a new city named after the emperor, Justiniana Prima. The large number of towns named after emperors in antiquity is a sign of imperial vanity, or sometimes the wish to gain imperial favour. The practice could be taken to extraordinary lengths, and the bestowing of an imperial name on a town was no guarantee that it would not be renamed: thus, Adrianopolis, named after Hadrian, was later renamed Justinianopolis. In Africa, the Vandal king Huneric had renamed Hadrumentum, the capital of Byzacena, Unuricopolis, but after the conquest of Africa it was renamed Justiniana; the town now bears the name Sousse. Carthage temporarily acquired the name Justiniana, as did various other towns. The inhabitants of another African town renamed it Theodorias, while the public bath at Carthage was named Theodorianae. After the suburb of Sykai, just across the Golden Horn from Constantinople, had been rebuilt, it was given the name Justinianopolis. Indeed, the second part of the name Justiniana Prima was necessary to distinguish it from a fortress nearby which received the name Justiniana Secunda.

The new town is probably to be identified with Caričin Grad, 45 kilometres south of Niš. Our one written account of the city (Procopius *Buildings* 4.1.19–27) is bursting with clichés, but we know from the work of archaeologists that its walls enclosed a small site noteworthy for its number of churches; as with many urban environments of late antiquity, Justiniana Prima possessed far more churches than pastoral or liturgical needs would seem to have required. In 535 Justinian issued a law which specified the privileges of the archbishop of Justiniana Prima (novel 11). The law stated that its bishop was to be not only a metropolitan but also an archbishop, and was to hold ecclesiastical power over a wide swathe of territory. This high-handed action, which was typical of Justinian's interventions in church affairs, elicited a cool response from pope Agapetus, but Justinian felt it was in keeping with the movement of the headquarters of the praetorian prefect of Illyricum. Traditionally this official had been based at Sirmium, but in the days of Attila he had retreated to Thessaloniki. We learn from a law of 535, however, of his relocation to Justiniana Prima, halfway between Sirmium and Thessaloniki.[5] The foundation of a new town where civil and ecclesiastical power was concentrated was a vote of confidence in the north. Indeed, in his law of 535 Justinian boasted that, with the help of God, the extent of the state had grown to encompass both banks of the Danube, and even named some towns north of the Danube subject to his power.

These were good days. But the situation gradually worsened. The splendid roads the Romans had built in the Balkans turned into a liability, for they allowed invaders from the north easy access. In 534 Chilbudius was killed in battle. Shortly after this the Gepids, a Germanic people, were able to seize Sirmium, and when Justinian sought to turn the Lombards, another barbarian people, against the Gepids, he had the indignity of seeing his new allies turn against another of his allies. In 540 the appearance of a comet was followed by an incursion by a large force made up of Bulgars, or a similar people. They captured thirty-two fortresses in Illyricum, breached the defences of the Gallipoli peninsula where they proceeded to create havoc, and, having forced their way through Anastasius' Long Wall, they proceeded to sack the suburbs of Constantinople and cause terror in the court. They also succeeded for the first time in capturing a walled town, generally a difficult operation for barbarian forces. The raiders were said to have retired with 120 000 captives; a later author wrote of an infinite number of wild beasts creating

---

5. In practice, however, the prefect may have continued to reside in Thessaloniki: P. Lemerle 'Invasions et migrations dans les Balkans depuis la fin de l'époque romaine jusqu'au VIIIe siècle' *Revue historique* 430 1954: 265–308 at 267–71. This study remains an invaluable guide to the literary evidence.

trouble in Thrace at that time, and the burial of two coin hoards which have been found in Bulgaria, one of them buried near Pazardzhik and the other near Pernik, has been plausibly associated with this invasion. At the pass of Thermopylai in Greece another group worked its way around the wall and went on to ravage the land to the south, as far as the Peloponnesos.

Worse was to follow. In the middle of the 540s a large force of Sklavinoi crossed the Danube and made its way into Illyricum, laying waste the country and enslaving the wives and children of soldiers from those parts who were fighting the Goths in Italy. They were defeated and the captives they had taken liberated, but four coin hoards which have been discovered in Serbia seem to bear witness to the fear they aroused. A few years later an army of Sklavinoi penetrated as far as Dyrrhachium (Durrësi). This town stood at the western end of the Via Egnatia, the main east/west road in the Balkans, and was important in communications with Italy, then an important theatre of war. Although the raiders made no attempt to take the town, merely devoting themselves to the more straightforward tasks of plundering and enslaving the local people, that they had penetrated so far was worrying, and an imperial army of 15 000 men which was in the region did not intervene. Early in 550 the Sklavinoi returned, crossing the Danube and advancing to the Maritza, effortlessly disposing of the Roman forces and capturing fortresses. The prisoners they took were said to have been beyond counting. One contingent made its way to the Adriatic coast where it captured a town which was, as contemporaries gloomily noted, just twelve days' journey from the capital. Later in 550 the Sklavinoi breached the border again, and the Romans learned from captives that they were hoping to capture Thessaloniki. It is highly unlikely that their siegecraft would have allowed them to do this, but Justinian ordered Germanus, who was then preparing his invasion of Italy, to deal with the problem. He died before he could take effective action, whereupon the Sklavinoi took the ominous decision to winter in imperial territory. The next year they split into three groups, one of which defeated a Roman force Justinian sent against them at Adrianople and pillaged as far as the Long Wall.

If this were not enough, trouble loomed from further to

the west. The Frankish king Theudebert, who had succeeded his father in 533, was a man whose public and private lives were both lived on the wild side. In 539 he had led an army into northern Italy, apparently on a plundering expedition. He was annoyed that Justinian had adopted such titles as Francicus, which implied his subjection to the emperor. At a later stage he occupied large tracts of northern Italy, not only Liguria but also the Cottian Alps and most of Venetia, with the approval of the Gothic king Totila. Theudebert celebrated his success, won in territory Justinian regarded as belonging to the empire, by issuing gold coins bearing his own portrait and the boastful slogan 'Peace and Freedom'. In Constantinople, people complained that not even the Persian king was capable of such arrogant behaviour. On one occasion Theudebert wrote to Justinian explaining that he ruled over a broad stretch of territory which extended from the frontier of Pannonia to the shores of the Ocean. But even this did not satisfy his ambition, for Theudebert set his sights on marching into Thrace and taking Constantinople. He went so far as to canvass the support of the Gepids, Lombards and other peoples, but Justinian invited the Lombards to settle in lands which would block his way, and in 547, before he could carry out his plan, Theudebert was killed in a hunting accident. But it proved difficult to dislodge the Franks from Italy. In 552 they informed one of Justinian's generals that Verona, still held by the Goths, by right belonged to them, and only in 556 did the lands which Theudebert had occupied come under imperial control.

. . .

JUSTINIAN'S RESPONSES

The preceding narrative may have given the impression that Justinian sat nervously in the palace year by year waiting for further bulletins of bad news from the Balkans. To nervousness may have been added a degree of guilt, for the presence in the Balkans of the troops he had committed to Africa and Italy would have been welcome. But the implication of futile resistance which the mere narration of events can easily give is false, for Justinian, as energetic as ever, offered three major responses to the problems which developed in this area. The first of these involved a tightening up of the administration.

Prior to 535 the administration of the Long Wall had been

entrusted to two officials named vicars, one with civilian and the other with military authority. But, as was so often the case, Justinian found this an untidy arrangement, and in 535 a law was issued which authorized the appointment of a new official, the praetor of Thrace, who, in accordance with the principle which underlay a series of reforms in other parts of the empire, would combine both areas of competence. Here, as elsewhere, it was hoped that greater efficiency would ensue. More important was the establishment of another new office, the quaestor of the army. This official, who is known from a law issued in May 536, was given responsibility for Moesia Secunda and Scythia, which were the two provinces adjacent to the lowest reaches of the Danube, and Caria, Cyprus and the islands of the Ionian Sea, all of which were to be detached from the praetorian prefecture of the East. It was an odd agglomeration of territory, and people living in its southern parts complained that it was a difficult business obtaining justice from the distant quaestor. This official was based at Odessos (Varna), a town on the Black Sea coast not far from areas being attacked; in 538 the bishop of the city was given permission to sell some of the many vineyards which had been left to the church and use the proceeds to buy captives their freedom. The rationale for such an awkwardly shaped administrative unit, which owed such cohesiveness as it possessed to its component parts all lying along coasts or the Danube, was probably the desire to make the defence of the lower Danube area more efficient and assure the reliability of supplies to the troops. There may also have been an expectation that the resources of Cyprus, a traditional centre for ship-building, would be used to strengthen the Danube fleet.

But Justinian's activities went far beyond this. The book in Procopius' *Buildings* which describes the fortifications erected south of the Danube is the longest in the work, occupying a quarter of the whole. At its onset, Procopius states that his subject in this book will be 'Europe'. Elsewhere in his writings he understands this term in its traditional sense, but here his focus is more narrow, Italy, in particular, being excluded from the book. But it is hard to know how to evaluate the mass of material it contains, and even the date at which the work was written is unclear, although about 554 seems likely. In particular the list of over 600 fortresses which Justinian is said to have built or, in the majority of cases, restored, in the Balkans is hard to assess. The data tend to be uncorroborated by other written or archaeological evidence, and as the purpose of the work is panegyric, one naturally suspects a heightening of the evidence.[6] In particular, it is clear that Anastasius had already begun to upgrade defences in this region, and Procopius, who is known to have attributed to Justinian works carried out in the reign of his uncle Justin, may be suspected of sometimes crediting Justinian with achievements which were not his. Further, Procopius, in accordance with the convention of the time, gives Justinian sole credit for works which he merely repaired or refurbished. There is also the more general question of Justinian's personal involvement, for it is certainly possible that works carried out on local initiative were credited to the emperor. Finally, works undertaken throughout Justinian's long reign are lumped together, making it almost impossible to see when various works were undertaken. The body of material we have is therefore hard to use.

Nevertheless, some patterns emerge which allow us to form some estimate of Justinian's enterprises at the time Procopius was writing. Defences were strengthened along the Danube itself. The town of Singidunum was fortified, and from there down to the mouth of the river an impressive line of fortifications was installed. Another zone of fortresses extended a fluctuating distance to the south of the river. Various considerations governed the location of these fortresses away from the frontier. Some were built along major roads, but many were placed in positions of no strategic importance, which suggests that they are to be seen as refuges for civilians. It is clear that the defences of Greece were a matter for special attention. Extra fortifications were erected at the key site of Thermopylai, where 2000 troops were installed. To the north, a pass between two mountains at Heraclea was closed by a wall. Near Corinth, an old wall across the isthmus was rebuilt, so the Peloponnesos would be secure, while a wall was built across the entrance to Pallene, the westernmost of the three

6. But not necessarily, for archaeological work at Bostra, the capital of the province of Arabia, suggests undertakings on a scale far greater than what a reader of Procopius (*Buildings* 5.9.22 ed. and trans. H.B., Dewing, London 1914–1940) would expect: J.-M. Dentzer 'Bosra' in *Contribution française à l'archéologie syrienne* Damascus 1989: 133–41. It is reasonable to expect that archaeological findings will cast more light on the reliability of Procopius in this regard.

promontories of Chalcidice. The strengthening of sites so far from the Danube may seem clear evidence of weakness, although on the other hand it could be argued that it suggests that raiding parties were heading so far south because they were finding it increasingly difficult to gain booty near the frontier, and hence that the defensive measures were working. A section at the eastern end of the Via Egnatia, the highway which ran westwards from Constantinople to Dyrrhachium, was repaved with large stones, while another project near the royal city saw the Long Wall strengthened. At the isthmus of Gallipoli an old wall was torn down and replaced by a high one, itself protected by a deep moat, and, in the event of this line of defence failing, towns in Gallipoli were provided with their own defences.

But Justinian had another way of dealing with the problems in the Danube basin. In accordance with traditional Roman tactics, he sought to divide and rule. The Lombards and the Gepids were two Germanic peoples who were the subjects of the emperor's duplicitous diplomacy. The capture of Sirmium by his old allies the Gepids and their subsequent hostile acts had been hard to take, and in response to this and the threat posed by Theudebert the Frank Justinian settled the Lombards, under their king Audoin, in Pannonia. When embassies from both peoples sought the aid of the empire in 548–549, Justinian decided for the Lombards, and, at least in the short term, he was well rewarded, for in 552 a substantial Lombard force made its way to Italy to help Narses in his showdown with the Goths. Later in the year further hostilities broke out between the Lombards and the Gepids, and again both sought the assistance of Justinian. Again he supported the Lombards, to whose assistance he sent a Roman force led by a general whose name, Amalafridas, indicates his membership of the old ruling family of the Ostrogoths, and indeed he was the great-nephew of Theoderic. Again, the Lombards were victorious over their enemies.

The principle was capable of infinite uses. In 545 Justinian proposed to the Antai that they settle in a town north of the Danube which had been built centuries earlier by the emperor Trajan, and enjoy the use of the surrounding lands. The town was in the old province of Dacia, which had been a part of the empire in the second and third centuries. But Justinian also committed himself to the payment of large sums of money to the Antai if they prevented the Huns (i.e. Bulgars) from entering the empire. More devious was his conduct in 551 towards two other groups who were apparently of Hunnic origin. He told the Utigurs, who were ravaging Roman lands, that they should be supporting the Romans in their strife with the Cotrigurs, who, despite being in receipt of Roman subsidies, were perpetually attacking Roman lands. The Utigurs were happy to oblige and defeated the Cotrigurs, but before long 2000 Cotrigurs crossed into Roman territory and were allowed to settle in Thrace. The Utigur ruler Sandilchus understandably took this badly, and sent ambassadors to complain to Justinian: why should the Cotrigurs be allowed to enjoy a life of leisure in the empire where they could get drunk, take baths and wear clothes with gold? Their case was unanswerable, but after Justinian had heard the ambassadors out he simply sent them on their way with fine words and a large quantity of gifts.

. . .

SUCCESS IN THE SHORT TERM . . .

Justinian therefore mounted a series of attempts to solve the problems in the Danube area. It would be possible to argue that he did not succeed. The failure of any bishop from Moesia to attend the council of Constantinople in 553 may well indicate disturbed conditions, and, Procopius, writing in 550, offered a very negative evaluation of the situation. From the time Justinian took over the government of the Romans, he claimed, the Huns, Sklavinoi and Antai attacked Illyricum and Thrace, which he defines as the territory from the Adriatic Sea to the suburbs of Constantinople, nearly every year, killing or enslaving at least 200 000 Romans on each occasion (*Secret History* 18.20f). It is hard to imagine a more gloomy perspective, but there is no reason to take it seriously, for it comes in a passage in which the author claims that in Africa ten thousand times ten thousand times ten thousand people perished because of Justinian's activities (18.4; shortly afterwards the estimate is revised downwards to a scarcely more plausible figure of 5 000 000: 18.8), while the fate of Italy was even worse (8.13), and the plague which followed carried off about half the survivors (18.44)! The comments of Procopius in this passage are nothing more than an exercise in hyperbole.

But when, in about 554, he came to bring to an end the

introductory material in the section of his *Buildings* which dealt with this area, Procopius' assessment of the situation was up-beat: because of Justinian's works, the barbarians who lived on the far side of the Danube were unable to cross the river (*Buildings* 4.1.14). Immediately before the list of forts in Thrace which concludes the book he is equally optimistic: the forts which Justinian founded throughout the area freed it completely from enemy attacks (4.11.20). Further, there is no reason to believe that Slavs were settling in Roman territory during the reign of Justinian. Archaeologists have found no evidence of Slav settlement there prior to the middle of the third quarter of the century, and attempts which have sometimes been made to identify Slavic forms lurking behind the placenames in the list of forts built or restored by Justinian which Procopius provides have failed: while some of the names are Celtic, and others of Germanic origin, there seem to be no names for which a Slavic origin can be plausibly argued. To be sure, there are oddities in the forms of the placenames given by Procopius, but these peculiarities can be explained by the author having had to turn the Latin names which he found in an original document into Greek.[7] The Danube provinces, then, remained firmly Roman.

It is therefore reasonable to see Justinian's measures as having largely contained the threat by the mid-sixth century. To be sure, there had been some displacement of the population: the evidence of coins suggests that a hill site near Sadovets which remained unoccupied throughout the fifth and early sixth centuries was again occupied during the reign of Justinian. But on the other hand, the people of Pirdop in Bulgaria seem to have completed their large church in brick during Justinian's reign.[8] In 545 the harvest in Egypt was poor, and it was clear that the grain which arrived in the royal city would not be enough for the needs of the capital, even after the fall in population caused by the plague. The praetorian prefect Peter Barsymes dealt with the problem by requisitioning grain from the nearby areas of Bithinia, Phrygia and Thrace, apparently foreseeing no difficulty in obtaining grain

7. V. Beševliev *Zur Bedeutung der Kastellnamen in Prokops Werk De aedificiis* Amsterdam 1970.

8. R.F. Hoddinott *Bulgaria in Antiquity: An Archaeological Introduction* London 1975 is a convenient presentation of some archaeological findings.

from the last-mentioned. Further, the years from 552 to 558 were free from attacks, and a tabulation of the coins in the museums of Serbia suggests that relatively peaceful conditions had existed in that area from the middle of the preceding decade.[9]

But the respite was only temporary. In March 559 a force of Cotrigurs and Sklavinoi, led by Zabergan, launched a major attack on imperial territory. The waters of the Danube had frozen, as sometimes occurred in that cold period, and the invaders rode their horses across the ice. One force advanced on Greece, to be repulsed at Thermopylai, while another part of the attacking host advanced on Gallipoli, only to be defeated by the wall which Justinian had built to protect the isthmus, which they were unable either to storm or sail around. In 540 invaders had penetrated the defences at both places, and their failure to do so in 559 was a tribute to the measures taken by Justinian. Meanwhile, Zabergan himself advanced towards the royal city with a force of cavalry estimated at 7000, plundering and taking captives as he advanced. The Long Wall, which may have been made less effective by an earthquake in 557, proved no obstacle; it was said that not even a dog barked by way of resistance. Justinian had committed many troops to Italy, Africa, Lazica and Egypt, and it was embarrassingly clear that there were not sufficient troops in the capital to deal with the emergency. Detachments of imperial guards, the scholarii, were available, but their function had long been merely ceremonial and they could not be expected to offer effective resistance; nor were members of the Blue and Green factions enough to deal with the threat. A mood of fear gripped the capital, and Justinian ordered that the churches outside the Theodosian walls were to be stripped of their costly ornaments. He finally dealt with the problem posed by Zabergan in an unexpected way.

Ever since his return from Italy in 549 Belisarius had been leading a quiet life in the capital. From Justinian's point of view, the services of this general had been a mixed blessing. His resolute action during the Nika rebellion, his victory over Gelimer and then his defeat of Vitigis were achievements for

9. The figures are tabulated by V. Popović, 'La Descente des Slaves et des Avars vers la Mer Égéé: Le Témoinage de l'archéologie' *Comptes rendus de l'Académie des Inscriptions et belles-lettres* 1978: 596–648 at 614.

which his sovereign could only be thankful. Yet the possibility that he had harboured imperial ambitions on more than one occasion, and his failure to make headway against either the Persians or the Goths in the 540s, could only have led to resentment, as may the failure of Belisarius and Antonina to allow their daughter Ionannina to go ahead with a marriage to Theodora's grandson Anastasius. But in his hour of need Justinian called on the veteran, and Belisarius once more rode into battle. He was no longer a young man and he had at his disposal just over 300 troops, supported by untrained townspeople and peasants. But his tactical skill had not deserted him. When some 2000 enemy horsemen attacked, Belisarius brought it about that they were ambushed and then turned to flight. His victory, however, had a familiar sequel. There were those in Constantinople who said that Belisarius was aspiring to imperial office, and Justinian, yielding or pretending to yield to gossip as he had decades before, recalled the general before he could inflict more damage on the Huns.

After Easter, Justinian left the city to supervise the rebuilding of the Long Wall, remaining in Selymbria, a town on the Propontis, until August. The period he spent seeing to the repair of the wall was the longest period he is known to have spent outside Constantinople during his reign, a circumstance which suggests that he was not greatly concerned about a threat from Belisarius. He also ordered the strengthening of the fleet on the Danube. This could have prevented Zabergan from returning home, and the Hun came to terms with Justinian. These included the payment of an annual subsidy to the Cotrigurs, but Justinian felt it was an excellent outcome, and when he returned to Constantinople it was in triumph. Early on a summer morning he entered the city through the Gate of Charisius, towards the northern end of the Theodosian Wall. Unlike Belisarius on his return from Africa in 534, Justinian did not walk: he rode through crowded streets to the Church of the Holy Apostles, where he dismounted and lit candles by the tomb of Theodora.

After Zabergan retreated from the walls of Constantinople Justinian presented him with a sum of gold as a ransom for prisoners and an incentive to leave the territory of the empire. He thereupon wrote to his old ally, the gullible Sandilchus, who was also in receipt of imperial subsidies, claiming that Zabergan had made off with the gold which was to be paid to him. The only thing for Sandilchus to do, it was suggested, was to make war on Zabergan immediately. As soon as Zabergan crossed the Danube he was set upon by Sandilchus, who relieved him of his gold and booty. Thereafter there was persistent enmity between Cotrigurs and Utigurs, and the empire was safe from their attacks.

The strategy of sowing dissent among dangerous barbarians had some brilliant successes, but in the long term it was risky. It depended on the payment of money which need not always have been available, particularly given Justinian's penchant for expensive buildings, and it may not be accidental that when Procopius was writing his *Secret History* in 550 he made the desire of Justinian and Theodora to gain control of the assets of wealthy private citizens one of his main themes (3.19, 4.16, 4.33, 5.20, etc.). Some historians have felt that the class affiliation of the author caused him to exaggerate, but it may be that Procopius' own perception, that much of the wealth gained from citizens was expended on barbarians (especially 19.10, 13, 16), as well as unnecessary buildings, was accurate. The success of Justinian's policy also depended on the gullibility of the barbarians, who could hardly be blamed for seeking to exploit the system once they had experienced the generosity of the emperor.

Further attacks were launched by Huns in the spring of 562 which saw the town of Anastasiopolis captured, despite the activity in the field of Marcellus, one of Justinian's nephews. But by then a greater threat was emerging. In 558 envoys from the ruler of an Asiatic people, the Avars, arrived in Constantinople. They were fighters on horseback who had made contact with Justin, the son of Germanus, then the imperial general in Lazica. Modern scholars have often credited the Avars with the use of the stirrup, and it was clear that, in military terms, they posed a far greater threat than the Slavs.[10] People gazed in amazement at the envoys, whose long hair, fastened with ribbons and tied into plaits, looked frighteningly like snakes; it is possible that the fashion in which they wore

10. This point was not lost on other barbarian peoples. However we may account for the interest of the Slav and Bulgar peoples in Roman territory during the sixth century, it is clear that the Avars were differently motivated in their attacks and more powerful in military terms. On them, see W. Pohl *Die Awaren* Munich 1988.

their hair owed something to their contact with the Chinese. In return for an alliance they sought land, gifts, and annual subsidies from Justinian. The emperor declined to grant them land but, as usual, was pleased to buy new friends. But the newcomers proved all too successful, and quickly established suzerainty over the Antai, Utrigurs and Cotrigurs. In 561 the Avars sent another embassy to Justinian with more ambitious demands: now they asked for land south of the Danube in Scythia, the modern Dobruja, ominously close to Constantinople. These were denied them, and an Avar plot to take the land by force was foiled by diplomacy. In the same year an Avar force attacked the Franks in Thuringia, an act which may perhaps be seen as an example of Justinian's far-reaching diplomacy, for at that very time Narses was mopping up Frankish resistance in Italy, and a diversion may have been opportune. But the Franks defeated their assailants, and the Avars were to remain a problem on the northern border of the empire.

The death of Justinian was followed by a radical change in policy in the Balkans. His successor, Justin II, issued a law in 566 which complained that the army had been deprived of resources, with the result that the state was toiling under countless invasions and attacks from barbarians. He denied them subsidies. It was a foolish move. In 567 the Avars and Lombards joined forces and won a mighty victory over the Gepids. But the Lombards were worried by the rising power of their allies, and in the following year these old friends of the empire invaded the recently won Italy. By the end of the century only one third of Italy remained in imperial hands. Worse was to follow in the Balkans. Coin hoards tell a story of mounting insecurity: Serbian museums hold 67 coins which passed out of circulation in the period 538/9–564/5, but their holdings for the reign of Justin (565/6–577/8) amount to 184.[11] Sirmium fell in 582, while Thessaloniki was besieged in 586 and again in about 615. In 626 a force of Avars and Slavs unsuccessfully besieged Constantinople itself. The proud town of Justiniana Prima was abandoned, apparently after a fire. The latest coin found on the site was minted in 615, by which time barbarians were among those living in the city. Niš had already fallen to Avars and the settlement of Slavs in what

11. Popović, 'La Descente': 614f.

had been imperial territory was proceeding apace. In desperation, Justinian's old policy of buying peace had been taken up again, and huge sums found their way to the Avars. In the seventh century they took to minting gold coins imitating those of the empire, and belt settings of solid gold were items of fashionable attire among them. When they were defeated by the Franks late in the eighth century their conquerors were astounded at the quantity of gold, silver and spoils the Avars had at their disposal. This was nothing more than a direct reflection of the failure of Byzantine policy in the Balkans.

The assessment of responsibility for these developments is a difficult exercise. Given that our written sources are Byzantine, one is naturally inclined to interpret them as a phase of Byzantine rather than Slavic or Avar history, in just the same way as the balance of our sources leads us to think of events in western Europe during the fifth century as 'the fall of Rome' rather than 'the rise of the Germanic peoples'. Perhaps the weakening of the position of the empire is to be explained not by its own feebleness but by factors specific to its enemies. In any case, it is clear that the position of the empire declined rapidly after the death of Justinian. Here, as elsewhere, a large part of our final assessment of his reign will be based on the degree to which we assign him the blame for the disasters which followed shortly after his death.

Chapter 7

THE END AND BEYOND

In many respects the last years of the reign of Justinian saw the continuation of practices and policies long in place. Impressive buildings were still being erected. In the period 561–564 a large military complex which included a two-storey palace and a domed church on basilican lines was erected at Qasr ibn Wardan near the frontier in Syria, and at some time during the latter part of the reign an enormous bridge, 429 metres long and nearly ten metres wide, was flung over the river Sangarius, not far to the west of the royal city. After an earthquake of December 557 caused the collapse of the dome of the cathedral of Hagia Sophia in May 558, Isidore, a nephew of the Isidore of Miletus who had been involved in the original construction, presided over the construction of a new, somewhat higher dome. The church was reconsecrated on 24 December 562. Paul the silentiary, a poet also known for his skill in composing erotic verse, wrote a long, detailed poem in which he described the completed work. It seems to have been delivered on the feast of the Epiphany, 6 January 563.

Adherents of non-Christian religions could still expect rough treatment. In 551, having heard from the bishop of Caesarea that the Samaritans had calmed down, Justinian enacted a law which removed some of the disabilities which had been imposed on them at the beginning of his reign, while retaining incentives for them to convert. But in July 555 these feisty opponents of the imperial will, aided by Jews, rioted at Caesarea. They attacked churches and murdered the proconsul of Palestina Prima. Justinian sent against them one of his generals, Amantius, who enacted stern reprisals: some of the rioters were hanged, others lost their right hands, while others saw their property confiscated. On another occasion Amantios visited Antioch, where pagans, Manicheans, astrologers and heretics felt his wrath. In the royal city pagans were arrested and forced to endure a parade of infamy; their books were burned.

Another theme of Justinian's reign to continue across the decades was the search for a lasting peace with Persia. Having come to power at nearly the same time, Justinian and Khusrau had grown old trying to take advantage of each other. After lengthy negotiations conducted by Peter the patrician and Isdigousnas, a treaty was concluded in 562. Lazica, which had remained a bone of contention, was to pass under Byzantine control, while Justinian agreed to pay just over 400 pounds of gold per annum, with the payments for the first seven years to be handed over as a lump sum in advance; when these years had passed the payments for the subsequent three years were also to be paid *en bloc*. The treaty was drawn up in meticulous detail. Among other matters, it dealt with the Arab allies of each party, who were not to make attacks, the conduct of trade between the states, and the status, always a problem, of the Roman town of Daras. The parties agreed that God would help those who abided by its terms and harm those who did not. A separate agreement concerned Christians living in Persia, who were accorded various liberties, including that of building churches, but were not allowed to convert the Magi. It is interesting to find Justinian concerning himself with the situation of Christians outside the empire, particularly given that most Christians in Persia were Nestorians.[1] But the result of the treaty was typical of those Justinian concluded. Although the parties had agreed that the treaty would expire on the three hundred and sixty fifth day of the fiftieth year, it lasted just ten years.

.   .   .

SILK

In one area, however, the last years of Justinian's rule saw a

---

1.   The detailed provisions of the treaty are known from R.C. Blockley ed. and trans. *The History of Menander the guardsman* Liverpool 1985 6.1. Menander had access to an account by Justinian's veteran negotiator Peter the patrician. On Justinian and the Nestorians of Persia, A. Guillaumont, 'Justinien et l'église de Perse' *Dumbarton Oaks Papers* 1969f 23f pp. 39–66.

major innovation. While the empire was largely self-sufficient, it imported a range of items which have a romance denied the more important and bulkier commodities traded internally. Chief among these was raw silk, an expensive item imported from China, where the silk worm had been domesticated at least two millennia previously. Silken clothes had connotations of luxury; Procopius took the taste which the Vandals developed while in Africa for wearing what he described as the Medic clothes nowadays called 'Seric' to be a sign of their decadence (*Wars* 4.6.7). An import of less importance was incense, for which southern Arabia was the traditional source. In pagan times it had been employed in the imperial cult, but the Bible seemed to give unquestionable authorization to its use in worship, and so it was undergoing a revival in Christian contexts. The costumes of the people depicted in the famous mosaics at S Vitale, and the thurifer who leads the procession of which Justinian is a member, suggest the uses to which these prestige products, for which the empire depended on foreign suppliers, could be put. Less dignified were spices, such as pepper and cinnamon, which played a role in the daily diet of the citizens of the empire similar to that they play in the diet of modern vegetarians. Barbarians as well as Romans came to value such items: Visigoths who besieged Rome early in the fifth century were given several thousand pounds of pepper, while a few decades later Indian pepper and dates were among the presents given to a widow of a king of the Huns. The empire produced a variety of spices, but some were imported from India and Indonesia.

Broadly speaking, the empire was linked to its suppliers by two routes. One of these proceeded by sea. The Alexandrian merchant and theologian Kosmas Indicopleustses is known to have sailed past Socotra, and he claimed to have sailed as far as Sri Lanka, where hoards of early Byzantine coins have been found.[2] From there goods originating in the east could be

2. We know of Kosmas' journeying through his work the *Christian topography* (ed. and trans. W. Wolska-Conus, *La Topographie chrétienne de Cosmas Indicopleustès*, Paris 1968–73; there is an older English translation by J.W. McCrindle, London 1897), in which he sought to disprove theories that the world is a sphere. Kosmas argued that it is shaped like the tabernacle which Moses instructed the people to build. A man of Nestorian convictions, he wrote against a gifted Monophysite thinker, John Philoponos.

forwarded across the Indian Ocean and up the Red Sea, from which they would find their way to Alexandria, or up the Gulf, from which they would be transported overland through Persian territory to the empire. The other was the famous Silk Route. It proceeded by land westwards from China across the steppes, and made its way across Persian territory to the border with the empire, across which silk could be imported. Disparate as they were, the routes shared a major disadvantage: each was at the mercy of Persia. The heavy involvement of Persia in the silk trade is implied by Procopius' use of the word 'Medic' to describe silken garments. During times of war with Persia this was intolerable, and even in peace it was hard to bear, because Persia, never averse to profiting from the empire, levied an impost on the trade.

Justinian struggled to overcome this problem. He maintained Justin's policy of cultivating good relations with Axum, a state on the coast of the Red Sea to the south of Egypt. There could be no doubt that Axum, which had adopted the Christian religion, was a part of Africa (a Byzantine ambassador was astonished at the sight of a herd of some 5000 elephants), but the Semitic language spoken by its people was similar to that used in southern Arabia, and it maintained close connections with the Arabs across the Red Sea. Already, Justin had given naval support when a ruler of Axum, Elesboas, a Christian enthusiast who had adopted the biblical name Caleb, crossed the sea and invaded the Arab state of Himyar, located where Yemen is now. Elesboas, who wore a turban and went about in a carriage on top of four elephants, was a colourful ally, but no less exotic in his own way was the king of the Himyarites, Dhu-Nuwas, who had converted to Judaism and adopted the name Yusuf. It would certainly be possible to interpret the invasion mounted by Elesboas in a religious light, for after his success in Arabia he was an active builder of churches and obtained a bishop from Timothy, the patriarch of Alexandria who seems to have been an acquaintance of Theodora. The activity of Elesboas can also be seen as answering to a Roman strategy of putting pressure on the allies of Persia, and Justinian was later to attempt to inveigle the Himyarites into anti-Persian activity, to no avail. But there may have been more to his strategy than this. We know that Dhu-Nuwas caused trouble for Roman traders, and the war can also be seen as an attempt by a Roman ally to gain control of the straits leading into the Red Sea. A few years afterwards Justinian sought to use the people of Axum to exclude Persian middlemen in the silk trade, but met with no success.

Another solution to the problem was the creation of a new overland route to the north of the Silk Route which would circumvent Persia. It may be that Justinian's interest in Lazica, where another war had been fought prior to the conclusion of peace with Persia in 562, was partly stimulated by his interest in such a route. But it would have involved a dangerous and long journey, for in the favourable conditions of the four-teenth century, the trip from the Crimea to Beijing lasted about nine months, and there is no sign that Justinian was able to make progress in this direction.

However, a major breakthrough was at hand. In the early 550s two monks came before Justinian, stating that they had been to a land to the north of India named Serinda, a word obviously connected with the name Procopius gave the clothes worn by the Vandals, 'Seric'.[3] There they had dis-covered that silk was made by worms, the eggs of which could be easily transported. Justinian asked them to return to Serin-da and bring back eggs, which they did. This story is known from only one source (Procopius *Wars* 8.17.1–8), but there seems no reason to disbelieve it. Although silk continued to be imported, thanks to its capacity to produce it, the empire was no longer totally dependent on its suppliers. Earlier in his reign Justinian had established a state monopoly in the pro-duction of silk cloth. Trade had suffered badly during the war with Persia in the 540s, and the praetorian prefect Peter Barsymes[4] had brought about a state monopoly of the produc-tion of goods from silk. So it was that advances in production and manufacturing allowed the foundations of the great By-zantine silk industry to be laid.

. . .

LAST YEARS

It is possible, then, to see in the last years of Justinian's reign

3. 'Seres' is the Greek for the suppliers of silk, and it is the root from which the English 'silk' is derived.
4. The name is a curious one, but Peter was a Syrian, so 'Bar' would have the force of 'son of'. Peter's father would therefore have been called Simeon.

the continuation of themes which had been important earlier, and even a major new development. But they were also in a period of lengthening shadows. In 554 Constantinople was struck by an earthquake, during which the spear ominously fell from a statue of Constantine. The games held in May 556 to celebrate the anniversary of the foundation of Constantinople were marked by chanting against Justinian provoked by a shortage of bread; embarrassingly, an ambassador from Persia was present. The shortage lasted for three months. In December 557 Constantinople was struck by a major earthquake. An honorary consul was killed in his home by a piece of falling marble, but more important was the subsequent collapse of the dome of Hagia Sophia, a symbol of the confidence of the 530s. Justinian did not wear the stemma for 40 days, and customary Christmas celebrations were curtailed. An indication of the scale of the damage was given in 559 when the emperor, returning to the city in triumph after the withdrawal of the army of Zabergan, entered through the Gate of Charisius rather than the Golden Gate, through which the Via Egnatia made its way into the city. The unexpected route answered to the damage the earthquake had done along the lower part of the Mese.[5] In November 562 fights broke out at the cisterns. The city was suffering from a drought, the impact of which may have been exacerbated by failure to keep the aqueducts in a good state of repair. As if this was not enough, northerly winds prevented the grain fleet from reaching the city, and the patriarch enjoined religious observances.

Other parts of the empire also suffered from civil unrest. In Antioch, for example, there were disturbances involving orthodox and Monophysite Christians. But Constantinople was the worst affected. In November 561 trouble broke out between the Blues and Greens, and in the following year the anniversary games were marked by rioting and incendiarism, the house of the praetorian prefect Peter Barsymes being among the buildings destroyed. Some of the ringleaders were beheaded. In 563 Andrew, the prefect of the city of Constantinople, was himself attacked, and after further violence another holder of this office was dismissed in 565. Indeed, during the last few years of Justinian's reign there was an extraordinary turnover of prefects of the city, presumably

5.   Michael McCormick *Eternal Victory* Cambridge/Paris 1986 p. 67.

reflecting desperate attempts on the emperor's part to maintain law and order in his capital.

Such conditions provided a natural background to political tension. One day in September 560 word spread around the city that Justinian's life had come to its end. He had returned from Thrace, perhaps after an inspection of defences, but because he was suffering from a headache he was seeing no-one. The bakeries were looted, and by nine o'clock there was no bread to be found anywhere in the city. Justinian had certainly been ill, and after he recovered a former praetorian prefect, Eugenius, accused two men, Aetherius and George, of having sought to replace him as emperor with Theodore, the son of one of his most respected and longest-serving civil servants, Peter the patrician. When enquiries proved the charge without foundation, Eugenius saved himself by taking refuge in a church.

A far more serious situation developed in November 562, when a plan to murder Justinian was uncovered. The plotters were Marcellus, a banker, Sergius, one of those whose names had been mentioned in connection with the alleged plot of 560, and a certain Ablabios, who was bribed to join the group. Their plan was breath-taking in its simplicity: one evening they would enter the palace and murder Justinian. Security certainly seems to have been lax at the palace; an earlier conspirator, Artabanes, is represented as having described Justinian as easy to murder, for he was in the practice of sitting late into the evening without a bodyguard in the company of elderly priests, unravelling the sayings of the Christians (Procopius *Wars* 7.32.9). But Ablabios passed word on to the military authorities. Marcellus was intercepted as he entered the palace with a dagger, which he then used to take his own life, while Sergius made his way in haste to a famous church, that of the Theotokos at Blachernai. Subsequently he implicated other people in the plot, claiming that Isaac, a moneylender who was associated with Belisarius, together with Vitus, another banker, and Paul, another associate of Belisarius, had all been involved.

For decades now Justinian had been worrying about Belisarius. Doubtless the thought that he could replace Justinian had passed through the general's mind, but there is no evidence that he ever took steps towards this end. Nevertheless, Justinian was alarmed. A round of questioning followed, as a result of which Belisarius himself was directly implicated.

The various depositions were read out at a meeting held on 5 December, and Belisarius was placed under house arrest. In later centuries Justinian's response was exaggerated, stories being told that he blinded his old general, who ended his days as a beggar. But there was no more foundation to this charge than there had been to earlier ones, and Justinian soon relented. Belisarius was restored to favour in July 563, and died in March 565, beyond suspicion at last.

One of the reasons for this turmoil was the increasing unpopularity of Justinian, which can be traced through the various works of Procopius. A careful study of the figures which Procopius gave for the sizes of military forces in that part of his *Wars* dealing with the Goths suggests that, at the beginning of his narrative, he attempted to create a false picture of the degree of Belisarius' successes, but that as time passed he ceased to do so.[6] Perhaps he simply lost heart. By the time he completed Book 7 of the *Wars*, the last book of this work in which different theatres of war are treated separately, he had taken the story of the Gothic war up to early in 551, and the story told in the last stages of this book is indeed depressing. When he began work on Book 8 it was with a heavy heart.[7] This book narrates the triumph of Roman arms under Narses, but the war in Italy had dragged on far longer than its historian would have thought possible in the sunny days of 540, and his hero Belisarius had faded from the scene. Indeed, if there is a hero in Procopius' narrative of the last stages of the war against the Goths it is Justinian's enemy, the doomed but strangely attractive Totila.

But at the very time when the narrative of Book 7 of the *Wars* was drawing towards its conclusion, Procopius was working on his famous *Secret History*, the work which included the extremely negative characterization of Theodora we have already considered (above pp. 19-21). The book also displays a powerful animosity against Belisarius, whose wife Antonina is portrayed as a scheming and unfaithful spouse at whose feet her husband lay, on one memorable occasion, licking her

6. K. Hannestad 'Les Forces militaires d'après la Guerre gothique de Procope' *Classica et mediaevalia* 21 1960: 136–83.
7. The verbal echoes of *Wars* 8.1.1f in *Secret History* 1.1.1 (ed. and trans. H.B. Dewing, London 1914–1940), a work discussed immediately below, are clearer in the Greek than in the Loeb translation of Dewing.

ankles, but it is even more hostile to Justinian. At one point
Procopius casually notes that, among the emperors, Justinian
looked most like Domitian (8.13), but he proceeds to state
that no representation of Domitian had been allowed to
survive, except for one preserved in Rome. It is possible that
Procopius had seen the statue when he was in Rome, but the
underlying point is surely an implication that Justinian was an
emperor of such deplorable quality that it could simply be
assumed that he looked like his dreadful predecessor.[8] He was
described as walking about the palace late at night without his
head, and more than once Procopius described him as the
Prince of Demons (12.26, 12.32, 30.34), using precisely the
form of words used by enemies of Jesus to refer to the Devil
(e.g. Matt 9:34).

Procopius also transferred to Justinian accusations which
in earlier writings he had levelled against others or only
applied to Justinian in the mouths of other people. Interesting
in this connection is his use of the adjective νεώτερος, a word
which has the sense of 'revolutionary' or 'innovatory'.
Together with its cognates it is used a number of times in the
Wars, almost always carrying a negative connotation.[9] On one
occasion it is applied to Justinian by his enemies, representatives of the Ostrogoths alerting Khusrau to his evil designs (*Wars* 2.2.6). But in the *Secret History* Procopius
persistently applies the term to Justinian in a hostile sense
(6.21, 8.26, 11.2, 30.21). He was now prepared to make the
accusation of Justinian's enemies his own.

The historian had moved a long way from the early days
when everything seemed possible. It would be interesting to
know to what extent his loss of faith arose from the unexpectedly protracted length of the wars in the West, and if so to
what extent his reaction was shared by other people. It would
indeed have been curious if the cool response we have suggested the wars ultimately met with in the West had been
matched by a perception in the East that they had turned out
to be an expensive waste of time. Perhaps some of Procopius'

8. Averil Cameron *Procopius and the Sixth Century* London 1985 pp. 58f.
9. It is used of Khusrau the Persian king (*Wars* 1.23.1), of the charge made
against Symmachus and Boethius before Theoderic (*Wars* 5.1.34), of
disloyal Roman soldiers (*Wars* 7.1.25); it refers to the kind of activity
Belisarius stated he had sworn never to engage in (*Wars* 6.29.20). It
may be admissible to cite *Wars* 3.9.21 as well.

sense of disillusionment also sprang from personal disappointment with Belisarius. But, while we have no reason to see Procopius as a typical figure whose changing views would have reflected those of his society at large, he is evidence for hostility towards Justinian occurring where it had not earlier in the reign, and as the emperor's life moved towards its close he was not the only person to demonstrate antagonism.

This feeling could have been connected with Justinian's slowing down. The restoration of Hagia Sophia had taken nearly as long as the erection of the original building. The flow of novels, the new laws which Justinian had published in such abundance in the years immediately after the Code had been issued, virtually ceased. During the 540s something like thirty-six were issued, but there were only thirteen during the 550s, and just three in the period 560–565. Increasingly, Justinian's thoughts turned towards religion. His last novel, issued a few months before he died, was concerned with ecclesiastical matters, and was bolstered with quotations from S Gregory the Theologian, S Basil, the council of Nicaea and S Paul. It could not be disputed that they were excellent authorities, but none of them had traditionally been cited on points of Roman law. As early as 548 the conspirator Artabanes poured scorn on Justinian for always sitting unguarded late into the night, discussing the contents of the scriptures with very elderly priests,[10] and as time passed his religious interests became stronger. A work written in praise of Justin II not long after Justinian died states that in his old age the emperor was completely cold; the love of the other life alone warmed him, and his mind was completely devoted to heaven (Corippus *In Laudem* 2:265–7). In October 563 he discharged a vow by journeying to Germia, a town in Galatia where there was a famous church dedicated to the archangel S Michael, and the bishop had various portions of the body of S George. It was an unexpected act for a man about eighty years old who had rarely left Constantinople.

10. *Wars* 7.32.9. Needless to say, the passage may express the sentiments of Procopius rather than Artabanes, but given that he was writing a few years later it can stand as indicative of feeling current at the time. In describing the priests as being in extreme old age, Procopius uses a favourite term: cf. *Wars* 7.39.7 (applied to Liberius when he was in his 70s or 80s), *Secret History* 9.50 (applied to Justin in his 70s).

Oddly enough at the end of his life Justinian, who was so scrupulous with regard to correct Christian belief, tumbled into what almost everyone regarded as heresy.[11] Given that over four decades previously he had already been putting pressure on the pope to accept a theological formula to which he was partial, and that he had retained an intense interest in theological questions, it is not surprising that his mind continued to work along such lines. It is, however, surprising that the position he finally adopted was such an exceptional one. Justinian came to believe that the earthly body of Christ had been incorruptible and impassable, so that the manner in which Jesus ate after the resurrection was not different to the manner in which he had eaten before the crucifixion. It seemed to most people that this teaching, technically known as Aphthartodocetism, could not possibly be reconciled with the teaching of the council of Chalcedon that Christ had a perfect human nature, and even by Monophysite standards it was thought an extreme position. Of course, the events of the Three Chapters controversy had made it clear that Justinian had means of making clerics see his point of view. Nevertheless, when the patriarch of Antioch was invited to adhere to the emperor's position, he prepared to resist, and Eutychius, the patriarch of Constantinople, had no trouble in showing that Justinian's views were heretical.

But Eutychius, who had risen to the office of patriarch so quickly in 552, had enemies.[12] In 558 he had been required to co-operate in an investigation into a plot against Justinian, and in January 565 two senators were on hand to turn Justinian against him. They were an unsavory pair, for one of them, Addeus, was later to admit to having killed a praetorian prefect by sorcery, while the other, Aetherius, had been among those accused by Eugenius of plotting against Justinian in 560. It is now impossible to disentangle the roles which concerns about doctrine and the jockeying for position, which must have become increasingly intense as Justinian grew older, respectively played in the affair. But Eutychius was quickly banished, to be replaced in office by the representative

11. It is strange to find A. Gerostergios *Justinian the Great Emperor and Saint* Belmont Mass 1982 denying this lapse into heresy by the emperor.
12. P. Van der Ven 'L'Accession de Jean le scholastique au siège patriarchal de Constantinople en 565' *Byzantion* 35 1965: 320–52 is helpful.

in Constantinople of the church of Antioch, John the scholastic. Not for the first time in Justinian's reign, high office was
thrust upon an ecclesiastic who happened to be in the capital
seeing to the interests of another see. John, however, enjoyed
close relations with Justin, the son of Justinian's sister, who
would clearly have strong claims to the throne when the
emperor died. In line with his customary way of seeing Christian doctrine as a concern of the state, Justinian expressed his
new convictions in an edict, but before the new patriarch was
placed in the embarrassing position of having to declare
himself on the issue the emperor died.

The difficulties which attended Justinian's last years were
not merely the consequence of unpopularity and his attention
being less taken up with earthly matters. It was clear to
everyone that before long there would be a new emperor, and,
inevitably, parties formed. A lot of trouble would have been
avoided had Justinian nominated a successor, but the canny
old man failed to take a step that would have weakened his
own position. So it was that, whereas it had become perfectly
clear in the 520s that he would succeed his uncle Justin,
no-one could be sure who would follow Justinian on the
throne. His marriage had been childless,[13] although even if
Justinian and Theodora had produced a son, he need not
have succeeded his father, for succession by a son was not
automatic; the last son to succeed his father in the East had
been Theodosius II, early in the fifth century. Justinian's
cousin Germanus would have been a strong candidate, and it
may be that when Justinian named him as commander of what
was to be the definitive campaign against the Ostrogoths in
550 his plan was for Germanus to become a junior emperor,
technically a 'caesar', residing in Italy, with a view to assuming
responsibility for the entire empire when the senior emperor
died. But the death of Germanus in 550 would have put an
end to thoughts along such lines.

13. Theodora was already a mother when she married Justinian. She had
    a son, John, whose father had taken him away to Arabia, but when he
    came to Constantinople and made himself known to Theodora at the
    palace she is said to have caused him to disappear. She was also the
    mother of a daughter, who herself bore a son, Anastasius. In 548 he
    married Ioannina, the daughter of Belisarius, but on the death of
    Theodora later in the year Ionnina's mother separated them. We know
    that she had another grandson, Athanasius, who became a monk.

Two strong contenders remained. One of them was Justin, the son of Germanus by his first wife and hence a relative of Justinian. He had enjoyed a successful military career, having held commands in the Danube region and Lazica, and in the early 560s was making a name for himself by his energetic steps against the Avars. But his series of postings away from the capital meant that he was unable to intervene in its political life to his own advantage, while his loyalty ensured that he would not be one of those generals whose response to being passed over took the form of war.

The other likely candidate, and as it turned out the successful one, also bore the name Justin. He was the nephew of Justinian, being the son of his sister Vigilantia, and had married well, for his wife Sophia had all the ability and resourcefulness of her aunt, Theodora.[14] His record was certainly not as distinguished as that of his namesake. Nowhere is he mentioned in the voluminous writings of Procopius, and the office he had held since 552, *cura palatii*, was a modest one. But it placed him in control of the palace and gave him the inestimable advantage of being on the scene. The holy man Simeon the Stylite was later said to have predicted his accession, and a Monophysite historian was to write that Sophia transferred from the communion of the Monophysites to that of the Chalcedonians with a view to easing her husband's passage to the throne, three years before this occurred. These stories may be true, or they may simply reflect tales which spread after Justin had become emperor. Corippus, in a work he wrote in praise of Justin, claimed that during his last years Justinian had done nothing without the counsel of Justin, and on numerous occasions metaphorically refers to Justinian as Justin's father. But the author of a work celebrating Justin may be suspected of having sought to invest his accession with an inevitability it may not have had in reality. It may be more significant that Justin was the patron of one Tiberius, the leader of the bodyguard, the very office which Justin had used as his launching pad to the purple in 518. Neither had Justin lost anything by the appointment of his friend John the

14. Vigilantia had two other children, Marcellus and Praeiecta; the latter, as we have seen, was successively married to Areobindus and John, a relative of Anastasius. But neither is known to have entered into the calculation in 565.

scholastic as patriarch early in 565 in a manoeuvre which may have had political overtones. He was certainly well-positioned to succeed his uncle, and as it turned out his coming to power was straightforward.

Justinian died on the night of 14 November 562.[15] While it was still dark the only witness of his death, an elderly patrician, Callinicus, made his way to the palace of Justin and Sophia in the presence of senators. The news he transmitted, whether accurately or not, was that he had heard the dying emperor name Justin as his successor. From there the party made its way to the imperial palace. They entered it as the birds were singing, and were made welcome by Tiberius and the guard. Having been crowned with a torque and raised on a shield, Justin was then crowned by the patriarch John. Only when these military and religious ceremonies had been completed and he had received the acclamations of those present in the palace did Justin proceed to the Hippodrome, where a crowd had gathered on news of the death of Justinian. There, as he took his seat in the kathisma, the factions acclaimed the new emperor. One has the feeling that the whole operation was managed very smoothly with a view to an uncontested succession. After this had been secured the body of Justinian was placed in a sarcophagus, and a funeral procession made its way amid crowds of people from the palace down the Mese to the church of the Holy Apostles, where it was placed in a mausoleum he had built in its precincts. There it remained, to be discovered by members of the fourth crusade in 1204.

. . .

FOR GOOD OR ILL

Justinian was buried in an embroidered funeral pall which Sophia, already displaying qualities which were later to stand the empire in good stead, conveniently had ready. While Corippus states that the pall depicted the whole series of Justinian's labours, the only scene he describes was one portraying Justinian in his court treading the king of the Vandals underfoot. The event alluded to what had occurred over thirty

15. Our source for the following events is Corippus, who may be suspected of endowing the accession of Justin with a degree of inevitability it did not have (*In Landem Justini Augusti Minoris* ed. and trans. Averil Cameron, London 1976)

years previously. When Justin and Sophia went on to sit down to a ceremonial banquet the gold plate on the table depicted scenes which Justinian had ordered to be displayed in 534. From the brooch which fastened the chlamys Justin put on hung jewels from Ravenna and Africa, presumably spoils from the Gothic and Vandal treasures conveyed to Constantinople after the victories of Belisarius. Was it really the case that nothing worth while had happened since 540? Indeed, could it be said that the reign of Justinian had ultimately dragged on far too long?

By 565 the empire was quite different from what it had been in 527. Constantinople had become central to its life in a way it never had been before. Most of our study of Justinian has been set in the royal city. This has been fitting, given that its subject rarely travelled beyond its walls, and reflects the emphasis given the metropolis in our sources, but it may have exaggerated the role of the capital within the empire. Any such distortion, however, will have become progressively smaller over the course of our study. We have seen the ceaseless flow of talented people from the provinces to the capital, where their skills were put to use designing buildings, recasting the laws, and administering the affairs of the empire. The city was a magnet for ambitious careerists and the scions of impoverished western families alike. In 533 the teaching of law was restricted to Rome, Constantinople and Beirut, but by the end of the reign it was clear that only the second had a future as a centre of legal studies, and by the middle of the century the city had come to hold sway as the undisputed centre of not only Greek but also, more surprisingly, Latin literature. The styles of architecture and liturgy fashionable in the capital would increasingly tend to influence the provinces. Justinian deserves much of the credit for the centrality his capital came to enjoy, as he does for the buildings with which it was adorned by the end of his reign, although there is no disguising the religious nature of those for which he was responsible, a characteristic such as to suggest to one eminent scholar the announcement of what he saw as the coming of the middle ages.[16] *Oh come on!*

Justinian's reign saw the beginning of a grim period in

16. Cyril Mango, *Le Développement urbain de Constantinople (IVe–VIIe siècles)* Paris 1985, p. 52.

intellectual life.[17] This was particularly true in the secular sphere. In Italy, fewer secular manuscripts were produced under Justinian than had been under the Goth Theoderic, and, strange to say, after the defeat of the Goths the production of Greek texts in northern Italy almost dried up. In the East secular books had enjoyed a lively circulation during the reigns of Anastasius and Justin, but not one text of an ancient Greek author is known to have been produced in Constantinople during the reign of Justinian. Oddly enough, more Latin manuscripts seem to have been produced there during the sixth century, but this may have been an aspect of the refocusing of Latin-based intellectual life which occurred during the Gothic war, and hence at least in part a consequence of the catastrophic state of Italy for which Justinian was to blame. The production of Christian texts held up comparatively well, but legal texts constituted the only area of growth.

We may therefore speak of a remarkable constriction of intellectual life during this period. Confronted with the intellectual sway of Christianity in the medieval period, and the success it had come to enjoy in the West by the early sixth century, one can easily underestimate the importance of secular and explicitly non-Christian modes of discourse within the empire at the beginning of Justinian's reign. The thinkers who had participated in the revival of non-Christian thought in the century prior to the migration of the seven philosophers to Persia were far more than summarizers, eptimators and commentators. But the lofty tradition they represented did not have a bright future. The pagan scholars who returned from Persia were indeed free to continue their work at Harran, but the town was scarcely central to the life of the empire.

It is not easy to account for these developments. Doubtless they were connected with the strengthening impress of Christianity, which can be demonstrated in such developments as the rising tide of Marian piety. The feast of the Presentation of the Lord was first celebrated in Constantinople on 2 February 542, and as we have seen many churches were dedicated to the Theotokos in this period. Similarly, the building of a shrine to SS Priscus and Nicholas by Justinian seems to

17. For the following I draw on G. Cavallo 'La circolazione libraria nell' età di Giustiniano' in G.G. Archi ed. *L'imperatore Giustiniano storia e mito* Milan 1978 pp. 201–36.

constitute the first evidence we have for the cult of the latter, who was to become one of the most loved saints of the Christian East. The tendencies operating in intellectual life involved both a contraction in overall scope and an intense flourishing of the genres into which intellectual energies were now poured.[18] It was simply the fact that many members of the generation of Romanos Melodos, while happy to accept secular and frankly mythological themes in visual arts, thought they had better things to do than concern themselves with the content of classical literary culture.[19] The increasing role of monasteries in intellectual life may also be relevant, for it would be reasonable to expect that the religious concerns of the transmitters of books were reflected in the kinds of books that were copied. The field of history ceased to attract authors in the early seventh century, with the unfortunate result that the rise of the Arabs in that century is described in contemporary accounts written in Egypt and Armenia, but not the surviving parts of the empire. Only in the early ninth century was a revival of historical writing to take place.

No-one could blame Justinian for these broad developments, but it must be said that he was a more than willing participant.[20] His campaigns against pagans, of which execution and suicide were results, the parade of infamy which suspects had to undergo, and, most ominously for intellectual history, book burnings, pointed the way to a grim future, and the society over which he presided came to be characterized by fear in some respects.[21] There must have been thinkers who

18. See, with particular reference to the West, Robert Markus *The End of Ancient Christianity* Cambridge 1990 p. 225.
19. This is not to deny that the vocabulary, syntax and general style of the works of Procopius are of an intensely classical nature, but by the early seventh century it was clear that the future lay along other paths. The sixth-century items published in K. Weitzmann ed. *The Age of Spirituality* New York 1979, include numerous sixth-century examples of Greek gods, popular heroes and mythological themes; further, it is clear that production of items with such themes was to continue.
20. Interesting is the perspective of Zonaras: Justinian spent the money which had formerly been used to pay the salaries of teachers in all the towns on the construction of churches, so causing ignorance (*Epitome* 14.6.31f, ed. M. Pinder 1897).
21. See the comments of Roger Scott 'Malalas, *The Secret History* and Justinian's propaganda' *Dumbarton Oaks Papers* 39 1985 pp. 99–109.

trimmed their sails to the wind. One wonders as well about the control the state exercised over the sources of knowledge. Justinian's first edict against the Three Chapters, for example, issued in 543–544, does not survive; perhaps care was taken that it did not. Documents written by deviate Christians were hard to get hold of: Leontius of Byzantium found it difficult to gain access to a copy of a book by Theodore of Mopsuestia, because custodians were reluctant to let the uninstructed see it.[22] Such policies could only make intellectual life more narrow. It could plausibly be argued that, even though the patronage of Justinian had brought about a flourishing of some kinds of literary production in the sixth century, his long-term influence in this area was negative.

This is not the only important area in which Justinian's policies constituted a clear break with tradition. The amalgamation of civil and military authority which he established in various areas defied late Roman practice, and anticipated the developments of later centuries, as did the rising authority he was prepared to concede bishops in their towns.[23] Increasingly, the military man and the bishop would be the holders of power in the regions. For medieval historians there is a tendency to take this, together with the Christianizing of intellectual life, for granted, and to see it as a kind of inevitable development, but it is worth insisting on the fact that during the reign of Theoderic (493–526) secular letters flourished in Italy, as evidenced by the extraordinary achievement of Boethius, just as the traditional separation of civil and military powers was adhered to fairly rigorously. Judged by such criteria, the Roman emperor anticipated the middle ages more than the barbarian king, and, paradoxically, the reabsorption of Italy into the empire took it away from classical ways.

Yet there is a further irony. These developments occurred in the reign of an emperor whose legal reforms, laws and wars were sometimes rhetorically justified as restoring the past. Indeed, such activities have sometimes formed the basis for estimates of Justinian as an arch-conservative motivated by the desire to revive old ways. But caution is called for. Not all the

---

22. *Patrologia Graeca* 86:1384.
23. A revealing case in G. Dagron 'Two documents concerning Mesopotamia' in A.E. Laiou-Thomadakis ed. *Charanis Studies* New Brunswick NJ 1980?: 19–30.

projects he energetically set under way in the years immediately following his accession were classical in tenor, and the reform of the laws began by imitating the work of Theodosius II; only when the first edition of the Codex had been published and a lawyer of great abilities, Tribonian, had come to light did Justinian set under way the greater work of the Digest. There is no need to see the justifiable boasting which announced the completion of the Digest as indicating the frame of mind with which work on the laws was begun. Similarly, there is no need to see the western wars as having been launched in accordance with a great strategy to restore the lost provinces of the empire, whatever hyperbole may have attended their success; it was simply the fact that contingent and unforeseen circumstances in Africa and then Italy confronted Justinian with possibilities which he exploited in an opportunistic way. Despite the rhetorical language in which they were described, neither Justinian's legal work nor the wars in the West can be seen as having been prompted by a great vision of restoration.

The period after the death of Justinian was one of intense change for the empire. Reacting against the apparently supine policies of his predecessor, Justin took a firm line and refused to pay the subsidies Justinian had extended to various barbarian peoples. Doubtless the step was prompted by financial considerations, for which the spend-thrift policies of Justinian must bear some of the blame. Whether directed towards buildings, Khusrau, or military expeditions, a lot of money had flowed from the treasury during Justinian's reign, and in 566 Justin complained that it was burdened with obligations but contained only a little.[24] His change in policy, however, was followed by military disasters, which meant that civilians like Justinian and himself were no longer appropriate heads of state. Within a decade of his death effective power was being wielded by a military man, and a line of soldier emperors was to follow.

They had their work cut out for them. As we have seen, it

---

24. Justin's complaint: novel 149pr. Note as well the comments of John of Nikiu on Justinian's generosity: *Chronicle* 90.50f trans. R.H. Charles, London 1916.

became impossible to hold the Danube frontier, and before long Slavic peoples had gone beyond raiding and begun to settle in the Balkans in large numbers. In 568 Italy was invaded by the Lombards, who had succeeded in occupying some two-thirds of it by the end of the century. Early in the following century Persians surged over the eastern parts of the empire; goalposts were erected in the Hippodrome at Gerasa so they could play polo. A mighty effort by the emperor Heraclius (610–641) was enough to drive them out of imperial territory, but the latter part of his reign saw the beginning of the rise of the Arabs, newly converted to Islam. By the end of the seventh century they had brought under their power a good half of the Mediterranean coastline, extending from the eastern part of the modern Turkish coastline to northern Spain, a great arc of territory which included the wealthiest parts of the empire. The bulk of these were never to be regained. Already they were beginning the massive re-orientation which would see them turn away from the Mediterranean and become subsumed in a territorial block centred from the 660s on the inland city of Damascus and, from the mid-eighth century, on far-away Baghdad. The Slavicization of most of the Balkans and the Arabization of the Middle East and north Africa, developments which meant that henceforth these lands would dance to rhythms so different from those to which they had become accustomed in classical times, were set in train comfortably within a century of the death of Justinian.

The proper context in which these developments should be seen remains tantalizingly obscure. But it seems likely that the momentous changes which followed the Arab conquest occurred in those lost provinces of the empire which had been improving their relative economic position. Much of our evidence for this is archaeological, and there can be no doubt that work still to be done will modify current understandings. Nevertheless, it is hard to escape the conclusion that in the sixth century the different parts of the empire were moving apart in terms of their prosperity. In post-conquest Italy, economic decline which had set in centuries earlier was exacerbated by the Gothic war. The show-piece buildings erected at Ravenna should not blind us to the limited nature of building activity in sixth-century Italy, the inhabitants of which displayed an extraordinary commitment to the recycling of centuries-old buildings, or components of them, rather than the erection of new ones, and the decline in urban populations was apparent to an observer such as Cassiodorus (*Variae* 8.31, 11.39). In Thrace and Dacia, it has been suggested that important deviations from the classical lay-out of cities were under way.[25] The pattern is different for Constantinople, founded comparatively recently and the recipient of much imperial largesse in the time of Justinian, but it was to follow the western regions into decline: whereas 92 monasteries are known to have existed in the royal city in the sixth century, just two were founded during the seventh and eighth centuries.[26] Further to the east, however, it was a different story. Antioch seems to have been rebuilt on a moderate scale after the Persian sack in 540, and excavations at a site inland from the city reveal a flourishing economy based on traditional Mediterranean mixed cultivation. Here, the most expensive houses were those built in the sixth century, with a slow decline only setting in by the beginning of the seventh century.[27] In other words, the lost territories, which included the wealthy Egypt, were precisely the ones an emperor would have wished to hold.

Such evidence is very hard to evaluate. Perhaps the relative economic strength of the eastern regions can be seen as having been connected to the main political developments of the late-antique world, which can be summed up in the move of the centre of power steadily westwards: from Rome, in the centre of the Mediterranean, it passed to Constantinople,

25. V. Velkov *Cities in Thrace and Dacia in Late Antiquity* Amsterdam 1977 p. 231f.

26. Peter Charanis 'The monk in byzantine society' *Dumbarton Oaks Papers* 25 1971 pp. 61–84 at 65f. The figures are based on the data supplied in the first edition of R. Janin *La géographie ecclésiastique de l'empire buzantine* 1 *Le siège de Constantinople et le patriarchat œcumenique* 3 *Les églises et les monastères* 2nd edn Paris 1969, and I wish to record that I have found this work most useful, despite its flaws. Of course both the military situation of the city and the degree of documentation was different during the centuries following Justinian.

27. On Antioch I follow J. Lassus, *Antioch-on-the-Orontes* 5 Princeton 1972, who is more optimistic than G. Downey *A History of Antioch in Syria* Princeton 1961. The inland site is discussed by J.-P. Sodini, G. Tate, B. et Swant je Bavant, J-L. Biscop and D. Orssaud. 'Déhès (Syrie du Nord) campagnes I–III (1976–1978) Recherches sur l'habitat rurale' *Syria* 57 1980: 1–304, proposing revisions to the classic study of G. Tchalenko *Villages antiques de la Syrie du Nord* Paris 1958.

thence to the Umayyad caliphate based in Damascus, and ultimately to the purpose-built Abbasid capital of Baghdad on the Tigris. It may not be coincidental that the most interesting churches erected anywhere in the Christian world in the seventh century were those built in Armenia. It would take centuries for the Mediterranean to regain its centrality in the lives of many of those living around it, and for the surviving rump of the empire to regain its morale.

And so we may return to the question foreshadowed at the end of the preceding chapter. To what extent can Justinian be held to blame for these developments? It has been argued that the rise of the Arabs, often seen as bringing about the end of late antiquity, was not so much a cause as a consequence of changes.[28] If this were to be accepted, and the changes seen as arising from imperial policies as well as such phenomena as earthquakes and the plague, the point would gain in force. Perhaps the resources Justinian lavished on the building of churches would have been better spent on the army; perhaps the military adventures in the West were a diversion of money and energies which compromised the empire's ability to defend itself. The *Notitia Dignitatum*, a text of the early fifth century, records that some 170 000 troops were stationed in the East and Africa, Pannonia and Italy, but Agathias estimated that the strength of the army had dwindled to barely 150 000 soldiers late in Justinian's reign (*Histories* 5.13). In other words, by the end of his reign the army defending the whole empire was smaller than the force which had not been able to hold the area during the preceding century.[29] Yet the plague, for which Justinian could hardly be held to blame, may have had much to do with this. More generally, it is surely the case that attempts to explain the major developments of the late sixth and seventh centuries should be located in a framework which gives weight to the strengths of the victors as well as the better-documented weakness of the defeated. Once this is done, Justinian's responsibility for the losses suffered by the empire is hard to establish.

28. See the important studies by Hugh Kennedy, 'From Polis to Madina: Urban change in late antique and early Islamic Syria' *Past and Present* 106 1985: 3–27, and 'The last century of Byzantine Syria: A reinterpretation' *Byzantinische Forschungen* 10 1985: 141–83.
29. A.H.M. Jones *The Later Roman Empire 284–602* Oxford 1964 p. 684.

In any case, Justinian's western conquests were evanescent, and it is hard to see how they could have been anything else. The toehold achieved in Spain fell to the strong Visigothic monarchy of the early seventh century, Africa was being eroded by the Moors before the coming of the Arabs, and it was beyond the resources of the empire to defend the greater part of Italy against the Lombards. The wars have certainly attracted attention at subsequent times: in 1470 the Italian humanist Leonardo Bruni produced a book on the Italian war against the Goths which was basically a reworking into Latin of the account of the Gothic war by Procopius.[30] But his concern may have been connected with the situation of Italy when he was writing. There could be no doubt that the wars in the West were, in the long term, an expensive diversion from the forward path of medieval history.

If we seek the positive aspects of Justinian's legacy we will look in two other directions. The beautiful church of S Marco in Venice was built during the eleventh century in imitation of the church of the Holy Apostles in Constantinople, but the most influential of Justinian's buildings was the greatest. After a visit in 1869, Mark Twain disparagingly referred to Hagia Sophia as 'the rustiest old barn in heathendom',[31] but his is a minority opinion, for century after century the building has continued to work its spell. Pieces of evidence can be accumulated, almost at random. In the eighth century it was felt that a church which a Lombard duke of Benevento had erected was a likeness of Justinian's church; it was said that in the tenth century a celebration of the liturgy there was enough to dispose Russian envoys, who allegedly did not know whether they were in heaven or on earth, to accept orthodox Christianity; in the eleventh century envy of this work was believed to have stimulated an emperor to erect a church which he hoped would be finer; in the twelfth century abbot Suger of S Denis was concerned at comparisons between his church and Hagia Sophia. Members of the fourth crusade, which captured Constantinople in 1204, were impressed, although

30. Leonardo Aretino *De bello Italico adversus Gothos* Foligno 1470, which was itself translated into English by Arthur Goldyng: *The Historie of Leonard Aretine, concerning the warres betweene the Imperialles and the Gothes fro the possession of Italy* London 1563.
31. Cited in R.J. Mainstone *Hagia Sophia* New York 1988 p. 12.

the comment of one of them, Robert of Clari, that Saint
Sophia meant 'Holy Trinity' is devastating evidence for the
ignorance of the crusaders. But the greatest compliment to
Justinian's masterpiece was paid in his own city, following its
capture by the Turks in 1453. The impact of Hagia Sophia
brought about a re-orientation in Turkish architecture which
came to its fruition in the work of the great architect Sinan,
whose large-domed mosques can still be seen at Erdine as well
as Constantinople, while the slightly later Mosque of Sultan
Ahmed (the 'Blue Mosque') seems to stand in conscious
rivalry to the nearby Hagia Sophia.[32] The money lavished on
the church continued to have an impact beyond the Byzantine
period.

Justinian's legal work also lived on. Thanks to the decline
in the knowledge of Latin as well as the inherent quality of the
work for which he was responsible, his legislative enterprise
would hereafter always stand between classical Roman law and
any Byzantine present. A Greek version of the Institutes was
available as early as 534, and in various forms it continued to
influence Byzantine law for centuries; the Basilika issued by
Leo VI, probably in 888, is largely based on Justinian's works.
But its destiny in the West was to be more important. Quoted
by Gregory the Great, used in the following centuries in the
Byzantine-held parts of Italy, and known to the Lombards, it
nevertheless came to play its historical role only after the
Byzantine political presence in Italy had come to an end.
Astonishingly, a sixth-century text of the Digest was being used
by Italian scholars at the end of the eleventh century, and the
revival of civil law which later occurred, first in Italy and then
elsewhere, would have been unthinkable without Justinian's
work. Western emperors such as Frederick Barbarossa and
Frederick II saw to the insertion of some of their laws into
copies of the Codex, and Justinian's legislative work has been
influential in European law until recent times. It was Justinian's achievement in the field of law which won the admiration of Dante in the early fourteenth century. In his *Paradiso*
(6:10–27), the Florentine poet describes Justinian, in heaven,
explaining that pope Agapetus had converted him from believing that Christ had only one nature. Thereafter he sent

32. It must be said, however, that antecedents to this style are to be found
in earlier Turkish buildings.

Belisarius off to war and devoted himself to working on the laws. The description of Justinian's activities is, of course, inaccurate and chronologically woeful, but it is an interesting pointer to the concerns of Dante: for him, Justinian was significant for his legal work rather than his wars, even though Dante was partial to the idea of an imperial invasion of Italy.

Justinian's Nachleben, as opposed to the fate of his achievements, is complex and far from properly understood. Early opinions as to the fate of the emperor after death varied,[33] and by the seventh century strange stories about him and Belisarius were being told in Frankland.[34] Some later Byzantine authors, such as Zonaras, provide details concerning his reign unknown from earlier sources, and it is difficult to establish whether these are based on trustworthy sources of information or whether they reflect unreliable traditions which had grown up. Obviously, the opinions people had concerning Justinian would have reflected the sources of information available to them, and so a proper study of Justinian's posthumous reputation would encompass such matters as the manuscript tradition of the various works of Procopius. In 703 a Khazar princess who married Justinian II took the significant name Theodora, but a description of Constantinople written early in the eighth century has scarcely anything to say of the great contribution of his predecessor to the city.[35]

Today we are in a different situation. If every generation finds its own concerns mirrored in the past, it may be significant that books are being written on Theodora, and that Gore Vidal, the author of several interesting works on classical themes, has recently written the screenplay for a film on her, to be directed by Martin Scorsese. But acknowledgment that

---

33. That he went to heaven: Corippus *In Iaudem Justini Augusti minoris* 1.245f (ed. and trans. Averil Cameron, London 1976. That he went to hell: Evagrius *Historia Ecclesiastica* 5.1 (*The Ecclesiastical History of Evagrius*, ed. J. Bidez and L. Parmentier, London 1898; trans. E. Walford, London 1851) See in general J. Irmscher 'Justinianbild und Justiniankritik im frühen Byzanz' in H. Köpstein and F. Winkelmann eds *Studien zum 7. Jahrhundert in Byzanz. Probleme der Herausbildung des Feudalismus* Berlin 1976 pp. 131–42.

34. G. Schreibelreiter, 'Justinian und Belisar in fränkischer Sicht' in *BYZANTIOΣ Fest. H. Hunger* Vienna 1984: 267–80.

35. Eds and trans. Averil Cameron and Judith Herrin *Parataseis syntomoi chronikai* Leiden 1984.

the preoccupations of the present affect our approach to the past need not drive us towards a kind of presentist solipsism. The achievements of Justinian have their own solidness, and I believe that at least one of his personal characteristics can still be detected. For good or ill, Justinian was a restless man. He was wakeful, being described in the preface to an important piece of legislation as giving thought to the welfare of his subjects into the nights, as if it were day (novel 8pr.), and was well known for getting by on a limited amount of sleep.[36] The initiator of a whirlwind of reforms in the late 520s and 530s, the flinger-up of impressive buildings over an astonishingly wide area, the sender of generals to make war in unlikely places, and the canny manipulator of ecclesiastics was the same person who, late in life, prowled around the palace by night and sat up until all hours probing into questions of theology and who, in his last months, thought that he had found the long-desired solution. Here, as occasionally elsewhere, he had misread the situation. But there can be no mistaking the energies which continued to carry this extraordinary man, then over eighty, into new directions.

36. For example, Procopius *Secret History* 13.28, 30 (cf. *Buildings* 1.7.8f ed. and trans. H.B. Dewing, London 1914–1940), 15.11; John the Lydian *Powers* 2.15 fin (ed. and trans. A.C. Bandy *On Powers* Philadelphia 1983) ; and the reference to him as 'sleepless' in an inscription (*Corpus Inscriptionum Graecarum* 8639, line 9 ed. E. Curtius and A. Kirchhoff, repr. Hildesheim/New York 1977).

BIBLIOGRAPHY

The most voluminous source of information on the reign of Justinian is the *Wars, Secret History* and *Buildings* of his contemporary Procopius, conveniently published with a usually but not invariably accurate translation by H.B. Dewing London 1914–1940. Procopius' *Wars* conclude with events occurring in 553, but his narrative was continued by Agathias, whose *Histories* (ed. R. Keydell, Berlin 1968) have been translated by Joseph D. Frendo (Berlin/New York 1975). Averil Cameron 'Agathias on the Sassasians' *Dumbarton Oaks Papers* 23/24 1969/70 pp. 69–183 provides a translation with excellent commentary of the section dealing with Persian affairs. *The History of Menander the guardsman* has been edited and translated by R.C. Blockley (Liverpool 1985).

Among other narrative sources, *The Chronicle of John Malalas* (ed. L. Dindorf, Bonn 1831) has been translated by Elizabeth Jeffreys, Michael Jeffreys and Roger Scott Melbourne 1986 (a useful supplementary volume is Elizabeth Jeffreys, with Brian Croke and Roger Scott, eds. *Studies in John Malalas* Sydney 1990), while the *Chronicon paschale* (ed. L. Dindorf, Bonn 1832) has been translated by Michael and Mary Whitby, Liverpool 1989. The *Chronographia* of Theophanes, a work of the early ninth century which draws some material from sources no longer extant, is edited by Charles de Boor (Leipzig 1883). The Latin chronicles of Marcellinus comes and Victor of Tunnunna are edited by Th. Mommsen (*Monumenta Germaniae Historica Auctores Antiquissimi* 11). *The Ecclesiastical History of Evagrius* has been edited by J. Bidez and L. Parmentier (London 1898) and translated by E. Walford (London 1851). Justinian's laws are available in a translation by S.P. Scott,

189

Cincinnati 1932; the standard edition of the Codex is that by P. Krueger, Berlin 1915; of the Digest, that by Th. Mommsen, Berlin 1870; of the Institutiones, that by P. Krueger, Berlin 1877; and of the Novellae, that by R. Schoell and G. Kroll, Berlin 1895. The texts of the Digest and Institutes are available with facing translations, respectively by A. Watson, Philadelphia Pa 1985–, and P. Birks and G. McLeod, London 1987.

For the church, there is material in C.J. Hefele *A History of the Councils of the Church from the Original Documents* trans. W.R. Clark 4 Edinburgh 1895, although readers should be alert for errors in the translation. The proceedings of the council of 553 are edited by J. Straub (*Acta Concilia Oecumenicorum* 4/1 1971). Theological texts by Justinian have been translated by Kenneth P. Wesche, *On the Person of Christ the Christology of Emperor Justinian* Crestwood NY 1991, although even those interested in theology may find these works daunting.

The *In Laudem Justini Augusti minoris* by Corippus has been edited and translated by Averil Cameron, London 1976, while the work of John the Lydian has been edited and translated under the title *On Powers* by A.C. Bandy, Philadelphia Pa. 1983. Cassiodorus' *Variae* (ed. Th. Mommsen, *Monumenta Germaniae Historica Auctores Antiquissimi* 12) have recently been translated by S.J.B. Barnish, Liverpool 1992.

Readers seeking a general introduction to the period in which Justinian lived could do no better than start with Peter Brown *The World of Late Antiquity* London 1971 (reprinted with updated bibliography 1989), in which the chapter devoted to Justinian retains its capacity to inspire and challenge. More detailed are the studies of J.B. Bury *History of the Later Roman Empire* 2 London 1923, and E. Stein *Histoire du bas-empire* 2 Paris 1949, although the latter's immense learning and power of analysis are perhaps not quite matched by breadth of vision. J. Martindale ed. *The Prosopography of the Later Roman Empire 3 527–641* Cambridge 1992 is an invaluable tool for research on individuals who lived during this period.

There have been a number of studies devoted specifically to Justinian. Charles Diehl *Justinien et la civilisation byzantine au VIe siècle* Paris 1901 is still worth consulting. Berthold Rubin *Das Zeitalter Justinians* 1 Berlin 1960 (no longer published) is an exhaustive study of aspects of its topic. P.N. Ure *Justinian and his Reign* Harmondsworth 1951 is interesting, while Robert Browning *Justinian and Theodora* 2nd edn London

1987 is a sound guide; the first edn, London 1971, is worthy of note for its excellent illustrations.

Italian history during this period is covered in parts of two very different classic studies with much broader horizons: Thomas Hodgkin *Italy and Her Invaders* 4 and 5 2nd edn Oxford 1896, and L.M. Hartmann *Geschichte Italiens im Mittelalter* 1 Leipzig 1897; for background, see recently John Moorhead *Theoderic in Italy* Oxford 1992. Christian Courtois *Les Vandales et l'Afrique* Paris 1955 is the standard treatment of its subject. For Persia, there is A. Christensen *L'Iran sous les Sassinides* 2nd edn Copenhagen 1944, and for Spain José Orlandis *Historia de España época visigoda (409–711)* Madrid 1987.

On ecclesiastical history, Judith Herrin *The Formation of Christendom* Oxford 1987 is a major study, while John Meyendorff *Imperial Unity and Christian Divisions: The Church 450–680 AD* Crestwood NY 1989 attempts to approach the field from a less western perspective than has been customary; it seems to me sounder on eastern than on western matters. L. Duchesne *L'Église au VIe siècle* Paris 1922 remains a classic, informed by deep learning.

The questions treated in chapter six are discussed in a collection of papers published under the title *Villes et peuplement dans l'Illyricum protobyzantin* Rome 1984 (=Collection de l'École français de Rome 77); for general background, consult Dimitri Obolensky *The Byzantine Commonwealth: Eastern Europe 500–1453* London 1971.

Alan Cameron *Circus Factions* Oxford 1976 is the basic study of its topic. I regret not having been able to consult R. Mark and A.S. Calcmat *Hagia Sophia from the Age of Justinian to the Present* Cambridge 1992.

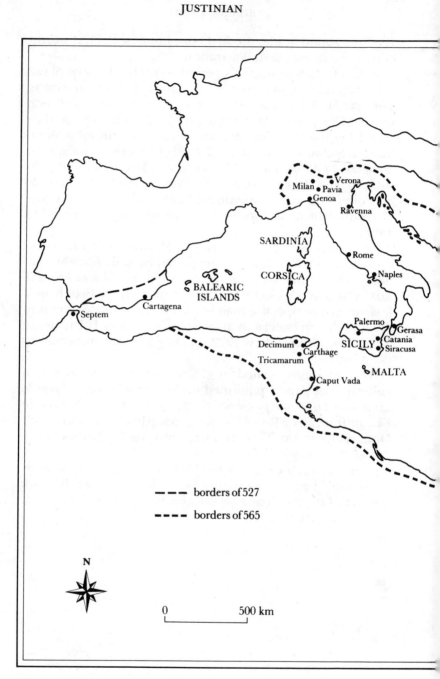

The empire under Justinian

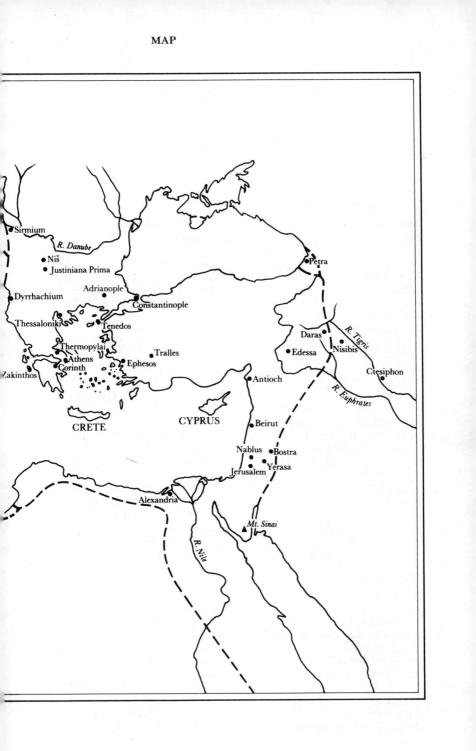

INDEX

Abbreviations: Alex. = Alexandria, Cp = Constantinople, emp. = emperor, kg = king, pat. = patriarch, bp = bishop